UNI
TD
T62
1991

W9-AVY-438

DOCUMENTS OFFICIELS

OCT 8 1991

GOVERNMENT
PUBLICATIONS

TRADE AND DEVELOPMENT REPORT, 1991

DÉPÔT
DEPOSIT

Report by the secretariat
of the
United Nations Conference on Trade and Development

UNITED NATIONS
New York, 1991

Note

- Symbols of United Nations documents are composed of capital letters combined with figures. Mention of such a symbol indicates a reference to a United Nations document.

- The designations employed and the presentation of the material in this publication do not imply the expression of any opinion whatsoever on the part of the Secretariat of the United Nations concerning the legal status of any country, territory, city or area, or of its authorities, or concerning the delimitation of its frontiers or boundaries.

- Material in this publication may be freely quoted or reprinted, but acknowledgement is requested, together with a reference to the document number. A copy of the publication containing the quotation or reprint should be sent to the UNCTAD secretariat.

UNCTAD/TDR/11

UNITED NATIONS PUBLICATION
Sales No.: E.91.II.D.15
ISBN 92-1-112309-7 ISSN 0255-4607

Contents

Part One

CURRENT DEVELOPMENTS IN THE WORLD ECONOMY

Chapter I

Part Three

SELECTED ISSUES IN THE URUGUAY ROUND

TRADE-RELATED ASPECTS OF INTELLECTUAL PROPERTY RIGHTS *179*

THE MULTILATERAL NEGOTIATIONS ON BANKING SERVICES: CONTEXT AND SELECTED OUTSTANDING ISSUES *195*

List of text tables

List of boxes and charts

Explanatory notes

Classification of countries and territories

Unless otherwise indicated, the following classification of countries and territories has been used in this Report. It has been adopted for the purposes of statistical convenience only and does not necessarily imply any judgement concerning the stage of development of a particular country or territory:

Developed market-economy countries (DMECs): Australia, Austria, Belgium, Canada, Denmark, Faeroe Islands, Finland, France, Germany [1] (former Federal Republic of Germany), Greece, Iceland, Ireland, Israel, Italy, Japan, Liechtenstein, Luxembourg, Netherlands, New Zealand, Norway, Portugal, South Africa, Spain, Sweden, Switzerland, United Kingdom, United States.

Central and Eastern Europe: Albania, Bulgaria, Czechoslovakia, Germany [1] (former German Democratic Republic), Hungary, Poland, Romania, USSR.

Socialist countries of Asia: China, Democratic People's Republic of Korea, Mongolia, Vietnam.

Developing countries and territories: All other countries, territories or areas not specified above.

Generally speaking, sub-groupings within geographical regions and analytical groupings (e.g. Major petroleum exporters, Major exporters of manufactures and Least developed countries (LDCs)) are those used in the UNCTAD *Handbook of International Trade and Development Statistics 1990.* [2]

Latin America corresponds to the *Handbook* grouping "Developing America" and thus includes the Caribbean countries.

South Asia includes Afghanistan, Bangladesh, India, Myanmar, Nepal, Pakistan, Sri Lanka and *East Asia* includes all other countries in *South and South-East Asia* as well as countries in *Oceania.* In general, data for the People's Republic of China exclude Taiwan Province.

Commodity classification

Unless otherwise stated, the classification by commodity group used in this Report follows generally that employed in the *Handbook of International Trade and Development Statistics 1990.*

---

[1] Through accession of the German Democratic Republic to the Federal Republic of Germany with effect from 3 October 1990, the two German States have united to form one sovereign State. As from the date of unification, the Federal Republic of Germany acts in the United Nations under the designation "Germany".

[2] United Nations publication, Sales No. E/F.91.II.D.11.

Other notes

In the tables and in the text: references to "countries" are to countries, territories or areas as appropriate. References to *TDR* are to the *Trade and Development Report* (of a particular year). For example, *TDR 1990* refers to *Trade and Development Report, 1990* (United Nations publication, Sales No. E.90.II.D.6).

The term dollar ($) refers to United States dollars, unless otherwise stated.

The term 'billion' signifies 1,000 million.

The term 'tons' refers to metric tons.

Annual rates of growth and change refer to compound rates.

Exports are valued f.o.b. and imports c.i.f., unless otherwise specified.

Use of a hyphen (-) between dates representing years, e.g. 1965-1966, signifies the full period involved, including the initial and final years.

An oblique stroke (/) between two years, e.g. 1980/81, signifies a fiscal or crop year.

One dot (.) indicates that the data are not applicable.

Two dots (..) indicate that the data are not available, or are not separately reported.

A dash (-) or a zero sign (0) indicates that the amount is nil or negligible.

A plus sign (+) before a figure indicates an increase; a minus sign (-) before a figure indicates a decrease.

Details and percentages do not necessarily add up to totals, owing to rounding.

Abbreviations

ACP	African, Caribbean and Pacific (Group of States)
ALADI	Latin American Integration Association
AMS	aggregate measurement of support
ASEAN	Association of South-East Asian Nations
BIS	Bank for International Settlements
CACM	Central American Common Market
CAP	common agricultural policy (of EEC)
CARICOM	Caribbean Community
CD	certificate of deposit
CEPAL	Economic Commission for Latin America and the Caribbean (Comisión Económica para América Latina y el Caribe)
c.i.f.	cost, insurance and freight
CMEA	Council for Mutual Economic Assistance
DAC	Development Assistance Committee (of OECD)
DMEC	developed market-economy country
ECA	Economic Commission for Africa
ECAs	export credit agencies
ECE	Economic Commission for Europe
ECGD	Export Credits Guarantee Department (United Kingdom)
ECLAC	Economic Commission for Latin America and the Caribbean
ECU	European currency unit
EEA	European Economic Area
EEC	European Economic Community
EFTA	European Free Trade Association
EMS	European Monetary System
ESAF	Enhanced Structural Adjustment Facility (IMF)
ESCAP	Economic and Social Commission for Asia and the Pacific
ESCWA	Economic and Social Commission for Western Asia
EXIM	Export-Import Bank (United States)
FAO	Food and Agriculture Organization of the United Nations
FDI	foreign direct investment
f.o.b.	free on board
FY	fiscal year
GATT	General Agreement on Tariffs and Trade
GDP	gross domestic product
GNP	gross national product
GSP	generalized system of preferences
ICCO	International Cocoa Organization
ICO	International Coffee Organization
IDA	International Development Association
IFC	International Finance Corporation
IIASA	International Institute for Applied Systems Analysis
ILO	International Labour Organisation
IMF	International Monetary Fund

INTAL	Institute for Latin American Integration
IPRs	intellectual property rights
LAIA	Latin American Integration Association
LDC	least developed country
LIBOR	London Inter-Bank Offered Rate
LME	London Metal Exchange
mb/d	million barrels per day
MERCOSUR	Southern Cone Common Market
MFA	Multi-Fibre Arrangement
MFN	most favoured nation
MTNs	multilateral trade negotiations
MYRA	multi-year rescheduling agreement
NAFTA	North American Free Trade Agreement (Canada-United States-Mexico)
NMP	net material product
NTB	non-tariff barrier
NTM	non-tariff measure
OAS	Organization of American States
ODA	official development assistance
ODF	official development finance
OECD	Organisation for Economic Co-operation and Development
OPEC	Organization of the Petroleum Exporting Countries
PSE	producer subsidy equivalent
QR	quantitative restriction
R and D	research and development
ROSCA	rotating savings and credit association
SDR	special drawing right
SEACEN	South-East Asia Central Banks and Monetary Authorities
SELA	Latin American Economic System (Sistema Económica Latino-Americana)
SEM	single European market (of EEC)
SIGMA	System for Interlinked Global Modelling and Analysis
SITC	Standard International Trade Classification (revision 1)
TNC	Trade Negotiations Committee
TNCs	transnational corporations
TRIMs	trade-related investment measures
TRIPs	trade-related intellectual property rights
UCC	Universal Copyright Convention
UNCTAD	United Nations Conference on Trade and Development
UNCTC	United Nations Centre on Transnational Corporations
UNDP	United Nations Development Programme
UNIDO	United Nations Industrial Development Organization
USAID	United States Agency for International Development
USDA	United States Department of Agriculture

USTR   United States Trade Representative
VER   voluntary export restraint
WIDER   World Institute for Development Economics Research

OVERVIEW
by the
Secretary-General of UNCTAD

The world economy is in recession. This has much to do with cyclical developments in several major economies. But a number of exceptional events and sources of rapid change are also affecting the level and pattern of economic activity. These include the recent war, the unification of Germany, and the political and economic restructuring under way in Central and Eastern Europe. Large parts of the world economy are also being influenced by the efforts of Governments to form larger economic spaces, to bring the Uruguay Round to a successful conclusion, and to protect their own trading interests whether or not the Round is successful. The time dimensions of these various forces are vastly different - some may be expected to spend themselves in the short run, while others could have effects for decades to come. But all are important to economic performance whether directly or through the expectations that they are generating.

The changes taking place come at a time when many economies are particularly vulnerable. Developed market-economy countries have experienced their first recession since the early 1980s, and although some of them are showing signs of recovery, the pace and extent of revival are clouded by a number of factors, including the heightened vulnerability of financial institutions in some countries. The economies of Central and Eastern Europe are weighed down by antiquated plant and equipment, lack of the institutional infrastructure required for a market economy - including an established system of private property rights - and insufficient experience with markets - in particular a paucity of entrepreneurship and of skill in handling risk. Many developing countries, too, are in the midst of a complex process of adjustment and reform, among which efforts at revising the trade regime and the internal financial system figure prominently. For all countries, the prospects for prosperity hinge on the intensity of their own efforts and on whether international cooperation is forthcoming to overcome the negative aspects of these events, and exploit the positive elements.

Aggregate world output is likely to advance by less than 1 per cent in 1991, following an expansion of 1.8 per cent in 1990. Last year poor growth performance was concentrated in parts of the western industrial world, in Central and Eastern Europe, and in Latin America. This year there should be an improvement in parts of Latin America (though growth will none the less remain unsatisfactory) and for developing countries as a whole. The slowdown in industrial countries will spread wider, while the fall in output in Central and Eastern Europe will be deeper.

In Latin America, recent economic performance has been shaped by the interaction of foreign exchange availabilities and domestic stabilization efforts. In general, the oil-exporting countries in the region have grown reasonably well, while the oil importers have not. The vicious circle of over-indebtedness, domestic financial disorder and low growth is being broken in a few countries which have succeeded in sustaining adjustment and reform, obtained negotiated debt reduction, and, in addition, enjoyed relatively high export prices and earnings. But it is still too early to conclude that the growth and debt crisis is being mastered. One of the key ingredients of success - favourable export prices and earnings - falls only in part, and sometimes only in small part, within the ambit of policy influence. The successes noted above will provide scant comfort to those in-debted countries that must seek to improve export earnings in the teeth of persistently low or de-clining terms of trade.

In Africa, too, performance has mirrored patterns of foreign exchange availabilities and do-mestic policy effort. Some countries suffered sharp declines in external earnings because of the Persian Gulf crisis. For oil exporters foreign exchange earnings rose briskly; in other countries export revenues stagnated or fell as the prices of their traditional commodity exports sagged. These changes were generally reflected rather directly in the pace of economic activity, although natural disasters, civil unrest, and the difficulties of coming to grips with the complex requirements of reform and adjustment also played a role in some cases. Growth performance in the period ahead will continue to be influenced by external earnings. For some countries, including notably oil exporters, prospects are fairly encouraging, but the overall outlook for the prices of commod-ities exported by African countries is not promising, and little near-term stimulus to growth can be expected from this quarter. Moreover, there are increasing signs that the availability of food may once again become an acute problem in parts of Africa.

Some parts of developing Asia are showing similar patterns of growth to those of Africa and Latin America: where external earnings were boosted by the Gulf conflict, growth accelerated, and where earnings declined, growth slowed down. For some economies in South Asia that have been performing well, losses in earnings, together with a number of domestic factors, have produced pressures on prices, the budget and the balance of payments that could influence future growth prospects. In one country this has recently triggered a strong policy response. For most of the countries in West Asia directly involved in or otherwise heavily affected by the conflict, the eco-nomic impact has been truly calamitous, with long-term consequences for the economy and social welfare.

As in the past, a number of economies in East and South-East Asia were able to use their underlying financial strength, increasingly sophisticated economic structures, and capacity to adapt policies rapidly to changing circumstances to avoid severe damage from external shocks. In countries with unusually large external surpluses, the slowdown in external earnings and the in-creased import bill implied by higher oil prices, while troublesome, were not entirely unwelcome, since they facilitated external adjustment. While growth prospects for these countries are some-what diminished, they none the less remain relatively bright.

The least developed countries are being influenced by many of the forces bearing on devel-oping countries as a whole, including in many cases the direct adverse effects of the Gulf crisis and a weakening of export prices. In addition, some have been hit by natural disasters - in one case of catastrophic proportions - and continued bad weather is endangering food supplies in several instances. Overall, prospects are for a continuation of inadequate rates of growth.

Economic performance in China continues to be dominated by the austerity programme put in place in 1988, which, together with good agricultural output, has brought down the rate of in-flation. The pace of activity has picked up, and recent advances in industrial output suggest that the economy will continue to strengthen in the period ahead.

Countries in Central and Eastern Europe continue to feel both the ill-effects of the command and control systems prevailing until recently and the costs of transition. In 1990 output declined in all these countries; in 1991 it will drop steeply. The process of transition to market-oriented economic structures is proving to be exceedingly complex, and is advancing in the various coun-tries at distinctly different paces. For those which have gone furthest down the path of reform, some positive results are now in evidence, but there have also been heavy costs, particularly in terms of unemployment. The process of restructuring, with all its social and political dimensions, cannot be accomplished in short order, and economic performance in most of these countries can be expected to remain relatively poor in the period immediately ahead.

The steady deceleration of growth that has characterized developed market-economy coun-tries since 1988 has now culminated in full-scale recession, with poor growth performance currently concentrated in North America and parts of Western Europe. A modest but convergent recovery is expected towards the end of this year, but its strength (and duration) are subject to a number of uncertainties, and in some countries fragility of financial institutions is creating considerable down-side risk (see below).

Recent Developments in International Trade

In 1990, the expansion of trade maintained its close correlation with the growth of output, slowing for the second consecutive year along with the deceleration in global economic growth. Although trade has been described as an engine of economic growth, the causality runs in both directions: the recession that afflicted a number of developed countries in 1990 was one of the negative influences on international trade during the year. It was reinforced by the disruptions to trade caused by the Gulf conflict and by the changes in Central and Eastern Europe. German unification resulted in a large increase in that country's import demand, to the benefit of world trade. For the other economies in transition, the severe economic reversals experienced during the year, combined with the disintegration of CMEA, resulted in large declines in import and export volumes.

The pattern of world trade was also influenced by changes in the exchange rates of the major trading nations. The depreciation of the dollar reinforced the effects of the recession in the United States in further reducing the rate of growth of that country's imports below the world average; the growth of United States exports also slowed, but continued to exceed the world average. In Europe, the rate of growth of EEC exports to third countries fell (and was well below the world average) whereas the growth of the Community's imports rose (and was well above the world average). In contrast to the 1980s, the same applied to each of the four newly industrializing economies in South-East Asia; exchange rate realignments have been one reason for this.

The behaviour of world energy prices and output in 1990 illustrates the importance of having a margin of unused capacity and the dangers of speculation. Despite the loss of output from two major producers, prices increased much less than during the crisis periods of the 1970s and 1980s. However, they reached extremely high levels for a short while because of panic buying. Although the panic subsided after a few months, the temporary rise in prices resulted in severe damage to the economies of many developing countries.

In contrast, the prices of non-fuel commodities dropped. The index of the annual average dollar prices for all such commodities fell for the first time since 1985; in relation to the prices of the manufactured exports of developed countries, the index has declined continuously since early 1989, and by early 1991 it had fallen by some 30 per cent.

Overall, the trade volume performance of developing countries in 1990 was mixed. There was a considerable deceleration in the growth of exports from South and South-East Asia for the second consecutive year, mainly owing to a sharp slowdown in the exports of the four more industrialized economies of the region. Also for the second consecutive year, Latin America recorded negligible export growth, particularly for non-energy products. However, results were highly varied among countries: those suffering from continued macroeconomic instability fared far worse than the remainder. In Africa, the volume of exports registered an unusual spurt in 1990, but much of it was due to higher oil exports by the region's few energy-exporting countries. Moreover, in commodity markets increases in export volumes are often associated with softness of prices. In China, after a setback in 1989 exports recovered the momentum characteristic of the 1980s, while imports fell substantially in response to restrictive macroeconomic policies.

Recent Developments in International Capital Markets and Debt

The year 1990 was marked by continuation of the recent disconnection of global trends in the international capital markets from lending to developing countries. Total borrowing in 1990 from these markets slowed, reflecting the influence of factors such as banks' efforts to improve their capital positions and the impact of the decline in Japanese equity values on issues of equity-related external bonds. Within the total the borrowing of developing countries remained marginal. The bulk of the funds raised continued to go to countries in South and South-East Asia whose creditworthiness has not been impaired by the debt crisis. The access of most other developing countries to the international capital markets is still restricted by unfavourable perceptions of creditworthiness and continuing difficulties with the servicing of external debt.

There have been limited improvements in the indicators of net debtor developing countries' external financial positions during the past two years, though their incidence has been uneven and the picture remains particularly unfavourable for sub-Saharan Africa. The improvements may help to explain the incipient recovery of export credits to developing countries in 1989 and 1990. In spite of this recovery, the levels of such lending remained well below those of the early 1980s. Moreover, official insurance cover from the export credit agencies of two major OECD countries continues to be unavailable, or available only at high cost and on restrictive conditions, for the great majority of countries in Africa and Latin America.

A number of the renegotiations of developing countries' debt to commercial banks since 1989 were designed to reduce debt and debt service in line with the current debt strategy. The reductions achieved in relation to outstanding bank debt have varied from high proportions for some countries to only 10-12 per cent for two of the largest borrowers. Evaluation of the impact of the agreements reached so far to reduce debt and debt service remains premature for the most part. However, there are indications that Mexico's agreement with its creditors has contributed to a climate of greater economic confidence which has led to a return of flight capital and a sharp rise in foreign equity investment. Nevertheless, the continuing slowness of progress in reducing developing countries' debt to commercial banks confirms the conclusion of *TDR 1990* that action needs to be taken to accelerate the process and extend its scope. In the absence of such action the debt overhang will remain an impediment to the success of policies undertaken to revive economic development in a large number of countries.

As regards official bilateral debt, the Paris Club has taken some significant steps to improve the terms of rescheduling. These steps have reinforced the trend which began in 1987 towards a differential treatment of debtors.

The 50 per cent debt reduction granted to Poland and Egypt advances significantly the international debt strategy by introducing the concept of debt reduction for middle-income countries, and by applying the reduction to the entire stock of debt. Furthermore, the combined size of debt forgiveness for these two countries (at least $24 billion) is extraordinarily large, equivalent to over twice the aggregate amount of ODA debt cancellations granted by OECD countries during the past 13 years. It is to be hoped that the debt reduction needs of other middle-income countries whose burden of official bilateral debt is excessively onerous will not be ignored. In order to reach its goal of fostering adjustment and growth, the international debt strategy must be governed by objective economic criteria, not political preferences or narrow financial concerns. Some lower middle-income countries have already benefited from the Houston terms. However, these involve primarily longer maturities and grace periods and not debt reduction (apart from a limited amount of voluntary debt swaps).

Growing recognition of the inadequacy of the Toronto terms has led Paris Club creditors to consider over the past year the bold proposals put forward by the Netherlands and the United Kingdom to remove the debt overhang in low-income countries. The London summit of the Group of Seven agreed that there was a need for additional debt relief measures for the poorest countries "going well beyond the relief already granted under Toronto terms". This is most welcome. The political consensus should impart a strong impetus to the Paris Club to conclude its consideration of this question. Budgetary problems faced by some creditor countries must not delay the adoption of much improved terms for the low-income countries. Their combined debt owed to the Paris Club is relatively small (being, for instance, well below that of Poland alone). There are, however, a number of issues that need to be settled:

- The *scale* of debt reduction. Implementation of the United Kingdom proposal (the Trinidad terms), which calls for a two-thirds cancellation, would go far towards reconciling debt service obligations of many of the potential beneficiaries with their capacity to pay. For several beneficiaries, however, debt burdens would still remain too high. Official creditors - both within and outside the Paris Club - could treat the two-thirds debt reduction as a benchmark and take additional measures for these countries, such as a higher percentage of debt reduction (up to 100 per cent, as advocated by the Dutch proposal) and increased ODA flows. For some countries, concessional refinancing of multilateral debt service and commercial bank debt reduction would also be required;

- The *modalities* of debt reduction and related policy conditionality. Debt reduction is most effective if it is implemented in a single operation, thus removing once and for all the investment disincentives associated with the debt overhang and the uncertainties generated by repeated rescheduling. If a policy of "tranching" is adopted instead, creditors' commitment to an overall amount of debt reduction should be made explicit from the start and the bulk of total forgiveness should be given "up front";

- *Eligibility* criteria. The intended beneficiaries appear to be those currently eligible for Toronto terms (i.e. debt-distressed IDA-only countries undertaking IMF adjustment programmes). But, as proposed in previous issues of the *TDR*, eligibility criteria should be widened to include all heavily indebted countries that are IDA recipients, even if they borrow from the World Bank. Consideration should also be given to avoiding moral hazard by attending to the needs of those countries that have managed to meet their debt service obligations, but only barely and at a high cost.

Financial policies

Much concern has been expressed in recent months that developed countries will not prove sufficiently thrifty to meet the new demands for financing from Central and Eastern Europe, the Middle East and elsewhere without adding to pressures on interest rates and to the financial difficulties of indebted developing countries. The fear that global savings will necessarily become increasingly scarce appears, however, to be unfounded. For one thing, there is ample scope to reduce military spending, the rationale of which is being rapidly eroded by the end of the Cold War. For another, the cost of investment goods has been falling sharply thanks to rapid technical progress, especially in computing. Moreover, household savings behaviour has not in reality been worsening, despite some appearances to the contrary.

Besides, when, as is frequently the case, the level of overall demand is insufficient to allow the world's productive potential to be fully utilized, investment can be stepped up without Governments and households having first to cut their consumption, since the investment itself will create the required savings by generating additional income. It is therefore more pertinent to focus on the factors presently constraining investment and pushing up interest rates, in particular the organization of the financial system and its impact on the cost and supply of finance.

Financial innovation and deregulation of financial markets have made interest rates and asset prices more variable and the supply of finance less predictable; they have also increased the potential for instability in the financial system. Governments have responded to this potential by requiring increases in banks' capital and other improvements in their balance sheets. However, a slump in the prices of assets held by banks in the world's two largest economies has worked in the opposite direction, thus greatly diminishing the ability of banks to increase lending to support investment and recovery. Both financial institutions and Governments now face the challenge of overcoming these structural weaknesses in the financial system. In the meantime, however, stresses and strains are likely to prevent the world's production potential from being fully utilized for some time. Until it is, the constraint on financing development will not be the supply of real resources but the institutional capacity to generate finance. One way of tackling the problem is to renew SDR allocations and "link" them to development finance. Japan has recently made such a proposal.

However, even with better access to external finance, developing countries will need to improve their own financial systems considerably. Indeed, efforts at financial reform are under way in all groups of countries, including those in Central and Eastern Europe. The thinking behind them stresses the benefits of market forces. It is opposed to regulation of interest rates and to limitations on competition among different types of financial institutions for each other's business. It is even more strongly opposed to government influence on the allocation of credit, and it stresses the benefits of developing, or further developing, capital markets.

This line of thinking has its logic, but it can easily be pushed too far. Finance must serve industry and commerce - not vice versa. It must therefore not be allowed to become too costly or uncertain for business.

Doing away with "financial repression" typically leads to a sharp increase in interest rates. In practice, this does little if anything to boost savings. Nor do high interest rates (whether due to deregulation or to tight monetary policies) induce firms to turn towards equity financing when the owners are reluctant to lose control or when they enjoy privileged access to bank credit. The consequences for debtors can be devastating, especially for those that have borrowed heavily to invest in plant and equipment, or in social and physical infrastructure. High interest rates not only accentuate stagflationary pressures but also harm competitiveness, since export and import-competing industries are generally unable to pass on cost increases. Devaluing the currency to compensate can set off a spiral of inflation and social conflict, especially when a large depreciation has already taken place. Experience also shows the dangers of liberalizing finance in the context of macroeconomic disorder. It aggravates the financial difficulties of firms and further weakens the balance sheets of financial institutions; and it can easily generate speculative excesses and end in a crash, producing even more government intervention than initially.

Careful consideration also needs to be given to the extent of external financial liberalization. Financial openness in a developing country typically pushes domestic interest rates above international rates, owing to the greater uncertainty attached to holding domestic assets. Besides, it exposes the economy to international financial flows that are inherently volatile and that tend to move in bandwagons. Inward movements of funds on a large scale can be as disruptive as outward ones. The loss of policy autonomy can be very costly for both growth and stability. While complete financial isolation is neither possible nor desirable, it is important to retain some insulation (though controls are not the answer to capital flight provoked by political or economic instability).

For government intervention in financial activity to be dispensed with there must exist institutions through which the "invisible hand" can operate, in particular private institutions capable of providing long-term finance. In most developing countries these are weak or even absent, while business firms tend to be under-capitalized. Consequently, entrepreneurship is stymied, and businessmen have to operate with very short time horizons, and hold back from "learning by doing" when the pay-off though high is distant. All latecomers to industrialization have encountered this problem, and successful ones (including some that are now highly advanced) have improvised techniques consciously to direct credit according to government priorities. In developing countries there may have been many more instances of misdirected interventionism, but the fact remains that practically no country that has modernized in recent decades has pursued purely market-oriented financial policies.

Why interventionism has produced disastrous results in some countries and brilliant ones in others is still something of a mystery. However, two factors stand out:

- Macroeconomic stability and budgetary discipline are especially important where the banking system is used extensively to finance long-term business expansion;

- The Government must not allow itself to become a prisoner of vested interests; it should ensure that any support it extends to enterprises (whether private or public) is fully matched by good performance, and withdraw it when obsolete.

Nevertheless, liberalization can bring benefits provided that certain conditions are met. It should be:

- adopted when considerable industrial advance has already been achieved, and strong institutions and markets and competitive industries are in place;

- undertaken gradually and without preventing the Government from pursuing an active industrial policy and from intervening in finance in the interest of stability;

- accompanied by strong prudential regulations and effective bank supervision.

Many Governments are taking active steps to help develop capital markets. They can do so by, for instance, providing tax benefits for equity issues and disincentives to short-term borrowing; preventing firms from controlling banks; and punishing fraud and other irregularities. However, equity markets cannot be expected to become the major source of investment finance swiftly.

Nor is the Anglo-Saxon model of financing (in which banks provide short-term finance while long-term funding is accomplished by issuing securities) necessarily the best option. In Germany and Japan, for instance, capital markets have historically played a much smaller role in financing business growth than have banks. Moreover, because the latter have had a voice in corporate decision-making, as well as much greater access than capital markets to information about corporate performance and prospects, they have been willing to provide capital at lower cost. Firms have also enjoyed greater confidence regarding the continued availability of funds for expansion and have therefore been able to plan further ahead. When firms depend on equity markets for outside finance, they are at the mercy of their share prices (which are especially volatile in developing countries), and management focuses on short-term financial results rather than long-term strategy.

Industrialized countries are now converging towards a common financial system in which capital markets will be of central importance. However, this does not mean that all other countries should be following suit. Until they achieve substantial economic advance, most developing countries have more to gain by improving the banking system (for instance via investment banks) and by upgrading the quality of government intervention, if necessary through drastic reforms.

Trade Policies

The developed market-economy countries have forfeited their position in the vanguard of trade liberalization: some developing countries and economies in transition (such as Chile, Mexico and Poland) have assumed the pioneering role, with many others following their example. Recent years have seen a widespread movement among developing countries towards trade liberalization, both unilaterally and within trading groups. As part of their transformation into market-oriented economies, there is now a similar trend in most of the former centrally planned economies.

Within the developed market economies, however, the commitment to trade liberalization has been eroded. Agreements were reached in the latter half of the 1980s on a number of arrangements that would reduce the trade barriers among these countries themselves. The Free Trade Agreement between Canada and the United States and the creation and potential enlargement of the Single European Market (SEM) are the most noteworthy examples; the trade-related discussions between Japan and the United States, referred to as the Structural Impediments Initiative, are another. Some measures have also been taken by developed countries to reduce the barriers to imports from developing countries. But these have usually been selective both in product coverage and in geographical scope (in part because they have been driven by political as well as economic motives) and have barely made a dent in the panoply of non-tariff barriers that faces a large proportion of the exports from developing to developed countries.

The gradual abandonment of the MFN principle that is implicit in the selective nature of these trade liberalization measures, together with the obdurate nature of protectionism in the developed market-economy countries, accentuate concerns of third parties about the emergence of regional trading arrangements among these countries. A major fear of trading partners is that these arrangements will become inward-looking - that efforts to protect weaker segments within the new groupings may result in further barriers being imposed against non-participating countries. The participants in the arrangements deny that they intend to become inward-looking, arguing that existing trading arrangements with third parties will not be made more restrictive. Moreover, it is claimed that the trade-creating effects of higher incomes within the groupings will outweigh the trade diversion from non-members to members that the groupings will inevitably bring about.

Even with unchanged policies, analysis suggests that, at least in the important case of the SEM, the additional and immediate net trade effects on non-participants are unlikely to be large. This is partly because the formal creation of the SEM represents the culmination of an integration process that is already well advanced, with many of the consequential adjustments in trade having already taken place. The same applies in large measure to the United States-Canada free trade agreement. Since any short-run benefits these arrangements may have for third parties are likely to be small, they would easily be overwhelmed by any tightening of restrictions towards non-participants.

Viewed in a longer-term perspective, a major driving force behind both the North American and the Western European trading arrangements has been the desire to foster overall economic growth by raising efficiency and promoting technological change, in part by increasing competition and realizing economies of scale. There is increasing awareness among countries that are not participating in these and similar arrangements that the direct negative consequences of being omitted, most of which will be of a one-time, short-run nature, are likely to be less important than the potential indirect gains they will forgo, particularly over the longer term. Higher overall growth within the new trade groupings will trickle down to other countries through imports, but these beneficial effects are likely to be far less than those that would result from sharing in the more dynamic growth that the members of the groupings can expect. The potential gains forgone by non-participants will be that much greater if the Uruguay Round does not succeed in fulfilling its objectives.

Fear of being deprived of the potential benefits of participation in a major trading group has been an important stimulus for the recent surge of interest in this form of international economic collaboration. The prospective emergence of a united market in Western Europe was one of many motivations for negotiation of a free trade agreement between the United States and Canada. That agreement, reinforced by the negotiations with Mexico and the Initiative for the Americas, has prompted a flurry of discussions about more collaborative trading arrangements within the Americas. Similarly, in Europe, recognition of the opportunities likely to be lost as a result of not being included in the SEM has prompted several non-members to seek a closer trading relationship with EEC.

Regional trading arrangements can help rationalize production and promote growth, but they cannot substitute for a properly functioning multilateral trading system. The differences of view among the developed market economies regarding, for example, agriculture and the matters under discussion in the Structural Impediments Initiative highlight two facts: that trade between the regions is perceived by the parties concerned to be vital to their respective interests and that a regional approach cannot provide a fully acceptable trading environment even for the developed market economies. At the same time, from a procedural point of view, the extensive efforts to enhance and expand regional trading arrangements are inevitably diverting the attention of politicians and negotiators from their attempts to improve the multilateral trading system.

Recent moves by industrial countries to set up or strengthen regional arrangements will have various effects on developing countries, not all of them positive. If the world market becomes more segmented, the present diversity (and complexity) of restrictions on trade in individual markets is likely to increase, further exacerbating difficulties of market access. Overall, there is a danger that the present regional trading arrangements, even if they do not become more inward-looking, will contribute to a further marginalization of the developing countries unable to participate in them. This is in part because the burden of adjustment to the arrangements by the members' weaker segments may inevitably be shifted onto non-members. Even participating countries will have to confront the stronger competition expected in the 1990s inside and outside regional arrangements.

Most developing countries are either already associated with one of the main trading groups or are actively seeking to become so. However, individual developing countries, or even groups of them, lack leverage, not only in negotiations for membership but also in subsequent discussions among the members of the groupings. The position of developing countries vis-à-vis such groupings will normally be even weaker than in GATT negotiations. Consequently, developing countries as a whole, and in most cases individually, could gain more from an improvement in the multilateral system than from participation in a geographically limited trading group. Indeed, a system of international review of the *modus operandi* of such groupings could help protect the interests of both weaker members and non-participants.

Regional trading groups may develop in such a way that they do not violate the legal niceties of international trade. World trade itself might not suffer the predicted breakdown in the absence of more substantial progress than has been apparent to date in the Uruguay Round. Nevertheless, the development of regional trading arrangements at the expense of the multilateral system would be contrary to both the spirit and the letter of recent undertakings by the international community to address the needs of its poorer members. The enhanced regional trading arrangements in place and in prospect must not be allowed to act as a stumbling block to a global compact on trade that fully respects the needs of the developing countries. These regional arrangements should be used as building blocks to revitalize the multilateral trading system and extend it to new areas in ways that meet the needs of all members of the international community.

Current State of Play in the Uruguay Round

The Uruguay Round of multilateral trade negotiations could not be concluded within the agreed time frame at the Ministerial meeting of the Trade Negotiations Committee, held in Brussels from 3 to 7 December 1990. The negotiations of the most ambitious and complex Round ever undertaken were suspended, leaving the international trading system in a period of uncertainty as to prospects for further liberalization and expansion of world trade and for strengthening multilateral trade rules and disciplines.

These events flowed from a number of political deadlocks in some of the major substantive areas of negotiation, in particular as regards agriculture, where participants could not agree on a common basis for reforming trade. Some other negotiating areas, such as trade-related investment measures (TRIMs) and anti-dumping, also lacked an agreed basis for negotiation, reflecting fundamental divergencies in the positions of participants and in their interpretation of the negotiating mandate. Moreover, practically all parts of the draft Final Act, which was submitted to Ministers in Brussels, contained some fundamental or technical points of disagreement.

Since then the efforts of participants have concentrated on finding the consensus needed to resume the negotiations. Difficult compromises finally emerged, and the Uruguay Round was formally restarted in February 1991 in all areas and is being pursued under a streamlined negotiating structure. In May 1991, Congress extended the "fast-track" authority granted to the Executive Branch of the Government of the United States, allowing the negotiations to resume in earnest.

The importance attached to a successful outcome is evidenced by the many declarations adopted at the highest political level. Most recently, the London summit of seven industrialized countries in July 1991 committed their leaders to an ambitious, global and balanced package of results, with the widest possible participation by both developed and developing countries, and to concluding the Round by the end of 1991.

There appears to be a clear understanding by all participants in the Round that, as recognized at UNCTAD VII, a balanced outcome is crucial to efforts to maintain an open multilateral trading system, something of vital importance to all countries. If the opportunities afforded by the Uruguay Round are missed, a severe blow will be dealt to multilateralism, paradoxically at a time when the multilateral trading system is becoming universal.

A positive and balanced outcome by the end of 1991 will require genuine efforts to resolve outstanding political and technical problems. Those exist in practically every negotiating area from market access to institutional issues. The technical complexities will present a formidable challenge, in particular in such areas as market access, agriculture, rule-making, services and textiles and clothing; in this last instance consensus is needed on modalities for bringing trade back under GATT rules and disciplines. Finally, the negotiations will also need to address the institutional implications of the Round and the implementation of its substantive results, including the specific proposals for a common institutional structure for the administration and execution of possible agreements in various areas, and to recognize the concern that this should not necessarily create links between the rights and obligations contained in the various instruments. Care also needs to be taken that any action in this area foster the overall objective of strengthening international organizations involved in multilateral trade, as provided for in General Assembly resolution 45/201.

Thus, if the Uruguay Round is to reach a balanced and substantial package of results in all areas, it should address and satisfy the vital interests of all participants, in particular those of developing countries, which are taking an active and constructive part in these negotiations. However, the current status of negotiations suggests that the real benefits to developing countries are likely to be limited.

In order to illustrate the complexity of the different issues facing the negotiators at present, *TDR 1991* reviews in detail three specific negotiating areas: Agriculture, where the credibility of commitments to trade liberalization is at stake; Trade-Related Aspects of Intellectual Property Rights (TRIPs), a test for the right of developing countries to acquire a competitive capacity; and Financial Services, the negotiation of which is a major challenge to the establishment of a multilateral framework for trade in services generally.

Agriculture

A satisfactory outcome to the negotiations on agriculture is of utmost importance, especially for developing countries. For the first time an attempt is being made to establish multilateral disciplines that would subject agricultural trade to a regime comparable to that governing trade in other goods. The negotiations have addressed not only border protection and export subsidization but also the fundamental problem of agricultural support policies in developed countries. They are complicated by the diversity of interests, including even among developing countries, some of which are being defended by alliances of participants in the Round, such as the Cairns Group and the net food importers.

Developed market-economy countries remain the major markets for the agricultural exports of the developing countries. However, these markets have grown relatively slowly, largely because of the impact of agricultural support policies. Such national support policies, including subsidy programmes, originally motivated by a desire for food security and to assist rural areas for social reasons, have in many cases led to structural overcapacity. Indeed, some developed countries that were previously major importers have not only become self-sufficient in agriculture but have even become large-scale net exporters of a number of products and are involved in export subsidy competition (while developing countries as a whole are large net importers of temperate zone agricultural products). The result has been to reduce, or shut off, the traditional markets for developing countries, thus displacing those countries on world markets. Export subsidies have reduced developing country exports of cereals, meat, dairy products, oilseeds/vegetable oils and sugar. By contrast, the general policy stance toward agriculture in developing countries has discouraged agricultural exports: in many cases domestic pricing and taxation policies have kept producer prices well below world prices.

The Uruguay Round represents a major attempt to come to grips with the problem by achieving substantial reform of agricultural support policies. The decision to enter into specific, binding commitments in the areas of market access, export competition and domestic support enabled the Trade Negotiations Committee to "restart" the Uruguay Round in February 1991.

However, if the Round is to be concluded by the end of 1991, early decisions will be necessary on unresolved issues and options for binding commitments in the main areas of the reform programme under consideration (i.e. domestic support, market access, export competition, sanitary and phytosanitary measures, and differential and more favourable treatment for developing countries).

The critically important role of agriculture in development should not be ignored in this process. The reform programme on agriculture should be framed in a such a way as to enable developing countries to expand and develop their agricultural sectors. This implies, for example, that in the areas of domestic support and border protection, developing countries should be able to retain the necessary flexibility to continue with, or to institute, public programmes to develop their agricultural sectors. In addition, in order to provide opportunities to raise export earnings, their market access will need to be significantly enlarged. It follows that there must be greater and/or accelerated liberalization of access to the markets of developed countries for products of export interest to developing countries (including non-traditional tropical products, both raw and processed). Finally, measures to deal with the possible effects of the reform programme on net food-importing developing countries will also need to be adopted, including financial assistance, food aid and improved market access to generate additional foreign exchange earnings.

Trade-Related Aspects of Intellectual Property Rights

The TRIPs negotiations constitute a comprehensive and far-reaching multilateral effort to establish international standards for intellectual property protection, as well as a first attempt to bring property rights into the multilateral system of trading rights and obligations. The current negotiating text contains uniform standards for the protection of intellectual property that would be universally applicable. This is one of the areas of the Uruguay Round which has been marked by strong divergencies between developed and developing countries with respect to the nature, scope and institutional implementation of the legal regime to be established.

A priority issue is the suppression of counterfeiting. Developing countries accept the need to establish international rules covering this matter in any agreement, recognizing that counterfeiting can deprive legitimate producers of sales and reputation and reduce incentives to maintain high quality standards, while it contributes nothing to national efforts to build up industrial and technological capabilities. However, they oppose the establishment of substantive and uniform standards involving greater protection for intellectual property rights, because of the implications for their own technological development. In countries that have already attained a certain degree of industrial and technological development, intellectual property protection may well be an important tool in fostering innovation: the grant of exclusive rights ensures that those who engage in R and D are able to exploit commercially its results. Developing countries, however, do not view the relationship between protection and innovation in the same light. They account for only some 3 per cent of world R and D expenditure, and their levels of domestic patenting are extremely low compared with those of the developed countries. Those few developing countries that have been industralizing rapidly show significant improvement in their innovative capacities, but have been criticized for maintaining relatively weak levels of intellectual property protection.

Strong systems of protection may limit the possibility of following an imitative path of technological development, based on reverse engineering, adaptation and the improvement of existing innovations. A premature strengthening of the international intellectual property system can therefore be viewed as skewed in favour of the developed countries, which possess a virtual monopoly in technological assets and innovation capabilities, and against broad-based technology diffusion to the developing countries through freer access to the existing stock of technologies. Furthermore, such strengthening of the system does not conform to the practices successfully followed by the present-day developed countries themselves in their earlier stages of development. It is, however, clear that at an appropriate stage developing countries will have to provide a certain degree of intellectual property protection that is development-oriented. The proper focus of discussion should therefore be on the type, extent and pace of relevant reforms and on the measures needed to mitigate their undesirable monopolistic effects.

While foreign firms are reluctant to transfer their knowledge to countries where technology can be easily copied, greater legal protection may not automatically lead to an enhanced process of technology transfer. Intellectual property protection by itself will not make up for a lack of trained personnel and of equipment and general infrastructure, nor for distance from major research centres. These are all key factors in decisions concerning technology transfer, including decisions on the location of R and D facilities. Equally, technology transfer may not occur, even with legal protection, if other conditions are not met, such as adequate market size and expected growth or ability of potential licencees to compete successfully. Stronger legal protection will only strengthen the bargaining position of property rights holders, which will be reflected in demands for higher royalties and in the imposition of restrictive clauses of various kinds, thereby retarding the technological progress of the developing countries.

The impact of intellectual property protection on consumers would also depend on market structure, on the characteristics of the products in question and on the extent of the property rights conferred. As a rule, the stronger and broader the exclusive rights, the higher is the risk of exorbitant prices and of other abusive practices. The high prices charged for patented pharmaceuticals are a classic example of such a phenomenon, often triggering corrective measures by Governments, including the establishment of special compulsory licensing mechanisms.

A TRIPs agreement along the lines currently before the negotiators would result in a regime that was stronger and better harmonized with the present system of intellectual property rights as practised in the advanced countries. Although significant disagreement persists, an accord may be reached if the needs and interests of developing countries are taken into account. Even so, such an agreement would necessarily complicate the task of developing countries in seeking improved access to technology, the attainment of social goals and a strengthened competitive position in world trade.

Banking within a Multilateral Framework for Trade in Services

The benefits and costs of liberalizing international trade in banking services were discussed in *TDR 1990*, along with the problems of applying to this sector certain key concepts and principles to which a central role has been attributed in the Uruguay Round in the elaboration of a multilateral framework agreement for trade in services. The present Report reviews various aspects of the more recent evolution of these negotiations, focusing particularly on unresolved issues of special concern to developing countries. A number of difficulties have arisen because of the need for such a framework to be sufficiently flexible to accommodate the objectives of countries at very different levels of development. On the one hand, the Uruguay Round is taking place at the same time as the broader movement in OECD countries towards more open financial markets and regulatory convergence in banking. On the other hand, the developing countries' attitudes towards financial liberalization are more cautious. While they do not deny the potential benefits from at least a measure of liberalization, they have none the less emphasized their need to maintain control over the process, so that its costs are minimized and their policy autonomy is not threatened. The negotiations have led to a better understanding of the problems of applying the key concepts and principles mentioned above to banking. As a result, the positions of the OECD and other countries have converged on certain issues, but on others major differences persist.

Progress on banking questions at the negotiations is closely connected to the scope and character of the overall framework agreement for international trade in services. Thus, for example, developing countries have supported an agreement which would include all service sectors so that countries prepared to make only limited concessions regarding one service (which might be banking) could receive offsetting credits for greater commitments in other sectors.

Under the heading of cross-border trade in banking services, developing countries have been particularly concerned that the agreed framework might be a vehicle for pressures to dismantle controls over international capital transactions. However, OECD countries have recently acknowledged that the provisions of the framework should not take precedence over the rights and obligations of member countries of IMF under its Articles of Agreement concerning such matters as the use of exchange controls and exchange restrictions.

Issues where significant disagreements among participants remain include the modalities of market access, the character of obligations under national treatment, and the handling of restrictive business practices. If countries limit the access of foreign banks for reasons of economic policy rather than according to standard licensing rules concerning aspects such as fitness to conduct banking business, the problem arises of how to allocate the resulting quota for such banks in a manner compatible with the MFN principle. Regarding national treatment, there has been disagreement between developing and OECD countries over the latter's efforts to include in the agreed framework obligations that go beyond non-discriminatory treatment under an importing country's internal taxes and regulations and comprise a broader, less precise concept of equality of competitive opportunity. With respect to restrictive business practices by private suppliers, the obligations in the current draft framework are limited to the exchange of information and other unspecified forms of cooperation, and do not provide for redress when services are dumped, a practice which in banking is a source of concern to certain OECD members as well as to developing countries.

K.K.S Dadzie

Part One

CURRENT DEVELOPMENTS IN THE WORLD ECONOMY

PROSPECTS FOR THE WORLD ECONOMY

A. Introduction and summary

1990 marked a significant further slackening of the pace of world economic activity, continuing a trend that had begun in 1989. Output rose by about 1.8 per cent, compared to 4.5 per cent in 1988 and 3.2 per cent in 1989 (see chart 1). Similarly, the growth of the volume of world trade slowed to 4.3 per cent, down from 8.5 per cent in 1988 and 7.0 per cent in 1989. Prices of primary commodities excluding fuels closely followed the state of world demand; relative to prices of internationally traded manufactures they declined by more than 6 per cent in 1990.[1] Nevertheless, in a number of countries and regions previous growth rates were by and large sustained; the overall slowdown in activity was largely the result of deceleration in some developed market economies, a slight decline in output in Latin America and a sharp drop in the level of activity in countries of Central and Eastern Europe. Indeed, the severity of the global downturn may have been considerably mitigated by the varied performance registered by the different regions.

1991 is likely to witness some further deterioration of output growth for the world as a whole, while in some regions economic activity should begin to strengthen. World output is forecast to grow by about 0.7 per cent, and the volume of world trade by about 3 per cent. Primary commodity prices will accelerate their decline relative to those of manufactures, falling in nominal terms as well. Again, the overall picture for 1991 masks considerable regional differences. In the developed market economies the slowdown appears to be rather more broadly-based than in 1990, while in contrast the developing economies are in many instances showing signs of improved growth. Thus 1992 could mark a reconvergence of growth trends in the world economy, with most regions able to achieve more normal rates of growth. However, the projected recovery for 1992 is rather modest and its extent is in some doubt, in part due to increased financial fragility in some major industrial countries.[2]

Among the main developing regions, only Latin America registered a decline in output in 1990 (of about 0.5 per cent) as some of those countries implemented adjustment programmes to contain inflation and deal with the burden of external debt. Growth in f Africaas somewhat above past experience due largely to the improved performance of petroleum-producing countries; in most other countries of the region lower, trend rates of growth were the rule. The Asian experience was mixed, with improved performance in some countries offset by sharply worsened growth in others, particularly in those countries in West Asia affected by the crisis in the Persian Gulf. For developing countries as a whole GDP growth in 1991 should be somewhat higher than in 1990, in particular in Latin America, where a resumption of growth should be possible.

---

1   See table 3 below and section A.5 of the next chapter, where developments in commodity markets are reviewed.
2   See part two below, chap. II.

In 1990 China's growth performance improved modestly, after the sharp deceleration of 1989 brought about by the 1988 austerity programme. A resumption of capital flows, together with an improvement in the trade balance in 1990, should allow for some further acceleration in 1991 and 1992. However, sustainable growth is likely to remain below the rates attained in the 1980s.

Chart 1

WORLD OUTPUT, EXPORTS AND COMMODITY PRICES [a] IN REAL TERMS: 1988-1990 AND FORECASTS FOR 1991 AND 1992

(Percentages)

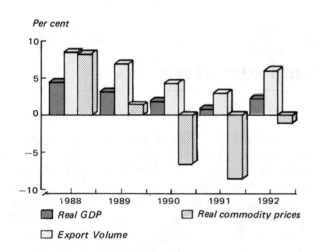

Source: UNCTAD secretariat calculations, based on national and international sources, and SIGMA for forecasts.
a World primary commodity prices, excluding fuels.

Output continued to decline in most countries of Central and Eastern Europe in 1990. While estimates are necessarily subject to a great deal of uncertainty, production appears to have fallen by about 4.8 per cent in 1990. In 1991 conditions are likely to deteriorate further, particularly in the Soviet Union. However, there are some signs that economic reforms are beginning to show results in a number of countries of the region, with prospects of a resumption of growth in certain cases.

Growth in developed market economies slowed further from the peak reached in 1988 and was less than 2.3 per cent in 1990. However, the slowdown was concentrated primarily in North America and the United Kingdom. The outcome for 1991 is likely to be a further worsening of performance in those countries and also slower economic growth in other developed market economies. Nevertheless, significant signs of recovery by mid-year indicate that the developed market economies should achieve a highly convergent, though modest, upturn in 1992.

The sharp decline in world trade in 1990 was due primarily to much weaker import demand in North America and, to a lesser extent, in Japan and EEC. The volume of imports by countries of Central and Eastern Europe fell sharply, reflecting in large part the collapse of trade among the former members of CMEA. In contrast, import demand in developing countries remained relatively strong, rising by 7.7 per cent. While of the same order as that of the previous year, in Latin America and in certain countries of South-East Asia import growth actually accelerated. Some acceleration also occurred in Africa, partly in response to increased oil revenues. 1991 is likely to see continued strength in import demand of developing countries, but with the sources of dynamism largely shifting to Asia.

The slowdown in world economic activity in 1990 was perhaps most vividly reflected in the sharp fall in primary commodity prices other than fuels relative to those of manufactures (see chart 1 and table 3). Among the broad aggregates, world food prices increased slightly, but there were severe declines for coffee, soyabeans and wheat. (Food export prices for developing countries fell by about 6 per cent.) Prices of agricultural raw materials increased somewhat, led by tropical timber and softwood. Prices of mineral ores again rose considerably in 1990, due to strong performance in the steel industry. However, the continued slowdown in world economic activity expected for 1991 as a whole is likely to be reflected in further, broadly-based declines in primary commodity prices. It is only with the modest recovery expected in 1992 that real prices of non-fuel primary commodities are likely to stabilize.

Table 1

WORLD OUTPUT, 1980-1990, AND FORECASTS FOR 1991 AND 1992

(Percentage change) [a]

Country group	1980-1985	1985-1990	1990	1991	1992
	Actual		Estimated	Forecasts	
World	2.6	3.2	1.8	0.7	2.3
Developed market-economy countries	2.4	3.2	2.3	0.9	2.7
Central and Eastern Europe [b]	2.9	1.1	-4.8	-8.9	-8.5 [c]
China	9.8	7.5	4.8	5.8	6.3
Developing countries	2.0	3.1	2.5	2.9	4.6
of which:					
Latin America	1.1	1.6	-0.5	1.6	3.7
Africa	1.8	2.3	3.5	3.8	2.8
Asia	2.7	4.4	4.2	4.1	5.9
Memo item:					
Least developed countries	2.4	3.2	2.5	2.7	2.9

Source: UNCTAD secretariat calculations, based on national and international sources, and SIGMA for forecasts.
  a Annual average or change over previous year
  b Net material product. For purposes of aggregation estimated GDP weights have been used.
  c Due to the uncertainties, it is assumed that the decline in Soviet NMP will be the same as in 1991.

Table 2

WORLD TRADE VOLUMES, 1980-1990, AND FORECASTS FOR 1991 AND 1992

(Percentage change) [a]

Country group	1980-1985	1985-1990	1990	1991	1992
	Actual		Estimated	Forecasts [b]	
World [c]					
Exports	2.1	6.0	4.3	3.0	6.0
Imports	2.2	6.2	4.5	3.0	6.0
Developed market-economy countries					
Exports	3.6	5.3	5.1	3.0	6.0
Imports	3.1	6.8	5.3	3.0	6.0
Central and Eastern Europe					
Exports	1.5	0.4	-14.5	-10.5	-3.0
Imports	2.6	0.5	-7.0	-7.0	-0.5
China					
Exports	12.7	10.3	13.0	13.0	10.0
Imports	19.7	4.5	-9.0	10.0	10.5
Developing countries					
Exports	-1.4	8.4	5.0	4.5	7.0
Imports	-0.1	6.7	7.7	7.0	8.5
Memo item:					
Least developed countries					
Exports	-0.0	1.0	1.5	1.0	7.5
Imports	-0.4	0.3	-3.7	4.5	3.0

Source: UNCTAD secretariat calculations, based on national and international sources, and SIGMA for forecasts.
  a Annual average or change over previous year.
  b Forecasts are rounded to the nearest half percentage point.
  a Differences between world exports and imports are due to unresolvable statistical discrepancies.

Table 3

WORLD PRIMARY COMMODITY PRICES, 1980-1990, AND FORECASTS FOR 1991 AND 1992

(Percentage change) [a]

	1980-1985	1985-1990	1990	1991	1992
Commodity group	Actual			Forecasts	
All food items	-8.0	5.9	1.1	-5.7	4.4
Agricultural non-food	-5.8	6.2	2.0	-1.6	1.7
Minerals excluding fuels	-4.3	8.5	20.4	-0.2	3.8
Fuels	-1.5	-4.3	26.4	-10.0	5.0
All primary commodities	-3.4	-0.6	15.1	-6.8	4.2
of which					
Non-fuel primary commodities	-7.0	6.2	2.5	-3.7	3.5
Memo item:					
Unit value index of manufactures [b]	-3.0	9.4	9.8	5.4	4.5

Source: UNCTAD secretariat calculations, based on United Nations, *Monthly Bulletin of Statistics,* and SIGMA for forecasts.
a Annual average or change over previous year.
b Unit value index of manufactured goods exported by developed market-economy countries.

B. Developing countries

1. Latin America

(a) Recent performance

1990 was a year of retrenchment in Latin America, with GDP falling by 0.5 per cent. The downturn, following several years of unsatisfactory economic performance, coincided with the widespread implementation of stabilization programmes aimed primarily at the containment of inflation and hyperinflation, which accelerated to almost 1,500 per cent in 1990, from over 1,100 per cent in 1989. However, in spite of these efforts fiscal adjustment proved difficult to achieve, particularly where external constraints remained binding. In such cases fiscal imbalances persisted, domestic debt accumulated, and inflationary pressures were exacerbated. In contrast, those countries whose external environment improved in 1990 generally outperformed the region as a whole, in terms of both growth and the control of inflation.

Latin American *oil-exporting countries,* performing relatively well, achieved an average GDP growth of 2.5 per cent in 1990 (4.5 per cent in Venezuela, 3.5 per cent in Colombia, 2.5 per cent in Mexico and 2.5 per cent in Bolivia). Inflation either decreased or remained relatively moderate (Mexico, Bolivia and Colombia). Peru proved an exception among the oil-exporting countries, posting a third year of severe economic decline. While all countries of the group benefited from the higher petroleum prices in 1989 and 1990, Venezuela, Ecuador and Mexico were able also to increase their export volumes as a consequence of the Gulf crisis. Thus, their purchasing power of exports strengthened considerably, permitting larger trade surpluses in spite of import volume growth of 12 per cent. Economic expansion thus proved possible simultaneously with reduced pressure on government budgets and

Table 4

WORLD CURRENT ACCOUNT BALANCES, 1981-1990, AND FORECASTS FOR 1991 AND 1992

(Billions of dollars)

Country group	1981-1985	1986-1990	1990	1991	1992
	Actual [a]		Estimated	Forecasts	
Developed market-economy countries	-15.2	-29.7	-79.1	-39.1	-25.1
Central and Eastern Europe	-0.7	-5.8	-12.9	-21.5	-28.7
China	0.6	-1.4	8.4	11.1	15.2
Developing countries	-51.5	-20.6	-8.8	-12.9	-1.0
of which:					
Latin America	-23.5	-16.7	-12.4	-13.2	-13.7
Africa	-17.2	-17.7	-21.3	-22.7	-22.9
Asia	-9.0	12.2	31.8	27.8	40.8
Statistical discrepancy	-66.8	-57.4	-92.4	-62.4	-39.6
Memo item:					
Least developed countries	-8.2	-10.5	-12.6	-13.9	-14.1

Source: UNCTAD secretariat calculations, based on national and international sources, and SIGMA for forecasts.
  a Annual average.

an enhanced capacity to service public external debt.

With regard to the external financial environment, Mexico enjoyed particular success in attracting additional capital, with an inflow amounting to $8.6 billion, consisting of direct investment, bond issues on international capital markets, repatriation of capital and short-term credits. In the case of Venezuela, improvement in its trading environment enabled the country to provide the means to guarantee the debt reduction agreement reached under the Brady Plan. The recovery of exports also allowed a recovery in public investment while at the same time nearly eliminating the fiscal deficit and allocating resources to a stabilization fund.

Economic performance in the *non-oil exporting countries* of Latin America was significantly worse, as GDP declined in 1990 by 2.8 per cent, whereas in the previous year there had been growth of 2.5 per cent. This was largely the result of a continued decline in Argentina, a reversal in Brazil from growth of 3.6 per cent in 1989 to a decline of 4.0 per cent in 1990 and deceleration in Chile from growth of 9.3 per cent in 1989 to 2.0 per cent. Inflation also increased, particularly in Brazil. The relatively poor record of these countries in 1990 was largely due to a conjunction of the implementation of domestic stabilization

programmes and developments in external trade and finance. The worsened trade outcome was in part due to the increased import bill for petrol in 1989 and 1990 caused by higher prices. However, a number of country-specific factors were also at play. In Brazil the trade balance was seriously affected by a substantial decline in export volumes resulting from an uncompetitive exchange rate, the effect of labour conflicts on exports of iron and steel and lower car exports. In addition, export financing was hampered by the existence of debt arrears. In Chile there was a major decline in the terms of trade as a result of a substantial fall in copper prices, the impact of which was only partly offset by a higher volume of exports of other commodities. Argentina's terms of trade also deteriorated in 1990, but were counterbalanced by an improvement in export volumes, especially for agricultural commodities, and by a lower level of imports.

(b) Outlook

Recent Latin American experience indicates that the implementation of stabilization programmes in an unfavourable external environment can be costly, achieving only slow progress in containing inflation. This being said, there are tentative indications of an improvement in trade and financial prospects which, together with determined monetary and fiscal policies, should allow some resumption of growth for the region as a whole.

Chart 2

ECONOMIC GROWTH IN LATIN AMERICA AND SELECTED COUNTRIES SINCE 1980

(Percentages)

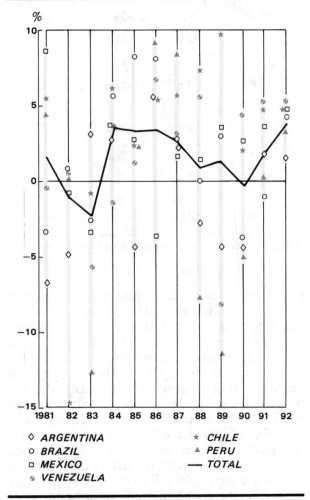

◇ ARGENTINA   ★ CHILE
○ BRAZIL   ▲ PERU
□ MEXICO   — TOTAL
❂ VENEZUELA

Source: UNCTAD secretariat calculations, based on national and international sources, and SIGMA for forecasts.

In spite of a considerable fallback of petroleum prices subsequent to the cessation of hostilities in the Gulf, it is expected that many of the oil exporters of the region will be able to consolidate their position and further improve their economic performance. For Venezuela, the recent decline in the terms of trade, the uncompetitiveness of the exchange rate, and the increase in growth-oriented domestic expenditures and related imports will probably result in a deterioration of the trade balance. However, possible demand-induced inflationary

pressures are to be fought by the issuance of zero-coupon bonds to absorb liquidity, while the improved macroeconomic climate is expected to induce reverse flows of flight capital and promote growth. Continued progress in Mexico is expected as the external financial situation is strengthened through increased foreign investment and better creditworthiness. Consequently, lower domestic interest rates should be sustainable, providing some relief to the budget deficit by reducing the cost of public debt and further stimulating economic activity. Lower inflation rates and further privatization should also serve to reduce the budget deficit. However, the trade balance will probably deteriorate somewhat, due to higher imports arising from increased domestic demand and a possible enhanced supply of external finance.

Prospects for the major non-oil exporting countries, while less promising, should improve as world trade recovers, although the debt overhang and renewed access to foreign capital remain important questions for policy-makers. In this context Argentina is pursuing vigorous domestic policies aimed at increasing its debt service capacity and creditworthiness in order to obtain fresh external finance from IMF and other sources.

In Brazil, both the trade and the financial sectors can be expected to be more supportive. Stable oil prices and firmer coffee prices should lead to significantly better terms of trade. In addition, in the first half of 1991 partial payment was made of interest due on external debt. In this context, efforts by Brazil to initiate negotiations on debt reduction along the lines of the Brady Plan, if successful, could lead to enhanced creditworthiness. However, there is a structural aspect to the debt-servicing problem of Brazil. Like most countries, its external debt is mainly owed by the public sector, but unlike many Latin American exporters the resources generated by exports accrue almost exclusively to the private sector. Thus a successful stabilization and adjustment programme needs to be supported by a tax system that would transfer more resources to the Government. All in all, the Brazilian economy should fare better than in 1990 but is not expected to achieve significant growth this year.

Progress in the control of inflation in Chile and a consequent easing of monetary policy should facilitate economic activity. At the same time, increased foreign investment, lower oil prices and firmer copper prices are permitting growth-oriented fiscal adjustment, with the prospect of higher growth in the coming two years.

Table 5

**DEVELOPING COUNTRIES: SOURCES OF FINANCING OF THE CURRENT ACCOUNT, [a]
1981-1990 AND FORECASTS FOR 1991 AND 1992**

(Billions of dollars)

Item	1981-1985 [b] Actual	1986-1990 [b] Actual	1990 Estimated	1991 Forecasts	1992 Forecasts
Current account balance	-62.2	-31.5	-44.2	-52.6	-48.7
Source of financing:					
Increase in official reserves	7.5	18.4	28.8	4.9	12.1
Total net capital flows	54.7	49.9	73.0	57.5	60.9
Official flows	46.6	36.2	39.7	34.9	32.7
Grants [c]	11.3	15.7	19.4	19.8	20.5
Medium- and long-term loans	35.3	20.5	20.3	15.1	12.2
Private flows	21.5	1.0	13.8	3.9	9.5
Direct investment	10.6	14.5	19.2	22.1	23.3
Private borrowing	10.8	-13.5	-5.4	-18.2	-13.8
Other capital, unrecorded flows, errors and omissions	-13.4	12.7	19.5	18.7	18.7

Source: UNCTAD secretariat calculations, based on national and international sources, and SIGMA for forecasts.
a Excluding oil-dominant countries (Iraq, Kuwait, Libyan Arab Jamahiriya, Oman, Qatar, Saudi Arabia, United Arab Emirates) and developing countries of Europe.
b Annual average.
c Excluding technical assistance.

2. Africa

(a) Recent performance

In spite of considerable improvement in the economic situation in some countries in recent years, African economic development remains largely blocked. Though GDP growth was somewhat higher in 1990 (3.5 per cent, reaching one of the highest rates of the last decade) the economic situation of the region remains precarious, and the combination of external and internal conditions is still unfavourable for narrowing the gap between Africa and other developing regions. The economies of most African countries are still dominated by weather conditions, and they confront a generally hostile world economic environment, problems of external indebtedness and, in a number of cases, political and social unrest. Domestic policy reforms and economic restructuring, which have been initiated in the majority of countries, have not so far had a major influence on overall economic growth despite some encouraging preliminary signs. In some cases these efforts have been undermined by natural disasters, civil unrest and inadequate implementation of the reforms.

The relatively good performance of developing Africa as a whole in 1990 masked, as in previous years, wide disparities among countries, and owed much to the unexpected stimulus to oil-producing economies arising from the Gulf crisis. Seven major African oil

Table 6

DEVELOPING COUNTRIES: [a] DEBT OUTSTANDING, 1988-1990, AND FORECASTS FOR 1991 AND 1992

(Billions of dollars) [b]

	1988	1989	1990	1991	1992
	Actual		Estimated	Forecasts	
Total debt outstanding	933.7	922.1	937.1	934.0	932.3
of which:					
Latin America	404.6	388.6	384.1	372.0	362.8
Africa	242.0	245.6	257.5	264.9	272.0
Asia	287.1	287.9	295.5	297.1	297.5
Memo item:					
Least developed countries	79.7	80.4	86.7	93.0	99.4

Source: UNCTAD secretariat calculations, based on national and international sources, and SIGMA for forecasts.
   a Excluding oil-dominant countries (see note a to table 5) and developing countries of Europe.
   b End of year.

producers,[3] accounting for 50 per cent of the GDP of African developing countries, both together and individually recorded the second highest growth rate of the last decade (1985 being the highest). Sharply increased export revenues, resulting from the oil price increase in the second part of the year, alleviated their international liquidity problems and offered short-term relief for the most indebted among them.

Although they are also oil producers and exporters, Egypt and Tunisia nevertheless suffered considerably from the Gulf crisis. In Egypt the balance of payments deteriorated seriously on account of the sharp fall in workers' remittances, tourism and Suez canal dues, which are normally important sources of the country's foreign exchange earnings. Tunisia suffered from important cuts in trade as a result of the United Nations embargo.

Non-oil producers in Africa recorded only modest progress, in keeping with their general growth performance over the last decade. Weather conditions, particularly important for this group, were reasonably favourable in 1990, permitting some improvement in the agricultural sector, which is basic to the economy. While the increase in oil prices exerted inflationary pressure, it did not significantly prejudice the achievement of previously forecast growth rates. However, higher import bills did affect the balance of payments, particularly of the low-income countries. Losses linked to the

Gulf crisis either through trade (caused by the embargo) or financial transfers (remittances of migrant workers, reductions in the flow of assistance, etc.) were confined to a limited number of countries, but where they occurred (e.g. Mauritania, Sudan and Seychelles) they were critical to the economy. In Mauritania the reduced volume of trade, higher oil prices and lower remittances and other transfers brought about a substantial recession. Sudan, already confronted by severe external payments difficulties, faced an increased oil import bill and a fall in remittances, compounding the problems. However, the situation was most serious for the Seychelles, which had had access to oil on concessional terms; the country also experienced a drastic fall in tourism due to rising transportation and insurance costs and general uncertainty.

(b) Prospects

Short-term prospects for growth in Africa are linked to continued strengthening of economic activity in the oil-exporting countries in the aftermath of the Gulf crisis, one of the consequences of which has been to increase oil output in almost all African oil-producing countries. A more extensive use of production capacity in the petrochemical industry is likely to contribute to overall economic activity in non-oil sectors. With higher oil prices (compared to the beginning of 1990), multiplier ef-

---

3   Algeria, Angola, Cameroon, Congo, Gabon, Libyan Arab Jamahiriya, Nigeria.

fects can feed through the economies of such countries as Angola, Gabon, Libyan Arab Jamahiriya and Nigeria which were not directly affected by the crisis. The strength of the oil sector in these countries, through its impact on investment and exports, can stimulate domestic demand, thus in some cases relieving pressure on their balances of payments and alleviating severe financial constraints. In 1991 GDP growth rates for this group of countries are expected to exceed those of the previous year, and thus contribute to an improved performance for African developing countries as a whole.

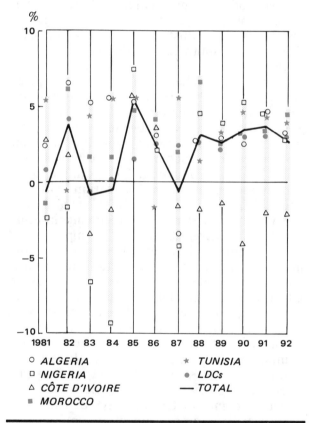

Chart 3

ECONOMIC GROWTH IN DEVELOPING AFRICA AND SELECTED COUNTRIES SINCE 1980

(Percentages)

○ ALGERIA   ★ TUNISIA
□ NIGERIA   ● LDCs
△ CÔTE D'IVOIRE   — TOTAL
■ MOROCCO

Source: UNCTAD secretariat calculations, based on national and international sources, and SIGMA for forecasts.

For the North African oil-producing countries, in particular Egypt and Tunisia, negative effects of the Gulf war will continue to be felt at least until the end of 1991. While oil production is expected to rise, recovery in earnings from invisibles may take some time, as regards both tourism (the volume of which is not likely to return to pre-Gulf levels before

1992) and workers' remittances. The resettlement costs for repatriated workers are likely to create additional economic pressures. However, remittances could increase as early as the second half of 1991 as a result of the reconstruction needs of the Gulf States.

Higher import costs in African oil-importing countries will not in general have a major influence on their economies, since in many of them oil consumption is relatively low. However, a limited number of countries, which had obtained oil supplies from Gulf countries on concessional terms, will suffer adverse consequences. In general, the prevailing higher oil prices (as compared to pre-Gulf levels) can be expected to have an inflationary effect on oil-importing countries.

The slowdown in world economic activity in 1991 is significantly affecting African countries through lower prices of primary commodities, higher interest rates, and reduced demand (notably in developed market-economy countries) for their exports. As in the past, this slowdown entails a reduced demand for minerals and metals. Since most African producers of such products are heavily dependent on the export of a particular metal, 1991 will be an exceptionally difficult year. Thus growth rates are expected to weaken in major African copper-producing countries.

Weather is a factor of particular uncertainty for many sub-Saharan countries, where agriculture accounts for as much as 45 to 50 per cent of GDP. The current agricultural season is assumed, in general, to be not worse than in 1990. However, a slightly lower increase in agricultural output is forecast. The food situation in most African countries is expected to be satisfactory, but the need for food aid will nevertheless persist. There is the possibility of a new drought in some Sahelian countries, such as Chad, Mauritania and Niger, where precipitation has so far been well below the normal. The food supply situation is also becoming critical in Ethiopia and Sudan, where a new famine cannot be ruled out.

World demand for non-food agricultural commodities remains of critical importance to African countries such as Kenya and Côte d'Ivoire. As noted in chapter II, section A.5, prices of cocoa and coffee continue to be depressed. Lower receipts are projected for almost all African countries supplying tropical beverages, further constraining their already limited import capacity.

Medium-term prospects for the majority of countries in the region depend on the successful implementation of domestic policy reforms and support for them by the international community. Despite considerable efforts undertaken by African Governments in recent years, the achievement of monetary and exchange rate equilibrium and the improvement of fiscal management remain main objectives of the restructuring process in many countries. Economic liberalization, an objective sought by most African countries, should be pursued through the further encouragement of small businesses, progress in market determination of prices, speedier progress in privatization and modifications in trade policies. Such steps are now all the more important if African countries are to sustain and attract an adequate flow of development finance.

3.   Asia

(a)   East Asia

(i)   Recent developments

In spite of the impact of the Gulf crisis and the slowdown in the world economy, East Asian countries continued to expand in 1990 at relatively rapid rates. Policy reforms undertaken by the major exporters of manufactures in past years helped them to absorb the shocks more easily than many other countries, and their average GDP growth rate rose from the previous year's level. Economic activity was led mainly by domestic demand, inducing an acceleration of imports, while export growth fell sharply, resulting in a large reduction of current account surpluses. Depressed external demand, rising production costs and the emergence of competition from other producers were among the factors explaining the slower growth of manufactured exports, particularly light industrial goods. Strong private consumption was accompanied by high investment in plant and equipment to restructure industrial production, while rising public expenditures to ease infrastructure bottlenecks and protect the environment from degradation further fuelled internal demand.

In the Republic of Korea an unexpectedly high GDP growth of 9.0 per cent was in part due to a construction boom, which strained domestic resources, in particular of labour, and drove up wages sharply. Inflation, which accelerated to 8.6 per cent, became a source of concern. The rapid growth of domestic con-

sumption, as well as surging imports of machinery and crude oil, resulted in the first current account deficit since 1985 ($2.2 billion), compared with a surplus of $5.0 billion in 1989. Growth in Hong Kong was marginally higher than the relatively low rate recorded in 1989, partly due to a recovery in entrepôt trade with China. Though some slowdown occurred in Singapore, the country continued to perform well, with strong growth in the financial sector and petroleum refining. On the other hand, the slowdown in Taiwan Province of China to 5.2 per cent, from 7.6 per cent in 1989, can be mainly attributed to sluggish exports and a sharp decline in private investment because of falling stock and property prices.

The ability of the highly trade-oriented countries of the region to maintain growth in the face of slackening world trade is a measure of their adaptability to changes in the pattern and pace of world production and trade. They can be expected to continue relocating light industrial export industries in lower labour-cost countries of South-East Asia and to China. At the same time, measures to promote the development of higher value-added industries, with emphasis on capital-intensive technology for upgrading production as well as for easing labour shortages, could be accelerated. Research and development for improving scientific capabilities may encourage the establishment of new lines of production. For example, plans to increase industrial specialization with the focus of investment on technology and productivity, with the aim of enhancing international competitiveness, are to be implemented in the Republic of Korea. It has been recognized that a greater diversification and an expansion of markets are necessary, so as to reduce the present high degree of reliance on certain major markets. At the same time, price stabilization measures and social peace are essential to create a favourable environment for maintaining stable export growth. Investment policy in Hong Kong and Singapore appears to be shifting towards the service sector. In Taiwan Province of China, heavy expenditures on infrastructure improvement are envisaged in the new six-year development plan, which places emphasis on new technological equipment in reducing environmental degradation, on improving the quality of life and on lowering regional disparities.

(ii)   Prospects

The major exporters of manufactures in the East Asian region are expected to have slower output growth in 1991, particularly in the Republic of Korea and Singapore, in part due to domestic capacity constraints, but also to continued relatively weak export demand. In the Republic of Korea an improvement in exports will involve increased imports in the short run, particularly of capital equipment, and the trade deficit is thus likely to be even larger than in 1990. Social unrest may also hamper manufacturing production. Prospects for Hong Kong are for an improved performance on account of higher re-exports and services related to entrepôt trade, which would arise from faster growth of the Chinese economy, and also because of further recovery in tourism. In Taiwan Province of China a substantial increase in government current expenditures and gross fixed capital formation, both associated with major infrastructure improvements, is foreseen. However, a growing labour shortage is likely to result in rising labour costs and retard the rate of implementation of projects. With imports growing faster than exports, the trade surplus will decline.

(b)   South-East Asia

(i)   Recent developments

The major economies of South-East Asia sustained their vigorous growth of preceding years and continued to outperform other Asian subregions. Policy reforms undertaken in many countries in the past five years have helped to create a favourable environment and encourage domestic and foreign investment. Although growth generally slowed down in 1990, the pattern differed among countries, in part according to their ability to cope with the Gulf crisis. Oil-exporting countries (Brunei Darussalam, Indonesia and Malaysia) generally benefited from the oil price increase while oil-importing countries suffered. Led by strong domestic demand, high industrial output and infrastructure investment expansion, growth in Indonesia and Malaysia was already accelerating prior to the Gulf crisis. Having received a further boost from the rise in exports of oil which made up for some slowdown of other exports, these two countries achieved growth rates of 7.1 per cent and 9.3 per cent, respectively. On the other hand, in the Philippines and Thailand growth slowed from 5.2 per cent to 2.6 per cent and from 12.2 per cent to 10 per cent, respectively. The economy of the Philippines was hard hit by a number of inauspicious events, such as the Gulf crisis, political uncertainty, severe natural disasters, weakening commodity prices and power shortages. Export expansion slowed considerably

while imports continued to grow rapidly, resulting in a widening of the current account deficit. Combined with a worsening budget deficit, the situation reflected the vulnerability of the economy to natural disasters and external shocks, and highlighted the need for further structural adaptation. Thailand was one of the fastest-growing economies in developing Asia for the fourth consecutive year, with strong increases in investment and consumer spending, particularly on durable goods, due to increased income and high employment levels. Though current account deficits widened in most countries, their external outstanding debt increased only slightly, as the deficits were largely financed by flows of FDI. In Indonesia, external debt declined by $8.7 billion.

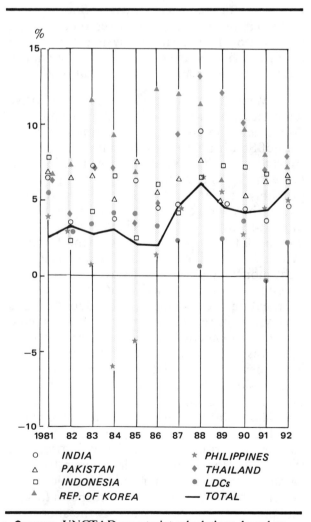

Chart 4

**ECONOMIC GROWTH IN DEVELOPING ASIA
AND SELECTED COUNTRIES SINCE 1980**

(Percentages)

○ INDIA	★ PHILIPPINES
△ PAKISTAN	◆ THAILAND
□ INDONESIA	● LDCs
▲ REP. OF KOREA	— TOTAL

Source: UNCTAD secretariat calculations, based on national and international sources, and SIGMA for forecasts.

(ii) Prospects

In many countries of the subregion, the diversification of the manufacturing base is well under way. However, some serious problems, ranging from inflation to poverty alleviation and environmental degradation, persist. Production of electricity, raw materials and industrial inputs needs to be expanded to ease shortages and supply disruptions. There is also a strong case for further stimulation of domestic saving, particularly in Thailand, where it has started to stagnate. With some expected slowdown in private investment, public investment in the subregion should remain relatively vigorous, reflecting, among other things, the need to overcome bottlenecks in transport and telecommunications. Uneven regional economic development and income distribution in these countries may have adverse social and economic repercussions in rural areas. Higher investment in the agricultural sector and efforts to introduce small business in rural areas are necessary for balanced growth. Shortages of skilled labour can in part be overcome through a reform of the educational system. In certain countries, greater attention needs to be paid to natural resources and environmental issues.

While the relocation of labour-intensive manufacturing activities from Japan and East Asia's newly industrialized economies to countries of South-East Asia will continue, there are signs that it will do so at a slower rate in 1991. Growth in these developing countries will probably decelerate, though it will remain well above the average for Asia as a whole, with a modest recovery in 1992. This outcome will be due in part to reduced world demand for their exports. Inflationary pressures and resulting tight monetary policies will slow the expansion of domestic demand and dampen speculative overheating. Growth rates in Indonesia and Malaysia will remain strong. Indonesia should continue to benefit from financial deregulation measures (implemented since 1988) and foreign investment inflows, while some credit shortage might slow the rapidly emerging export-oriented manufacturing sector. The rapid industrialization of these two countries, together with labour shortages in Singapore, have motivated the formation of a "growth triangle", through exploitation of their comparative advantages and cooperation in various joint industrial and tourism projects. Prospects for the Philippines are set to improve as the shocks of 1990 are absorbed and with the disbursement of fresh IMF loans and recent foreign assistance pledges from aid donors. However, efforts to contain the growing budget and current account deficits are necessary - a difficult task,

given the need to cope with the most recent natural disaster. It is expected that FDI will revive now that more liberal terms are offered, while reforms agreed for the banking sector await implementation. Signs that interest and inflation rates are beginning to subside have given some impetus to business investment in anticipation of an economic recovery. New expansion plans will depend on the success of policies in reducing imbalances and early restoration of investment confidence. Thailand is projected to face some slowdown as both domestic and export demand soften, while infrastructure constraints and cost-push factors will adversely affect production.

(c) South Asia

(i) Recent developments

Growth in South Asia was slightly lower than in 1989. While the economies of Bangladesh, Pakistan and Sri Lanka grew rapidly, growth in India decelerated. The rise in Bangladesh (6.2 per cent) was due mainly to agriculture and manufacturing (especially ready-made garments), while the rise of 5.1 per cent in Sri Lanka resulted from a gradual return of social stability and an associated recovery of tourism and from high garment and tea exports. In Pakistan, some recovery in manufacturing was responsible for a slight improvement in economic growth (from 5.0 per cent to 5.3 per cent), despite a slowdown in agriculture. A strong expansion of textile goods accounted for most of the 18.6 per cent increase in the value of exports. Whereas growth accelerated in India during the first half of 1990, the rate was not sustained in the second half, and for the year as a whole GDP increased by about 4.3 per cent, compared with about 5 per cent in 1989. Sluggish industrial production and low investment were in part attributable to social unrest and to shortages and high costs of inputs.

South Asian countries have been particularly affected by the Gulf crisis. The severe repercussions on their balances of payments, inflation and employment are already evident. High import bills for oil, which constitute a large share of total imports, are a major concern for many countries and will remain an important factor limiting growth rates. The decline in remittances from overseas workers in the West Asian (Gulf) region and in export earnings from those countries widened current account deficits and compounded debt servicing difficulties. The return of expatriate workers further affected the employment situation. Some of these countries also faced higher transportation costs and losses from tourism, though conditions in this respect should gradually return to normal.

Domestic policy reform is necessary to create a favourable and stable environment for more private capital inflows to meet external financial requirements. In Pakistan, for example, the Government initiated in 1989 a three-year structural adjustment programme with the assistance of IMF to redress macroeconomic imbalances. Since then, progress has been made in reducing significantly both the current account and the fiscal deficits. To keep the programme on track, other measures, including those to increase productivity through major structural reforms in the real as well as in the financial sectors, were taken. While some liberalization of the banking system has been implemented to encourage private initiatives in industrial production, incentives to reinforce business confidence and to attract foreign investment have been introduced and are gathering pace. Giving greater priority to the export sector, with selective fiscal and credit support, is essential. In India, the Government has recently announced an extensive programme of stabilization and reform. Steps to be included are the liberalization of the trade regime and of the systems of investment controls and of industrial licences and permits, the easing of restrictions governing foreign direct investment, a reduction of government spending and subsidies, and increased taxes.

(ii) Prospects

Growth prospects for the developing countries in South Asia vary significantly from country to country; important constraints in many cases will continue to be the need to reduce budgetary and trade deficits and the decline in foreign exchange reserves. While some slowdown is to be expected in Bangladesh and India, due to a combination of factors, Pakistan and Sri Lanka should enjoy higher growth due to the expansion of the industrial and export sectors. In Pakistan, the current process of import liberalization, privatization and deregulation of industrial investment should contribute, together with an increase in agricultural production, to the achievement of a growth rate of around 6 per cent, and the budget deficit should continue to narrow. The economy of Sri Lanka should benefit from the Government's continuing economic stabilization programme, and the liberalization of the private business environment. Growth in India

is projected to slow down to less than 4 per cent, mainly because of constraints imposed by large budget and current account deficits. Although agriculture is expected to maintain its growth rate, the difficult balance of payments situation will constrain imports and could slow down industrial expansion. However, the recently announced liberalization programme and possible large-scale external support can be expected to have a significant impact.

(d) West Asia

(i) Recent developments

All West Asian countries were, to varying degrees, affected by the Gulf crisis and the subsequent military conflict. Through its direct effect on the output of petroleum the crisis had major consequences for balances of payments. Three groups of countries can be distinguished in this regard: Iraq and Kuwait, where production and exports of oil were severely disrupted; other major oil exporters, who generally increased their output to make up for the absence of Iraq and Kuwait from the world oil market; and minor oil exporters (Syrian Arab Republic and Yemen) or net oil importers (Jordan), where results depended on the movement of their oil production and the intensity of their trade relations with Iraq and Kuwait.

For the subregion as a whole GDP declined by about 3.0 per cent, essentially the result of the substantial fall in Iraq, Kuwait and, to a lesser extent, Jordan. The decline would have been sharper had it not been for the increase in oil production of the other oil-exporting countries of the subregion, notably Saudi Arabia, where GDP growth of 10 per cent in 1990 exceeded that of 1989. Because of its excess capacity, Saudi Arabia was able to increase its oil production to make up for the shortfall caused by the eruption of the Gulf crisis and to mobilize resources to meet crisis-related military expenditures. By the end of 1990 those expenditures amounted to $20 billion, and by June 1991 another $35 billion had been committed. The increase in Saudi defence expenditure has been financed from gains in export revenues and a drawing down of international reserves, supplemented by borrowing. Borrowing proved necessary because the gains from trade were less than expected, as some of the extra oil produced was used domestically for the war effort. In addition, while the country's international assets are large, a high proportion appears to be owned by the private sector. The Government accordingly decided to borrow from the international markets ($4.5 billion) and appears also to be approaching local banks for another $2.5 billion. In consequence, it has been able by and large to avoid any growth-restricting measures of adjustment.

Among the third group of countries - minor oil exporters or net oil importers - Jordan was the most seriously affected by the Gulf crisis. Real GDP declined by about 8 per cent in 1990 reflecting, in the main, the effect of the United Nations embargo. One quarter of Jordan's exports normally go to Iraq, and much of the latter's imports normally transit through Jordan. In addition, financial flows to Jordan were greatly reduced because of the return of expatriate workers from the Gulf region (who were furthermore unable to repatriate their savings) and the virtual cessation of official assistance. Some estimates put the resultant loss in foreign exchange for Jordan as equivalent to about one-third of GNP in 1990.

Output in Yemen was relatively insulated from the effects of the Gulf crisis for two reasons. First, its oil production rose in 1990, and second, unlike Jordan, it does not have very close trading relations with Iraq and Kuwait. Nevertheless, its external balance deteriorated sharply as workers' remittances fell drastically and financial assistance to Yemen was curtailed; these two reduced flows amounted to about 10 per cent of Yemen's GNP. In addition, the expulsion of Yemeni workers from Saudi Arabia aggravated the unemployment situation in this least developed country. Growth in the Syrian Arab Republic was apparently not adversely affected by the Gulf crisis, and was higher (at 6 per cent) than in 1989 (4 per cent), thanks to increased oil production and higher exports from the non-oil sector. In addition, the country does not have close trading relations with Iraq and enjoyed continued assistance from the Gulf States.

In both Iraq and Kuwait real GDP declined by about one-third in 1990, as a result essentially of the cessation of oil output and of the United Nations embargo. As reconstruction proceeds, the economy of Kuwait should revive, but a return to normal levels of oil output is not an immediate prospect in view of the damage to oilfields during the military conflict. The financial situation of Kuwait has also been affected by war-related expenditures (some $22 billion) financed from its considerable international reserves. Kuwait has recently opted for borrowing in the capital market to help finance postwar reconstruction, to the extent of some $20 billion, rather than further liquidating its foreign assets.

The United Nations embargo reduced Iraq's exports of oil by about 25 per cent in 1990 as a whole, while the effect on imports was even greater, so that the trade surplus was larger than in 1989. However, the reduction in imports had major repercussions on industrial output and on the consumption of food, three-quarters of which is normally imported. Although the ban on food imports has been lifted, food consumption remains precarious since Iraq is unable to finance imports. The shortage of domestic supplies in general is such that increases in the price level have taken on hyperinflationary proportions. In order to finance its current expenditures, the Government is believed to have resorted to the printing press, thereby exacerbating the pressure on prices and the rate of exchange, which currently stands in the black market at almost 20 times its official value.

(ii) Prospects

While activity in some countries is likely to pick up in the coming year and the high level of oil production in Saudi Arabia is likely to be sustained for the time being, there are factors that might dampen growth prospects. Oil production will probably be much below the 1990 average in Iraq because of the continued embargo, and it is not expected that Kuwait will reach in 1991 even the average production level of 1990. Economic activity in Iraq is unlikely to recover significantly during 1991. Even if the embargo were lifted, oil production would at best average 1.0 mb/d in the latter part of 1991, or one-half the average 1990 figure, of which roughly 0.4 mb/d would probably be destined for domestic consumption. Comparing its prospective export earnings in 1991 ($1.7 billion) with its import requirements (for consumption, investment and reconstruction) and debt service requirements ($49.3 billion), the Government of Iraq claims that there will be a deficit of $47.6 billion. However, the major part of Iraq's debt service payments in 1991 relates to arrears. For 1992-1995 the average debt service/export earnings ratio is projected to be at least 75 per cent and the average current account deficit for the same period to be about $23 billion.[4] These balances do not include the

---

4   Details concerning these aggregates are to be found in a report submitted to the Secretary-General of the United Nations by Iraq on 29 April 1991, on the basis of which it requested a moratorium of at least five years before the start of the required deduction for war reparation under Security Council resolution 687 (1991). See *Middle East Economic Survey*, 13 May 1991.

30 per cent of oil export revenue that Iraq is required to set aside for the war reparation fund. Therefore, even when sanctions are lifted and Iraq resumes exports of oil, that alone will not be sufficient to meet the country's financial requirements in the short and medium term unless it is supplemented by a significant amount of external finance and debt relief.

The medium-term outlook for the subregion seems, in general, to be brighter. World demand for oil is expected to strengthen, and West Asia is thought to be the only region capable of meeting any major increment in world demand, which may henceforth emanate not only from traditional oil consumers but also from Central and Eastern Europe. Postwar reconstruction in Iraq and Kuwait may also provide an important stimulus.

4. Least developed countries

The economies of the LDCs for the most part remain weak, unstable and bereft of positive trends. They remain ill-prepared to cope with the external hazards to which they are regularly subjected, often at the cost of years of painful work. With the agricultural sector generally contributing more than half of GDP, and despite continuous and sustained efforts to strengthen the technological content of agricultural production, weather conditions continue to be a key factor in economic performance. In 1990 many LDCs were also adversely affected by the economic consequences of the Gulf crisis.

1990 was a particularly poor year for African LDCs as a group, with GDP growth rates falling to about 1.6 per cent, their lowest level since 1985. The encouraging performance of some countries, such as Botswana and Cape Verde, was offset by the disappointing levels of economic activity in the majority of countries and the absence of a basis for real economic advance in a number of them. In addition, an important effect of the Gulf crisis was to raise import costs in the majority of countries. Botswana, Chad, Sudan, and the United Republic of Tanzania were among the most affected, their total resultant losses exceeding 2.5 per cent of GNP. Nevertheless, the United Republic of Tanzania, despite a middling agricultural season and adverse external conditions, achieved reasonably stable growth. Certain domestic activities in LDCs, dependent on oil inputs, in particular manufacturing and transport, contracted. Export earnings, under pressure from low world commodity prices,

remained at about the same level as in 1989 and thus the overall trade and current account deficit of the group widened further.

The performance of the Asian LDCs was also mixed in 1990. At one extreme Bangladesh did well (see box 1), but GDP growth in many countries remained low as they were faced with severe adjustment problems, including inflationary pressures and lack of capital for basic infrastructure development, a situation complicated by the virtual absence of domestic savings. The slowdown in Bhutan and in Myanmar was attributable to both agriculture and industry. Economic activities in Samoa were disrupted by a cyclone early in 1990, causing severe damage to the country and a sharp setback to growth. Both Maldives and Vanuatu witnessed an increase in tourist arrivals and improved export performance. On the other hand, Nepal suffered not only from trade and transit difficulties, but also from fuel shortages, which affected agricultural activities such as irrigation. Growth in 1989 and 1990 fell to 2.3 per cent and 2.0 per cent, respectively, from a high of 7.8 per cent in 1988. Industrial production was disrupted due to lack of raw materials and electricity resulting from transportation problems, and consequently exports decelerated sharply. In contrast, the Lao People's Democratic Republic continued reforms to promote economic growth and stimulate investment, having recorded output growth of around 10 per cent annually in the preceding two years.

To restore economic growth and address the deteriorating balance of payments situation, domestic currencies were devalued, government spending was trimmed and monetary policies tightened in various LDCs. Some of these problems may in part be approached with policies encouraging export-oriented industries. For example, in Nepal, to attract foreign investors, the Government plans to provide tax incentives and import liberalization measures to speed up purchases of machinery. Although good weather has been the main reason behind gains in food output, it appears that in some countries, such as the Lao People's Democratic Republic, the economic reform process (crop diversification incentives and measures affecting agricultural prices and the availability of inputs) has also been an important contributory factor.

The paucity of reliable statistics makes any assessment of prospects for African LDCs necessarily precarious. A number of countries, accounting for an important share of overall GDP of African LDCs (Ethiopia, Mozambique, Somalia and Sudan) are suffering from the effects of past or current regional or internal military conflicts, causing dislocation of traditional economic links and having a devastating influence on further development. Prospects for African LDCs as a whole continue to be uncertain, though some recovery is forecast and overall growth should be at least one percentage point higher than in 1990. Agricultural output, which is vital for the economic development of the majority of countries of the group, depends largely on weather conditions, and many of them (for example Mali, Mauritania and Niger, not to mention Ethiopia and Sudan, where there is a considerable risk of renewed famine) have poor harvest expectations and are likely to face a critical food situation. The effects of the Gulf crisis will continue to be felt during 1992, especially in those African LDCs which had been granted concessional terms for their oil supplies or had special aid arrangements with Gulf States. The economies of most countries will thus continue to suffer from costly oil imports and the contraction of demand for their commodity exports due to the slowdown of the world economy. A further worsening of their trade and current account balances is thus also likely.

The economic momentum of the Lao People's Democratic Republic will be sustained in the next two years, but at a less rapid rate, and activities in Nepal should revive, following the agreement reached with India on trade and transit problems. The Samoan economy is likely to take some time to recover due to last year's damage to agriculture and forestry, which are the source of most exports.

In most LDCs, as the industrial sector is relatively small, interlinkages with the agricultural sector need to be reinforced to develop processing industries for the production of finished or semi-finished products with a high value added. Restoring the efficiency and profitability of State enterprises or pursuing further privatization would help contain the growth of public expenditure and probably stimulate the establishment of new manufacturing enterprises. Reforms to develop a banking system capable of mobilizing and allocating resources efficiently are necessary. In general, despite the repeated need to divert energies and scarce resources for the repair of damage caused by natural calamities, prospects for economic development will depend upon successful stabilization and implementation of structural reforms. In addition, foreign assistance on highly concessional terms is necessary for growth-enhancing investment programmes.

C. China

The three-year austerity programme initiated by the Chinese Government in 1988 has achieved some success in curbing high inflation rates, reducing serious imbalances between supply and demand, and slowing the growth of current account deficits. In 1990 the inflation rate fell to 2.1 per cent, in contrast to 17.8 per cent in 1989 and 19.5 per cent in 1988. Monetary and credit policies could therefore be relaxed somewhat. As a result, industrial production accelerated after mid-year and for 1990 as a whole was 7.6 per cent over the previous year; for light industry the increase was as much as 9.1 per cent. Shipbuilding continued to expand, with almost half of the output exported. Combined with a good performance in agriculture, including a record grain crop, this led to an increase in the overall growth rate to around 4.8 per cent, against 3.7 per cent a year earlier. The value of exports grew by as much as 18.0 per cent, reflecting the lagged ef-

fect of devaluation and official efforts to stimulate exports. Imports fell, in part owing to efforts to economize on foreign exchange. The outcome was China's first trade surplus since 1984. With a surplus in invisibles trade, the current account balance registered a substantial improvement (a surplus of $8 billion, in contrast to a deficit of $4.5 billion in 1989). This, in turn, allowed for some build-up of foreign exchange reserves ahead of next year's bulge in scheduled debt service payments.

Many Governments and international organizations resumed loans to China in 1990. Foreign banks are expected to open branches in Shanghai later in the current year. Steps towards some financial reforms, such as setting up stock exchanges and allowing a syndicate of financial institutions to underwrite bond issues, have been taken to help mobilize savings. In an effort to attract more foreign high tech-

Box 1

NATURAL DISASTERS IN BANGLADESH: A CONTINUING THREAT TO DEVELOPMENT

Bangladesh, with its remarkable economic recovery of 1990, until very recently appeared to be embarked on a path of sustainable economic growth. In 1990, following the serious setbacks of 1988 and 1989, GDP grew by 6.2 per cent (led by the agricultural and manufacturing sectors). Sizeable increases in exports and a slower growth of imports resulted in a narrowing trade deficit. Benefiting from good weather, the performance of the economy also was supported by significant reforms in economic policies and programmes, including improved agricultural policies, trade liberalization, investment incentive schemes, measures to better balance the public and the private sectors and financial reforms.

Despite serious direct and indirect costs stemming from the Gulf crisis, and complications associated with the process of transition to democracy, projections earlier this year remained generally optimistic, expectations being that the economy would be able to maintain reasonable growth with continued export expansion and a sustainable current account deficit, thus achieving significant gains in income per capita.

However, the May 1991 cyclone largely invalidated those projections. The Joint Task Force of the Government of Bangladesh and the United Nations has estimated the total loss due to the catastrophe at $2.4 billion. [1] As a consequence of widespread damage to standing crops, the loss of a cropping season in the coastal area due to severe salinity and destroyed government and private food stocks, considerable additional food imports are required. Damage to buildings and houses, physical infrastructure and industrial plants implies significantly increased imports of capital goods and other manufactures. The virtual disappearance of the shrimp hatcheries of the country will entail a major loss of export revenue. There also has been extensive damage to textile plants, with the possibility that a good part of ready-made garment production, recently the largest export earner, will be lost.

As a result, the need for external resources will intensify in the short term, and the need for additional assistance may continue even after completion of immediate relief and rehabilitation efforts. Even if the economy were able to continue to sustain recent growth rates of around 3.5 per cent per year, it would take nearly six years to recover from the direct and indirect losses caused by the cyclone. [2] However, additional and sustained aid flows of about 30 per cent above real current levels would allow Bangladesh to overcome the losses in about three years. At the recent Aid Group meeting donor commitments for the current fiscal year stood at $2.3 billion, close to suggested levels. Expected additional commitments by some donors would increase that total. A number of other international actions in favour of Bangladesh, including alleviation of its debt and debt service burden and withdrawal or significant dismantling of trade barriers, particularly with respect to textiles, would also be of benefit.

The issues relating to the reconstruction and development needs of Bangladesh stemming from the recent disaster having been addressed, it must be emphasized that, of the last four years' economic performance, three have been dominated by the impact of natural phenomena. Clearly, issues of direct relevance to its environment and ecology (and those of the neighbouring region) need to be quickly and adequately addressed. Recurrent disasters not only negate the gains of domestic effort, but also reduce the effectiveness of donors' contributions to development. The challenge of meaningful disaster mitigation, preparedness and prevention cannot be met by the efforts of Bangladesh alone, or those of the region, and must be adequately supported by the international community. In the Programme of Action for the LDCs for the 1990s [3] support was pledged for implementation of a flood control programme in Bangladesh. In particular, the Action Plan on floods, prepared by the World Bank and adopted at a conference in London in 1989, needs to be fully and timely implemented and adequate external resources provided for the purpose.

---

1 *The 1991 cyclone in Bangladesh: Impact, Recovery and Reconstruction* (SG/CONF.6/1).
2 *External sector of Bangladesh: Recent performance and near-term prospects* (UNCTAD/RDP/LDC/Misc.21), prepared for submission to the Bangladesh Aid Group Meeting, Paris, 29-30 May 1991.
3 *The Least Developed Countries. 1990 Report* (TD/B/1289), United Nations publication, Sales No.E.91.II.D.3, annex I.

nology investment flows in manufacturing, large tax incentives will be granted to foreign investors. Some of them have already started new joint ventures in such areas as consumer electronics and component assembly.

Although the economy is gradually recovering, and while small experimental reforms are carried out all over China on a local basis, the emergence of some difficulties will have to be addressed in the period ahead. A sharp inventory build-up, brought on by weak retail sales, forced a number of business closures and worsened the employment situation in 1990. The closures also strained the budget deficit by decreasing corporate tax revenues and increasing government subsidies to State-run enterprises and urban workers, resulting in a deficit wider than expected. Productivity, as well as the quality of goods, needs to be enhanced so as to reduce subsidies and help ease the decline of profitability of public enterprises. The money supply increased rapidly during the second half of 1990, through domestic bank loans to stimulate industrial production, particularly of intermediate inputs. Prices of some essential food items have been raised closer to market prices to avoid imbalances between farm and non-farm incomes and also to reduce food subsidies to the urban population.

The economic momentum which started to gather in China after July 1990 is projected to continue in the next two years. The recovery is being led by the industrial sector, which grew by 13.7 per cent in the first quarter of 1991 over the same period of 1990. Expenditures on new equipment are likely to be raised for modernizing existing plants, such as textile and garment industries, to enhance product competitiveness. The contract responsibility system of production in enterprises, recently introduced, will give State managers more autonomy to deal with inefficiencies and infrastructure improvement and to make expenditures in new special economic zones, such as Pudong in Shanghai. Small steps also are being tried that would permit more independence to invest profits and sell

goods produced above plan commitments. Increased agricultural investment and loans, as well as increased farm inputs, will be made available to maintain stable output growth. Purchase prices of some farm products are likely to be raised progressively to stimulate an enlarged production base. Construction of warehouses and new storage facilities will soon be accelerated. Emphasis on purchase and marketing of grain may facilitate distribution.

Economic prospects will depend to some extent on the world economic situation and also on progress in price, enterprise and other policy reforms. Keeping inflation under control, and limiting it to single-digit growth in 1991, could be within reach, as State bank lending has been severely cut back since January. Depressed consumer spending will pick up moderately in response to some income growth; there are signs of recovery in retail sales, primarily for basic necessities such as foodstuffs. The removal of export incentives accorded to some provinces can be expected to dampen the expansion of trade, but will also reduce the budget deficit. Protectionist measures abroad will also hinder export expansion. Import growth is likely to accelerate faster than export growth, with increased purchases of equipment and machinery for technological improvements in industry. Consequently, the trade surplus will probably decline. Agricultural output may increase less than in 1990; the grain harvest is likely to suffer because of heavy crop damage due to torrential rain and floods in the northern part of the country, while severe drought has left rice fields dry in southern regions. The Government is likely to continue implementing adjustment measures under a cautious economic policy, with control of credit expansion. However, much will depend on price movements, given the need to prevent renewed inflation, and also on measures introduced to reduce the budget deficit. The rapid acceleration of industrial output in the second half of 1990 is likely to maintain growth momentum, and overall economic activity is projected to increase by about 6 per cent in 1991.

D. Central and Eastern Europe

In 1990 the economies of Central and Eastern Europe continued to regress. Macroeconomic indicators reveal a confirmation of adverse trends in almost all countries of the re-

gion. After modest growth in 1989, NMP fell by about 4.8 per cent in 1990 for these countries as a whole, and by even more if the USSR is excluded. Production fell in most major sectors. In most countries exports also declined in both volume and value. Intra-regional trade, traditionally representing a large part of the external economic relations of these countries, declined sharply.

In many cases, the transitional difficulties faced by the economies of the region are due to serious imbalances accumulated in earlier years. However, these problems are also being exacerbated by new destabilizing factors which have emerged during the transition to market-oriented economic structures. Widespread social and political changes, conflicts and strikes are seriously affecting the transition process.

Overall output fell in all countries in 1990. NMP fell by 13.6 per cent in Bulgaria, 13 per cent in Poland, and 10.5 per cent in Romania; in Hungary and Czechoslovakia the decline was limited to less than 5.5 per cent. A steep decline in industrial production was recorded by Poland (on account of the deep recession in the State sector), Bulgaria and Romania. In addition to internal economic difficulties, some countries (Bulgaria, Czechoslovakia and Hungary), which are net importers of petroleum products, were severely hit by the Gulf crisis.

However, 1990 witnessed certain positive developments in those countries more deeply involved in the reform process. An expansion of exports to world markets was recorded in Hungary and Poland, which both attained a modest current account surplus in 1990 instead of the previously expected deficit. Poland's hard currency exports increased impressively (by nearly 40 per cent) in both volume and value. The evolving market system in Hungary contributed to a considerable increase of manufactured exports; the country also confirmed its creditworthiness, continuing to service large debt obligations. Agricultural output and private sector activity were stronger than expected in these two countries, reflecting the start of the process of economic recovery.

Industrial output in the USSR, which in previous years was a major source of growth for the economy, declined in 1990, and the process of disintegration of internal economic links became more pronounced by the end of the year. Agricultural output fell by 2.3 per cent after very modest growth in the previous year, thus worsening an already tense situation in the internal consumer market. Another destabilizing factor has been the profound imbalance of the budget. For the first time in many years an absolute decline in both GNP and national income was recorded. The depression also touched upon external economic relations, with overall export values and volumes con-

tracting significantly, partly reflecting the 6 per cent drop in crude oil production. The trade deficit thus more than tripled.

The economic prospects of the region are subject to considerable uncertainty due to internal political, social and economic problems in most countries. The commitment to serious economic reform remains to be confirmed in some countries; partial reform will not be sufficient. The short-term outlook is bleak, both on the domestic front (NMP in 1991 for these countries as a whole is expected again to decline, though for countries other than the Soviet Union the decline may be less than in 1990) and as regards the external sector (a further deterioration of trade and current account balances is forecast for most countries). Nevertheless, the economies of those countries which have progressed furthest in institutional reform, such as Hungary and Poland and, to some extent, Czechoslovakia, are expected to recover over the medium term (3-5 years).

Another important uncertainty dominating the regional outlook is the collapse of intra-regional trade. This has been caused by the transition to a new settlement mechanism among former CMEA member countries, implemented in January 1991, which entails hard currency payments at world market prices in mutual trade. This is likely to further worsen the already difficult payments position of the heavily indebted countries, and to have repercussions on the industrial output and economic activity of those branches which have been traditionally oriented to the intra-regional market. Spillover effects could result in substantial losses in GDP growth, although their scope for the moment is difficult to quantify.

Hungary seems to be in the most favourable position as far as prospects are concerned. The process of institutional and other market reforms (creation of goods, labour and capital markets) is at an advanced stage, although signs of a certain slowing of "large-scale" privatization have emerged. The fall in GDP in 1990 may level off in the current year, although a further fall in industrial output and a persistent rise in unemployment cannot be excluded. The Hungarian economy may return to modest growth in 1992, given a continuation of present policies. However, the renewed growth of industrial production, a curtailment, or at least a reduction, of the growth of external indebtedness, an increase in consumption and a fall in unemployment are not expected before 1993. Large gains in exports to the convertible-currency areas achieved in 1990 may help the country to offset the fall in trade with the USSR, although uncertainty with regard to new price patterns and new conditions of supply will persist at least throughout 1991.

The progress towards restoration of market equilibrium made in Poland during the implementation of the government programme in 1990 justifies a cautious optimism. A return to positive growth rates may be possible already in 1991, with a further recovery subsequently. In the area of foreign economic relations, however, prospects are not so bright. The previous year's upsurge of exports is unlikely to be repeated, in part because important further declines in exports to other countries of the region are probable. A general increase of import prices and values, especially in trade with the USSR, is possible in this regard. The trade balance is expected to worsen, even turning into a deficit with the former CMEA partners.

The outlook for the USSR is dominated by uncertainties linked to internal political problems, in particular the evolving relationship between central and regional political authorities. Prospects essentially depend on the adoption of consistent economic reforms, agreed upon by all participants of the new Union Treaty. Whatever economic policies are followed, the economic crisis has almost certainly not yet bottomed out, and depressed conditions are likely to continue over the next few years. The first quarter of 1991 saw a further decline in industrial output, with real GDP and national income falling by 8 per cent and 10 per cent, respectively. The investment process slowed sharply, thus undermining the longer-term economic prospects of the country. Increased social tension, partly reflected in strikes in basic branches of the economy, may have unpredictable influences on future economic developments. It is difficult to assess the depth of the recession in 1991, estimates of the decline in GNP varying from 1.5 per cent (official estimate of November 1990) to 11 per cent or more. Industrial output is variously assessed to fall by up to 15 per cent and agriculture by as much as 5 per cent. The results for the first quarter of 1991 seem to confirm the most pessimistic forecasts.

External factors add to the current uncertainty and could seriously influence the economic situation in 1991. Already in 1990, the Soviet economy was unable to take full advantage of the oil price increase; because of output constraints, exports of oil actually fell in volume by 14 per cent. Official estimates envisage a further reduction of oil exports, which could lead to more than a 20 per cent fall in total export receipts.[5]

The new requirements for payments in hard currency and at market prices may not alleviate the pressures on the external accounts. It is possible that difficulties linked with the new settlement mechanism will even tend to aggravate the economic crisis in the Soviet Union, because many Soviet enterprises used to benefit from cheap supplies of raw and semi-processed materials and equipment parts from other Central and Eastern European countries. The termination of such imports due to the lack of convertible currency in most Soviet enterprises may lead to sharp cutbacks in the output of light industry, which traditionally depends on imported inputs. On the other hand, in the longer run, the USSR could gain substantially from this transition, because its primary commodities are easier to sell for convertible currency than the manufactured products of the other countries of the region.

High debt service obligations of the USSR are another matter for concern in the short run. Although the debt burden of the country is relatively modest, 1991 may witness an aggravation of debt servicing problems as the external debt obligations constitute almost a quarter of projected hard currency revenues. Therefore the question of external financial support is highly relevant.

As far as the other countries of the region are concerned, prospects depend crucially on the coherence of economic policy decisions. In this context, Czechoslovakia seems well placed and its chances of a relatively quick transition to a market economy are good, bearing in mind its relatively low level of indebtedness and high industrial potential. Nevertheless, a substantial fall in GDP growth is forecast for 1991. Bulgaria may face one of the most difficult years in its economic history. Not only the consequences of the Gulf crisis, which were particularly severe, but also the level of integration with the USSR, highest among the countries of the region, will play a significant role in the short term. Thus, disintegration of traditional economic links will raise sharper problems for Bulgaria than for any other Central or Eastern European country. Since much of the country's industrial potential depends upon imports of Soviet primary commodities, the new settlement mechanism is likely to seriously compromise industrial output. Current projections indicate a further important decline in NMP in 1991. The process of economic reform being still in its initial stages, the medium-term prospects for the country are uncertain, particularly in view of serious debt

---

5   In the first quarter of 1991 external trade turnover was 34 per cent below the same quarter of 1990, but this result can also be partially attributed to import cuts.

servicing problems. The outlook for Romania may also be characterized as uncertain, although the country does not have any serious debt obligations. Its economic prospects are very difficult to assess at the moment, taking into consideration the particularly disappointing performance in 1990 and the current serious disequilibria in the economy.

E. Developed market-economy countries

The combination of a steady deceleration of growth for developed market-economy countries as a whole since 1988, coupled with increasingly divergent performance among the major economies, culminated in a somewhat unexpectedly sharp slowdown in the current year, now projected to be replaced by a modest, but convergent, recovery beginning towards the end of 1991. As a result, while the average outcome for 1991 is likely to be an increase in GDP of just under 1 per cent, a rise of 2.7 per cent is expected in 1992.[6] For 1991 as a whole continental Western Europe and Japan will see a significant slowdown of growth, with some revival likely in 1992, while the recession in North America, the United Kingdom (and also most of the Nordic countries) which started in 1989 may bottom out in the second half of the current year (see chart 5). The effects of the Gulf crisis seem to have been a weakening of output growth at a time when demand growth was already slowing down. The subsequent ending of hostilities has helped to reduce the general level of uncertainty and boosted confidence but this alone may not be enough to outweigh the factors at work which caused the slowdown in the first place. Moreover, financial fragility poses a threat in a number of countries (see part two, chapter II). With the exception of Germany, inflation is not expected to pick up markedly. In particular, the inflationary effect of the Gulf crisis proved rather ephemeral, in contrast to the oil price increases of the early 1970s and the 1980s.

The increased desynchronization of national growth cycles in recent years has been reflected in differences in monetary policies among the three major developed market economies. The Federal Reserve Board in the United States, amidst rising fears of an impending recession, started easing its monetary stance in the latter half of 1990 and short-term interest rates fell by about 2 percentage points in the 12 months up to April 1991. The rapid end to the Gulf war and the drop in fuel prices has contributed to a lowering of inflationary expectations and a revival of consumer confidence, which are expected to facilitate an upturn in the latter half of 1991. In contrast, Germany and Japan have been experiencing buoyant growth and rising interest rates. The monetary authorities in Germany feel that a reduction in interest rates is not compatible with perceived inflationary pressures related to the strength of domestic demand; these fears are compounded by serious concern about the budgetary position following the higher than expected costs of unification. Germany's short-term interest rates are now fully 3 percentage points higher than those of the United States. The monetary authorities of Japan, which had been reluctant to lower interest rates, announced a half-point cut in the official discount rate in the beginning of July, signalling the end of an era of rising rates which started at the beginning of 1989.

In the United States unemployment reached 6.9 per cent in May 1991, the highest level since 1986, and capacity utilization has fallen considerably. Private consumption and investment have been sluggish since mid-1990. Non-residential investment declined at an annual rate of 15.9 per cent from the fourth quarter of 1990 to the first quarter of 1991. GDP contracted by 2.6 per cent in the first quarter of 1991 at an annual rate, compared with a 1.6 per cent decline in the preceding quarter, and overall growth for 1991 is expected to be negative. The cut in the discount rate to 5.5 per cent by the end of April 1991, which brought it to its lowest level since 1977, was taken in the light of continued weakness in the economy. The budget deficit for the fiscal year 1990/91 is expected to be larger than in the previous year mainly because of lower tax revenues due to the cyclical downturn and increased outlays for the bail-out of the savings and loan institutions. Without the latter, the

---

6 Figures for the developed market economies include GDP estimates reflecting the unification of Germany.

deficit has been estimated to reach 3.6 per cent of GNP, up from 3 per cent in fiscal 1990. In 1990 the weakness of the dollar against the currencies of its main trading partners stimulated United States exports, which grew by about 8.2 per cent in value terms, while imports increased much more modestly (4.7 per cent). In the first quarter of 1991 the trade deficit narrowed from $25.8 billion in the preceding quarter to $16.9 billion, the smallest deficit since 1983. However, if the economy recovers in 1992 a renewed surge in imports can be expected, particularly in view of the recent strengthening of the dollar. Thus, for 1991 a significant improvement in the current account deficit is to be expected, but a reversal of this trend seems likely in 1992.[7]

Chart 5

SELECTED DEVELOPED MARKET-ECONOMY COUNTRIES: DEVIATION OF ANNUAL GDP GROWTH RATES FROM THE GROUP AVERAGE

(Percentages)

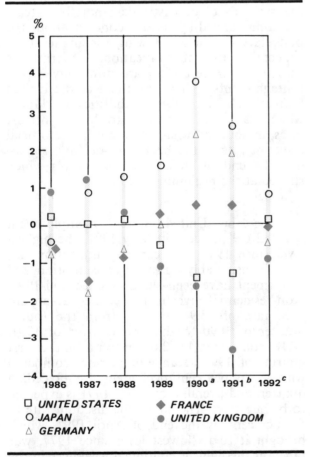

□ *UNITED STATES*   ◆ *FRANCE*
○ *JAPAN*   ● *UNITED KINGDOM*
△ *GERMANY*

Source: Calculations by the UNCTAD secretariat, based on data of the United Nations Statistical Office.

In Japan there has been some concern about the slump in equity prices, which fell by 33 per cent from the fourth quarter of 1989 to the first quarter of 1991, and its potential effect on the financial sector and on business activity in general. Investment is likely to weaken as the effects of higher interest rates and lower equity values assert themselves. Long-term interest rates have been 2-3 percentage points higher since the beginning of 1990 than in any year since 1986. Private consumption will remain the main source of domestic demand growth. The trade surplus is expected to widen again as Japan benefits from a significant improvement in its terms of trade due to the fallback in oil prices and from the recent strengthening of the yen. At the same time, imports may not rise as fast as anticipated due to the slowdown in demand. While the trade surplus with the United States fell recently, the surplus with EEC seems to have risen substantially. Output growth is expected to slacken to 3.5 per cent in 1991, with some acceleration possible in 1992.

In Western Europe, there is recession in the United Kingdom, Sweden and Finland; investment is expected to decline in these countries and to become sluggish in the other Western European countries. The growth of private consumption is also expected to be slower in 1991 as the rise of real disposable income slackens, partly on account of tax increases in several countries. Intra-Western European trade lost its momentum in spite of vigorous import growth in Germany, and exports to developing countries and North America are unlikely to provide any major stimulus. Average growth in 1991 may therefore slow to 1 per cent, or less than half the 1990 rate. The recession in the United Kingdom will be longer and deeper than in any other of the major industrial countries. Unemployment in that country is expected to increase to beyond 2 million in 1991, from 1.8 million in 1990. In most other Western European countries the employment situation is also expected to deteriorate due to the slowdown in economic activity.

In EEC member countries inflation seems to be resisting a fall to below an average of 5 per cent, a fairly high rate given that demand growth is weakening and that the terms of trade have improved since 1989. However, differentials within the Community are being reduced as inflation rates are expected to continue rising in Germany and to remain high in the United

---

7 The definition of the current account balance used here does not include government transfers. Therefore there will be no shift in current account balances of the major OECD countries due to contributions to the multinational force in the Gulf as long as those are recorded as government transfers.

Kingdom and in Southern Europe, whereas the increase in consumer prices in France, excluding energy, in 1990 was the smallest for over 20 years and the rise in 1991 may even remain below that in Germany. As a result, the French monetary authorities have not been obliged to react to the repeated rise in German interest rates in order to avoid a depreciation of the franc. The strength of the franc has had, however, a dampening effect on export growth and led to a deterioration in the external balance in 1990 which is likely to persist, given the weakness of world export demand.

In Germany economic developments reveal a sharply contrasting picture between the eastern and western parts of the country. In the latter, growth has been at its highest since 1976, employment increasing by over 3 per cent from January 1990 to March 1991, with only a modest increase in inflation. For 1991 as a whole, however, a weakening of growth or a downturn is expected, mainly because of a slower rise of private consumption and exports. The public sector deficit (of unified Germany) is projected to rise to 5 per cent of GNP, but medium-term fiscal policies already in place are set for a consolidation by 1995.[8] There is con- tinued progress in reducing the current account surplus, mainly due to the surge in imports due to unification and high capacity utilization in western Germany. Together with the slow- down in export growth, this has resulted in the trade surplus falling from DM36 billion in the first quarter of 1990 to DM15 billion in the last quarter. For 1991 a further decline is expected and a deficit in the current account balance cannot be excluded. The main external benefi- ciaries of these developments were other EEC countries.

The situation in the former German Democratic Republic has deteriorated dramat- ically since unification. About one third of the labour force is either unemployed or main- tained on company payrolls with state funds while virtually idle. Industrial production may fall by 40 per cent in 1991. Exports, which formerly were mainly to other Eastern European countries, have collapsed. GDP generated in the eastern part of Germany is expected to fall by 17 per cent in 1991 while prices may rise 11 per cent. The upward pres- sure on prices is likely to remain heavy in coming years as relative prices adjust to those of western Germany.■

---

8 Starting in July 1991 petrol taxes have been raised substantially and there has been a temporary surcharge of 7.5 per cent on income taxes, intended to cover the costs of unification and the commitments to the multinational force in the Gulf.

Chapter II

INTERNATIONAL MARKETS AND DEVELOPING COUNTRIES

The recent past has been characterized by a slowing in the expansion of world trade and of international financial flows, and a weakening of commodity prices. These developments occurred against the background of the slowdown in the world economy described in the preceding chapter. The deceleration in economic growth in some major industrialized countries, especially the United States, was the principal cause of fatigue in world trade. The deep recession in Eastern Europe and the Gulf crisis were additional factors. In Germany, sharply increased import demand coincided with weakening export growth, with a favourable net impact on world trade.[9] The export expansion of most developing countries slackened under the impact of faltering economic growth in the developed countries. A number of developing economies with important trading relations with Eastern Europe were hard hit by the economic downturn in this region; others were adversely affected by the Persian Gulf crisis. The dynamics of import growth in some developing countries in South-East Asia and oil-exporting developing economies were, on the other hand, favourable to trade expansion.

The weakening of commodity prices in recent months reflects in part the economic slowdown in industrial countries. For many commodities, however, rapid growth of output has been a significant source of downward pressure on prices. There is mounting evidence that debt servicing difficulties are a key factor explaining the apparently perverse link between lower world market prices and expanding output.

As in previous years, financial flows to developing countries have been driven by forces particular to them, rather than by overall trends in world lending. Flows to developing countries continue to be tempered by the acute debt problems that plague many of them, and the continued high level of arrears and pace of debt rescheduling indicate that, overall, these problems continue unabated. There are, however, some signs of improvement: export credits to developing countries appear to be expanding after several years of contraction; a small number of the heavily indebted countries have been able to attract funds from capital markets; and imaginative proposals for dealing better with Paris Club debt are receiving serious consideration.

The remainder of this chapter takes up these and related issues.

A. Recent developments in international trade

The growth of world trade decelerated (from 7 per cent to 4.3 per cent) in 1990 (see table 7), a trend that was apparently continuing in 1991. At the same time, non-fuel primary commodity prices fell by about 6 per cent. The major economic and political events of the recent past - the Gulf crisis, recession or feebler economic growth in developed countries, systemic change in Central and Eastern Europe, and German unification - had major

[9] See section A.3.

impacts on world trade and on international prices as a whole, and on the trade of specific groups of countries.

1. The impact of the Gulf crisis

The overall effect of the crisis in the Persian Gulf on the growth of world trade has not been dramatic. The two countries under the United Nations embargo (Iraq and occupied Kuwait) account for only 1 per cent of world imports, and the loss of their oil exports was compensated quickly by increases in supplies from other countries. On a global basis, estimates for 1990 indicate that merchandise exports from developing countries were reduced by about 1 per cent ($6 billion) as a result of hostilities in the Gulf region.[10]

The adverse effect on individual developing countries has, however, in many cases been much more severe. There was a temporary deterioration of the terms of trade for oil importers (and a parallel improvement for oil exporters) as oil prices rose sharply in the second half of 1990, but fell back almost to their pre-crisis levels during 1991. Some countries had to endure more lasting adverse impacts. Those developing countries for which Iraq and Kuwait were important markets, most notably Jordan, suffered losses in their merchandise exports. Other important suppliers to Iraq and Kuwait include India, Romania, Turkey, and Yugoslavia. Moreover, a number of developing countries in the Middle East, North Africa and Asia lost workers' remittances on a large scale and were, in addition, burdened with the cost of repatriating their nationals. Several developing countries in the Middle East and neighbouring regions incurred heavy losses in income as tourism declined sharply. Reduced traffic through the Suez Canal and the Red Sea involved an important loss of foreign exchange earnings for some countries, in particular Egypt.

These various losses of foreign exchange earnings required the countries concerned to reduce their imports. Some of the secondary effects are likely to be lagged and will also have a dampening effect on the world economy in 1991.

For at least 40 developing countries, the total cost inflicted upon them by the Gulf crisis has been estimated to exceed 1 per cent of their GNP in 1990 alone - an impact "akin to a widespread natural disaster".[11] The war and the way it was waged have been devastating for Iraq and Kuwait, which face the task of a major reconstruction of their economies.

2. Trade of developed market economies: major trends and imports from developing countries

The trade of the developed countries in 1990 recorded yet another deceleration both in the volume growth of exports and in the pace of import expansion (see table 8). The volume growth of exports from the United States slowed down, but was still faster than in most developed market economies. A depreciating dollar, which reached a postwar low, supported export growth. The volume growth of imports, on the other hand, decelerated further in 1990 as the economy entered a recession and a lower dollar dampened import demand. The deficit in the United States trade balance continued to fall, to a level of around $100 billion.

Growth in the volume of Japan's exports gained new momentum, while the pace of import expansion decelerated for the second consecutive year, even though Japan recorded the strongest economic growth among the major industrialized countries in 1990. The trade surplus narrowed further in 1990, to $52 billion. Most of the reduction was due to a fall in the surplus with the United States, mitigating the major problem in economic relations between the two countries. However, preliminary data point to a renewed and possibly strong increase in Japan's overall trade surplus in 1991. Its surplus with Western Europe soared by nearly 55 per cent in the first quarter of 1991 compared to the corresponding period in 1990, and the surplus with the United States increased slightly over the same period.

The volume growth of exports from EEC slackened in 1990, while import growth (excluding intra-EEC trade) became more dynamic. The Community recorded the slowest growth in exports and the fastest import expansion among the major developed countries. These developments were influenced by

---

10 See "The impact of the Gulf crisis on developing countries", Briefing paper, Overseas Development Institute, London, March 1991.

11 *Ibid.*

Table 7

GROWTH OF EXPORT VOLUMES IN SELECTED GROUPS OF COUNTRIES, 1980-1992

(Average annual rate of growth in per cent)

Region/group	1980-1990	1988	1989	1990 [a]	1991 [b]	1992 [b]
World	4.0	8.5	7.0	4.3	3.0	6.0
Developed market economies	4.5	8.3	7.5	5.1	3.0	6.0
Europe	3.7	6.3	7.2	4.2	2.0	5.0
EEC	4.0	6.5	7.5	4.2	2.0	5.5
Intra-EEC	5.2	7.5	8.0	4.8	3.0	..
Extra-EEC	1.6	2.5	5.0	1.8	1.0	..
EFTA	5.3	6.0	8.5	4.0	3.0	4.5
Japan	5.0	4.3	4.2	5.5	5.5	7.0
North America	4.3	18.6	9.4	7.5	4.0	7.0
United States	4.4	21.6	12.5	8.5	5.0	7.0
Canada	3.9	9.7	0.1	4.4	-0.5	6.0
Australia/New Zealand	5.0	1.0	3.8	11.0	7.5	4.0
Developing countries	3.5	11.3	7.2	5.0	4.5	7.0
Africa	-1.0	0.5	1.9	5.6	3.5	3.5
North Africa	-0.6	-3.0	2.0	4.0	4.0	4.5
Sub-Saharan Africa	-1.4	1.6	1.9	7.2	2.5	3.0
Oil-exporting countries [c]	-3.2	5.2	7.2	15.0	4.5	2.0
Other countries	0.5	-3.9	-1.6	2.0	1.0	4.5
Latin America	3.9	9.1	2.5	2.0	4.0	4.0
South and South-East Asia	10.0	14.0	9.2	6.0	7.5	8.0
East Asia [d]	11.7	14.1	8.3	5.5	7.0	7.5
ASEAN [e]	7.0	14.4	11.5	7.0	8.5	9.0
South Asia [f]	4.0	11.8	10.0	9.0	9.5	9.5
West Asia	-2.2	12.0	11.5	4.0	-2.5	8.0
Central and Eastern Europe	1.3	4.4	-1.6	-14.5	-10.5	-3.0
USSR	1.0	4.8	-0.3	-14.0	..	..
Other countries [g]	1.5	3.7	-2.1	-14.8	..	..
China	15.0	14.4	8.0	13.0	13.0	10.0

Source: UNCTAD secretariat, based on data from various issues of: UNCTAD, *Handbook of International Trade and Development Statistics*; OECD, *Economic Outlook*; Eurostat, *External Trade*; CEPAL, *Balance Preliminar de la Economia de America Latina y el Caribe*; African Development Bank, *Annual Report*; IMF, *World Economic Outlook*; ECE, *Economic Survey of Europe*; and on SIGMA for forecasts.

a Estimates.
b Forecasts (rounded to the nearest half percentage point).
c Angola, Congo, Gabon, Nigeria.
d Hong Kong, Republic of Korea, Singapore, Taiwan Province of China.
e Indonesia, Malaysia, Philippines, Thailand only.
f Bangladesh, India, Nepal, Pakistan, Sri Lanka.
g Bulgaria, Czechoslovakia, German Democratic Republic until 1990, Hungary, Poland, Romania.

Germany's trade performance, which reached a turning point in 1990 as exports decelerated and imports started to soar. Furthermore, the more export-oriented industries in EEC were less successful in 1990 than in previous years, due in part to the fairly strong appreciation of major European currencies against the dollar. The growth of intra-EEC trade also slowed down, but remained stronger than the Community's export expansion in the world market.

Table 8

GROWTH OF IMPORT VOLUMES IN SELECTED GROUPS OF COUNTRIES, 1980-1992

(Average annual rate of growth in per cent)

Region/group	1980-1990	1988	1989	1990 [a]	1991 [b]	1992 [b]
World	4.0	8.5	7.0	4.5	3.0	6.0
Developed market economies	5.4	8.3	7.7	5.3	3.0	6.0
Europe	4.7	7.3	7.8	6.5	4.5	5.0
EEC	4.7	7.9	8.1	6.7	5.0	5.0
Intra-EEC	5.2	7.5	8.0	5.7	4.5	..
Extra-EEC	3.5	9.0	6.5	8.5	6.0	..
EFTA	4.8	4.0	7.1	4.3	2.5	4.0
Japan	5.7	16.7	7.9	6.0	7.0	8.0
North America	7.2	7.8	6.4	2.8	-1.0	7.0
United States	7.4	6.5	6.4	3.5	-1.0	7.5
Canada	6.0	13.6	6.5	-0.6	-2.0	5.0
Australia/New Zealand	6.8	12.9	18.0	-2.0	-1.0	4.0
Developing countries	3.4	14.7	7.0	7.7	7.0	8.5
Africa	-3.5	1.2	-0.8	3.6	3.0	3.5
North Africa	-3.5	3.3	-1.3	6.0	4.0	5.0
Sub-Saharan Africa	-3.5	-1.3	-3.2	1.0	2.0	2.5
Oil-exporting countries [c]	-6.0	-6.0	-6.2	15.0	5.0	2.5
Other countries	-0.5	0.6	-0.7	-2.5	1.5	3.0
Latin America	-1.5	7.9	2.5	7.5	3.0	6.0
South and South-East Asia	9.0	21.5	10.5	10.0	9.0	9.0
East Asia [d]	11.0	23.0	11.0	10.0	9.0	9.5
ASEAN [e]	5.5	22.6	14.4	13.0	10.5	10.5
South Asia [f]	7.0	10.0	7.0	2.2	5.5	3.5
West Asia	-1.6	-0.2	2.0	2.0	8.0	13.0
Central and Eastern Europe	1.4	7.4	4.1	-7.0	-7.0	-0.5
USSR	3.6	9.5	7.1	-5.0	..	..
Other countries [g]	0.5	3.0	0.6	-9.6	..	..
China	11.5	16.9	6.5	-9.0	10.0	10.5

Source: As for table 7.
  a Estimates.
  b Forecasts (rounded to the nearest half percentage point).
  c Angola, Congo, Gabon, Nigeria.
  d Hong Kong, Republic of Korea, Singapore, Taiwan Province of China.
  e Indonesia, Malaysia, Philippines, Thailand only.
  f Bangladesh, India, Nepal, Pakistan, Sri Lanka.
  g Bulgaria, Czechoslovakia, German Democratic Republic until 1990, Hungary, Poland, Romania.

The relatively faster expansion of intra-EEC trade reflects the progressive economic integration within the Community, particularly the drive towards a single internal market by 1993.

In 1990, the United States and EEC each imported products worth some $190 billion from developing countries, while for Japan the figure was about $90 billion (see chart 6). The dynamics of import growth differed substan-tially in value terms in the three markets, and if purchases of mineral fuels are excluded, the differences are striking. Import growth slowed in the United States, where weakening economic activity, combined with a depreciating dollar, exacted its toll. In EEC, imports from developing countries benefited from the strong demand situation and accelerated significantly, recording impressive growth. In striking contrast, imports from developing countries by

Japan declined in value, reflecting, in particular, the sharp fall in manufactured imports from major developing country exporters and manufacturers in the South-East Asian region.

Chart 6

**EEC, UNITED STATES AND JAPAN:
IMPORTS FROM DEVELOPING COUNTRIES BY
MAJOR COMMODITY GROUPS, 1988-1990**

(billions of dollars)

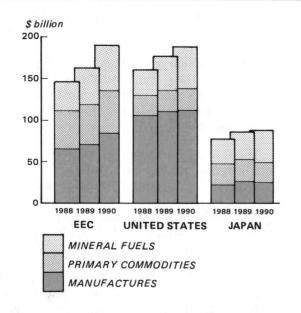

Source: UNCTAD secretariat calculations, based on data from the United Nations Statistical Office.

The United States remains the largest importer of manufactured goods from developing countries. In 1990, these imports reached $113 billion, representing nearly one third of United States total manufactured imports. EEC, with a larger population and similar GDP, imported manufactures worth $86 billion from developing economies in 1990, nearly one quarter of the Community's total imports of manufactures. The corresponding figure for Japan was $26 billion, slightly more than one quarter of its total manufactured imports.

While Japanese imports from developing countries were significantly lower in value than those of both the United States and EEC, the difference is explained, in part, by the smaller size of Japan's market, but also by the relatively greater self-sufficiency of Japanese industry. However, the share of manufactures in the country's total imports from developing economies has expanded significantly over the past decade, from less than 7 per cent in 1980 to about 30 per cent in 1990. Manufactured imports have also become more diversified and greater specialization in the pattern of Japan's trade with developing countries is emerging.

3. German unification and imports from developing countries

In Europe, German unification was the dominant event. The implementation of German economic, monetary and social union took place in mid-1990, and full political union was completed on 3 October. The shock to the east German economy proved to be devastating. The decline of its industry gathered momentum, with a rapid fall in industrial ouput and a steep rise in unemployment. The agricultural sector also plunged into disarray. These trends continued in 1991.

The process of unification had immediate implications for Germany's trade. Exports were replaced by domestic consumer spending as the engine of growth. As unification injected substantial purchasing power into east Germany, the enormous pent-up demand led to an unprecedented boom in consumption. Its striking feature was the consumer preference for western-style products, with an almost complete rejection of locally produced goods. Many west German companies reached the limits of their production capacities. As a consequence, strong domestic demand dampened exports and drove up imports. The reorientation in German trade flows was dramatic. From 1989 to 1990, the volume growth of imports soared from 7 per cent to 12.7 per cent, while the volume growth of exports declined from 7.3 per cent to 3 per cent, and appears to be falling further in 1991.[12]

The export gains from this expanding market were unevenly distributed among developing countries. The growth of exports of raw materials and food products (excluding mineral fuels) from developing economies into Germany slackened considerably (table 9). Sub-Saharan Africa and India suffered declines

---

12 All data refer to the trade performance of the former Federal Republic of Germany within its pre-unification boundaries as there is as yet no statistical base covering all of Germany. However, as foreign demand for east German products ebbed away in the course of 1990 and imports into east Germany were largely channelled through west German traders when the import boom set in, west German trade data cover a good deal of Germany's overall trade performance in 1990.

in their exports, while the growth of China's commodity exports to the German market decelerated sharply. It was the member countries of EEC which turned out to be the big winners.

Exports of manufactured products from developing countries, on the other hand, performed well. The value of imports of manufactures by Germany from South and South-East Asia, Latin America and Africa grew by between 20 per cent and 30 per cent in 1990. The best performers, with increases of around 50 per cent, were a number of developing countries in South-East Asia (Indonesia, Malaysia and Thailand) as well as China. However, the countries members of EEC once again reaped the largest gains; their exports of manufactures to Germany increased by $26 billion in 1990, equal to the total value of German imports of manufactures from all developing countries in that year.

The boom in consumer goods imports into Germany is unlikely to continue unabated. Pent-up demand will weaken as time passes. Moreover, a move back to locally produced goods became apparent in consumer preferences in eastern Germany in mid-1991. Expenditure on investment goods, on the other hand, will increase once investment comes on stream. The main beneficiaries can be expected to be producers in western Germany and other Western European countries. Export gains of the few developing countries which have competitive supply capabilities in this sector are likely to be marginal.

4. Basic trends in the trade of Central and Eastern European countries

The economic downturn in the countries of Central and Eastern Europe assumed a daunting dimension in the course of 1990. Their economies went into disarray and sustained significant losses of production under the disruptive impact of political turbulence, rapid systemic changes and the collapse of the CMEA trade and payments system. The downturn was exacerbated in many cases by shortages of energy. The higher energy bill resulting from the switch to world prices in intra-CMEA trade and reduced oil supplies from the Soviet Union represented an additional burden for other countries of the region.

The effects on trade have been severe; both exports and imports suffered sharp volume declines in 1990 in all the countries (tables 7 and 8). The contractions reflected primarily the dramatic setback in trade among these economies as their trade relations switched to world pricing and payments settlements were made in convertible currencies. Sharply reduced deliveries of manufactured goods, in particular machinery and equipment, to the Soviet Union brought many factories in these countries to a near standstill, and their exports to developing countries also recorded a large fall.

The breakdown of CMEA has severely affected a number of developing countries. The impact was greatest on those which were CMEA members (Cuba, Mongolia, and Viet Nam), but countries such as Afghanistan, Angola, Cambodia, Ethiopia, and Mozambique, which previously enjoyed preferential terms in their trade with the European CMEA countries and received most of their development assistance from those countries, were also greatly affected.

The trading partners with the USSR face the challenge of finding new outlets for many of their products to compensate for losses in the market of the Soviet Union, which had in the past readily absorbed their goods in large quantities in exchange for raw materials and energy. A significant deterioration of their terms of trade has resulted from the breakdown of intra-regional trade arrangements. The search for new outlets has begun. Measured in value terms, most of the countries concerned, in particular Hungary and Poland, substantially increased their agricultural and manufactured exports to EEC in 1990, thanks to easier access to the EEC market (see chapter III below). However, their total exports to the United States declined, as did their exports of manufactures to Japan. Moreover, the absolute value of exports to all three markets remains small. The export performance of the Soviet Union in East-West trade continued to deteriorate in 1990.

5. Developments in commodity markets

For the first time since 1985 the combined index of dollar prices for the principal commodities exported by developing countries fell in 1990 (see table 10). Agricultural raw materials as a group registered an improvement. The most seriously affected commodities were tropical beverages and vegetable oilseeds and oils. When deflated by the prices of manufactured goods exported by developed market-economy countries, the fall in prices in

Table 9

MERCHANDISE IMPORTS INTO GERMANY BY MAJOR REGIONS OF ORIGIN AND COMMODITY GROUP, a 1988-1990

| Imports from: | Primary commodities (excluding mineral fuels) | | | | | | Manufactures | | | | | |
| | Growth of value (Per cent) | | | Value ($ billion) | | | Growth of value (Per cent) | | | Value ($ billion) | | |
	1988	1989	1990	1988	1989	1990	1988	1989	1990	1988	1989	1990
World	12.3	5.9	10.0	45.0	50.5	58.9	12.3	8.5	26.3	173.1	187.9	237.3
EEC	10.6	3.0	17.6	26.0	26.7	31.4	11.0	7.6	26.3	92.6	99.7	125.9
Developing countries	11.6	6.0	1.9	10.6	11.2	11.4	13.6	7.6	29.2	19.2	20.6	26.6
Africa	-4.5	2.7	-1.1	2.0	2.0	2.0	6.1	14.1	26.2	1.0	1.1	1.4
North Africa	13.3	-8.4	4.2	0.2	0.2	0.2	2.8	17.5	30.9	0.7	0.9	1.2
Sub-Saharan Africa	-6.6	4.2	-6.6	1.7	1.8	1.7	16.7	4.5	9.5	0.2	0.3	0.3
Latin America	24.2	5.5	4.5	5.6	5.9	6.2	15.5	15.9	29.5	1.3	1.6	2.1
South and South-East Asia	2.3	6.2	0.7	1.8	1.9	2.0	16.4	3.8	28.3	11.8	12.3	15.8
East Asia b	-19.4	-5.3	4.5	0.2	0.2	0.2	16.4	0.2	22.9	8.7	8.7	10.7
ASEAN c	4.4	9.2	-0.3	1.3	1.5	1.4	16.4	19.2	50.1	1.5	1.8	2.7
India	18.9	10.3	-8.6	0.1	0.1	0.1	16.0	17.8	33.1	0.9	1.1	1.5
Developing Europe d	1.7	6.4	13.1	0.8	0.8	0.9	9.3	13.9	34.4	4.5	5.2	7.0
China	5.4	14.3	2.4	0.4	0.5	0.5	36.3	28.6	57.1	2.0	2.5	3.9

Source: UNCTAD secretariat, based on data from the United Nations Statistical Office.

    a Refers to western Germany only. Estimates for 1990 are based on data for Jan.-Sept. 1990 (see text, footnote 12).

    b Hong Kong, Republic of Korea, Singapore, Taiwan Province of China.

    c Indonesia, Malaysia, Philippines, Thailand only.

    d Cyprus, Malta, Turkey, Yugoslavia.

Note: In terms of ECUs, the average value of the dollar depreciated by 2.4 per cent in 1988, appreciated by 7.3 per cent in 1989 and depreciated by 15 per cent in 1990.

1990 was even more pronounced and there was a further drop in the first half of 1991.

Tropical beverage prices dramatically illustrate the plight of commodity-producing developing countries. World market prices for coffee, cocoa and tea, as a group, have been falling at an average annual rate of 11 per cent since 1982. Coffee prices reached a 15-year low in 1990 and, while the volume exported increased by 4 per cent, export earnings collapsed by 22 per cent. This was catastrophic for many countries in Africa and Central America for which coffee accounts for the bulk of export revenue. Although global cocoa consumption has continued to grow strongly compared to most other commodities, 1990 was the seventh consecutive year of surplus production; the consequent further growth in stocks has inten-

sified the downward pressure on prices, which hit a new low in early 1991.

Prices for basic food items exported by developing countries fell by 6 per cent in 1990. They rose only for bananas, supplies of which were disrupted by cyclones in Central and South America and a banana workers' strike in Honduras, the second largest exporting country. Sugar production losses from dry weather in Australia and Thailand and harvest delays in Cuba were quickly replaced by abundant yields in Western Europe and India. Moreover, China, the world's second largest importer, reaped an unexpectedly large crop and implemented an import curtailment policy, further limiting upward pressure on the world price. The decline in rice prices in 1990 was the result of increases in production in industrialized

Table 10

PRICE INDICES OF NON-OIL PRIMARY COMMODITIES EXPORTED BY DEVELOPING COUNTRIES, 1989-1991

(1985 = 100)

	1989	1990	1990		1991	
	Year	Year	Third quarter	Fourth quarter	First quarter	Second quarter [a]
Combined index [b]	135	127	128	123	125	120
Food	161	151	144	137	145	142
Tropical beverages	70	62	62	63	61	57
Vegetable oilseeds and oil	85	74	73	77	78	75
Agricultural raw materials	129	137	140	142	138	130
Minerals, ores and metals	164	149	159	148	142	137
Combined index in real terms [c]	94	80	81	74	74 [a]	69
Memo items:						
Unit value index of manufactured exports of DMECs	143	158	159	167	170 [a]	173
Unit value of fuel imports of DMECs	67	85	82	100	87 [a]	85

Source: UNCTAD, *Monthly Commodity Price Bulletin;* United Nations, *Monthly Bulletin of Statistics.*
  a Estimates.
  b Derived from data in dollar terms.
  c Prices deflated by the unit value index of manufactured goods exported by developed market-economy countries (1980 = 100).

countries and in some developing exporting countries, particularly Viet Nam, and unexpectedly large crops in some traditional rice-importing countries. In early 1991, however, rice prices rose considerably as import demand increased in some Far Eastern and Middle Eastern countries while production declined in the main exporting countries (Thailand and Viet Nam and some countries in South America).

For vegetable oilseeds and oils, prices in 1990 fell even more sharply (an average of 13 per cent), affecting items produced principally by developing countries, whereas those produced by developed countries, such as sunflower and soya bean oils, enjoyed stable or rising prices. Prices for copra, coconut oil, palm oil and palm kernels and derivative oils registered sharp drops owing to pressures of both increased supply and weakening import demand. China and India, two of the largest importers of palm oil, have increased domestic supplies substantially. The market for tropical oils is further threatened by the likely increased

supply of temperate zone oils from Central and Eastern Europe.

Among agricultural raw materials, lower world production and expanding consumption kept cotton prices relatively high, while strengthened timber export restraints in producer countries raised prices of tropical logs and sawnwood by 25 per cent. The price of natural rubber, on the other hand, drifted downward as a result of diminishing demand from the ailing automobile and tyre industries.

Prices of minerals, ores and metals dropped by 12 per cent in 1990. Tin prices fell by 40 per cent, despite production cuts. The combination of large supply and weak demand also depressed the price of aluminium. Production problems in several producing countries cushioned the decline in copper prices in response to the economic slowdown in most industrialized countries. The price of iron ore, on the other hand, rose, pursuant to negotiations between major producers and consumers, by 16 per cent. Prices of other minerals, ores and metals were relatively stable.

The world crude oil market in 1990 was characterized by significant instability and high price volatility. In the first half of the year, production exceeded demand and petroleum prices declined from almost $20 per barrel in January to about $14 in June. However, with rising tensions in the Middle East and the subseqeunt outbreak of hostilities, prices increased sharply. Monthly average prices peaked at about $33 per barrel in September - October, although world crude oil supplies were not seriously disrupted. Crude petroleum prices have since stabilized in the region of $17 - $20 a barrel.

While the slowdown in economic activity in 1990 and in 1991 has affected demand for some commodities, it is not the only factor. The more rapid growth of production and the consequent increase in the level of stocks has also played an important role in several instances. For most foods and beverages, for example, the rising trend in consumption has been maintained but has been generally outpaced by production. For certain agricultural products, a major explanation is improved productivity, in particular as a result of the use of new hybrid varieties and, in the case of perennial crops such as cocoa, coffee and tropical oils, of their reaching maturity.

Production of commodities does not automatically respond to international price signals for a number of reasons. For basic foodstuffs and certain vegetable oils, production, and particularly the quantity available on world markets, is heavily influenced by agricultural support policies, especially in industrialized countries. In OECD member countries, for example, the total cost of supporting agriculture reached $300 billion in 1990[13] and output increased strongly, despite the fall in world prices.

For tropical products, international market signals are transmitted to domestic producers to a much larger extent than previously because of the introduction of more market-oriented pricing systems in many countries. Coupled with changes in export tax policies, the result has been for producer prices to follow world market conditions more closely. Nevertheless, producers in developing countries often have difficulties in cutting back production. This is in part because current output of such products is the result of past, and therefore "sunk", investment and in part because they are often under pressure from their Governments to increase supplies, given the importance of the sector as a foreign exchange earner and the acute foreign exchange shortages faced by most developing countries.

There appears to be a strong relationship between commodity export behaviour and debt-servicing pressure, especially in those developing countries which continue to depend on commodities for the bulk of their export earnings. When total debt service rises, commodity-dependent indebted countries tend to increase the volume of their commodity exports, as illustrated by the examples of Ghana and Mauritania during the 1980s. The need to service foreign debt leads to the introduction of macroeconomic policies, notably devaluation, to encourage overall exports. In most of these countries, the commodity sector is usually better able to respond than manufacturing, although there is evidence that devaluation does not necessarily result in higher export earnings and, in some cases, does not even increase the volume of commodity exports.

There is a close relationship between world economic growth, particularly in industry, and demand for minerals and metals, although in recent years record stock levels have also had a major influence on prices. After the slower growth in world industrial production and depressed prices in 1985-1986, most metals enjoyed strong demand and higher prices in the succeeding two years, largely as a result of the return to faster growth of industrial production in the developed market economies. Gross fixed investment and the output of metals-intensive capital goods expanded even faster than industrial production. This trend was reversed in 1990 and 1991, when industrial demand, and especially investment, slackened in these countries, contributing to the decline in the prices of metals.

In 1991 the strengthening dollar has also contributed to weaker commodity prices. Changes in many commodity prices to a large degree tend to move in an inverse fashion to the exchange rate of the dollar against currencies of other major importers. During the first half of 1980s, when the dollar appreciated by almost one third against the SDR, the combined index of commodity prices expressed in current dollars decreased by approximately 40 per cent. On the other hand, during 1986-1990, when the dollar depreciated by 25 per cent against the SDR, there was a 27 per cent increase in commodity prices. This inverse relationship seems to hold particularly well for petroleum, basic foods, metals and agricultural raw materials.

---

[13] *Agricultural Policies, Markets and Trade: Monitoring and Outlook 1991* (Paris: OECD, 1991). See also part three, chap. II, sect. B.

Box 2

COMMODITY STOCKS

Faster growth of production than of consumption and the resulting high stock levels have been exerting a depressing influence on commodity prices, as illustrated by data on the consumption, production, stocks and prices for coffee and cocoa for the past decade (see the two charts below). In both cases, world consumption has been rising - in the case of cocoa quite strongly. Because of the more rapid growth of production, however, cocoa stocks, already high, have risen sharply since the mid-1980s, resulting in record low prices.

Stocks of many metals are also high, and a significant proportion is not held by producers. These non-producing owners can influence prices through their decision to withhold or buy. On the London Metal Exchange (LME), for example, stock levels continue to dominate trading, resulting in widely fluctuating prices. In May 1991, LME stocks of aluminium and zinc had reached record levels and copper stocks were at a seven-year high. These stock increases coincided with sharp drops in prices.

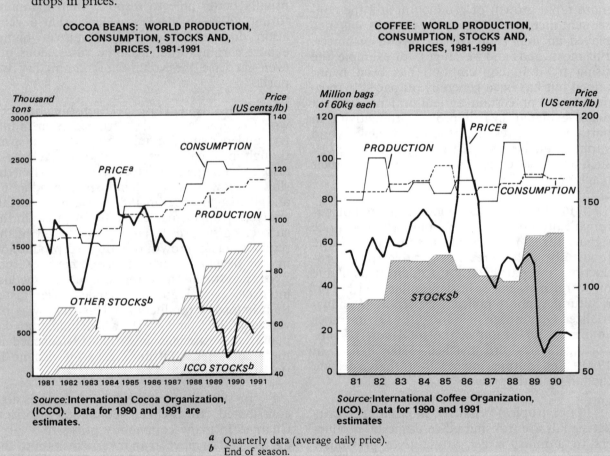

COCOA BEANS: WORLD PRODUCTION, CONSUMPTION, STOCKS AND, PRICES, 1981-1991

COFFEE: WORLD PRODUCTION, CONSUMPTION, STOCKS AND, PRICES, 1981-1991

Source: International Cocoa Organization, (ICCO). Data for 1990 and 1991 are estimates.

Source: International Coffee Organization, (ICO). Data for 1990 and 1991 estimates

a Quarterly data (average daily price).
b End of season.

In addition, the depressed levels of economic activity and the shortage of foreign exchange in the countries of Central and Eastern Europe have led to a contraction in their demand for tropical products. While the potential exists for substantially increased imports of such products into these countries, and hence for a reduction in surplus stocks, it is unlikely to be realized in the near future. Indeed, increased supplies by these countries of such products as meat, sugar, vegetable oils and cereals could depress their prices even further. More generally, the high level of stocks of most commodities is likely to keep commodity prices at depressed levels in the short term, irrespective of the length of the current recession in various parts of the world economy (see box 2).

6. Salient features of the trade performance of developing countries

For the developing countries, 1990 was an unsatisfactory year. The volume growth of their exports fell from some 7 per cent in 1989 to about 5 per cent in 1990 (table 7). The weaker growth can be traced back to a slowdown in the expansion of exports of mineral fuels and manufactured products. The era of double-digit growth of exports of manufactures, which reached its peak in 1988, has seemingly come to an end. Exports of food and beverages, on the other hand, grew dynamically (table 11).

The developing countries maintained relatively strong volume growth of imports, at a rate of 7.7 per cent, well above the average for the developed market-economy countries (table 8). This performance provided a stimulus to world trade, and was essentially the result of the dynamic import growth experienced by some developing countries in South-East Asia (see below) and several oil-exporting developing economies. The imports of many other developing economies continued to be constrained by foreign exchange shortages, heavy debt burdens and stringent structural adjustment programmes.

The trade performances of the major developing regions varied, but the picture was marked by faltering growth. The volume growth of exports from South and South-East Asia decelerated for the second consecutive year, reflecting mainly the dramatic slowdown in the four established exporters and manufacturers (Hong Kong, Republic of Korea, Singapore, Taiwan Province of China). The growth rate of their (combined) volume of exports, which consist essentially of manufactured products, fell from 14 per cent in 1988 to 5.5 per cent in 1990. In the same year, the value of their exports of manufactures to the United States and Japan actually declined. These economies are apparently settling for less spectacular export growth than hitherto. The growth of their (combined) import volume, on the other hand, was still strong in 1990, distinctly faster than the expansion in world trade, but the unprecedented import boom of the second half of the 1980s has subsided.

A number of factors on the supply side contributed to these developments. These economies have, by now, built up relatively well diversified industrial structures, and further progress in expanding their supply capabilities - and hence their export potential - is likely to

be at a slower pace. Furthermore, there has been a shift in some of these economies from a policy of stimulating exports to one of giving more impetus to the expansion of domestic demand. In addition to the consequent increase in imports of consumer goods, imports of investment goods also rose, on account of the need to build competitive positions in new areas of production with higher technology and quality standards.

Other developing countries in South-East Asia, such as Indonesia, Malaysia and Thailand, are emerging as important exporters, particularly of manufactures, where relatively low labour costs provide a competitive edge. Both their exports and their imports continued to record strong volume growth in 1990, reflecting in the latter case buoyant activity in their domestic economies.

The considerable decline in the growth of manufactured imports by Japan affected these countries much less than it did the four traditional exporters, reflecting, in part, a reorientation in Japan's procurement strategies in response to changes in the competitive positions of its neighbouring developing countries. Labour-intensive production is increasingly being phased out in the more advanced developing economies and relocated in those which still possess labour-cost advantages. Thus, a "second generation" of developing countries is moving into the pattern of inter- and intra-industry specialization between countries in the region.

South Asia, with India and Pakistan as important exporting countries, maintained the rapid growth in the volume of exports of recent years. A slower increase in exports of manufactures to the United States and Japan was more than offset by a steep rise in such exports to EEC. The volume growth of imports of South Asia slowed considerably in 1990, reflecting in particular growing balance of payments constraints in India and Pakistan, which brought about a setback to their import liberalization programmes.

The volume growth of exports from West Asia declined significantly, mainly due to the disruption of oil exports from Iraq and Kuwait. On the other hand, import growth is recovering and is expected to accelerate as the reconstruction of Kuwait proceeds.

Latin America, whose export performance deteriorated once again, recorded the slowest volume growth of exports among the developing regions in 1990, in part due to faltering economic growth in the neighbouring market of the United States. By contrast, import volume growth rose strongly, reflecting

Table 11

WORLD EXPORTS AND EXPORTS FROM DEVELOPING COUNTRIES, BY MAJOR PRODUCT GROUP, 1980-1990

	Percentage change in volume				Value ($ billion)	
	1980-1990 (Average)	1988	1989	1990 [a]	1980	1990 [a]
World exports						
All products	4.0	8.5	7.0	4.3	2001	3417
Manufactures [b]	5.5	9.5	7.5	5.0	1085	2450
Food and beverages	5.7	3.0	3.5	6.0	221	321
Agricultural raw materials	4.0	1.5	6.0	3.5	74	108
Minerals, ores and metals	0.5	-13.0	11.0	8.0	93	127
Mineral fuels	0.6	6.0	3.0	0.5	481	336
Exports from developing countries						
All products	4.3	11.3	7.2	5.0	558	739
Manufactures [b]	12.0	16.4	7.5	5.5	99	375
Food and beverages	5.8	3.0	2.0	8.0	63	87
Agricultural raw materials	3.2	5.7	8.0	6.5	20	27
Minerals, ores and metals	1.5	-7.0	5.0	3.0	24	30
Mineral fuels	0.0	12.0	11.0	4.0	350	215

Source: UNCTAD secretariat, based on data from UNCTAD, *Commodity Yearbook,* and United Nations Statistical Office, *Monthly Bulletin of Statistics,* various issues.
   a Estimates, partly based on import data of developed market economies.
   b SITC 5 to 8 less 68.

increased imports by some major oil-exporting countries.

With the exception of Peru and Ecuador, the oil-exporting countries of the region achieved strong overall export growth, due essentially to oil. Performance among oil importers was much more varied.[14] In these countries, as well as in some oil exporters with a large debt overhang, export growth continued to be influenced by differences in the conduct of domestic economic policies and in the availability of foreign exchange. A number of countries which recorded strong export growth had also made good headway with reforms of their economic structures, supported in some cases by a reduction of their external indebtedness (e.g. Chile, Bolivia, Uruguay, Venezuela). In some other countries (e.g. Argentina, Brazil and Peru), reforms have not yet achieved the desired results and severe macro-economic imbalances, in particular uncontrolled inflation and exchange rate instability, defeat any attempt by enterprises to engage

in sustained efforts to develop their export potential. The debt overhang has also played a role, since the resulting import compression has made it very difficult for these countries to increase investment in the production of exportables.

In 1990, roughly half of the value of Latin America's exports (excluding mineral fuels) to developed market-economy countries consisted of raw materials and food products, the remainder being essentially manufactured goods. EEC remains Latin America's major outlet for raw material and food exports, while the United States once again confirmed its position as the region's most important market for manufactures.

The bulk of Latin America's manufactured exports continues to come from only a few countries, especially Mexico and Brazil, which accounted for three quarters of the total value of manufactures exported to developed

---

14 See CEPAL, *Balance Preliminar de la Economía de América Latina y el Caribe,* Santiago, December 1990, table 8.

market-economy countries in 1990. The machinery and transport equipment sectors have come to occupy a prominent position in exports from Mexico and Brazil, which in 1990 supplied almost the totality of such exports from the region to the United States. Strengthening and diversifying the manufacturing export sector remains a major challenge for almost all the Latin American countries.

The volume growth of Africa's exports rose strongly in 1990, due mainly to higher oil exports, particularly from sub-Saharan Africa. Moreover, exports of raw materials (excluding mineral fuels), food products and manufactures from countries in North Africa benefited greatly from strong demand in EEC, by far the most important market for Africa.

The volume of imports into Africa rose moderately in 1990, after a decline in the preceding year. However, this performance was due mainly to strong import expansion in oil-exporting countries. In most African economies, import constraints persisted unabated in 1990. In oil-importing countries in sub-Saharan Africa, import volumes continued to decline. The prevailing import constraints continued to have an adverse impact on new investment, impeding growth in future capacity and export supply capability.

Manufactured products gained considerably in importance in the product composition of Africa's exports in the second half of the 1980s. Their share in the value of exports (excluding mineral fuels) doubled, from 20 per cent in 1985 to 40 per cent in 1990. However, the picture is less encouraging than it appears to be. Africa remains a small exporter of manufactures (about $10 billion to developed market-economy countries, which is slightly more than 4 per cent of the total imports of manufactures by those countries from developing countries). Furthermore, product concentration is still a salient feature of the structure of Africa's manufactured exports. In 1990, the four leading export products (clothing, textiles, chemical elements and compounds, and non-metallic mineral manufactures) accounted for 80 per cent of the total value of manufactured exports to developed market-economy countries. Exports from more skill- and technology-intensive sectors such as machinery and transport equipment still play a small role. Moreover, there is a geographical concentration of exports; in 1990, three countries (Mauritius, Morocco, and Tunisia) accounted for over 90 per cent of Africa's clothing exports to the developed market economies and four (Côte d'Ivoire, Egypt, Morocco and Tunisia)

for 70 per cent of the exports of textiles. Most African countries continue to struggle against stagnation in the process of industrialization.

7. China

The volume of China's exports continued to expand in 1990, and at a rate (13 per cent) distinctly faster than in the preceding year. The volume of imports, on the other hand, declined sharply, reflecting retrenchment measures to improve the country's external financial position. Over the past decade, China has been actively developing its international markets. As a result, total exports increased from $18 billion in 1980 to about $62 billion in 1990. The increase in exports is likely to continue in the years ahead.

China's export performance varied considerably between major markets in 1990. In value terms, the growth of exports (excluding mineral fuels) to EEC accelerated while it slowed in the case of the United States and was virtually nil in Japan. The United States nevertheless remains China's major market for manufactured exports, while Japan continues to be its largest market for raw materials and food products. Overall, manufactures accounted for about three-quarters of the value of imports by the developed market economies from China in 1990, compared to some 45 per cent in 1985. China has thus considerably strengthened its position as an exporter of manufactures to the developed countries.

The product concentration of China's manufactured exports has remained high. Textiles and clothing accounted for about half of the total manufactures exported to developed market-economy countries in 1990, and machinery and transport equipment for only 15.5 per cent, although this contrasts with a mere 1 per cent in 1980. The dominant role of labour-intensive goods in exports to developed countries is in line with China's comparative advantage, but raising the technology component of exports will be crucial to ensuring continued export expansion in the longer term.

8. Outlook

The growth of world trade will continue to slow down in 1991 (to about 3 per cent), along with a further deceleration in the expansion of world output. However, there should be an acceleration in 1992 to about 6 per cent. There are indications that world output will also grow more rapidly in 1992. The end of the Gulf war has inspired new business confidence. There are good prospects that the United States will escape from the grip of recession, and that economic growth will pick up in most developed market-economy countries. On this basis, it is expected that the volume growth of exports from the developed countries will, after a slowdown in 1991, accelerate in the following year. In particular, Japan should maintain relatively strong export growth, reflecting its solid competitiveness and increased demand in major markets, including some large developing economies in South-East Asia. The United States is likely to record equally fast export expansion, benefiting especially from stronger demand in Latin America and the Persian Gulf region. Furthermore, recent improvements in productivity in the United States have strengthened the country's competitive position. On the import side, Japan could experience an acceleration in volume growth in 1991, in advance of the reversal of the global trend. Among the contributory factors are strong economic growth, the continued pursuit of policies to bolster domestic demand, and improved conditions of market access. In the United States, import growth is expected to recover together with economic growth in 1992.

The trade performance of the developing countries remains linked to the fortunes of world trade. As a group, these countries will also sustain a further slowdown in exports in 1991, before export growth accelerates in the year thereafter with the upswing in the world economy. The picture will, of course, vary according to region.

The main explanation for the significant slowdown in Africa's export growth and for the steep decline in exports from West Asia in 1991 is the slackening performance of oil exports, reflecting weaker demand as economic growth decelerates. In 1992, export growth in West Asia could resume. In most of Africa export gains in 1992 will be modest, at best, reflecting prevailing weaknesses on the supply side. A sustained growth of exports will require that development efforts focus to a greater extent on improving production capabilities. Fur-

thermore, Africa's poor infrastructure, as well as the high transport costs to major overseas markets, remain formidable obstacles to export expansion and export market diversification.

The volume growth of exports from South and South-East Asia may increase in both 1991 and 1992, but the improvements are likely to be due mainly to somewhat stronger, though still moderate, export growth of the few larger trading economies in the region. Some other developing countries in South-East Asia which are emerging as substantial exporters of manufactures are expected to record relatively strong export growth, although not at as dynamic a pace as in the late 1980s. Intraregional trade is likely to continue to play an important role. The expansion of trade within the region, with Japan as its dynamic centre, is already faster than that of world trade, and is being propelled by a significant amount of intra-regional foreign investment that is likely to continue to increase vigorously. Moreover, the economic integration of China within the region of South-East Asia can be expected to progress in the years ahead, with increasing foreign investment in China from neighbouring countries, including Japan, and a growing participation of China in intra-regional trade.

Improvements in the export performance of Latin America are expected to be modest in both 1991 and 1992. A level of investment higher than at present will be necessary to build a broader and more competitive export base. As noted in the next section, several countries in this region have undertaken profound economic reforms aimed at integrating their economies more closely with world markets. However, in most countries sustainable growth in manufactured and other non-traditional exports is likely to remain elusive until they can restructure their economies through investment. This will require an easing of current foreign exchange scarcities.

The economic situation in Central and Eastern Europe will remain highly disconcerting in 1991-1992. Intra-regional trade is likely to suffer a further setback, while some countries may improve their export performance in western markets. The Soviet Union is likely to suffer another steep decline in the volume of its exports, owing mainly to supply-side problems.

B. Borrowing by developing countries from the international capital markets and external debt

1. Recent trends in international lending

The growth of borrowing from the international capital markets slowed in 1990, all major categories of financing losing dynamism (as can be seen from table 12). This movement reflected, on the one hand, a general deterioration of the economic climate due to lower economic growth in OECD countries and the uncertainties resulting from the crisis in the Persian Gulf and, on the other, circumstances specific to the capital markets themselves such as efforts by banks to improve their capital positions, frequently at the expense of lower growth in their balance sheets, and the adverse impact of the decline in equity values in Japan on issues of equity-related external bonds.

Fluctuations in aggregate borrowing from the international capital markets during recent years have been disconnected from the course of external financing for developing countries from this source, which has remained marginal in relation to global totals. The relatively low pace of lending to such countries is indicated by tables 12, 13 and 14. In the case of both issues of external bonds and newly-signed syndicated credits much the largest part of this lending was accounted for by countries of South and South-East Asia whose creditworthiness was not impaired by the debt crisis. Nevertheless, Mexico and Venezuela, for which access to financing from the international capital markets was sharply restricted during much of the 1980s,[15] were able to raise money in 1990 on a "voluntary" basis in the form of external bonds and bank credits. This return to "voluntary" borrowing had begun in earlier years but for Mexico the sums raised were markedly higher in 1990. None the less, re-entry into the international capital markets of developing countries recently affected by the debt crisis remains very much the exception. For the great majority other than those of South and South-East Asia the dominant influences on access are still unfavourable perceptions of creditworthiness and continued difficulties in servicing external debt.

The effects of these influences are evident in the slow or negative expansion during 1990 of the external assets of banks in the BIS reporting area vis-à-vis different developing country regions shown in table 13 (though the contraction in Latin America also reflects the decrease in banks' claims on Mexico resulting from the country's debt reduction package as well as smaller contractions of their exposure to certain other countries of the region resulting from debt reduction operations). The effects of low perceived creditworthiness, generally accompanied by depressed levels of demand (particularly for capital goods) due to external financial stringency, can also be seen in recent trends in the amount and terms of financing closely linked to particular trade transactions. As shown by table 14, 40 per cent of developing countries were still experiencing net outflows of export credits in the first half of 1990. Nevertheless, the figures in this table (together with those for net flows of medium-term and long-term export credits in 1989 in table 15) point to a possible revival in this form of external financing for developing countries. But provisional figures for medium-term and long-term net flows for the whole of 1990 raise doubts as to whether the revival has been sustained. Moreover, even the net flows in 1989 were well below those of the early 1980s, and data concerning official insurance in two OECD countries discussed below in subsection 4 point to the continuing prevalence of high costs and restrictive conditions for export credits to developing countries.

---

[15] During this period Mexico was the recipient of "managed" loans as part of restructuring agreements for its external debt.

Table 12

SELECTED CATEGORIES OF INTERNATIONAL FINANCING AND SHARES
OF DEVELOPING COUNTRIES THEREIN, 1983-1990

Category	1983	1984	1985	1986	1987	1988	1989	1990
External bond offerings								
Total ($ billion)	77.1	109.5	167.8	227.1	180.8	227.1	255.7	228.8
Share of developing countries (per cent)	3.4	3.2	3.7	1.3	0.9	1.5	0.9	1.6
Syndicated credits								
Total ($ billion)	67.2	57.0	43.0	52.4	91.7	125.5	121.1	118.2
Share of developing countries (per cent) *a*	47.8 (26.5)	39.6 (20.2)	37.4 (20.9)	19.1 (19.1)	18.3 (7.9)	10.2 (6.1)	12.1 (12.1)	12.5 (12.5)
Committed borrowing facilities *b*								
Total ($ billion)	9.5	28.8	42.9	29.3	31.2	16.6	8.4	6.3
Share of developing countries (per cent)	7.4	21.5	4.7	8.5	4.2	7.8	10.7	27.0

Source: OECD, *Financial Market Trends* (Paris: OECD), various issues, and UNCTAD secretariat estimates.

    a Figures in parentheses exclude managed loans - i.e. new money facilities extended by banks in the context of debt restructuring agreements.

    b Multiple-component facilities, note issuance facilities and other international facilities underwritten by banks, excluding merger-related stand-bys.

2.   Debtor countries' external financial positions and recent policy responses

As shown in table 16, during 1990 there were improvements in key indicators of the external financial positions of net debtor countries as a whole and of the group of 15 highly indebted countries[16] but not in those of the countries of Sub-Saharan Africa. The improvements applied to the debt-to-exports ratio, the interest-to-exports ratio (in this case reflecting, *inter alia*, the lower interest rates exemplified in table 17), and net financial transfers.[17] Recent relevant figures for sub-Saharan Africa are still provisional but show a sharply unfavourable movement in the debt-to-exports ratio and little change in the interest-to-exports ratio. Other features of continuing strains in relations between debtor and creditor countries persisted in 1990.

Arrears continued to accumulate, and there were 18 reschedulings of official bilateral debts.

Alleviation of the debt crisis has been the objective of a series of recent major initiatives. Progress under the initiative put forward by United States Treasury Secretary Brady with the aim of reducing developing countries' debt and debt service obligations to commercial banks is discussed in subsection 3, and a series of initiatives to improve the terms in reschedulings of such countries' bilateral official debts are examined in subsection 5. Additional steps in this area have also been under consideration in the General Assembly of the United Nations. In order to assist the General Assembly in its efforts to enlarge the area of international agreement on policy approaches to the problem of developing countries' debts, at the end of 1989 the Secretary-General of the United Nations appointed Mr. Bettino Craxi, former Prime Minister of Italy, as his Personal Representative on Debt. After extensive consulta-

---

16 The 15 highly indebted countries are those whose external debt positions were the target of the Baker Plan of September 1985. Continuing use of the group for convenience of analysis should not be taken to imply that some of the countries included have not made substantial progress in handling their external debt problems.

17 The changes during 1990 in these two ratios are not greatly affected by the substitution of exports at 1981 prices for those at current prices, a procedure designed to give an idea of the effect on the two indicators of depressed commodity prices during much of the 1980s.

Table 13

EXTERNAL ASSETS OF BANKS IN THE BIS REPORTING AREA [a]
VIS-A-VIS DEVELOPING COUNTRIES, 1983-1990

	1983	1984	1985	1986	1987	1988	1989	1990	Stock (end of 1990)
	Percentage rate of increase [b]								$ billion
All developing countries [c]	5.2	0.7	4.9	4.2	6.5	-4.0	-1.1	-1.6	499
Of which in:									
Latin America	3.1	0.1	3.0	0.8	1.4	-5.3	-4.9	-12.8	204
Africa [d]	1.6	-4.4	14.8	10.3	8.8	-8.0	-3.9	1.8	54
West Asia [d]	20.0	3.2	0.0	4.6	17.0	3.7	9.4	3.6	96
South and South-East Asia [e]	7.9	3.3	8.3	6.4	10.9	-4.2	1.4	15.4	136
Europe [f]	-2.0	-1.3	7.6	-2.1	0.4	-9.5	-14.1	-4.6	8
Memo items:									
All borrowers: Total [g]	4.0	3.2	19.1	27.0	28.5	7.4	14.3	14.7	5907
15 highly indebted countries [h]	3.1	21.5	2.8	2.9	1.6	-6.6	-6.2	-8.5	236
Central and Eastern Europe	-8.2	-1.4	25.9	18.7	17.3	2.9	13.0	-20.2	78

Source: Bank for International Settlements, *International Banking Statistics, 1973-1983* (Basle, April 1984) and *International Banking and Financial Market Developments*, various issues.
a Including certain offshore branches of United States banks.
b Based on data for end-December.
c Excluding offshore banking centres, i.e. in Latin America: Barbados, Bahamas, Bermuda, Netherlands Antilles, Cayman Islands and Panama; in Africa: Liberia; in West Asia: Lebanon; in South and South-East Asia: Hong Kong and Singapore.
d Libyan Arab Jamahiriya is included in West Asia up to 1982 (since it could not be separated from this area in the BIS series). Since 1983, it is included in Africa.
e Including Oceania.
f Malta and Yugoslavia.
g Including multilateral financial institutions.
h Argentina, Bolivia, Brazil, Chile, Colombia, Côte d'Ivoire, Ecuador, Mexico, Morocco, Nigeria, Peru, Philippines, Uruguay, Venezuela and Yugoslavia.

tions, Mr. Craxi submitted his report[18] in October 1990. Salient features of the report are shown in box 3.

3. Renegotiations of external debt owed to commercial banks

Of the agreements reached during renegotiations since mid-1990 some were designed to reduce external debt and debt service, while others involved rescheduling obligations along more conventional lines. The first group of agreements comprises those of Venezuela, Uruguay, Niger and Nigeria, and the second those of Madagascar, Jamaica and Senegal. The other agreement recently negotiated, that of Morocco, involves two phases: the first restructures outstanding debt but also makes possible buybacks once the country has obtained the resources required for the purpose; and the second, which is conditional on Morocco's reaching agreement with IMF on an Extended Fund Facility, provides for re-

18 A/45/380, annex.

Table 14

DEVELOPING COUNTRY RECIPIENTS OF NEGATIVE NET FLOWS OF TOTAL EXPORT CREDITS [a]

(Percentage of developing countries - in each region or grouping - for which figures are available)

	1986	1987		1988		1989		1990
	(2nd half)	*(1st half)*	*(2nd half)*	*(1st half)*	*(2nd half)*	*(1st half)*	*(2nd half)*	*(1st half)*
All developing countries	49	50	47	43	42	35	45	40
Africa	56	56	54	38	40	28	42	40
Latin America	42	39	35	38	38	32	54	35
West Asia	53	60	67	60	53	50	43	43
South and South-East Asia [b]	48	52	38	45	45	45	41	45
Memo item:								
Highly indebted countries [c]	33	53	67	60	60	33	47	40

Source: BIS and OECD, *Statistics on External Indebtedness. Bank and trade-related non-bank external claims on individual borrowing countries and territories*, new series, various issues.
  a After adjustment for the effect of movements of exchange rates.
  b Including Oceania.
  c See note *h* to table 13.

ductions in debt service through an exchange of outstanding debt for bonds at par.[19]

The objective of reducing debt and debt service is to be achieved in the agreements under the current debt strategy through various options of a broadly similar character (though those chosen and their precise terms vary from one agreement to another). These options are buybacks of outstanding debt, its replacement at a discount with collateralized bonds, and its replacement at par by bonds carrying reduced rates of interest. The reductions in interest payments may be achieved through fixing the rate of interest at a level below the current one for the bonds' entire maturity or only during the early years of their maturity (the so- called "step down, step up" formula). The options mostly entail credit enhancements, for example through the collateralization or guaranteeing

of interest payments. Finance for the provision of these enhancements is obtained through borrowing from IMF, the World Bank and bilateral sources, or out of foreign exchange reserves.[20] The options in some agreements are interdependent: for example, that of exchanging outstanding debt for bonds on more favourable terms may be available only to creditor banks willing to tender their loans for buyback at a minimum level of discount.

The reductions in bank debt less the sum of new debt incurred and exchange reserves expended for credit enhancements amounted to about 10 per cent of the outstanding stock for Venezuela, almost 20 per cent for Uruguay and 100 per cent for Niger.[21] These agreements involving debt and debt service reduction followed analogous ones under the Brady Initiative for Costa Rica, Mexico and the

19 In late 1990 Colombia agreed with creditor banks on a loan for the refinancing of $1.8 billion of repayments of principal in 1991-1994.

20 Novel features of the agreement for Niger were the guaranteeing of the principal of zero-interest-rate bonds exchanged at par for outstanding debt by zero-coupon bonds purchased by the Banque Centrale des Etats de l'Afrique de l'Ouest, and the provision of financial support under the IDA Debt Reduction Facility (a Facility through which $100 million was made available for the reduction of the bank debt of heavily indebted IDA-only developing countries).

21 IMF, *International Capital Markets. Development and Prospects* (Washington, D.C.: IMF, 1991), p.76.

Table 15

**NET FLOW OF MEDIUM-TERM AND LONG-TERM EXPORT CREDITS TO
DEVELOPING COUNTRIES, 1983-1990**

(Millions of dollars)

Net flows to:	1983	1984	1985	1986	1987	1988	1989	1990
All developing countries								
Total	7429	5055	871	-3041	-6752	-4698	4007	- b
Private	4802	3728	1002	-1932	-4266	-3484	4273	..
Africa								
Total	3009	1070	635	-875	-2801	-2738	1545	..
Private	2499	717	541	-281	-2244	-2200	1350	..
Latin America								
Total	2243	855	-146	-716	-859	279	1286	..
Private	1284	461	-240	-965	-1037	256	1450	..
West Asia								
Total	456	1201	260	-309	246	997	1334	..
Private	523	1377	477	-226	217	1071	1471	..
South and South-East Asia [a]								
Total	1687	1869	198	-651	-2884	-1850	568	..
Private	585	1196	333	-94	-821	-1345	664	..

Source: Estimates by the UNCTAD secretariat, based on OECD figures.
    a Including Oceania.
    b Provisional.

Philippines, which were discussed in *TDR 1990.* Several other countries are currently attempting to reach similar agreements with their creditor banks.

It is difficult to evaluate the size of the contribution made by agreements involving reductions of debt and debt service to improving the external payments positions of the countries in question, and to reducing the adverse effects of their debt overhangs. Even in the case of the agreements discussed in *TDR 1990,* (those of Mexico, Costa Rica and the Philippines) many relevant data are still not available. Moreover, the impact of the agreements is often obscured by the effects of other recent developments such as the Gulf crisis and slower economic growth in many OECD countries. Nevertheless, it is of special interest to examine various features of the experience of Mexico and Venezuela, two highly indebted countries which negotiated agreements under the current strategy and, as mentioned in subsection 1, have recently raised money from the international capital markets in the form of "spontaneous" borrowing.

At the time of writing complete up-to-date balance of payments figures for the two countries, and thus full pictures of recent changes in their external financial positions, are not available. But there are various indications of the improving creditworthiness that has accompanied their re-entry into the international capital markets. For both countries there have been sharp improvements in the balance of their borrowing from, and deposits with, BIS reporting banks.[22] For Mexico this was due largely to the reductions in its creditor banks' exposure under its debt restructuring agreement. Venezuela has decreased its indebtedness in a similar way through the options in its restructuring agreement and, thanks also to higher oil prices, during 1990 changed its position vis-à-vis BIS reporting banks from one of net indebtedness of almost $8 billion to that of a net creditor to the tune of more than $3

---

[22] See, for example, BIS, *International Banking and Financial Market Developments,* May 1991, table 5A.

Table 16

SELECTED INDICATORS OF EXTERNAL FINANCIAL POSITIONS OF NET DEBTOR DEVELOPING COUNTRIES, [a] 1981-1990

	1981	1982	1983	1984	1985	1986	1987	1988	1989	1990
Ratio of debt [b] to exports of goods and services (per cent)										
All net debtor countries [a]										
Actual	152.1	192.8	214.9	207.7	227.6	264.6	249.6	220.7	208.2	203.1
In 1981 export prices	152.1	180.7	185.0	178.4	198.4	198.5	207.6	183.1	172.4	175.5
Highly indebted countries [c]										
Actual	211.3	283.3	321.8	300.8	306.3	374.7	366.5	310.8	283.3	265.7
In 1981 export prices	211.3	260.3	267.6	254.4	249.0	273.8	289.2	250.9	234.2	234.9
Sub-Saharan Africa										
Actual	130.5	188.3	233.3	224.2	252.2	347.0	372.7	375.0	359.4	387.9
In 1981 export prices	130.5	165.6	192.2	185.4	207.3	268.8	310.9	313.9	314.3	345.0
Ratio of interest payments [d] to exports of goods and services (per cent)										
All net debtor countries [a]										
Actual	16.0	17.2	16.9	16.7	16.7	16.5	13.6	14.1	11.7	10.9
In 1981 export prices	16.0	16.2	14.6	14.4	14.2	12.4	11.3	11.7	9.7	9.4
Highly indebted countries [c]										
Actual	26.8	30.6	29.7	28.4	27.1	27.0	22.9	24.0	17.7	15.7
In 1981 export prices	26.8	28.1	24.7	23.9	22.0	19.8	18.0	19.4	14.7	13.8
Sub-Saharan Africa										
Actual	9.4	10.8	11.7	12.9	12.3	12.4	9.5	11.9	10.0	10.3
In 1981 export prices	9.4	9.5	9.6	10.7	10.1	9.6	7.9	9.9	8.7	9.2
Net financial transfers [e] ($ billion)										
All net debtor countries [a]	27.7	23.3	-30.8	-28.8	-46.0	-51.8	-33.3	-28.5	-16.3	-9.8 [f]
Highly indebted countries [c]	19.6	3.3	-44.1	-35.6	-49.0	-47.4	-17.5	-24.9	-17.7	-10.1 [f]
Sub-Saharan Africa	4.7	4.5	6.1	2.1	0.1	2.7	5.0	3.3	2.4	1.4 [f]

Source: Figures for total external debt and interest payments for 1981-1989 were taken from The World Bank, *World Debt Tables 1990-1991* (Washington, D.C., 1990); figures for 1990 were estimated on the basis of data in IMF, *World Economic Outlook May 1991* (Washington, D.C., 1991). Figures for exports of goods and services at current prices are data of the UNCTAD secretariat; exports of goods and services at 1981 prices are extrapolations of 1981 figures at current prices on the basis of data of the UNCTAD secretariat for export volumes; figures for exports at current and 1981 prices in 1990 were estimated on the basis of data in IMF, *op. cit.* The figures for net financial transfers for 1981-1989 were estimated from data in The World Bank, *op. cit.*, and those for 1990 were estimated on the basis of data in *ibid.*, and IMF, *op. cit.*

a Excluding Islamic Republic of Iran, Kuwait, Libyan Arab Jamahiriya, Oman, Qatar, Saudi Arabia, Taiwan Province of China, and United Arab Emirates.
b Total short-term and long-term debt.
c See note *h* to table 13.
d Interest on total short-term and long-term debt.
e Disbursements of, minus repayments of principal and interest on, total short-term and long-term debt.
f Preliminary estimates.

billion. Both countries were accorded an improvement in the terms on insurance for short-term borrowing from one of the export credit agencies (ECAs) of the two OECD countries whose recent practices in this regard towards developing countries are discussed below in more detail in subsection 4. Such terms, though in some cases influenced by broader policy considerations, usually reflect perceptions of risk associated with the financing and

Table 17

SELECTED INTERNATIONAL INTEREST RATES

LONDON INTER-BANK OFFERED RATE (LIBOR) ON DOLLAR DEPOSITS
(Period averages in per cent per annum)

Year/period	Maturity 3-month	6-month		Maturity 3-month	6-month
1975-1978	6.86	7.36	1985	8.40	8.64
1979	12.09	12.15	1986	6.86	6.85
1980	14.19	14.03	1987	7.18	7.30
1981	16.87	16.72	1988	7.98	8.13
1982	13.29	13.60	1989	9.28	9.27
1983	9.72	9.93	1990	8.31	8.35
1984	10.94	11.29	1991 (1st quarter)	6.87	6.91

MATRIX MINIMUM INTEREST RATES UNDER THE OECD ARRANGEMENT ON GUIDELINES FOR OFFICIALLY SUPPORTED EXPORT CREDITS
(Per cent)

Rate as from:		Maturity: 2 to 5 years Group I	Group II	Group III	Maturity: over 5 years Group I	Group II	Group III
July	1976	7.75	7.25	7.25	8.00	7.75	7.50
July	1980	8.50	8.00	7.50	8.75	8.50	7.75
November	1981	11.00	10.50	10.00	11.25	11.00	10.00
July	1982	12.15	10.85	10.00	12.40	11.35	10.00
October	1983	12.15	10.35	9.50	12.40	10.70	9.50
July	1984	13.35	11.55	10.70	13.60	11.90	10.70
January	1985	12.00	10.70	9.85	12.25	11.20	9.85
January	1986	10.95	9.65	8.80	11.20	10.15	8.80
July	1986	9.55	8.25	7.40	9.80	8.75	7.40
January	1988	10.15	8.85	8.00	10.40	9.35	8.00
July	1988 [a]	..	9.15	8.30	..	9.66	8.30
July	1990 [a]	..	10.05	9.20	..	10.55	9.20

Source: IMF, *International Financial Statistics*; OECD press releases and publications.

Note: Under the OECD Arrangement Group I consists of relatively rich borrower countries, Group II of intermediate borrower countries, and Group III of relatively poor borrower countries.

[a] As from 15 July 1988 matrix minimum interest rates for Group I countries were abandoned.

payments arrangements of a borrowing country.[23]

The "spontaneous" borrowing from the capital markets mentioned above was in the form of bank loans of $0.2 billion for Venezuela and $0.5 billion for Mexico, and of publicly announced external bond issues respectively of the same amounts, supplemented in both cases by further sums raised through private placements (bringing Mexico's total issues to more than $2 billion). Mexico has also recently experienced a sharp rise in foreign investment, inflows under this heading rising to more than

---

[23] In both cases the improvements were accorded by the Export Credits Guarantee Department (ECGD) of the United Kingdom, from which the countries can now obtain insurance on "normal" terms for short-term borrowing (that is to say without special restrictions or surcharges). Insurance on "normal terms" was already available to Mexico from the Export-Import Bank (EXIM) of the United States for both short-term and long-term borrowing. Restrictive conditions still apply to insurance from EXIM on short-term and long-term borrowing by Venezuela, and to insurance from ECGD on long-term borrowing by both countries. (This characterization is based on data in the March issue of *Trade Finance*).

Box 3

THE CRAXI REPORT ON DEBT

The Craxi report on debt contains an extensive analysis of the origins, evolution, scope and character of debt problems facing developing countries and proposes policy remedies. It also sets the debt crisis in the context of international economic relations and deals thoroughly with the need for increasing financial flows to developing countries.

Recommendations

The major recommendations of the report are the following:

- The *Brady plan* should be strengthened and provided with more resources, so as to raise the degree of debt and debt service reduction to 50 per cent. The plan should be managed by an agency within the international financial institutions, working closely with the regional banks. Consideration should also be given to an increase of the resources of the international financial institutions and to an allocation of SDRs, both to be used to finance operations under the Brady Plan. Tax and accounting regulations should be revised to favour those creditor banks which reduce interest and provide new financial flows to developing countries. In those indebted countries endowed with a wide range of industrial assets or natural resources, incentives should be provided for debt conversion operations that would set up joint ventures and promote the participation of external capital in privatized public enterprises. Innovative approaches should be considered, such as the payment of part of debt service in bonds expressed in local currency and indexed to prices of commodities, with the option of using them to purchase shares and other marketable securities.

- As regards *official bilateral debt*, following the Toronto agreement (described in box 7 of *TDR 1989*) further alleviation should be achieved through long-term debt rescheduling (30-40 years) and greater concessionality in a measure reflecting debtors' poverty levels. For the poorest IDA-only countries ODA debt service should be fully written off. For lower middle-income countries, the degree of concessionality should be increased by applying, as a first measure, the Toronto terms to their rescheduling at reduced interest rates. It should be made possible for debtor countries to pay interest on bilateral debts into trust funds in indexed local currencies, to be used for the financing of development projects for environmental protection and human resources development. As for the debt (both bilateral and private) owed by the countries of Central and Eastern Europe, consideration should be given to innovative financing options and the conversion of debt into shares of privatized companies.

- As regards *new flows*, ODA should gradually increase towards the target of 0.7 per cent of GNP; greater use should be made of innovative financial instruments for project financing, such as build-operate-transfer (BOT) schemes, and for commodity-related financing, such as commodity bonds; and consideration should be given to the establishment of a bank for the Mediterranean region.

Follow-up

This initiative was a major element of support for the General Assembly in its endeavours to enlarge the area of international agreement on policy approaches required to overcome the debt crisis. In line with the recommendations of the Craxi report, the Paris Club has increasingly encouraged the conversion of official bilateral debt into local currency obligations, in the framework of debt-for-nature, debt-for-culture, debt-for-aid, and debt-for-equity swaps. These schemes were launched in the context of agreements with lower-middle income countries under the Houston terms. They were later included in the debt reduction packages for Poland and Egypt, and in the agreement with Senegal under the Toronto terms. On-going negotiations within the Paris Club for a significant improvement of the Toronto terms are also consistent with the tone and spirit of the Craxi report.

The UNCTAD secretariat is currently executing a programme of research into the technical aspects of debt conversions and new financial instruments, as a follow-up to the Craxi report on debt. A comprehensive study of mechanisms involving the conversion of official bilateral debt (including debt-for-equity, debt-for-bonds, debt-for-nature, debt-for-goods or other local currency debt conversion schemes) is under way, with a view to enabling the secretariat to assist debtor countries in designing and implementing appropriate debt conversion packages.

$4.5 billion in 1990 from $3.5 billion in 1989[24] and to a level in the first quarter of 1991 corresponding to an annual figure of more than $6 billion.[25] The rise in 1990 was due to equity investment, whereas FDI was actually lower than in 1989. This expansion of foreign investment may reflect partly the return of flight capital, which official sources in Mexico believe has led to inflows of about $4 billion since August 1990.[26]

Both Mexico and Venezuela benefited from the rise in oil prices in the latter half of 1990. The close coincidence of this rise with Venezuela's debt restructuring (agreed in principle in June 1990) precludes even a provisional assessment of the respective contributions of the two events to improvements in the country's external payments position. However, Mexico's agreement antedates the rise in oil prices by a much longer period. Many observers now believe that while the relief provided under the restructuring of Mexico's debt to banks was small in relation to the total amount outstanding, this agreement has none the less helped to create a climate of greater confidence in the country's economy. This confidence, which is also associated with the prospect of a North American Free Trade Agreement with Canada and the United States, has been associated with relaxation of the pressures on Mexico's external payments. Such confidence reflects economic expectations which, as emphasized elsewhere in this Report, can be volatile.[27] But so long as it continues to generate inflows of foreign capital, it may contribute to a more sustained improvement in economic performance.

4. The costs and other terms of private export credits[28]

As noted in subsection 1, the flow of export credits to developing countries reflects the interaction of factors on the demand side (principally levels of macroeconomic activity and policies towards external payments), on the one hand, and the costs and other terms on which such financing is available, on the other. These costs consist of interest and the premiums on official insurance provided by ECAs. The other terms on export credits comprise the proportion and amount of credit for which insurance cover is available, the limit on the amount of financing below which the exporter can exercise discretion in granting insured credits, the length of the period after the occurrence of non-payment before claims are met (the claims-waiting period), and the types of security required.

Owing to the diversity of movements of national interest rates, generalizations about their impact on export credits to developing countries are not possible. Rates of interest for medium- and long-term export credits under the OECD Arrangement on Guidelines for Officially Supported Export Credits (the OECD Consensus) rose in 1990 (see table 17). But the increase is likely to have had less impact on such lending than unfavourable perceptions of creditworthiness. Such perceptions are reflected in premiums on official insurance for export credits and the other terms of such insurance (though changes in the premiums and terms may also be influenced by more general policy considerations). Furthermore, movements in the charges and terms of export credits provide a useful indication of conditions in the markets for financing and payments arrangements for developing countries' trade more generally, as exemplified by charges on banks' letters of credit, the premiums on private credit insurance, and the margins over inter-bank interest rates for *à forfait* financing.

As shown in table 18, official credit insurance from the Export-Import Bank of the United States (EXIM) and the Export Credits Guarantee Department of the United Kingdom (ECGD) continues to be available only on restrictive conditions or unavailable on any terms in the great majority of instances[29] for countries of Africa. In Latin America restrictive conditions apply in the majority of instances for short-term credit, and to almost a majority of instances for medium- and long-term credits.

---

24 *Latin American Weekly Report,* 23 May 1991, p.5.

25 *Latin American Economy and Business,* May 1991, p.4.

26 *Ibid.,* June 1991, p.4.

27 See part two, chap. III, sect. F.2.

28 The export credits in tables 14 and 15 include not only the private lending carrying official insurance or guarantees which is discussed in the present subsection, but also direct lending by OECD Governments (whose determinants are not discussed in this Report).

29 As is also explained in note *a* to table 18, the term "restrictive conditions" for this purpose includes both surcharges on official insurance premiums and other restrictions on the availability of insurance such as those mentioned above. As explained in note *b*, an "instance" corresponds to the terms on official insurance cover either for short-term or for medium- and long-term credits available from one or the other of EXIM and ECGD.

Table 18

TERMS [a] OF INSURANCE COVER AVAILABLE TO SELECTED DEVELOPING COUNTRIES FROM THE EXPORT-IMPORT BANK (EXIM) OF THE UNITED STATES AND THE EXPORT CREDITS GUARANTEE DEPARTMENT (ECGD) OF THE UNITED KINGDOM

(Number of instances [b] in which EXIM or ECGD applied specified terms)

Region/period	Normal terms [a]		No cover [a]		Restrictive conditions [a]	
	Short-term [c]	Medium- and long-term [d]	Short-term [c]	Medium- and long-term [d]	Short-term [c]	Medium- and long-term [d]
Africa						
Late 1986/early 1987	6	4	14	18	50	48
Late 1988/early 1989	9	8	18	21	43	41
Late 1989/early 1990	9	8	18	18	43	44
Late 1990/early 1991	9	8	18	19	43	43
Latin America						
Early 1987	7	7	5	8	40	37
Late 1988	7	7	6	9	39	36
Late 1989	7	7	6	8	39	37
Early 1991	15	8	5	20	32	24
South and South-East Asia [e]						
Early 1987	16	14	5	5	27	29
Early 1989	16	16	3	3	29	29
Early 1990	16	16	3	3	29	29
Early 1991	16	16	3	3	29	29
Memo item:						
Highly indebted countries [f]						
Late 1986/early 1987	2	1	3	4	25	25
Late 1988/early 1989	3	3	4	5	23	22
Late 1989/early 1990	3	3	4	4	23	23
Late 1990/early 1991	8	3	4	9	18	18

Source: Exporter's regional guides in *Trade Finance*, various issues.

  a Normal terms apply when cover is available to a borrower subject to no restrictive conditions. Such conditions include surcharges and restrictions on the availability of insurance cover and reflect the perceived riskiness of the provision of financing to the borrower in question (or in certain cases other considerations). The number and stringency of the conditions vary. For some borrowers cover is not available on any terms.

  b Each country for which information is available corresponds to two instances for the terms available on its insurance cover for short-term credits, one for EXIM and one for ECGD, and likewise to two instances for the terms available on its cover for medium- and long-term credits.

  c Insurance cover for credits with maturities up to 180 days except in the case of credits from EXIM for certain equipment goods and bulk agricultural commodities, for which maturities up to 360 days are also classified as short-term.

  d Insurance cover for credits other than short-term.

  e Including Oceania.

  f See note *h* to table 13.

In general, table 18 points to the persistent prevalence of adverse perceptions of creditworthiness. However, as shown in table 19, countries of Latin America experienced in 1990 an exceptionally large number of changes in the conditions available from EXIM and ECGD, mainly in the form of a rise in instances where official insurance is available for short-term credits on normal terms (i.e. without any restrictive conditions), counterbalanced by an even sharper increase in those where it was completely unavailable for medium- and long-term credits.

Favourable changes were concentrated among the highly indebted countries of Latin America, nine out of 11 such changes applying to this group (including the instances for Mexico and Venezuela discussed above in subsection 3). Unfavourable changes were experienced more widely, in only four instances applying to highly indebted countries. All 13 of the unfavourable changes in Latin America refer to the terms on insurance cover for medium- and long-term credits from ECGD, and many of them may well reflect a tightening of its conditions in response to a long period of losses rather than changes in the creditworthiness of the borrowing countries in question.

Conditions in the market for private credit insurance were more inert than those for official insurance from EXIM and ECGD. No significant shifts in the terms on which it was available were reported by the source used for tables 18 and 19 for any of the countries covered therein. There has thus been a lack of response so far in the form of improved terms from the private insurance market to agreements on debt restructuring under the Brady Initiative.

As mentioned above, losses are capable of leading ECAs to impose higher charges and more restrictive conditions on official credit insurance independently of shifts in borrowers' creditworthiness because of their obligations to be self-supporting in their commercial operations in the medium term. Table 20 shows how widespread are the continuing losses among ECAs in OECD countries. Premium income has been depressed by declines or slow growth in developing countries' imports since 1982, while claims have increased owing to disruptions of debt service. Loss makers have fallen below 70 per cent of the samples in table 20 in only one year since 1983. Moreover, the records of the ECAs of France, Germany, Japan, the United Kingdom and the United States have been particularly unfavourable, only one of the ECAs of the group avoiding losses in more than one year since 1986.

Officially insured export credits represent a substantial part of developing countries' total external debt. The prevalence of restrictive conditions on such insurance is part of the broader picture of such countries' difficulties in servicing their debts to private and official lenders which was described above in subsection 1. Another consequence of these difficulties has been the continuation of the rapid

pace of reschedulings of bilateral official debt at the Paris Club, as discussed in the following subsection.

5. Rescheduling of official bilateral debt

During the past decade, debt owed to official bilateral creditors trebled. At $318 billion by 1990, it accounted for about one-third of the total stock of developing countries' debt, as compared to one-fourth in 1980. The growing importance of official bilateral debt is attributable to a large extent to workouts of existing debt, such as the taking over by official guarantors of debts to private lenders, the capitalization of interest in debt reschedulings, the accumulation of interest arrears, and bilateral borrowing in the context of the Brady initiative. However, the expansion of bilateral debt would have been somewhat higher if debtor countries (mostly low-income) had not benefited from forgiveness of ODA debt to DAC countries amounting to about $11 billion during 1978-1990, in accordance with Trade and Development Board resolution 165 (S-IX).

Since the onset of the debt crisis, the frequency of Paris Club meetings (where debt owed to OECD Governments is usually rescheduled) increased steadily: 21 agreements were signed on average in 1989-1990, against 16 in the previous six years. The amounts consolidated grew from an annual average of $5 billion in 1984-1985 to $17 billion in 1989-1990. The majority of rescheduling countries came repeatedly to the Paris Club. This acceleration in official debt rescheduling is a symptom of both the protracted nature of the problems of many debtor countries and the short-term approach of the Paris Club, whereby the consolidation period (the period in which debt service payments to be rescheduled fall due) has been - until recently - typically 12-18 months. Moreover, debt service due on previously rescheduled debt accounted for an increased share of the consolidated amount, reflecting the inadequacy of the terms of the original rescheduling agreements. In addition, there were several new rescheduling countries - 12 since 1988, a figure which far exceeds that of debtors which have graduated from the Paris Club in recent years. For most rescheduling countries, debt relief from the Paris Club has become the largest source of exceptional external financing.

In the first half of 1991, Paris Club activity slowed down, as only 7 agreements were

Table 19

CHANGES IN TERMS [a] ON INSURANCE COVER AVAILABLE TO SELECTED DEVELOPING COUNTRIES FROM THE EXPORT-IMPORT BANK (EXIM) OF THE UNITED STATES AND THE EXPORT CREDITS GUARANTEE DEPARTMENT (ECGD) OF THE UNITED KINGDOM

(Number of instances)

Region	More favourable terms [a]			Less favourable terms [a]		
	Late 1986/ early 1987- Late 1988/ early 1989	Late 1988/ early 1989- Late 1989/ early 1990	Late 1989/ early 1990- Late 1990/ early 1991	Late 1986/ early 1987- Late 1988/ early 1989	Late 1988/ early 1989- Late 1989/ early 1990	Late 1989/ early 1990- Late 1990/ early 1991
Africa	14 [b]	3	-	15 [b]	-	1
Latin America	3	1	11 [c]	6	-	13 [c]
South and South-East Asia [d]	4	-	-	-	-	-
Memo item:						
Highly indebted countries [e]	4 [b]	1	9	3 [b]	-	5

Source: Exporter's regional guides in *Euromoney Trade Finance Report, Trade Finance* and *Trade Finance and Banker International*, various issues.

    a All instances in which there has been a change in the terms of export credit insurance cover available to a borrower from EXIM or ECGD between the categories "normal cover", "no cover", and "restrictive conditions". (For "instances" and these three categories see table 12.) Such changes are recorded separately for short-term and for medium- and long-term credits.

    b Including the case of one borrower for which a favourable change in the terms of insurance cover available from one agency for long-term credits was accompanied by an unfavourable change in the terms for short-term credits.

    c Including the case of two borrowers for which favourable changes in the terms of insurance cover for short-term credits were accompanied by unfavourable changes in the terms for long-term credits.

    d Including Oceania.

    e See note *h* to table 13.

signed. This did not reflect a significant lessening of pressures for debt relief. By mid-1991, there were about 30 countries whose Paris Club agreements had expired and that were candidates for future reschedulings.[30] These delays rather reflect the problems faced by a number of debtor countries in obtaining new IMF arrangements, a pre-condition for concluding an agreement with Paris Club creditors.

Since mid-1990, significant progress has been made in improving the terms of Paris Club debt rescheduling. The trend towards a differentiated treatment of debtors, which started in 1987 with the adoption of the Venice terms for the poorest sub-Saharan African countries, has been given additional impetus by three important measures: longer maturities (Houston terms) for lower middle-income countries; exceptional debt reduction packages for Poland and Egypt; and negotiations among official creditors on proposals to improve the Toronto terms. As a result of these actions, four distinct categories of Paris Club debtors have emerged: (i) low-income (defined as IDA-only) countries, which are eligible for the Toronto terms; (ii) lower-middle income countries, which are eligible for the Houston terms; (iii) countries - mostly upper-middle income - that would continue to receive the standard Paris Club terms;[31] and (iv) the exceptional cases, such as those of Poland and Egypt.

---

30 For about three quarters of these countries, the agreement had expired for at least six months.

31 Rescheduling at market interest rates, with a 10-year maturity, including a grace period of 5 years.

Table 20

PROPORTION OF EXPORT CREDIT AGENCIES IN SELECTED DEVELOPED MARKET-ECONOMY COUNTRIES THAT INCURRED LOSSES [a] ON INSURANCE ACTIVITIES, 1981-1989

(Percentage)

	1981	1982	1983	1984	1985	1986	1987	1988	1989
Proportion:	50	60	85	70	65	70	70	75	73

Source: 1981: D. Bowen, D. Mills and M. Knight, *The Euromoney Guide to Export Finance* (London: Euromoney Publications, 1986), Part I; 1982-1988: M. Knight, J. Ball and A. Inglis-Taylor (eds), *The Guide to Export Finance 1988* (London: Euromoney Publications, 1988), Part I; J. Ball and M. Knight (eds) with the assistance of R. Saxena, *The Guide to Export Finance 1989* (London: Euromoney Publications, 1989), Part III; J. Ball and M. Knight (eds), *The Guide to Export Finance*, Fifth Edition (London: Euromoney Books, 1990); and F. Carnevale, "ECAs sing the blues", *Trade Finance*, January 1991.

a Losses occur when claims exceed the sum of premium income and recoveries (adjusted in some cases for the inclusion of other factors). The number of loss-making agencies is expressed as a proportion of the total number of agencies for which data were available (18 in 1981, 20 in 1982-1988 and 15 in 1989).

Following bilateral initiatives by France and the United States and the recommendations made at the Houston Summit, the Paris Club adopted in September 1990 a more favourable treatment for lower-middle-income countries with high levels of official debt (Houston terms).[32] Six countries (Congo, El Salvador, Honduras, Morocco, Nigeria and Philippines) have so far benefited from this initiative. The new treatment consists of a lengthening of repayment terms whereby (a) ODA loans are rescheduled with a 20-year maturity, including up to 10 years of grace and (b) non-concessional loans are rescheduled with a 15-year maturity and up to 8 years of grace. It should be noted that these easier repayment terms do not entail concessionality, as market-related rates continue to be applied to non-concessional debt. However, the Houston terms contain one element of debt reduction, as they include, as a major innovation, the possibility for creditor Governments to sell or swap ODA loans as well as a limited amount of non-concessional credits through debt-for-nature, debt-for-aid, debt-for-equity, or other local currency debt conversions.[33]

Important advances involving significant debt reduction have been made in the treatment of the official bilateral debt of Poland and Egypt. In April-May 1991, official creditors agreed to reduce by 50 per cent the entire stock of eligible (i.e. pre-cutoff date) Paris Club debt owed by these two countries.[34] The debt reduction will be effected through a menu of options, including principal reduction, interest reduction, and partial interest capitalization on concessional terms. In addition, creditor countries agreed to a voluntary debt swap facility, which could include up to an additional 10 per cent of outstanding claims.

These deals - which creditors have described as exceptional - constitute a major advance in the international debt strategy by introducing the concept of official debt reduction for middle-income countries and by applying the reduction to the entire stock of debt. Furthermore, the size of debt forgiveness - about $24 billion for the two deals combined - is extraordinarily large. It is equivalent to over twice the aggregate amount of ODA debt cancellations granted by OECD countries during the past 13 years.

32 Low-income countries that are not "IDA-only", and thus not eligible for the Toronto terms, may also benefit from this treatment. In deciding on eligibility for the Houston terms on a case-by-case basis, the Paris Club considers three criteria: per capita income, the ratio of bilateral debt to commercial bank debt, and the debt and debt service burdens, as measured by the ratios of debt to GNP, debt to exports and scheduled debt service to exports.

33 The amount of non-concessional debt that can be converted has been set at 10 per cent of the outstanding claims or $10-20 million, whichever is higher.

34 For Poland, the debt reduction will occur in two stages: 30 per cent "upfront" and 20 per cent after three years. For Egypt, the reduction will take place in three stages: 15 per cent "upfront", 15 per cent after 18 months, and 20 per cent after three years. In both cases, the implementation of the stages following the "upfront" reduction is conditional upon successful completion of an IMF arrangement.

Box 4

A COMPARATIVE ANALYSIS OF THE TORONTO OPTIONS AND THE TRINIDAD TERMS

The chart below shows the debt service profiles resulting from the implementation of the Toronto options and the Trinidad terms (the latter with two different rates of growth of debt service payments: 5 per cent and 8 per cent). The debt service reduction that would be obtained with the Trinidad terms is substantial. In fact, the Trinidad terms entail high concessionality, as the resulting grant element would amount to about 67 per cent, while the combined grant element of the three Toronto options is only 20 per cent. Moreover, in the Toronto scheme debt service obligations generally need to be rescheduled repeatedly, sometimes every year (the assumption used in the chart). The resulting debt service would sharply increase from year 9 (reaching a level slightly below the debt service due in the absence of debt relief) and would peak in year 14 at a level almost four times higher than the debt service under the Trinidad terms.

DEBT SERVICE PROFILES: TORONTO OPTIONS AND TRINIDAD TERMS *a*

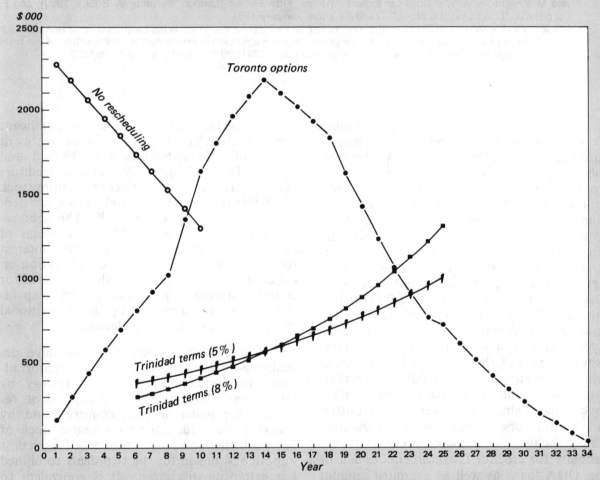

a Debt service payments are derived from a hypothetical loan of $12 million, with a maturity of 10 years and an interest rate of 9 per cent.

In order to evaluate the adequacy of the Trinidad terms in relation to the debt-servicing capacity of debtor countries, the UNCTAD secretariat has assessed the impact of these terms on the scheduled debt service of 18 low-income African countries which are eligible for the Toronto

---

The growing recognition of the inadequacy of the Toronto terms[35] has led Paris Club creditors to consider over the past year bold

proposals giving further impetus to the principle of debt reduction for low-income countries. At the Second United Nations Conference on

Box 4 (concluded)

options. Estimates have been made on the basis of the following assumptions: (1) the Trinidad terms are applied to the stock of Paris Club debt as of end-1989, including post-cutoff date debt; (2) exports grow by 5 per cent annually; and (3) the "nominative" debt service ratio, which is taken to reflect the debt-servicing capacity of debtor countries, is set at 20 per cent. The analysis has produced the following results:

- For a group of countries (Benin, Central African Republic, Chad, Malawi, and Togo) whose debt service ratios originally did not exceed 20 per cent, the Trinidad terms would result in a small reduction of the ratios (a few percentage points). For these countries, the great bulk of their debt is on concessional terms;.
- For a second group of countries (Guinea, Niger, Senegal, Zaire) the Trinidad terms would have a significant immediate impact, as they would lower their debt service ratios to less than 20 per cent by the second year of the scheme, from levels which were originally in the 25-35 per cent range;
- For a third group of countries (Madagascar, Mali, Mauritania, Uganda and United Republic of Tanzania), the debt service ratios after implementation of the Trinidad terms would fall to below 20 per cent from years 6-8 onwards. Therefore, for the first 5-7 years, these countries would continue to be afflicted by the debt overhang, although in some cases (Madagascar and United Republic of Tanzania) the immediate debt service reduction would be considerable. In this group, about 40 per cent of total debt is owed to Paris Club creditors;
- The fourth group includes those countries which would maintain high, sometimes extremely high, debt service ratios (Guinea-Bissau, Mozambique, Sao Tomé and Principe, Somalia). For most of these countries, the Trinidad terms would have a significant impact on debt service ratios; nevertheless, they would still remain far above 20 per cent. For instance, in the eighth year of the scheme, debt service ratios in Guinea-Bissau and Mozambique would be about 60 per cent and 30 per cent, respectively. In Sao Tomé and Principe and Somalia, these ratios would be in the 30-40 per cent range. In all countries belonging to this group, much of the debt is owed either to non-Paris Club bilateral creditors or to multilateral institutions. In Guinea-Bissau, for example, about three-quarters of official bilateral debt is to non-Paris Club creditors, and about half of its total debt is to multilateral institutions.

It follows from the above that if the United Kingdom proposal is implemented, half of the countries in the sample (i.e. the nine countries belonging to the first and second group) would register debt service ratios lower than the "normative" level of 20 per cent within two years. But for the remaining countries, this initiative is not enough. This conclusion is reinforced by the fact that debt service projections do not include debt contracted after 1989 and assume that the reduction would also apply to post-cutoff date debt, a scenario more favourable to debtors than that which would prevail if the Trinidad terms were adopted.

---

the Least Developed Countries, in September 1990, the Netherlands called for the cancellation of all official bilateral debt owed by LDCs and other low-income countries facing severe debt problems. The cancellation would be gradual and conditional on the implementation by debtor countries of sound economic policies in the context of IMF programmes. Shortly thereafter, at the meeting of Commonwealth Finance Ministers held in Trinidad, the United Kingdom proposed that Paris Club creditors should cancel two-thirds of the stock of debt owed by eligible countries in a single operation, with the remaining debt rescheduled over 25 years (including 5 years of grace) and interest payments capitalized for the first 5 years. The repayment schedule would be linked to the debtor country's export capacity. Eligibility for this scheme, known as the Trinidad terms, would be the same as for the Toronto terms.

As shown in box 4, for many low-income countries the Trinidad terms, if implemented, would go far towards reconciling debt-servicing obligations with their capacity to pay. But for several other poor countries saddled with an extremely heavy debt burden, this initiative will not, by itself, remove the debt overhang.∎

---

35 For a detailed assessment of the Toronto terms, see *TDR 1989*, box 7.

Chapter III

RECENT DEVELOPMENTS IN TRADE POLICIES

Recent trends in trade policies have been characterized by an increasing resort to selectivity and the persistence of protectionism in developed market-economy countries and by the embrace of trade liberalization in a large number of developing countries as well as in Central and Eastern Europe. The differences in the evolution of trade regimes are unmistakable and at the same time unique in historical terms. Therefore, as one observer put it, "for the first time in economic history the impetus to trade liberalization is not coming from industrial countries which profess to accept liberal norms, but rather from countries whose past tradition has been to reject them".[36]

Overall measures of trade covered by non-tariff measures (NTMs) in developed countries have not exhibited major changes in recent years. Certain measures of liberalization have been accompanied by a tightening of controls elsewhere, so that the end result has been an erosion of the MFN principle rather than a decisive move away from trade controls, as promised at the start of the Uruguay Round in the Punta del Este Declaration. NTMs cover a larger proportion of imports today than they did at the beginning of the 1980s or at the launching of the Uruguay Round in 1986.

It is in this context that one must appraise the recent movement towards greater economic integration in Europe and the Americas. While each of these arrangements could bring benefits to a particular group of developing countries - economic integration in the Americas would benefit mainly the countries in Latin America - they could have powerful impacts on the allocation of investment resources which would not necessarily be related to long-term comparative advantage or to development needs.

Regional integration is considerably more advanced in Europe, but its future impact, particularly as regards third countries, remains highly uncertain. It is estimated that the one-time net trade creation effects for the developing countries as a group of the establishment of a single EEC market by 1992 will be roughly equivalent to the annual increase in exports that such countries could expect in a "normal" year in present economic conditions. This limited gain could be readily offset if trading partners attempt to pass on the costs of adjustment that the integration process will involve. The way in which trade policies and measures towards non-participating countries are actually applied will be crucial.

The characteristics of wider European integration are still uncertain. None the less, its impact on non-participating countries will also depend more on the nature of trade policies toward third countries than on the process of integration as such.

This chapter explores some of these developments. It does not deal with recent developments in the Uruguay Round, which are the subject of part three of this Report.

---

[36] David Henderson, Head of the Economics and Statistics Department of OECD, speaking at the Institute for International Economics, Washington D.C. (*IMF Survey,* 27 May 1991).

A. Protection in developed and developing countries

1. Persistence of managed trade in industrialized countries

In the recent past, there have been some trade-liberalizing moves in the major industrialized countries in favour of selected groups of countries. The extension of the United States' Caribbean Basin Initiative in 1990 (CBI II) made the scheme permanent and provided for improved market access conditions for beneficiaries, especially on products assembled from United States parts. Both the United States and EEC improved benefits for four Andean countries under their respective GSP schemes. Since the mid-1980s, there has been a gradual phasing out of national quantitative restrictions (QRs) in EEC member countries. In selected cases, textile restrictions have been replaced by less restrictive arrangements.[37] However, national QRs have in some cases been superseded by voluntary export restraint arrangements (VERs) at the Community level. For example, VERs on footwear were concluded with the Republic of Korea and Taiwan Province of China in June 1990, and it appears likely that the VERs applied on automobiles in four member States (France, Italy, Portugal, and Spain) will also be transformed into Community-wide restrictions.

Perhaps the greatest beneficiaries of selective liberalization have been the countries of Central and Eastern Europe. Until the mid-1980s, these countries were at the bottom of the hierarchy of EEC's trade preferences. Since then, however, improved access to the EEC market has begun to be granted. This rapprochement, originally planned in small steps, was significantly accelerated by the revolutionary changes in these countries in recent years. Both EEC and several other industrialized countries have recently extended the application of their GSP schemes to Bulgaria, Czechoslovakia, Hungary and Poland.[38]

The importance which the countries of Western Europe attach to support for Central and Eastern Europe is reflected in their willingness to increase market access even in the traditionally "sensitive" product areas - textiles, steel, agriculture - despite resistance from some Governments and interest groups. In November 1989, EEC decided to lift specific (discriminatory) QRs on Polish and Hungarian goods as of the beginning of 1990. However, non-discriminatory QRs were to remain in place and sectoral agreements in textiles, steel and agriculture were not to be affected. Subsequently, the EEC Commission proposed additional liberalization measures: a one-year suspension of remaining QRs on products such as cars, footwear, and toys; quotas on imports of textiles above the levels agreed upon within the MFA framework; and finalization of a new agreement with the two countries on steel products, which would pave the way for the eventual elimination of the QRs applied by a number of EEC member countries. In spite of these measures, the incidence of NTMs in industrialized countries' imports from Central and Eastern Europe is still higher than on imports from any other group of countries, partly because of the relatively large share of agricultural and other sensitive products in the total exports of Central and Eastern European countries to their principal markets.

The measures selectively liberalizing trade in favour of some countries (most often only in some product categories) have gone side-by-side with measures restricting the exports of other countries. This is nowhere more evident than in the textile and clothing sector. While in Europe imports of textiles and clothing may have become slightly more liberal, in North America restrictions on imports of these goods have increased, owing mainly to the extended product coverage of certain agreements - including MFA - but also because more countries have become subject to restraint agreements. Even small exporters, with "infant (exporting) industries", such as Fiji and Myanmar, have

---

37 Since 1 January 1988, restraints under the Multifibre Arrangement with Colombia, Egypt, Guatemala, Haiti and Mexico have been discontinued and replaced by administrative arrangements. Arrangements with Bangladesh and Uruguay no longer include quantitative restrictions.

38 Romania (and to a lesser extent Bulgaria) already enjoyed GSP benefits in the schemes of most developed countries.

been brought within the scope of application of textile restraints (see annex 1 to this chapter).

Another disturbing trend in the growing selectivity of the industrialized countries' trade policies has been the steady rise in the number of outstanding anti-dumping cases, particularly those involving developing countries. The persistent use of anti-dumping actions and the widening of the scope of their application create concern that anti-dumping laws are being used for protectionist purposes. As shown in annex 1, even very small exporters with marginal market shares, such as Papua New Guinea, have become subject to anti-dumping investigations in recent years. The harassment to trade for new and small exporters resulting from the time and costs involved in anti-dumping investigations can be very large.

As regards longer-term trends in the application of NTMs in industrialized countries, an increase can be observed up to 1987, with a levelling off in subsequent years (see chart 7). Trade restrictions affect a larger proportion of imports into developed market-economy countries now than in the early 1980s, and they are disproportionately imposed against the exports of developing countries. Only Australia, Japan, New Zealand and Norway make less use of NTMs; in the United States and EEC, resort to such measures is more widespread now than at the beginning of the 1980s.

2. Trade liberalization in developing countries

Tariffs in developing countries have traditionally been high in order to generate government revenues and to provide protection to domestic industries. Due to industrialization policies with a strong sectoral bias, tariff structures have tended to be complex, with large variations in the levels of duty by sector in combination with rebates or exemptions for inputs not produced domestically or which are needed for the production of exports. Tariff policies have often created distortions as well as an anti-export bias which has had to be compensated by subsidies.

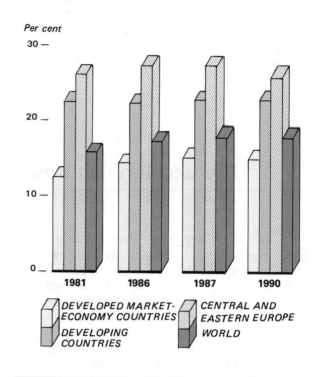

Chart 7

TRADE COVERAGE RATIOS OF NON-TARIFF MEASURES APPLIED BY DEVELOPED MARKET-ECONOMY COUNTRIES IN SELECTED YEARS

(Percentage of imports)

Per cent

DEVELOPED MARKET-ECONOMY COUNTRIES
DEVELOPING COUNTRIES
CENTRAL AND EASTERN EUROPE
WORLD

Source: UNCTAD Data Base on Trade Control Measures.

Note: Ratios have been computed using 1988 trade weights.

In recent years, many developing countries have liberalized their tariff regimes by simplifying tariff structures, reducing rates and increasing the share of duty-bound items in GATT (see annex 2 to this chapter). A salient feature in this context in recent years has been the far-reaching process of tariff liberalization in Latin America, where in almost all countries tariff structures were simplified and rates reduced significantly. Bolivia, Costa Rica, Chile, Mexico and Venezuela have bound their full tariff schedules in GATT.

In recent years, and as part of packages of trade policy reforms, many countries reduced or even discontinued most of their NTMs (see annex 3 to this chapter), particularly in Latin America, where the changes in tariffs and the elimination of NTMs, taken together, represent a radical liberalization of trade policy. Several countries in other regions (e.g., Morocco and the Republic of Korea) have also reduced their NTMs considerably.

in the ways in which developed and developing countries use NTMs. Those of developed countries are intended to provide relief from import competition for specific domestic sectors; therefore, they tend to affect specific import categories and to remain in place for a long time. They are frequently discriminatory, affecting only selected countries. Trade actions by developing countries are more frequently much broader in product coverage, and they are used for the management of foreign ex-

dustrial development. They are most often applied on a general, non-selective basis.[39] Unlike in many industrialized countries, NTMs in developing countries tend to be applied on a MFN basis without discriminating against specific groups of trading partners. Selective NTMs, such as VERs and MFA restrictions, are not applied, although a few countries have used anti-dumping actions to some extent.

B. The accelerating trend towards economic integration

In the recent past, several developments in Europe and in the Americas have increased the likelihood that the structure of the international trading system will be altered very significantly in the near future. In Europe, the completion of the single European market (SEM), scheduled for January 1993, is proceeding on schedule. In addition, negotiations between EEC and EFTA on closer economic links are nearing completion, and three countries in Central Europe (Czechoslovakia, Hungary and Poland) are in the process of negotiating association agreements with EEC and free trade agreements with EFTA. In the Americas, Mexico has started negotiations with the United States and Canada on the formation of a North American Free Trade Area, and President Bush launched in June 1990 his Enterprise for the Americas Initiative, one of its objectives being the negotiation of free trade areas with groups of countries in Latin America and the Caribbean. At the same time, and apparently under the stimulus of the United States initiative, several Latin American countries have entered into ilateral or plurilateral negotiations among themselves or ave decided to strengthen existing integration agreements.

It is difficult to say what these recent moves portend for developing countries as a whole, for different groups of developing countries, or for the international trading system. Developing countries have a clear stake

in the strengthening of the multilateral trading system. While this or that group of countries may obtain temporary gains from preferential access to one of the main markets, in the long run all countries will lose if the international trading system is split up into a few large economic blocs characterized by managed imports. The recent moves aimed at forming or strengthening integration groupings could represent either building blocks towards a more open trading system or stumbling blocks in the way of its achievement. Everything will depend on the policies of the groupings towards imports from non-participating countries.

1. Developing countries and greater European integration

(a) Recent policy developments

As noted above, the transformation of EEC into a true common market within which goods, services and factors of production are able to move freely is on course. Negotiations between EEC and EFTA countries on the formation of a European Eco-

---

[39] See Sam Laird and Rene Vossenaar, "Why We Should be Worried About Non-Tariff Measures", Special Issue on Non-Tariff Measures, *Información Comercial Española* (Madrid), 1991 (forthcoming); and R. Erzan, K. Kuwahara, S. Marchese and R. Vossenaar, "The Profile of Protection in Developing Countries", *UNCTAD Review*, Vol.1, No.1, (United Nations publication, Sales No.E.89.II.D.4).

nomic Area (EEA) are in their final stages. At present, EFTA and EEC constitute a free trade area in manufactured goods. The free trade agreement entered into by EFTA and EEC in 1973 has already significantly reduced tariffs and has abolished most quantitative restrictions on trade in manufactures between the two groups of countries. Although the precise contents of the EEA agreement are not yet settled, its objective is to extend the provisions of the SEM to EFTA countries by ensuring the free movement of goods, services, persons and capital throughout EEC and EFTA countries. It is envisaged that the EEA will come into being at the same time as the completion of the SEM (1 January 1993).

The EEA agreement is expected to bring major benefits to EFTA countries. The extension of the current EFTA-EEC free trade agreement to cover measures other than tariffs and quotas (e.g., the harmonization of technical standards and competition policies and the liberalization of public procurement), essentially on the basis of EEC norms, will prevent the erosion of the competitiveness of EFTA firms in EEC which would otherwise result from the 1992 programme. Moreover, the EEA will give service companies from EFTA countries access to the EEC market. However, it is becoming increasingly evident that the creation of an EEA would involve a considerable loss of autonomy for EFTA countries without providing them with the full benefits that would be associated with their being members of EEC and their being able to influence the evolution of Community-wide policies. Partly for this reason, Austria and Sweden have applied for EEC membership and other countries may follow suit in the near future.

As already noted in section A above, trade restrictions on exports from Central and Eastern European countries to those of Western Europe have been eased. Moreover, three of these countries (Czechoslovakia, Hungary and Poland) are seeking association agreements with EEC which would gradually extend to them the SEM's "four freedoms" over a period of ten years. The agreements would also call for the three countries' "ultimate, though not automatic", membership in EEC. The full details of these agreements are still to be worked out. Ties are also becoming closer between the countries of Central and Eastern Europe and those of EFTA. In late 1990, the latter countries, on the one hand, and Czechoslovakia, Hungary and Poland, on the other, began negotiations aimed at signing free trade agreements. Both the free trade agreements with EFTA countries and the association agreements with EEC are asymmetric, in the sense that trade liberalization and the removal of obstacles will be reciprocal, although the timetables will differ.

(b) Impact on developing countries

These developments suggest that, during the 1990s, an essentially integrated market covering most of Europe will emerge, with major consequences for the rest of the world. The trade of developing countries with Europe is bound to be affected, and groups of developing countries will be affected in different ways, depending not only on the composition of their exports to Europe but also on the position they are able to negotiate within Europe's scale of preferences.

Most of the short- and medium-term effects on developing countries of these changes will be the result of the growth of demand and the evolution of market access conditions in EEC. The extension of the 1992 programme to EFTA countries will have lesser consequences for non-European trading partners because it involves a much smaller market than EEC (see chart 8). The EEC market is crucial for individual countries both of EFTA and of EEC (it absorbs 60 per cent of EEC members' combined exports and over 55 per cent of those of EFTA countries); on the other hand, the EFTA countries constitute a relatively marginal market not only for EEC but also for their own exports. The effects of European integration on Central and Eastern Europe will be of a long-term nature, largely because the current economic dislocation in these countries rules out any significant increases in imports. Special trading relationships with Western European countries could, in the long run, contribute to their economic recovery and, to the extent that this is so, their demand for tropical beverages, raw materials, simple manufactures and capital equipment will rise. If trade policies towards non-European partners remain open, developing countries could eventually be in a good position to increase their exports to Central and Eastern Europe.

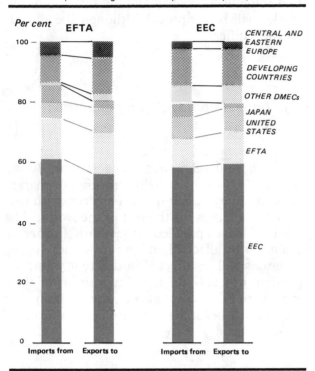

Chart 8

**SHARE OF DIFFERENT COUNTRY GROUPS
IN THE TRADE OF EFTA AND EEC IN 1988**

(Percentage of total imports or exports)

Source: Calculations by the UNCTAD secretariat, based on data of EFTA and EEC.

Much of the current interest in European integration focuses on the completion of the SEM, which is expected to have a fairly quick impact on developing countries. In fact, many of the effects may have already occurred.[40] Most of the EEC Commission's proposals to the Council for new laws or modifications to existing law have already been adopted, and business firms within the Community have already taken action in anticipation of 1992. One sure sign is the wave of mergers and take-overs, many for the purpose of rationalization, which has swept Europe since the launching of the SEM programme in 1985. There has also been a sharp increase in domestic and foreign investment in EEC, partly induced by the SEM. These trends will undoubtedly continue. Other effects will be of a longer-term nature and will depend, *inter alia,* on how trade policies in

Europe evolve in response to adjustment pressures.

The SEM is expected to have trade-creating and trade-diverting effects on developing countries.[41] Increases in income in the Community as a result of the SEM will raise demand for imports from developing countries. These are the trade-creation effects. On the other hand, the essence of the programme is to reduce costs within the Community by increasing competition (e.g., through the opening up of public procurement) and by reducing existing national barriers to trade such as border controls or eliminating differences in technical standards. In the longer run, the creation of a unified market is also expected to induce significant economies of scale. The lower costs of producing in the Community would shift demand away from imports and towards EEC producers. These are the trade-diversion effects.

One of the impacts of the SEM may be a higher rate of investment and an intensified flow of innovations, new processes and new products; in that event, the completion of the internal market would lead to an increase not merely in the level but also in the rate of growth of EEC income.[42] Both trade-creation and trade-diversion effects would thus be commensurately greater. The magnitude of such effects is, however, difficult to estimate.

In primary commodities, the Community is a net importer of most non-food products or, in the case of agriculture, protects domestic producers through the CAP. Therefore, cost decreases in these sectors are likely to be negligible and no trade diversion effects are likely to arise from the 1992 programme. On the other hand, the demand for primary commodities exported by developing countries will rise together with EEC incomes, although at a slower pace since the income elasticity of demand for most raw materials is lower than unity (with the major exception of petroleum, where it is relatively high).

Although efficiency gains are likely to be significant in several service industries, they will have little impact on developing countries, since the latter are not large exporters of services (except for tourism) to EEC. In manu-

---

[40] See Michael Davenport with Sheila Page, *Europe: 1992 and the Developing Countries* (London, Overseas Development Institute, 1991), pp. 1-5.

[41] The meaning of the terms "trade creation" and "trade diversion" as used here (and in much of the recent writings on the SEM) differs from that given to them in the literature on customs unions. In the latter, trade creation is defined as the union-induced shift from consumption of domestic products to the consumption of imports from other members, and trade diversion is the union-induced shift in demand from outside the union to higher-cost products from within the union. Here the terms are used to reflect the positive ("trade creation") and negative ("trade diversion") impacts on the exports to EEC by non-EEC countries.

[42] Richard Baldwin, "The Growth Effects of 1992", *Economic Policy,* No.9, October 1989.

factures, the trade diversion effects on exports from developing countries could be important; the sectors which would probably secure the strongest gains in efficiency from the SEM are those which are particularly affected by the current segmentation of EEC into national markets (office equipment, electrical goods, motor vehicles, telecommunications equipment, chemicals and pharmaceuticals and engineering goods). These sectors are also likely to have the largest potential for economies of scale. The scope for efficiency gains is more modest in traditional sectors, which account for the bulk of developing country exports of manufactures (e.g., textiles, clothing, footwear, leather, iron and steel, cork products). Some of these sectors have already undergone severe structural adjustment in the Community. Moreover, access to the EEC market is tightly controlled, by the MFA in the case of textiles and clothing and by VERs in the case of iron and steel. The evolution of imports into EEC in these sectors will depend more on the results of the Uruguay Round than on the effects of the SEM. In particular, the effective phasing out of the MFA would have considerably more powerful effects on developing country exports than the establishment of the SEM.

At the same time, trade creation effects will also be significant in manufacturing, since income elasticities of demand are, on average, higher than for primary commodities. Both the income elasticities and the trade diversion impacts are positively correlated with the degree of technological sophistication of the sectors involved.

In order to estimate the net trade creation effects on different groups of developing countries, it has been assumed that the SEM would cause EEC incomes to increase by 5 per cent, which is roughly the mid-point of the range estimated in a report prepared for the Commission (4.3 per cent to 6.4 per cent).[43] In addition, income elasticities of demand for imports from developing countries were calculated,[44] and sectoral trade diversion effects as estimated by the Community were used. Since the effects of the 1992 programme are likely to have begun to be felt around 1988-1989, net trade creation is estimated on the basis of 1988 exports of developing countries to EEC.

For developing countries as a whole, the SEM could induce an increase in exports to EEC of about $10 billion, or 7 per cent of their exports in 1988 (see table 21). The biggest gainers are the oil exporters of West Asia and North Africa and the economies of South-East Asia, which export predominantly manufactures and are the Community's major developing country suppliers of high-technology manufactures. The estimated net trade creation for ACP and Latin American countries is likely to be much more modest.

While an increase of $10 billion may appear large, it needs to be placed in perspective. During the period 1985-1989, developing country exports to EEC grew at an average annual rate of 8 per cent in volume. Therefore, the estimated overall export gain of 7 per cent for developing countries represents an average of about one year's export growth, and considerably less than the year of peak export growth during the past decade (10 per cent in 1988).

The SEM may have other favourable, but less measurable, effects. The terms of trade of primary commodity exporters are likely to improve. This is because EEC demand for primary commodities will rise together with incomes and, other things being equal, primary commodity prices will be higher; at the same time, the prices of manufactures exported by EEC will decline. Moreover, the elimination of national quotas for textile and clothing imports (even if they are replaced by their equivalents at the Community level) would result in a greater utilization of MFA quotas by exporting countries which at present are being constrained by the application of national quotas. Excise taxes on tropical beverages will also be harmonized and reduced, to the benefit of developing countries. These positive impacts have not been included in the estimates shown in table 21.

On the other hand, the trade diversion effects of the SEM could have also been underestimated, since the impact of economies of scale has not been taken into account. If there are important economies of scale to be reaped, their effects on the competitiveness of EEC firms could be considerable, and the displacement of supplies from third countries could be much larger than assumed here. Also, there is no way of taking into account the trade diversion effects of the incorporation of Spain and Portugal into the Community. The 1992 programme is being implemented in conjunction with the staged process of full integration into the Community of these two countries, a

---

43 Paolo Cecchini *et al.*, *The European Challenge 1992. The Benefits of a Single Market* (Aldershot, Wildwood House, 1988), p. 84

44 The income elasticities were obtained through the estimation of demand for import functions (at one- and two-digit SITC levels), where imports by EEC from developing countries were regressed against EEC income and the prices of imports from developing countries relative to a composite EEC deflator of GDP.

Table 21

ESTIMATED NET TRADE CREATION EFFECTS OF THE SINGLE EUROPEAN MARKET ON DEVELOPING COUNTRY EXPORTS BY REGION AND COMMODITY GROUP

(Millions of dollars)

Region/group	Primary commodities	Fuels	Manufactures	Total	As percentage of 1988 exports to EEC
All developing countries	1 923	3 306	4 920	10 149	6.9
Of which:					
ACP	491	443	85	1 019	5.2
Mediterranean [a]	225	694	754	1 673	6.4
South-East Asia [b]	266	-	2 587	2 853	6.8
Latin America [c]	894	261	404	1 559	5.4
West Asia [d]	24	1 346	177	1 547	9.1

Source: UNCTAD secretariat estimates, based on official international data.

   a   Algeria, Cyprus, Egypt, Lebanon, Malta, Morocco, Syrian Arab Republic, Tunisia, Turkey, Yugoslavia.
   b   Hong Kong, Indonesia, Malaysia, Philippines, Republic of Korea, Singapore, Taiwan Province of China, Thailand.
   c   Excludes Caribbean countries and territories (which are included in ACP).
   d   Bahrain, Iran (Islamic Republic of), Iraq, Kuwait, Oman, Saudi Arabia.

process which will be completed more rapidly than it was for the older EEC members. Furthermore, Spain and Portugal compete more directly with imports from developing countries than do the other Community countries.[45] Hence, the potential for trade diversion is large.

Other effects of the SEM could be to shift import demand from one group of developing countries to others. The abolition of national trade restrictions would be detrimental to producers from ACP countries and overseas territories of EEC member States, who at present enjoy preferential access to specific EEC markets for commodities such as bananas, rum and sugar. The abolition of national quotas would probably be accompanied by a shift in demand to lower-cost suppliers among developing countries which now face national trade restraints.

All in all, the effects of the SEM on developing country exports are likely to be positive, but relatively small, assuming that EEC trade policy towards non-members remains unchanged. As already argued in earlier reports

in this series, the evolution of policy toward non-EEC countries will be a fundamental determinant of the size, and even the direction, of its effects on developing countries.[46] In this respect, the handling of national quantitative restrictions - whether they will simply be eliminated, or whether they will be replaced by Community QRs, and how restrictive would be the latter - will be crucial.

At present, there are two kinds of national QRs: those on horticultural and fishery products, applied mainly by France, Italy, Greece and Belgium/Luxembourg on imports from many developing countries; and those applied under article 115 of the Treaty of Rome by several EEC countries, affecting mainly the more industrialized developing economies of Asia and China and which cover mostly footwear and consumer electronics products.

It is not clear how these restrictions will be handled after 1992. The optimal solution would be their elimination, but that outcome is far from certain, particularly in the current trading environment. In this connection, recent

---

45   Michael Davenport with Sheila Page, *op.cit.*, p. 21.
46   See *TDR 1990*, part one, chap. III, sect. A., and *TDR 1989*, part one, chap. III, section. B..

resort to Community-wide VERs in sectors undergoing structural adjustment and the upsurge of anti-dumping actions are a cause for concern. The temptation to use VERs and anti-dumping action at the Community level to pass on to trading partners the costs of adjustment to the SEM should be strongly resisted.

The extension of the SEM to EFTA countries could have some trade diversion effects on developing countries, since an EEA agreement would extend the cost-reducing benefits of a single market to EFTA producers of manufactures. Any trade diversion that does take place will fall mostly on non-European developed countries, which are EFTA's major competitors in EEC. The exports to EEC of only a few developing countries compete with those of EFTA. Sectors where there could be trade-displacing effects for developing countries are iron and steel, metal manufactures and electrical machinery. However, these effects are likely to be small. As regards trade creation in EFTA itself, even if incomes in its member countries are given a boost by European integration, the small size of the EFTA market suggests that the the positive trade impact on developing countries will not be of great consequence.

The effects of the extension of European integration to Central and Eastern Europe will be felt as the latter's trade with Western Europe increases. Trade flows between these two groups of countries are already important, the latter region taking almost 90 per cent of the former's exports to developed market economies. As noted above, since the beginning of 1990, Central and Eastern European exports to Western Europe have risen sharply and are expected to continue a rapid pace of expansion during the 1990s.

No comprehensive assessment of the impact of the recent trade liberalization measures in favour of Central and Eastern European countries is presently available. Preliminary estimates show meaningful although small gains. It is estimated that EEC's GSP scheme represents a potential gain of some ECU 100 million for Hungary and Poland combined. Tariffs applied to their industrial goods (which at present range from 8 per cent to 22 per cent) will be completely abolished. The Community's concessions on textiles are estimated to be worth approximately ECU 80 million to Poland and ECU 50 million to Hungary. For Hungary alone, it has been estimated that EEC's concessions on industrial products could yield an additional $60-80 million annually in export

revenues. More generally, Hungarian economists have attributed some one-third of the rather rapid growth of exports to EEC in the first half of 1990 to the Community's liberalization of trade.[47]

In the short to medium term, however, the response of Central and Eastern European countries to their newly granted trade preferences and to the even closer ties with Western European countries which are likely to be knitted in the 1990s will be severely limited by supply constraints. Therefore, developing country exporters of manufactures are unlikely to face any significant competition from those countries in Western European markets for some time to come. In the long term, preferential access to Western European markets, combined with the advantage of physical proximity, could well have an impact on export-oriented foreign investment in sectors where Central and Eastern European countries have a comparative advantage. The high levels of educational attainment in those countries, together with low wages, suggest that they could eventually gain competitiveness in technology-intensive manufactures and in some modern services.

Foreign companies have already expressed an interest in investing in Czechoslovakia, Hungary and Poland. So far, actual investment flows have been small, but they are expected to grow sharply as some of the obstacles to private investment, such as uncertainty over property rights, are removed. Some fairly sizeable foreign investments in Czechoslovakia and Hungary have been in high technology and automobiles, with the Western European markets partly in mind.

2. Liberalizing trade in the Americas

In section A above it was illustrated that, although selective protectionism remains widespread in the United States, there is a concurrent trend towards freer trade between that country and its neighbours. A landmark in this respect was the United States-Canada Free Trade Agreement. This has been followed by discussions of a similar arrangement with Mexico. Meanwhile, as also described above, individual countries throughout Latin America have been independently liberalizing their trade; they have also stepped up joint discussions about freer trading arrangements among themselves.

---

[47] Presentation by B. Kadar, Minister of Foreign Trade, in ECE, *Reforms in Foreign Economic Relations of Eastern Europe and Soviet Union* (United Nations publication, Sales No. E.91.II.E.5).

Trade relations throughout the western hemisphere are dominated by the presence of the United States. That country is the leading trading partner of most of the other countries, with the result that regional trade is heavily influenced by economic conditions in the United States and by the policies and measures it adopts. Trading partners are affected not only directly by actions taken regarding their trade with the United States but also indirectly, both positively and negatively, by actions by the United States directed at others. The renewed interest in more liberal trading arrangements that currently characterizes the region is thus, in part, a response to the several new departures in United States trading arrangements in recent years. The fear of being subjected to the trade sanctions that the United States is able to impose under the so-called "Super" and "Special" provisions in section 301 of its Omnibus Trade and Competitiveness Act of 1988[48] is an important example of the effect that United States measures have had on trade policies in Latin America.

The United States, in turn, has been prompted to strengthen its trading relationship with the rest of the Americas at least in part by changes in the trading environment elsewhere in the world. The emergence of a united market in Europe and, to a larger extent, the development of another closely integrated set of rapidly growing economies in East Asia pose a challenge to the United States position as the world's largest economy. The establishment of closer economic relations with its neighbours is part of its response. By the same token, many countries in Latin America feel that they may become marginalized in the world economy of the 1990s if they do not associate themselves with one of the world's three poles of economic activity. North America is a logical first choice.

(a) The pattern of intra-American trade

Latin American exports to the United States grew faster than to other markets during the 1980s and the United States is now the single most important market for the region, absorbing almost 40 per cent of its exports. The United States also supplies about one-third of Latin American imports. However, there are large differences in the importance of the United States among the regional sub-groupings and individual countries. More than two-thirds of Mexico's total trade is with the United States, while the proportion is about one-fifth for such countries as Chile, Paraguay

and Uruguay. For countries of the Andean Pact and the Central American Common Market, the United States accounts for somewhat less than 40 per cent of exports (see chart 9).

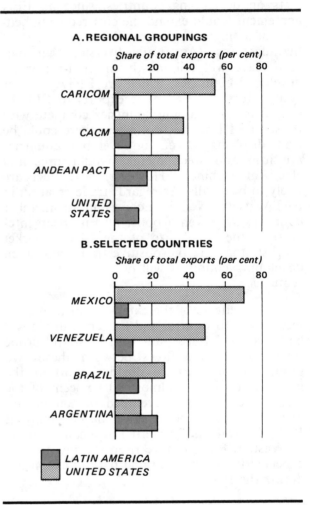

Chart 9

TRADE WITHIN THE AMERICAS BY SELECTED GROUPINGS AND COUNTRIES IN 1989

Source: United Nations Statistical Office.

Viewed from the perspective of the United States, Latin America accounts for about one-eighth of total exports and imports, with Mexico being responsible for about half of that share and Brazil and Venezuela (together) for about another quarter. Manufactured goods dominate United States exports to the region, accounting for 81 per cent in 1989; agricultural products represent another 11 per cent. Imports by the United States from Latin America consist mainly of manufactured goods (55 per cent), fuel (25 per cent) and agricultural

---

48 See *TDR 1990*, box 11, for a summary of these provisions.

products (14 per cent). Over two-thirds of the manufactured imports are supplied by Mexico under the special rules for the *maquila* industry, which has registered high growth over the past decade. The most important fuel supplier is Venezuela, which accounts for 40 per cent of the region's fuel exports to the world and 11 per cent of United States total fuel imports.

The importance of Latin America as a trading partner for the United States has declined over the past decade, largely as a result of the overall economic slowdown in the region and the inability to finance imports.[49] Nevertheless, the region as a whole remains an important market. On the other hand, trade with individual countries, with the possible exceptions of Mexico and Venezuela, is not of great importance to the United States. In contrast, exports from most countries in Latin America are heavily dependent on the United States market and have become more so in recent years; for these countries, their trading relationship with the United States is vital to their economic growth. These varying trading stakes have a major bearing on the trade negotiations that are under way.

(b) Regional trade barriers and preferences

As a result of successive GATT negotiations, the unweighted average tariff rate applied by the United States to imports from developing countries is now only 5.3 per cent. Slightly more than one-fifth of United States imports from developing countries were duty-free in 1989, but tariffs well above average apply to a wide range of goods.

The main obstacle to exports to the United States are non-tariff measures (NTMs).[50] Such measures apply to about one-fifth of total United States imports, though for Latin America the ratio is only 15.7 per cent because of the different composition of imports (see table 22). Moreover, the ratio varies widely among countries and sectors; in trade with Mexico, for example, NTMs apply to only 6.7 per cent of exports to the United States. The proportion is generally highest for manu-

factured goods, in particular for so-called traditional exports. Latin American exports of glass, leather and textiles are especially affected by such measures, while Mexican clothing also has a high coverage ratio.

Most imports from developing countries, including all of those from Latin America, are eligible for preferential treatment under the United States GSP scheme. A number of other preferential schemes have also been introduced by the United States for individual developing countries or groups of countries in the region. These include the Caribbean Basin Initiative and the Andean Initiative (benefiting in differing degrees exports from Bolivia, Colombia, Ecuador, Peru and Venezuela). The scope of these preferential agreements remains limited by their many restrictions.

Although most countries in Latin America have been liberalizing their trade in recent years, overall protection remains relatively high in several of them, and their average tariffs are higher than those of the United States. NTMs, while reduced, continue to be used in some countries.

There are currently four trading groups in the region: the Andean Pact countries (Bolivia, Colombia, Ecuador, Peru and Venezuela), the Central American Common Market (CACM, comprising Costa Rica, El Salvador, Honduras, Nicaragua), the Caribbean Common Market (CARICOM, comprising 12 countries in that area) and the Latin American Integration Association (LAIA, comprising Argentina, Brazil, Chile, Mexico, Paraguay, Uruguay and the Andean Pact members). The mechanisms of these groupings vary from full integration, including the creation of a customs union, to a free trade area; all embrace the principle of MFN treatment as regards non-Latin American third parties. Even though most of these arrangements have been in existence for many years, there was negligible progress in increasing the share of intra-trade in any of the groupings during the 1980s (see chart 10), partly because of the import compression that characterized Latin America at that time but also because of the slow progress in eliminating trade barriers.

49 According to official United States sources, the depressed economic conditions in Latin America resulted in a loss of United States exports of as much as $1 billion between 1982 and 1988. (Statement by USTR in the OAS Assembly, as reported in SELA, "Compendio de documentos sobre la Iniciativa para las Américas", Meeting of experts in their personal capacity on the Initiative for the Americas, Caraballeda, 6-8 February 1991, Working Paper No.5.)
50 In addition, there is an embargo on United States trade with Cuba.

Table 22

COVERAGE OF NON-TARIFF MEASURES APPLIED BY THE UNITED STATES TO EXPORTS FROM LATIN AMERICA, AND SPECIFICALLY TO MEXICO, BY SECTOR, IN 1990

(Percentage of total value of exports of the sector to the United States)

Sector	Latin America	Mexico
Food, beverages and edible oils	9.9	2.2
- Food	10.0	2.3
- Fish	0.4	0.0
Agricultural raw materials	15.5	0.3
Minerals and metals	22.1	23.9
- Iron and steel	65.2	67.0
Fuels	10.2	2.2
Chemicals	5.8	5.6
All other manufactures	11.4	7.3
- Glass and glassware	44.6	49.1
- Leather	33.9	0.1
- Textiles	66.0	80.7
- Clothing	60.7	93.0
- Footwear	1.0	0.0
- Road vehicles and parts	3.9	5.1
Other	3.0	3.6
All exports	11.6	6.7

Source: UNCTAD Data Base on Trade Measures.

Chart 10

TRADE WITHIN THE REGIONAL ECONOMIC GROUPINGS IN LATIN AMERICA, 1980-1981 AND 1988-1989

(Percentage of total exports)

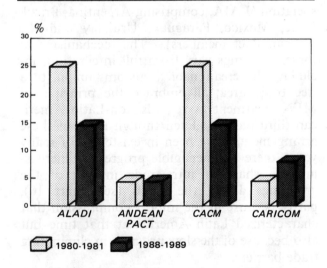

1980-1981   1988-1989

Source: INTAL, *El Proceso de Integración en América Latina* (Caracas, 1989).

(c)   The Enterprise for the Americas Initiative

The Enterprise for the Americas Initiative, generally referred to as the Bush Initiative, was announced by the United States in June 1990. The Initiative has three pillars - trade, investment and debt. This underlines not only the interrelationships between these three policy areas but also the crucial role of each in the growth and long-term recovery of Latin America. Nevertheless, the most wide-ranging proposals in the Initiative relate to trade.

As an immediate measure, the United States offered to negotiate deeper tariff reductions on products of special interest to Latin America in the Uruguay Round.[51] As a longer-term objective, recognition of the *de facto* interdependence of the United States and Latin America resulted in the Initiative's proposal to establish a free trade area covering the whole western hemisphere. While the Initiative is not clear on how such an arrangement is to be achieved, the United

---

[51] The offer subsequently made by the United States proposed cutting tariffs on such products by 27.3 per cent. The largest cuts were offered for agricultural products (70.8 per cent) and the smallest for textiles (7 per cent).

States has indicated its willingness to enter into free trade agreements either with individual countries or with groups of countries that have trade liberalization agreements among themselves. The bilateral "framework agreements" that already existed with Bolivia and Mexico were regarded as initial steps towards such trade arrangements with the United States. Sixteen countries have since signed "framework agreements" and several have also expressed interest in initiating negotiations on bilateral trade agreements with the United States.

The framework agreements identify mutual interests and set out general principles for mutual trade relations. They also establish a joint negotiation council and propose an immediate agenda. This agenda is usually wide-ranging, including such topics as barriers to trade in goods and services, investment-related questions and protection of intellectual property. Finally, the agreements set forth principles and procedures for consultations on trade and investment issues.

An immediate reaction to the Bush Initiative has been the new impetus given to integration in Latin America, as reflected in the various trade agreements that have been signed among the Latin American countries since its announcement. In March 1991, Argentina, Brazil, Paraguay and Uruguay signed the treaty of Asunción. This is a transitional agreement to liberalize trade, the objective being to lay the ground for the creation of a Southern Cone Common Market (MERCOSUR) starting in 1995. This will provide for the free circulation of goods, services and factors of production, the co-ordination of macroeconomic policies, a common trade policy towards third countries and the introduction of a common external tariff.

In May 1991, the Andean Group adopted the Acta de Caracas to accelerate the establishment of a free trade zone, which is to come into effect on 1 January 1992.[52] A common market is to be established by the end of 1995, by which time the exceptions granted to the less advanced members of the Group will be phased out. Article 3 of the Act refers to the Bush Initiative: members of the Group decided to proceed with a joint undertaking to establish more balanced and dynamic relations with the United States without adversely affecting the actions taken by members at the bilateral level.

Regular meetings between the member countries involved in such negotiations will also be held.

Representatives of Colombia, Mexico and Venezuela have also discussed the mutual elimination of tariffs with a view to reaching zero tariffs on a wide range of products by July 1994, starting with the establishment of maximum levels to be applied from 1 July 1991. Chile also has initiated negotiations to liberalize trade with several countries in the region.

These efforts to create free trade areas and to reinforce integration within Latin America can be seen as a first step in preparations for trade and related negotiations with the United States. However, it is unclear how the negotiations for a free trade area for the Americas will proceed and what final form it will have. Nevertheless, negotiations between the United States and Mexico on a free trade area have been initiated. Canada has decided to join these negotiations. A free trade area including these three countries would comprise 360 million people with a GNP of $6,000 billion - a market much larger than that of EEC. This new, unified market would have important consequences for the world trading system as a whole, but particularly for Latin American economies. Moreover, the way in which the negotiations for this and other trade arrangements in the region are conducted could have profound consequences for the eventual outcome.

(d) The experience of the Canada-United States Free Trade Agreement

It is premature to evaluate the economic effects of the free trade agreement between the United States and Canada because the negotiations ended less than two years ago and full implementation is not due before 1998. Furthermore, the main objective of the agreement is to increase competitiveness and economic growth: these effects can be measured only in a longer-term perspective. Although the outcome is difficult to assess at this stage, an evaluation of the experience of Canada in negotiating the agreement with the United States, comparing the initial objectives with the final results of the negotiations, could be useful to

[52] Signed by the Presidents of the member States of the Andean Group in Caracas on 18 May 1991. For the text see document JUN/di 1429 of the Andean Group (20 May 1991).

Latin American countries as they contemplate a similar exercise.[53]

A main objective for Canada was to ensure stable access to the United States market, where tariffs were less of an obstacle than NTMs;[54] especially the anti-dumping, countervailing and emergency safeguard rules but also government procurement and dispute settlement. In particular, Canada hoped to gain exemption from the provisions of the United States Omnibus Trade Act of 1988. However, the two countries were unable to resolve these questions, with the result that the agreement provides for negotiations on subsidies, unfair pricing and anti-dumping to continue for the next five to seven years, with national laws applying in the interim. Latin American countries are also unlikely to be able to obtain exemption.

Canada also had to make various concessions regarding its initial position on government procurement. The simple removal of restrictions on procurement was not regarded as sufficient by the United States because it stood to gain access to a much smaller market than would Canada.[55] Similar arguments about relative market size could also be applied to Latin American trading partners: compared with Canada, they have larger markets in terms of population but limited purchasing power.[56]

The Canada-United States negotiations also suggest that such issues as services and certain market access problems cannot be totally settled through bilateral agreements. The two countries agreed that it was not possible to resolve, for example, agricultural issues without the co-operation of other countries and therefore agreed to work together in the Uruguay Round to enhance trade in agriculture. This suggests that it is unlikely that the quotas affecting many Latin American agricultural products can be addressed in a satisfactory way in bilateral trade negotiations with the United States.

Overall, it is evident that the Canada-United States agreement will result in Canada's moving closer to United States regulations and arrangements than vice versa. It seems unlikely that any developing country that enters into negotiations with the United States will be able to do any better, largely because bilateral leverage is such an important feature of such negotiations. The United States is generally better able to achieve its objectives if the partners are dependent on continued access to its markets or capital, as is the case for almost every country in Latin America. In addition to the Canadian agreement, this is illustrated by the concessions that have been obtained from the Republic of Korea on investment and from Japan on steel and automobiles.[57]

(e) The nature of a free trade arrangement for the Americas

The question remains as to the eventual shape of free trade agreements between the United States and other countries in the Americas. The negotiations could be conducted purely bilaterally, in which case the result would be that the United States would be trading freely with each partner but the partners would not be trading freely among themselves. This has been referred to as a "hub" (the United States) and "spokes" (the individual trading partners) arrangement.[58] A different situation would result from a plurilateral agreement whereby all partners would trade with each other without restriction within the free trade area. The latter arrangement would avoid the distortions and inefficiencies of a "hub and spokes" relationship and therefore would provide participating countries with higher incomes.

At present, it is impossible to forecast which of these outcomes will materialize. Canada has decided to join the negotiations between Mexico and the United States, agreeing to the basic outline that the latter two

53 Some of these aspects are discussed in "The Free Trade Agreement between Canada and the United States", *Economic Bulletin for Europe*, vol. 42/90 (United Nations publication, Sales No.E.90.II.E.37), chap. 5.

54 When negotiations started, 80 per cent of Canada's exports entered the United States duty-free and the average duty ranged from 0.7 per cent to 2.8 per cent; only 5 per cent of exports had a tariff of more than 5 per cent.

55 The result was that no new sectors were added to already existing arrangements enabling producers to bid on contracts in each other's country, although the ceiling for bids was lowered.

56 Canada has a population of 26 million and a GDP per capita of around $17,000 while in Mexico and Brazil the populations are 84 million and 145 million and per capita GDP is $1,800 and $2,200, respectively.

57 See P. Morici, *Making Free Trade Work* (New York: Council of Foreign Relations Press, 1990), p. 31.

58 R.J. Wonnacott, "United States Hub-and-Spoke Bilaterals and the Multilateral Trading System", *CD Howe Institute Commentary*, Ottawa, Oct. 1990.

countries have proposed. The three countries have decided that any new accord will remain separate from the agreement between the United States and Canada,[59] implying a "hub and spokes" arrangement. Thereafter, it is not clear how other potential participating countries will be treated. The case-by-case approach implied by the eligibility criteria contained in the Bush Initiative suggests that the United States will negotiate a series of separate bilateral agreements with individual countries or groupings. Since it would be difficult in practice to negotiate with all interested countries simultaneously, the question arises of the priority which the United States will attach to the negotiations with a particular country.

An important element will be the sequencing of the negotiations, i.e., whether the agreement with Mexico will be concluded before other countries are invited to negotiate. In any event, it seems likely that the results of the negotiations with Mexico will largely determine the extent of negotiations with other countries. Because of their different interests, Latin American countries have often found it difficult to negotiate jointly. Nevertheless, it is now important for them to elaborate a common position on issues that are a priority for many of them so that the benefits of an initial agreement are not eroded through its extension to new partners. It is also necessary for Latin American countries to reach agreement on how to safeguard the commitments associated with the different integration schemes if a member country enters into bilateral negotiations with the United States.

3. Regional arrangements: building blocks or stumbling blocks?

There are two opposing views on the impact of regional liberalization on the international trading system. One view is that the new or strengthened regional arrangements represent moves away from multilateralism in trade and will be "stumbling blocks" to any attempt to reconstitute an open trading system. The other view, espoused particularly in North America, is that regional liberalization will promote globally freer trade by setting precedents which can later serve as a basis for multilateral agreements and by breaking new ground in areas such as services or investment.

In this view, regional arrangements would be essentially transitory and would constitute "building blocks" for a more liberal and open system.

Reality contains elements to support both of these views. The fact that regional liberalization is taking place concurrently with persistent protectionism, increasing selectivity and uncertainties with regard to the conclusion of the Uruguay Round lends credence to the more pessimistic approach. On the other hand, it must be recognized that the forces working for regionalization are quite different today from those of the 1930s, when the impulse was to create trading blocs behind high tariff walls. In both Europe and North America, the objective is to achieve a "deep" integration which reaches beyond border measures and seeks the reconciliation of divergent national laws and practices affecting trade in goods and services. In Latin America, the recent interest in reviving regional integration and in negotiating free trade agreements with the United States comes at a time when there are also far-reaching programmes of trade liberalization. Moreover, all three major candidates for regional blocs - Europe, the western hemisphere and Japan plus South-East Asia - depend too much on extra-regional markets to become self-contained "fortresses" (see table 23). The internationalization of production on a world scale through foreign direct investment also militates against the regionalization of the trading system.

There are some clear conditions for regional arrangements to be building blocks rather than stumbling blocks to freer multilateral trade. The major condition is that barriers toward non-participants be reduced concurrently with the establishment of the new regional arrangements. At the same time, a decisive move away from the recent trend toward selective preferences would do much to allay current fears. As regards EEC, national NTMs must not be replaced by Community-wide restraints or, at least, any new restrictions at the Community level must be strictly transitional and dismantled within a reasonable period of time. As regards the proposals for new arrangements in the Americas, these would foster freer trade if they were negotiated simultaneously among all (or most) countries. The alternative - a crazy-quilt pattern of bilateral agreements - would serve only to strengthen recent moves away from the MFN principle. Plurilateral negotiations would be facilitated by the strengthening of integration among the Latin American countries themselves. In addi-

---

[59] *Business International*, 18 March 1991, p. 90.

Table 23

INTRA- AND EXTRA-REGIONAL EXPORTS OF MAJOR REGIONS, 1973-1988

(Percentage of total exports)

Region	1973	1980	1985	1988
Western hemisphere [a]				
Intra-regional	47.3	46.7	52.7	48.1
Extra-regional	52.7	53.3	47.3	51.9
Total exports ($ billion)	129	405	421	559
Western Europe [b]				
Intra-regional	68.5	67.5	65.2	71.3
Extra-regional	35.1	32.5	34.8	29.7
Total exports ($ billion)	260	816	779	1 268
Japan and South-East Asia [c]				
Intra-regional	33.3	32.7	29.6	31.1
Extra-regional	66.7	67.3	70.4	68.9
Total exports ($ billion)	69	272	348	575

Source: UNCTAD secretariat, based data from official international sources.
   a North America and Latin America.
   b EEC and EFTA countries.
   c South-East Asia: Hong Kong, Indonesia, Malaysia, Philippines, Republic of Korea, Singapore, Taiwan Province of China and Thailand.

tion, the principal selective barriers in the United States and Canada affecting Latin American exports must be liberalized on a multilateral basis. Trade liberalization in Latin American countries in favour of regional partners must also be accompanied by the lowering of trade barriers toward all countries, a process which is already under way.■

Annex 1 to Chapter III

NON-TARIFF MEASURES APPLIED SINCE 1987 BY DEVELOPED MARKET-ECONOMY COUNTRIES TO DEVELOPING COUNTRIES NOT PREVIOUSLY AFFECTED BY SUCH MEASURES *a*

AUSTRALIA

Anti-dumping and countervailing duty actions

Colombia	AD and CVD action on woven polypropelene, primary carpet backing fabric, in January 1990.
Indonesia	AD action regarding woven bags of polylefin, in March 1990

CANADA

Textile restraints

Colombia	Quantitative restraint on exports of terry towels, since April 1990.
Dominican Republic	Restraint on fine suits, sportcoats, blazers, since 1988.
Democratic People's Republic of Korea	Unilateral restraint on clothing , since 1987.
United Arab Emirates	Unilateral restraint on winter outerwear, since 1990.

Anti-dumping and countervailing duty actions

Indonesia	AD action on photo albums, since June 1990.
Philippines	AD action on photo albums, since July 1990.
Thailand	AD action on carbon steel welded pipe, since November 1990.
Turkey	AD action on certain steel welded pipe, in September 1987.
Venezuela	AD action on carbon steel welded pipe, since November 1990.

EEC

Anti-dumping and countervailing duty actions

Algeria	AD duty on steel coils for re-rolling, since May 1987.
Indonesia	AD action on glutamic acid and salts since June 1988. AD action on denim, in March 1989.
Kuwait	Price undertaking on urea, since November 1987.
Libyan Arab Jamahiriya	AD duty on urea, since November 1987.
Macau	AD action on denim, since March 1989.
Saudi Arabia	AD duty on urea, since November 1987.

Voluntary export restraints

Venezuela	Steel products, in April 1987, in return for suspension of anti-dumping duties. Not renewed in 1990.

Source: UNCTAD Data Base on Trade Control Measures.
Note: AD = anti-dumping action; CVD = countervailing duty action;
a The list of countries and of measures is not exhaustive.

NON-TARIFF MEASURES APPLIED SINCE 1987 BY DEVELOPED MARKET-ECONOMY COUNTRIES TO DEVELOPING COUNTRIES NOT PREVIOUSLY AFFECTED BY SUCH MEASURES (continued)

NEW ZEALAND

Anti-dumping and countervailing duty actions

China	AD action on hog bristle paint brushes, since January 1988.
Malaysia	AD action on sugar, in May 1988.
Papua New Guinea	AD action on sugar, in December 1988.
Thailand	AD action on sugar, in May 1988.
	AD action on plasterboard, since July 1989.

SWEDEN

Textile restraints

Turkey	Quota on sweaters, pullovers, t-shirts, long trousers, dresses, skirts and bed linen, since May 1988.

UNITED STATES

Textile restraints

Argentina	Quotas on wool slacks, breeches and shorts, since June 1990.
El Salvador	Quotas on certain textiles, since January 1987.
Fiji	Quotas on nightwear and pyjamas, since February 1990.
Myanmar	Quotas on shirts and blouses, since January 1987.
Panama	Quotas on sweaters, since 1 April 1987.
United Arab Emirates	Quotas on dresses, shirts, blouses, skirts, trousers, breeches shorts, nightwear, pyjamas, underwear, terry towels, since June 1989

Anti-dumping and countervailing duty actions

Bangladesh	AD action on shop towels, since May 1991.
Ecuador	CVD and AD duties on fresh cut flowers, since January 1987.
Kenya	AD duty on standard carnations, since April 1987.
Zimbabwe	Countervailing duty on carbon steel wire rod, since August 1987.

Annex 2 to Chapter III

DEVELOPING COUNTRIES: RECENT TARIFF REDUCTIONS, BINDINGS AND SIMPLIFICATION OF TARIFF STRUCTURES *a*

Argentina	Tariff duties on imports of a wide range of products were reduced in October 1988. The tariff average, which was 38.2 per cent in 1988, fell to 29.4 per cent in 1990 for rates ranging from 5 per cent to 40 per cent. In 1991 a new tariff structure was introduced, establishing three levels of tariffs: zero, 11 per cent and 22 per cent *ad valorem*.
Bolivia	Tariff rates for capital goods were reduced from 10 per cent to 5 per cent in January 1990 followed, in April 1990, by a reduction from 15 per cent to 10 per cent for rates on imports of all products except capital goods. On accession to GATT in 1990 all import duties were bound at a ceiling rate of 40 per cent; duties for some capital goods are bound at 30 per cent.
Bangladesh	Tariff rates were reduced and the tariff structure simplified. The maximum tariff, applied on imports of textiles, engineering goods, chemicals and electronics was lowered from 20 per cent to 125 per cent.
Brazil	In February 1991, the average tariff which was 37 per cent in 1990 was reduced to 25 per cent, and will be further reduced, to 14 per cent by 1994.
Colombia	The average tariff of 26 per cent in 1989 was reduced to 22 per cent in 1990. A surtax of 18 per cent was reduced to 13 per cent in November 1990. Other import charges were reduced in March 1991.
Costa Rica	At present, tariffs range from 1 per cent to 40 per cent except for some items which are subject to higher rates. The entire tariff schedule has been bound at a maximum of 60 per cent (duties are to be bound at 55 per cent on the third year after accession to GATT, i.e. in 1993). Additional import taxes and surcharges exceeding the bound tariff rates were eliminated.
Chile	A uniform import duty of 15 per cent is applied since January 1988, instead of the previous 20 per cent. The entire tariff schedule has been bound at a maximum rate of 35 per cent. In mid-1991 the uniform tariff was reduced to 11 per cent.
Ecuador	In January 1991 the Government announced the implementation of a new customs tariff schedule with duties ranging from 5 per cent to 35 per cent.
Egypt	The average tariff was reduced by almost 50 per cent in August 1986 and further reduced by 30 per cent in June 1989.

Source: UNCTAD Data Base on Trade Control Measures; SELA secretariat; GATT; and World Bank.
  a The list of countries and of actions taken is not exhaustive.

DEVELOPING COUNTRIES: RECENT TARIFF REDUCTIONS, BINDINGS AND
SIMPLIFICATION OF TARIFF STRUCTURES (continued)

Honduras	Tariff duties are being reduced according to the following schedule: from 2 per cent to 40 per cent, until 31 December 1990; from 4 per cent to 35 per cent, until 31 December 1991 and from 5 per cent to 20 per cent, after 1 January 1992.
Indonesia	The simple average of tariff rates (including surcharges) was reduced from 26 per cent in 1989 to 22.2 per cent in 1990 (or from 12 per cent to 10 per cent when weighted by import values).
Jamaica	Tariffs range from 5 per cent to 30 per cent as from 1 January 1991.
Mexico	In 1988 the maximum tariff rate of 45 per cent was lowered so that rates now range from zero to 20 per cent. The entire tariff was bound in 1986 at a ceiling rate of 50 per cent.
Morocco	Prior to April 1984, tariff rates ranged from zero to 400 per cent, with many products subject to percentage rates of 70, 80, 100, 120 and 150. The top rates were brought down to 100 per cent in April and to 60 per cent in April and July 1984, respectively, and then to 45 per cent in February 1986. The import-weighted tariff average for all imports, excluding temporary admissions, was 13 per cent in 1988. Tariffs for 156 headings, representing 1,328 six-digit lines of the Moroccan General Product Nomenclature and covering around one-third of total imports, were bound in mid-1987.
Nicaragua	In September 1990, tariff rates up to 5 per cent were reduced to zero, those from 10-40 per cent to 5 per cent, and those from 40-60 per cent to 10 per cent. Rates above 60 per cent were reduced to a maximum of 20 per cent.
Nigeria	The comprehensive tariff review implemented in 1988 resulted in a general lowering and restructuring of tariff rates.
Pakistan	The maximum tariff of 225 per cent was reduced to 125 per cent in 1990.
Peru	In September 1990, tariffs were reduced substantially and the tariff structure was simplified. Tariff rates were set at 15 per cent, 25 per cent and 50 per cent, the rate for most items being 25 per cent. In March 1991 a further reduction set two levels of tariffs: a minimum rate of 15 per cent which applies to approximately 80 per cent of the customs tariff and a maximum rate of 20 per cent which applies to the remaining products.
Philippines	Further adjustments to the tariff reform programme implemented in 1981 and 1985 were made in 1989 and 1990, mainly through reduction or elimination of duties on a wide range of products. In July 1990 the tariff structure was radically revised, setting a 3 per cent minimum tariff with a maximum of 10 per cent on raw materials, 20 per cent on intermediate goods and 30 per cent on finished products (except on products for which quantitative restrictions were removed, which are subject to a 50 per cent duty). Weighted and simple tariff averages were thus reduced from 20 per cent to 14 per cent and from 28 per cent to 19 per cent respectively.

DEVELOPING COUNTRIES: RECENT TARIFF REDUCTIONS, BINDINGS AND SIMPLIFICATION OF TARIFF STRUCTURES (continued)

Rep. of Korea	The second phase of a 10-year programme of import tariff reduction, which would reduce the average tariff rate from 18.1 per cent to 7.9 per cent by 1993, was announced in 1988.
Thailand	A proposal to streamline the tariff structure, involving the replacement of the currently applied 36 different rates with six tariff rates, is under consideration. In September 1990 the statutory tariff on several items of machinery and equipment was brought down to 5 per cent and tariff changes in other sectors are under consideration.
Tunisia	Tariffs on capital goods were reduced in 1988 and 1989, involving a lowering of the maximum rate of 220 per cent to 43 per cent and raising the minimum rate from 5 per cent to 10 per cent. At the time of full accession to GATT in 1990, some 1,000 tariff headings were bound, at levels ranging from 17 per cent to 52 per cent.
Venezuela	Most tariff rates above 10 per cent were reduced substantially in May 1990. The maximum rate was brought down from 80 per cent to 50 per cent. The entire tariff schedule was bound at the maximum rate of 50 per cent upon accession to GATT in 1990. The ceiling level of binding will become 40 per cent two years after accession.
Yugoslavia	The average rate of tariff weighted by the value of imports declined from 7.8 per cent in 1987 to 7.1 per cent in 1990. Other charges levied on imports were also substantially reduced, from 21 per cent in 1989 to 16 per cent in 1990.

DEVELOPING COUNTRIES WHICH HAVE ELIMINATED ALL OR MOST QUANTITATIVE IMPORT RESTRICTIONS AND/OR OTHER NON-TARIFF MEASURES HAVING HAVING SIMILAR EFFECTS *a*

Algeria	All import licensing procedures were abolished in 1991.
Argentina	Import licensing and other non-tariff restrictions were abolished except for 22 items (vehicles and parts, which remain subject to quota). GATT article XVIII is no longer invoked to apply import restrictions for balance of payments reasons.
Bolivia	Elimination of all import restrictions, except those maintained for public health and safety reasons.
Bangladesh	The number of items subject to quotas or prohibitions was reduced in line with the reform programme applied since 1985 which, *inter alia*, would phase out all quantitative restrictions.
Brazil	The suspension of issuance of import licences (affecting 1,200 items) was discontinued and the "prohibited list" of products was removed. Company import quotas were eliminated in June 1990.
Central African Rep.	Import licensing procedures and quantitative restrictions have been eliminated.
Colombia	Import prohibitions have been eliminated and discretionary licensing has been almost completely phased out. The proportion of items under automatic licence increased from 30 per cent in 1989 to 96.7 per cent in 1990.
Costa Rica	Gradual elimination, or application in accordance with the GATT, of import licences and removal of quantitative restrictions within four years after accession, *i.e.*, before the end of 1994.
Chile	Imposition of import quotas is prohibited by law (Ley Organica Constitucional 18840). All products can be freely imported, except certain second-hand motor vehicles and goods for which imports are prohibited for reasons such as public health or public morals.
Egypt	In May 1990, 21 items were removed from the list of products subject to conditional import prohibition.
Indonesia	A series of trade reform packages has been introduced since 1986 which, *inter alia*, reduced by more than one-half the number of tariff lines subject to restrictive licensing, covering at the end of 1988 only 16 per cent of all tariff items or slightly more than 20 per cent of the total import value.
Madagascar	The market-opening measures implemented since 1986 include provisions for the removal of quantitative restrictions for protective purposes.

Source: As for annex 2.

a The list of countries and of actions taken is not exhaustive.

DEVELOPING COUNTRIES WHICH HAVE ELIMINATED ALL OR MOST QUANTITATIVE IMPORT RESTRICTIONS AND/OR OTHER NON-TARIFF MEASURES HAVING SIMILAR EFFECTS *a* (continued)

Malawi	In September 1988, the Goverment announced the liberalization of 30 per cent of imports. With the exception of several strategic items, all imports are scheduled to be liberalized by 1991.
Mexico	The gradual elimination of licences started in mid-1985. In 1990 import licences were required for some 330 items, or 3 per cent of the total number of tariff items. Licences for computers and pharmaceutical products were abolished in 1990. Decrees signed in December 1989 allowed for the free importation of automobiles, although imports in 1991 and 1992 will be restrained to 15 per cent of the market share. The local content requirement for imports of passenger cars was lowered in 1989.
Morocco	Gradual reduction of goods subject to import control, since 1987. On the basis of the 1989 General Import programme, 78 per cent of tariff positions (88 per cent of the country's total imports in 1988) are on the list of goods for which licencing is automatic.
Nigeria	The programme of reform initiated in mid-1986 included removal of import licensing and reduction of the list of prohibited imports. The number of products included in the "prohibited list" was further reduced in 1989.
Pakistan	In July 1988 a programme of reform was initiated providing for the shifting from non-tariff measures to tariffs as the main trade policy instrument. Import restrictions remain on certain products for balance of payments purposes; import licensing has been eliminated for other products as of March 1991.
Peru	Import prohibitions imposed for balance of payments reasons and other non-tariff measures, such as licensing, were lifted in August and September 1990. Trade was further liberalized in March 1991 through a Presidential Decree which, with exceptions for reasons such as public health and security, repealed most non-tariff restrictions.
Philippines	Under the import liberalization programme initiated in 1981, import licensing on 2,462 items has been removed as of mid-1990. Nearly 2,000 items were liberalized between 1986 and 1990, leaving 439 items still subject to restrictions, of which 323 will be liberalized in phases by the end of 1994.
Thailand	In 1990, most types of passenger cars were removed from the list of products requiring non-automatic import licensing.
Republic of Korea	The import surveillance system, introduced in 1979, was abolished as from January 1989. Between July 1986 and January 1991 quantitative restrictions affecting imports of 1,106 products were eliminated. A three-year import liberalization programme for 1992-1994, announced in March 1991, provides for the phasing out of restrictions on 133 products, mostly agricultural. Restrictions on the remaining 150 items will be either liberalized or brought into conformity with GATT by 1997.

DEVELOPING COUNTRIES WHICH HAVE ELIMINATED ALL OR MOST QUANTITATIVE IMPORT RESTRICTIONS AND/OR OTHER NON-TARIFF MEASURES HAVING SIMILAR EFFECTS *a* (continued)

Togo	As part of a reform programme initiated in 1988, import and export licences were substantially eliminated.
Tunisia	The programme of economic liberalization established for 1986-1991 provides for the gradual liberalization of foreign trade, including elimination of quantitative restrictions. More than one-half of the number of items for which there were import limitations were free by mid-1990.
Venezuela	As part of the major economic reform introduced in 1989 quantitative restrictions started to be phased out. Import prohibitions, restrictive import licensing and other quantitative restrictions will be completely removed by 1995.
Uruguay	These are non-tariff measures restraining imports.
Yugoslavia	The regime of conditionally free imports, which included imports restricted for balance of payments reasons, was phased out in August 1989 and most of the items were shifted to the free import regime. A large number of items were removed from the system of quotas and several items were removed from the "import accordance" regime. By the end of 1990, the free import regime covered nearly 88 per cent of all imports of goods (some 80 per cent of all tariff lines), 12.5 per cent was subject to quotas and a negligible percentage to import licences.

Part Two

FINANCE, INVESTMENT AND SAVINGS

Introduction

That finance is intimately connected with investment is unquestionable. But what the linkages between finance and investment consist of and how they operate remain subjects of debate between different schools of thought. This part of the present report seeks to add to the understanding of the dynamics of financing, savings and growth, and to identify how financing might best be reformed to the benefit of the world economy as a whole and the developing countries in particular.

The subject is highly topical. The idea has now gained ascendency that prospects for meeting the financing needs of recovery, reconstruction and development worldwide may well be endangered by an increasing scarcity of world savings. Moreover, mainstream thinking and official advice emphasize the foolishness of interventionism and the wisdom of laissez faire even regarding finance. The orthodox view therefore sees the answer to the investment needs of the world and of the developing countries in a tightening of the fiscal reins and a loosening of the fetters on financial institutions.

Chapter I begins by questioning some of the key empirical assumptions underlying the "global savings shortage" hypothesis. It then goes on to examine the theory that the rate of interest is the price which brings the supply of and demand for savings into balance and that the level of investment is determined primarily by the volume of savings - a theory which denies that monetary policies can have an enduring impact on the real economy. It sets out an alternative approach, which starts from the fact that investment can generate new savings by creating additional incomes, and which, instead of putting almost exclusive emphasis on thrift as the determinant of investment, gives equal or greater weight to the way finance is organized. The chapter goes on to show that finance has been organized very differently in different developed countries, and to point out that systems characterized by indirect, or market, relations between private lenders and borrowers have tended to be less efficient in providing low-cost long-term finance than some others in which relations between lenders and borrowers have been more direct.

The challenge of reforming financial systems better to meet the needs of growth and development is taken up in the following two chapters. Chapter II (which represents an extension of the study of the internationalization of finance contained in part two, chapter I, of *TDR 1990*) focuses on the structure and functioning of the financial systems of some developed countries. It examines the impact of the globalization and deregulation of the United States banking industry on interest rates, the stability of financial flows, and the transmission of monetary policy, as well as the stresses and strains on the Japanese financial system. It then goes on to discuss how far financial weakness and fragility may affect the balance of expansionary and recessionary forces in the world economy, and how the shortage of finance may be mitigated.

Chapter III contains a wide-ranging analysis of financial policies and the organization of finance in developing countries, a subject of critical importance given the difficulties of attracting external funds. It takes a critical look at both the interventionism of the past and the current emphasis on deregulation, and argues in favour of building on the happy as well as the unhappy instances of interventionism and on the examples of harmful as well as of beneficial liberalization. The main conclusion is that in order to contribute effectively to industrialization, diversification and development generally, the financial system must avoid both laxity and "short-termism". Therefore, activist government policies as well as market forces are usually needed.

There is thus a common theme running throughout: finance must serve industry and commerce, not the other way around; no single model suits all countries at all times; policy must be pragmatic, and be based on a realistic understanding of how monetary and financial variables interact with real ones. Textbooks are for training minds; they do not give recipes for action.■

Chapter I

THE CONCEPT OF SAVINGS SHORTAGE AND THE ROLE OF FINANCE

A. Introduction

Real interest rates on international capital markets have been exceptionally high for over a decade, giving rise to widespread concern regarding the implications for world investment and the developing countries. During the 1980s, the problem was largely viewed as resulting from the behaviour of government budgets, especially in the United States. Similarly, the large current account imbalances among industrialized countries were ascribed to disparities in their fiscal positions. More recently, as budget deficits have been brought under greater control and current account imbalances curtailed, concerns have been expressed that personal savings rates are declining, whereas the demand for funds is growing, especially in Central and Eastern Europe and the Middle East. Fears have therefore been expressed that, unless fiscal performance improves, the supply of global savings may prove insufficient, pushing up interest rates and further increasing the financing difficulties of developing countries.

This line of reasoning is vulnerable. It is questionable whether personal thrift is indeed declining significantly. Besides, the cost of investment is being reduced by technical progress. In any event, savings do not always determine the level of investment, but are themselves determined by the level of investment when, as now, production capacities are less than fully utilized. Moreover, interest rates and investment can be strongly influenced by the way the financial system is organized, something that has been changing rapidly in recent years. This chapter therefore argues that, in order both to meet the existing financing needs of developing countries and to respond to new ones, the main challenge is to make the international financial system function better, rather than to depress non-investment expenditures.

B. Private savings

Although there is a substantial difference in savings ratios across countries (see table 24), the gross private saving ratio as derived from national accounts has risen in the United States and the United Kingdom from the 1960s to the 1980s, while it has fallen in Japan and Germany. While there was a fall in the private net saving ratio in the United States, the decline

Table 24

SAVINGS RATIOS AS PER CENT OF GROSS AND NET NATIONAL PRODUCT IN MAJOR OECD COUNTRIES

Country/sector	1960-1970		1971-1980		1981-1987	
	Net	Gross	Net	Gross	Net	Gross
United States						
Total	10.6	19.6	8.9	19.5	3.9	16.3
Government	0.6	1.8	-1.3	0.3	-4.2	-2.4
Private	9.9	17.7	10.2	19.2	8.1	18.7
Personal	6.3	9.3	7.6	10.7	6.0	9.6
Corporate	3.6	8.4	2.6	8.5	2.1	9.1
Japan						
Total	25.6	35.6	24.6	34.4	20.2	31.1
Government	6.7	6.3	4.6	4.4	4.3	4.3
Private	18.9	28.7	20.1	29.9	15.9	26.8
Personal	12.0	13.5	16.7	18.5	13.3	15.9
Corporate	7.0	15.3	3.3	11.4	2.6	10.9
Germany						
Total	19.9	27.3	14.3	23.7	10.7	21.8
Government	6.3	6.2	3.3	3.5	1.3	1.8
Private	13.5	21.1	11.0	20.2	9.4	20.0
Personal	7.8	-.-	9.7	-.-	8.9	-.-
Corporate	5.8	14.1	1.3	11.6	0.6	12.3
United Kingdom						
Total	11.2	18.7	8.2	18.1	6.2	17.5
Government	3.2	4.0	0.5	1.7	-1.7	-0.3
Private	6.4	13.2	8.1	16.7	8.6	18.4
Personal	4.0	5.5	5.3	7.1	5.1	7.2
Corporate	2.7	8.0	2.8	9.7	3.5	11.2
France						
Total	-.-	26.3	-.-	25.4	-.-	19.6
Government	-.-	-.-	-.-	3.5	-.-	0.8
Private	-.-	-.-	-.-	22.0	-.-	18.8
Personal	-.-	-.-	-.-	13.6	-.-	10.9
Corporate	-.-	-.-	-.-	8.3	-.-	7.9

Source: OECD, Department of Economics and Statistics, "Saving Trends and Behaviour in OECD Countries", *Working Paper*, No. 67, June 1989, p. 68.

has been smaller than in Japan and Germany, suggesting a slow process of convergence over time.

These figures do not suggest that private saving behaviour in the United States has shifted dramatically; indeed, the deterioration in Germany has been even greater. Rather, it is the fall in personal or family savings (see table 25) which has generated the most attention and produced the widespread belief that a basic change has occurred in the savings behaviour of United States families. Measures of household savings derived from data on the flow of

funds confirm that there has been a decline in the ratio (see table 26).

Nevertheless, concern that families are becoming less thrifty appears to be exaggerated. The observed decline in personal savings ratios is indicative not so much of a real change in household savings behaviour as of other factors, such as changes in financial structure, which have produced anomalies in the way incomes, expenditures and savings are imputed in the national accounts, and the cyclical nature of household borrowing and spending (see box 5).

Table 25

NET PERSONAL SAVINGS RATES IN MAJOR OECD COUNTRIES, 1973-1989

(Percentage of disposable personal income)

	United States	Japan	Germany	France [a]	Italy [a]	United Kingdom	Canada
1973	9.6	20.4	13.9	19.1	28.3	10.0	10.7
1974	9.5	23.2	14.6	19.8	26.3	10.6	11.3
1975	9.4	22.8	15.1	20.2	26.9	11.4	12.7
1976	7.8	23.2	13.3	18.2	25.7	10.7	11.8
1977	6.7	21.8	12.2	18.7	23.3	9.1	11.4
1978	7.3	20.8	12.0	20.4	25.6	10.6	12.6
1979	7.0	18.2	12.6	18.8	24.7	11.9	13.3
1980	7.3	17.9	12.7	17.6	21.6	13.1	13.6
1981	7.7	18.3	13.5	18.0	20.5	12.5	15.4
1982	7.0	16.5	12.7	17.3	19.0	11.4	18.2
1983	5.5	16.3	10.8	15.9	19.8	9.8	14.8
1984	6.3	16.0	11.4	14.5	20.4	10.5	15.0
1985	4.5	16.0	11.4	14.0	17.8	9.7	13.3
1986	4.3	16.4	12.2	12.9	15.3	7.9	10.7
1987	3.0	15.1	12.6	11.1	14.3	6.6	9.4
1988	4.3	14.8	12.8	12.1	14.2	5.4	10.0
1989	4.7	15.0	12.5	12.3	13.9	6.7	11.0

Source: OECD, *Economic Outlook*, No. 48, December 1990 (table R.12).
a Gross figures.

C. Real investment

A fall in the ratio of savings to income should also be reflected in a decline in the ratio of investment to income. This has indeed occurred in a number of countries in the 1980s. However, just as for savings, national accounts do not accurately reflect the behaviour of the investment ratio. If this ratio is measured in constant 1982 prices, it shows an increase rather than a decrease in the United States over the 1980s.

The fact that nominal and real shares of investment moved in opposite directions suggests that an important movement has taken place in the supply price of capital goods. In fact, in the 1980s the price deflator for plant and equipment expenditures diverged significantly from the deflator for overall GNP. The latter had risen by over 30 per cent between 1982 and 1990, while the deflator for invest-

ment equipment had actually fallen by 4 per cent. (This implies that an increase of one percentage point in the ratio of investment to GNP in 1990 is the equivalent to over 1.3 percentage points at the beginning of the decade). Making such an adjustment, the fall in the ratio of investment in equipment to GNP from 3.9 per cent in 1982 to 3.6 per cent in 1990 becomes a rise to over 4.7 per cent.

Figures given by OECD for prices of computing machinery show a decline of around 70 per cent from 1981 to 1988 for the United States,[60] whereas the share of computers in the country's total business investment rose from 5 per cent to 25 per cent. Thus, while savings measures were being distorted by changes in financial asset prices, investment measures were likewise being distorted by changes in capital asset prices, in particular the spectacular fall in

---

[60] *OECD Economic Outlook*, No. 48, December 1990.

Table 26

UNITED STATES NET NATIONAL SAVING MEASURED FROM FLOW OF FUNDS

(Per cent of GNP)

Period	Personal saving	Corporate saving	Private saving	Government saving	Net national saving
1953-1961	5.6	1.9	7.5	-0.9	6.7
1962-1973	5.6	2.2	7.8	-0.5	7.3
1974-1979	5.6	2.7	8.3	-1.5	6.8
1980-1989	4.7	1.5	6.1	-2.9	3.2
1980-1984	5.5	1.6	7.0	-2.9	4.1
1985-1989	3.9	1.4	5.2	-2.9	2.3

Source: Federal Reserve Bank of New York Quarterly Review, Winter 1991, p. 4.

prices in the high technology and communications sectors, which account for a growing proportion of overall investment expenditures. Most analysts now agree that the investment ratio calculated on the basis of current prices underestimates the change of productive capacity brought about by investment in the 1980s.

The experience of the 1980s thus suggests that factors other than the behaviour of real rates of interest have dominated the behaviour of savings and investment. It also suggests that investment was not limited by a scarcity of savings. Consequently, the explanation of the behaviour of interest rates in the 1980s must be sought elsewhere. One of the most obvious explanations is the changes in the organization of financial markets which occurred in the 1980s, which have brought about substantial changes in the way investment is financed in both developed and developing countries.

D. Theory of savings, investment and finance

The difficulties of interpreting the behaviour of the various measures of the savings ratio are linked to more fundamental problems. The various accounting measures of savings provide specific information required by differing interpretations as to how the economic system functions. The definition used in national accounts is based on the *ex post* equality of savings and investment. If all household incomes are either spent on consumption or saved, while all final output is classified as being either for consumption or for investment (including unintended inventory changes), savings must necessarily equal investment for the circular-flow identity between national income and national output to be respected. Any change in the savings ratio therefore always represents an equal and opposite change in the "consumption ratio" or the propensity to consume. For a given level of national output, a fall in the savings ratio implies a rise in the level of consumption and a decline in the ratio of investment to national income; and investment can only be higher if the proportion of income saved is also higher.

But these relations hold only if the level of national output is taken as given, whereas the theory upon which the accounts were established sought to identify the factors that cause national income to change. Just as *potential production* is defined as the level of output that can be reached when there is full employment, so *potential savings* can be defined as the value of all employable resources that are not being used in the production of consumption goods; they are therefore equal to the measure of savings recorded in the national ac-

Box 5

MEASURING PERSONAL AND CORPORATE SAVINGS IN THE UNITED STATES

One of the major structural changes that has occurred in financial markets in the post-war period is the increase in contractual relative to discretionary savings by households. These payments include payments to state and private pension and social security funds, insurance premiums, and private contributions paid regularly to investment and mutual funds. This shift has put into a dominant position in financial markets large institutional investors representing public and private pension funds, insurance companies and mutual funds managing private savings plans.

Since the measurement of national income is based on real national production accounts the contribution of financial institutions, which do not produce real outputs, has always created difficulties. The problems are usually resolved by netting out financial transactions within the production sector, or by imputing the services of financial institutions to other sectors. Imputations of financial sector services in the United States national income and product accounts affect the measurement of both personal consumption expenditure and personal disposable income. Consequently, they have a direct impact on the figures for personal saving, measured by the difference between the two. The behaviour of the prices of financial assets and housing services in the 1970s and 1980s has changed the magnitude of these imputations in ways which produce differential effects on income and expenditure. The impact on the measure of savings, and in particular the personal savings ratio, has been a spurious reduction which makes comparison with earlier estimates difficult. The fall in the personal savings ratio observed in the 1980s results more from anomalies in the way changes in financial structure have affected imputed incomes and savings than from any actual change in household savings behaviour.

Contributions to social insurance and pension funds by private sector firms on behalf of their employees are included in personal incomes for national accounting purposes. When the value of a private fund's assets exceeds its future pension obligations, firms may (and in many cases are legally obliged to) reduce their contributions.

Capital gains on fund assets resulting from the rise of prices in financial markets in the 1980s led to substantial over-funding, and a decline in employer contributions credited as household incomes. Thus "contractual" personal savings as measured by employers' contributions declined in the 1980s. However, since these savings are also included as "other labour income" in constructing personal incomes, the same amount is removed from both the numerator, savings, and the denominator, personal income. Since the former is much smaller than the latter the measured savings ratio is reduced.

Contributions are treated as personal income only while employees are at work. By contrast, for retired workers only the net investment income (interest and dividends) earned by the funds, rather than the actual benefits paid, is included in disposable income. When paid-out benefits exceed fund investment income (as is usually the case) there is an adjustment added to personal incomes which has the effect of reducing the measured savings ratio without any change in actual saving behaviour. The reduction in household income between 1980 and 1987 due to the decline in employers' contributions and the adjustment factor has been estimated at $60-$75 billion, or 2-2.5 per cent of disposable income, all of which would have appeared as a decline in the savings ratio. [1]

In the United States employers' contributions to public sector pension funds at the state and local level (one of the largest institutional investors in the United States is the California public employees pension fund) are ascribed not to the household sector, but to the government sector, resulting in an underestimate of the personal savings ratio of as much as 2 percentage points. [2]

Since national accounts data do not include realized capital gains, some of which may be viewed much like income, and since real gains may be used to increase expenditure without reducing household wealth or increasing indebtedness, the use of capital gains to finance consumption would increase household expenditure without increasing measured personal income, reducing recorded savings and the savings ratio.

Part of the capital gains which accrued to households in the 1970s and 1980s were due to the rise in prices of residential property. Household expenditure on owner-occupied housing as measured in the national accounts is determined by the cost of equivalent rental housing, while household income from ownership of housing deducts maintenance costs, taxes, insurance, mortgage interest

Box 5 *(concluded)*

and depreciation from this figure. The imputation for housing services thus increases household expenditures more than it increases household incomes. As a result of inflation in the 1970s and 1980s in house prices and in costs in the construction industry, depreciation adjustments to rental incomes increased to the point that they exceeded imputed rental payments. The result was a negative adjustment to personal income and an increase in expenditures which rose with market rentals, leading to a reduction in measured savings and the savings ratio. [3]

Finally, capital gains on assets or on real property can be used to finance additional borrowing, which increases consumption and reduces savings, without increasing incomes. Figures for the post-war period suggest that household borrowing is pro-cyclical. Thus, past behaviour suggests that household indebtedness should have been expected to rise, and measured savings ratios to decline, during the long cyclical expansion in the 1980s. However, over the cycle the effect of borrowing on savings should cancel out, i.e. the borrowing in the boom simply brings forward savings which will be made in the slump. If deregulation and financial innovation have made it easier for households to adjust the time profile of their consumption to their expected real or permanent income, the nominal measured savings figures overestimate savings in a slump and underestimate them during a cyclical boom such as that of the mid-1980s.

Since national accounting systems differ across countries, as do their benefit systems, an alternative method of comparing one particular aspect of these adjustments, relating to capital gains, has been suggested by the Bank for International Settlements. It combines savings ratios with capital gains and losses across countries. For the period 1979-1986 this combined measure is 14.6 per cent for the United States, 18.5 per cent for Japan and 14.2 per cent for Germany.

Most of the discussion of the fall in the savings ratio has concerned personal saving. But a full discussion should include private saving, i.e. personal saving plus saving by non-financial corporations. Historically the largest proportion of gross private savings in the United States has come from the corporate, rather than the personal, sector. Gross corporate savings (defined as net retained after-tax profits plus depreciation), which is the most relevant measure of the internal savings available to firms to finance new investment, averaged 8.6 per cent for the period 1980-1988, up from 8.1 per cent for 1970-1979. [4]

Most of the decline in net corporate saving can be traced to an increase in the corporate capital consumption allowance. In addition, there was an increase in interest and dividend payments to households during the 1980s due to changes in financial regulations and monetary policy. Since retained earnings are fully saved, when they are used to increase unearned income payments to households, who will generally save a lower proportion, this will produce a decline in the overall private savings ratio.

All of these factors taken together suggest that the behaviour of savings and savings ratios in the 1980s should be approached with a great deal of caution.

1 See J. Steindl, "Capital gains, pension funds and the low saving ratio in the United States", *Banca Nazionale del Lavoro Quarterly Review*, June 1990.
2 See F. Block, "Bad data drive out good: The decline in personal savings re-examined", *Journal of Post-Keynesian Economics*, Fall 1990.
3 See T. Scitovsky, "An anomaly in the United States personal income and savings statistics" in John Cohen and Geoffrey Harcourt (eds.), *International Monetary Problems and Supply Side Economics* (London: Macmillan, 1986).
4 See R. Blecker, "Low savings rates and the 'twin deficits': Confusing the symptoms and causes of economic decline", in P. Davidson and J. Kregel (eds.), *Economic Problems of the 1990s*, Elgar Publishing, 1991.

counts plus the value of the production forgone because of the unemployment of resources. On this definition, as long as potential savings exceed actual savings, the latter cannot be a constraint to investment. When output is below potential, the level of both savings and invest-

ment can be raised even if the savings ratio is lowered and the consumption ratio raised; similarly, the level of consumption as well as savings can be raised by increasing investment and lowering the consumption ratio. Here it is the increase in expenditure which, by increasing incomes, raises savings; and since consumption expenditures are generally financed by household incomes, the constraint on consumption is a paucity of personal income. In an economy which depends on bank financing for the production of new investment goods, the existence of idle resources employable in the production of capital goods implies that actual savings are below potential savings either because bank financing is inadequate or because investment opportunities are not sufficiently attractive. When potential savings exceed the national accounts measure of actual savings, both actual investment and actual savings can be enlarged if entrepreneurs become more optimistic or if financing is made available on a larger scale or on more favourable terms.

The view that savings reflect the supply of real capital is based on the idea that financial markets equilibrate the supply of loanable funds, representing the real resources made available by individuals for investment by choosing to postpone present consumption, with the demand for investment funds as determined by the rate of return on investment (see box 6). According to this view, savings are becoming deficient owing to the sudden increase in the demand for capital in the Middle East and in Eastern Europe, plus the needs of the developing countries; moreover, in order to avoid a global scarcity of savings in the decade ahead, savings will have to increase in order to free the real resources required for the new investment. This argument is based on the assumption that the current level of world production is the maximum possible in the short term. However, the major industrialized economies as a whole are experiencing recession, i.e. productive capacity is in excess supply.

To understand the role played by financial organization and the provision of finance in the investment process requires an explanation of the relation between savings and investment and the rate of interest which allows monetary variables to influence real factors. In an economy with a sophisticated financial system, it is the power to create money, not the supply of loanable funds, which generates the power to command the use of real resources for investment purposes (see box 2). This power lies in the decision of banks to grant loans, not in the decision of households to postpone current consumption. It is the decision of banks and other financial institutions to finance investment projects and other expenditures which determines the allocation of claims to real resources.

In order to provide long-term funding for investment projects, firms sell liabilities in the capital markets. Given the quantity of existing assets and the preferences of portfolio owners, the capital market confronts the various assets created by firms seeking long-term funding for projects with the liquidity preferences of portfolio holders. The outcome determines the final prices, and the associated interest rates, at which the newly created financial assets find homes in investor portfolios. If households or portfolio managers have a high liquidity preference (i.e. are attracted by short-term assets), the prices of long-term financial assets will have to fall, and interest rates to rise, in order to induce portfolio holders to purchase them. The new investment will then be more costly to fund and bring a lower net return. That is how high long-term interest rates dampen investment.

The role of the capital market in financing investment is not to balance savings and investment, but rather to co-ordinate the process whereby the savings created by new investment are channelled to the firms that have incurred short-term debt in order to carry out the investment which generated the additional income and saving. The capital market is responsible for ensuring that the short-term indebtedness of firms to banks is replaced by long-term indebtedness of firms to households either directly or via pension funds, insurance companies, etc. Investment expenditures, therefore, do not require final savers first to decide to provide real resources. Rather, they depend on the decisions of bankers to provide short-term finance to firms, which they then use to generate income and savings by making investment.

E. The efficiency of financial markets

The increase in real and nominal interest rates over the past decade may have been due to a significant extent to the changes financial deregulation has made in the way money and capital markets provide short-term finance for investment.

The rationale for deregulating financial markets is that freeing financial institutions from controls on interest rates and types of lending activity increases the allocative efficiency of the system, by allowing scarce savings

Box 6

REAL AND MONETARY FACTORS IN THE RELATION BETWEEN
SAVINGS AND INVESTMENT

Economists have long been divided concerning the relationship between monetary and real variables. Until the beginning of the Great Depression, money was considered as simply a veil covering the real variables in the economy, which could not have any permanent influence on economic decisions which were taken with reference to real values - i.e. by abstracting from changes in nominal prices. The Depression brought a reversal of these ideas and economists such as Keynes and Fisher argued that money and nominal values could influence real economic activity permanently and directly. "The classical theory supposes that the readiness of the entrepreneur to start up a productive process depends on the amount of value in terms of product which he expects to fall to his share; i.e. that only an expectation of more "product" for himself will induce him to offer more employment. But in an entrepreneur economy this is a wrong analysis of the nature of the business calculation. An entrepreneur is interested, not in the amount of product, but in the amount of "money" which will fall to his share. He will increase his output if by doing so he expects to increase his money profit, even though his profit represents a smaller quantity of product than before." [1]

These two diverse approaches to the relation between money and real variables also differ in terms of their analysis of the role of saving. If money has no permanent influence, then saving must be considered as a supply of real resources made available for investment. On the other hand, if monetary factors are important, then it is the ability to create purchasing power which determines the ability to command resources, irrespective of decisions concerning real savings. The current concern with a shortage of saving seems to be motivated by the former view to the exclusion of the latter.

The supply of real saving

The idea that the appropriate measure of savings should reflect the supply of real resources available for capital formation is based on the view that personal saving is determined by the tradeoff between present and future consumption. This tradeoff is expressed in the rate of individual time preference, and will be compared to the terms at which an individual can convert present income into future income by saving and investing today's income to provide for increased future consumption. The demand for productive investment as a vehicle for saving will then be determined by the available production technology, which determines the rate of transformation between present saving and future consumption. This is often expressed as the marginal physical productivity of investing in capital equipment.

The marginal physical productivity of capital thus represents the rate at which individuals can exchange present income saved for future consumption, or the "real" rate of return to saving. It is also assumed that there are diminishing returns to investment. Facing an inter-temporal budget constraint of the possible distribution of consumption between present and future dates achieved by borrowing against future income or lending future income in the money market, the individual borrows and lends so as to bring the actual temporal distribution of consumption into line with his time preference. The optimum behaviour will be to borrow and lend in both the money market and the capital market to adjust the time profile of consumption to time preference. This should cause the rate of interest on loanable funds to move to equality with the marginal productivity of capital, with both equal to individual rates of time preference. The supply of saving thus represents the supply of real productive investment. A rise in the preference for present over future goods or in productivity leads to a relative scarcity of saving.

Money, investment and saving

On the other hand, in financial intermediated economic systems the allocation of resources is not determined in a true market, but is the result of a bilateral negotiation between a bank and a borrowing firm. The allocation of finance which provides the power to command resources takes place within a financial institution rather than via the capital market. It is the willingness of banks to create money by extending a business loan which allows non-financial firms to command resources.

In general, bank financing is short-term; it finances current production of output which is expected to generate the cash flows required to repay the loan and pay interest thereon as the output is sold. The short-term financing which leads to the construction and implementation of

Box 6 (concluded)

productive capacity must be replaced by the sale of long-term assets which allow operation over a sufficiently long period to fully recover investment costs through expected future revenues. It is this long-term funding which takes place in the capital market. (Firms may also finance current production or investment via retained earnings, in which case both the short- and long-term financing decisions are internal to the firms, whose owners are lending their earnings directly to the firm without either money or capital market intermediation.)

The sale of long-term assets by firms in the capital market typically represents the funding of real resources already "allocated" to the firm via the spending and production decisions undertaken with short-term bank lending. The borrower's new investment expenditure increases national income. The proportion of this income saved will provide the demand for long-term financial assets in the capital market. While it is the role of the banks in the money market to allocate finance which allows investment projects to take place, it is the role of the capital market to ensure that the investment expenditures already initiated are funded on a long-term basis via the sale of long-term financial assets to those whose savings have increased as a result of the increase in income due to the additional investment expenditure.

Since the overall increase in private savings will equal the new investment expenditures, the role of the long-term market rate of interest (or its inverse, the market price of long-term financial assets) cannot be to ensure equality of saving and investment; rather, it is to ensure the necessary funding to cover the short-term financing, in the form of the sale of long-term financial assets. The prices necessary to ensure that these financial assets are held in investors' portfolios will determine the interest rate on long-term finance and thus the expected profitability of the investment project. The rate of interest may differ from what was expected when the project was first initiated. Similarly, the return from the investment may also differ from the original expectation.

Since the flow of new long-term financial assets to finance new net investment is small relative to the existing stock of assets, prices will have to adjust to ensure not only that all new assets are sold, but also that all existing assets continue to be held in portfolios. For this reason new flows of assets will generally have a smaller impact on asset prices and interest rates than decisions on the purchase and sale of existing assets.

Changes in investors' liquidity preference can cause investors to adjust their stock holdings of different types of assets and may cause major shifts in asset prices, independent of changes in the flow of new assets to the capital market. Thus, not only does the interest rate not equate current flows of savings and investment, it may also not be directly influenced by those flows if there are sizable offsetting movements in the preferences of the public leading to adjustments in their holdings of existing financial assets.

Nor does the flow of new assets result from an increase in new expenditures on investment. Innovation and deregulation in financial markets in the 1980s has shifted lending from the banks to the capital market via "securitization". Since this increase in the supply of financial assets has occurred without any new investment, it has not created additional income and saving, and thus represents a net increase in asset supplies. The result is pressure on interest rates unrelated to changes in saving and investment.

---

1 J.M. Keynes, *Collected Works, XXIX* (London: Macmillan, 1979), p. 82.

to be channelled more easily to those borrowers with the most productive use for them, as measured by the real rate of return on investment. According to this theory, individuals can only reach more desirable combinations of present and future consumption if they can borrow and lend in financial markets at interest rates that reflect the real rate of return as given by the marginal productivity of capital. Consequently, any controls on money market interest rates, or restrictions on access to financial markets, that impede individuals from achieving their preferred consumption patterns will distort saving decisions and misallocate real resources between present consumption and future investment. Thus, allocations of loanable funds to alternative investment projects will not be made in the optimal manner and both investment and national income will be lower than otherwise.

According to this line of reasoning, the efficiency of a financial market depends on how far it produces interest rates equal to the real return or the marginal physical productivity of capital. Regulations in financial markets which control interest rates are thus inherently inefficient, for they prevent them from adjusting to changes in the marginal productivity determined in the real productive structure of the economy. The rise in real rates of interest following the removal of regulations during the 1980s would, according to this theory, merely reflect the real rates of return on investment.

However, as already suggested, if the initial financing of investment expenditures is considered separately from the role of financial markets in funding the investment, the question of efficiency must be approached in a different way. The efficiency with which the money market "finances" the investment expenditure of firms and with which the capital market "funds" this by allowing firms to repay short-term debt by selling longer-term financial assets to private portfolio holders must be looked at separately. The overall allocative efficiency of the system in providing finance to investors whose projects offer the highest expected real rates of return requires both the banking system and the capital markets to operate efficiently.

The short-term bank financing of investment may be conceived of as a process whereby banks change their balance sheets so as to offset the deficits and surpluses of households and firms - i.e. to allow firms to command resources without a prior household decision to "save" real resources. The efficiency of the banking system may then be evaluated in terms of the costs charged by banks for adjusting their balance sheets. These costs will depend on the overall reserve policy of the central bank and the liquidity preference of the banks themselves - i.e. their willingness to increase their assets relative to equity and liabilities relative to assets.

Similarly, the efficiency of the operation of capital markets depends on the costs associated with the process of matching the deficit and surplus spending units' balance sheets so as to allow the banks to restore their initial balance sheet position.

The determinants of the long-term rate of interest may be divided into two elements:

- The pure risk produced by uncertainties over future interest rates and over factors outside the control of the borrower affecting the profitability of investment projects. The latter can be reduced by better information and stabler economic conditions, but cannot in practice be entirely eliminated.[61] The pure risk element requires a "liquidity premium" to be paid to the lender and the efficiency of a financial system can be gauged, *inter alia*, in terms of the size of this premium;
- The "lender's risk", reflecting the possible failure of payment by the borrower. Part of this risk is a "moral" one due to the possibility of dishonesty but most of it is due to the possibility of mismanagement by the borrower. An efficient financial market will keep the latter to a minimum by ensuring appropriate discipline over management.[62]

In short, the efficiency of the financial system will be reflected in its ability to minimize the liquidity premium and the risk of erroneous investment decisions. The more stable are long-term asset prices, the lower is the liquidity premium. Consequently, because lifting regulations constraining the operation of financial markets will tend to produce greater variability of asset prices, it will increase the pure risk element of the rate of interest, and may ultimately lead to lower investment and growth performance. Moreover, as explained below, capital markets tend to provide weak discipline over borrowers and to be dominated by unduly short time horizons.

61 For various types of risks and liquidity premium see J.M. Keynes, *The General Theory of Employment, Interest and Money* (London: Macmillan, 1967).

62 If investors are institutions, such as pension funds or mutual funds, which are themselves under market pressure to maximize the value of their portfolio over each reporting period (usually quarterly) their assessement of risk will be related to changes in capital values rather than to long-run earnings. This means that lender's risk will be high in markets with high price variability unless lenders have a longer-term horizon and are more concerned with future income flows. The type of lender will therefore be a factor in determining cost efficiency.

F. Alternative ways of organizing the financial system

Increased variability of asset prices has also made it more difficult for banks to provide finance. A bank can raise funds from depositors only if its checking accounts serve as a perfect substitute for cash. If these are not covered by deposit insurance, a bank faces the potential for a sudden deposit or reserve "drain". Besides, a bank typically lends by creating new deposits to the credit of the borrower, who is free to use the loan to make a payment to another bank, in which case again the lending bank will suffer a reserve "drain". A bank which stands to lose a large proportion of its deposits needs to hold larger overall reserves, which represents a loss of income; thus, it needs to hold secondary reserves - i.e. assets which can be converted quickly into reserves and yet earn income. To serve as secondary reserves, assets must have stable prices and be saleable at short notice. In the United States bank regulations have restricted the asset choices of banks to short-term lending and assets having a stable capital value.

In the United States the probability of a reserve drain for a bank is enhanced by the fact that banks are unit banks and severely restricted in developing large branch networks within or across states.[63] The smaller the bank, the greater the need to keep the prices of its assets stable and their maturities short. A banking system with a small number of very large multi-branch banks requires much less formal regulation over the asset side of its balance sheet and fewer direct price controls on its liabilities. The German "universal banking system", which combines investment banking with deposit-taking, is an example of a system with a relatively small number of large multi-branch banks. Short-term financing is provided by banks, just as in a unit bank system. But there is a basic difference in the funding of long-term investment, since the same banks act both as the primary intermediaries and as investors in the long-term financial assets issued by firms. As a result, the bond and stock markets are much less important sources of funding than in countries with the "Anglo-Saxon" financial model, a very small proportion of industrial investment is funded by means of share issues held by the non-bank public, and a relatively high proportion is funded by fixed interest lending, primarily by the banks.

In Germany, because both short-term financing and long-term funding are organized within the banking system, rather than through the money and capital markets, changes in asset prices and in interest rates play a much smaller role in the process of ensuring that the financial assets created to fund investment find homes in investor portfolios. It is common for the controlling interest in industrial companies to be held by banks or banking groups who provide company directors (who may simultaneously hold directorships in other companies in the same sector of the economy). In such a system information about the firms' performance and prospects is not transmitted to potential financiers indirectly, namely by the prices determined in stock markets, but directly by means of direct knowledge of the condition of companies taken from banks' involvement in their day-to-day operations. It is thus common for financing to be made available to companies at rates which compare very favourably with "market" rates.

Interest rates in a capital-market-based financial system and a universal-bank-based system can differ significantly if the transaction costs associated with arranging long-term funding via free capital markets are substantially above those associated with the organization of financing within the banks themselves. These costs of market organization, and their impact on the cost efficiency of the financial system, are seldom considered in the evaluation of the allocative efficiency of the financial system. But when they are, it becomes doubtful that decreased regulation will increase allocative efficiency. In the German system banks, by organizing the capital market internally, can reap the economies of scale in information that come from providing both short-term project finance and long-term funding, and exert discipline in management. As a result, lender's risk is reduced, allowing capital to be offered at lower cost.[64]

---

63 The United States banking system has also had the problem that many firms have been raising much of their short-term credit by means of sales of short-term commercial paper and note issuance facilities in the money market. This has reduced the asset base of banks, while unrestricted competition for deposits from other financial institutions has reduced their deposit base. The enhanced role given to the market in allocating funds in order to increase allocative efficiency has resulted in a decline in cost efficiency.

64 While these arguments suggest that there are benefits to be gained from allowing banks greater freedom to take equity positions in industry, the relation is not symmetrical. The ownership of a bank by a non-financial corporation would

International comparisons of capital costs suggest that in countries, such as Germany, where internal bank capital markets dominate, firms' funding costs of investment are lower.[65] This implies that different types of financial organization will have different combinations of allocative and cost efficiency and structures of financial assets and liabilities. It is interesting to note that countries with market-based systems seem to be moving towards a universal system, and vice versa. The United States is currently discussing legislation which would lead to a system of large, multi-branch banks and financial holding companies able to operate over a wide range of financial activities, while Germany is seeking to provide a more important role for free capital markets by limiting bank investments in non-financial companies.

The discussion of cost efficiency also has a bearing on the question of the relationships between banks and industry. In the United States banks have been forbidden to make direct equity holdings in industrial companies since the inter-war stock market crash. However, as the German experience suggests, the risks associated with bank ownership of corporations depend on the size of banking units. The closer are the identities of the borrower and the lender, the closer is the identity of management and shareholders' interests, and, other things being equal, the more cost-efficient is the financial system. In theory, a capital-market-based system contains an extremely effective, albeit indirect, means of disciplining management, namely low share prices, which encourage hostile takeovers. However, share prices are often depressed not because of managerial inefficiency but because management is operating with a longer time horizon than the capital markets. A bank-based system, by contrast, can succeed in imposing a more direct discipline on management which is both less crisis-prone and more long-term in its perspectives. When a bank is both a big shareholder and an important lender, it is in a position to oblige the corporate management to act in the long-term interests of the shareholders and to change management if necessary without this involving any major change in ownership.

The universal bank organization is not the only way of obtaining a confluence of borrowers' risk and lenders' risk and of merging shareholder and stakeholder interests. The post-war Japanese financial system was founded on regulations similar to those in the United States based on market segmentation or single-purpose financial institutions. However, unlike in the United States, banks are allowed to hold up to 5 per cent of the stock of a non-financial company, while other financial institutions such as insurance companies may hold up to 40 per cent. Direct ownership of shares by private individuals usually amounts to less than 30 per cent. A Japanese company will generally be the client of a "main bank" which is a "city" (large commercial) bank that leads a consortium of banks extending long-term lending to the firm. The main bank also serves as the fiscal agent or principal paying agent on behalf of the consortium. It usually holds equity participation in the company, as do the other banks in the consortium. Thus, both the short-term financing and the long-term lending and equity holding for the firm will be organized through the banking system rather than in the capital market. Consequently, despite its low direct participation as either an owner or a lender, the lead or main bank of a Japanese firm will represent the interests of both the majority of the shareholders and the lenders, leading to the same confluence of shareholder and stakeholder interest as in Germany. This conclusion is supported by empirical studies which suggest that Japanese firms enjoy the same interest cost advantages as German firms relative to borrowers in the market-organized system. Japanese main banks also are involved in the day-to-day financing of a firm and are thus able to appraise both borrower and lender risk. They appear to exercise the same arm's length control function as German banks, although where a firm's performance is very unsatisfactory, they may intervene directly.

Another aspect of a bank-based system is that by reducing the variability of lending flows to borrowers, it allows firms to formulate and execute long-term plans. By contrast, "short-termism" seems to dominate the Anglo-Saxon system. This does not mean that in the bank-based system firms are not subject to monitoring and control; but their performance is measured against long-term profit and growth objectives, rather than by quarterly earnings.

produce an even sharper separation of shareholder interest from those of the banks' creditors, especially under a system of deposit insurance. As pointed out by the President of the Federal Reserve Bank of New York, Mr. G. Corrigan, "the mere fact of permitting commercial firms to own and control banking organizations carries with it at least the implicit transfer of some elements of the safety net to such firms" (*Federal Reserve Bank of New York Quarterly Review*, Spring 1991, vol. 16, No. 1, p. 9).

65 R.N. McCauley and S.A. Zimmer, "Explaining international differences in the cost of capital" (*Federal Reserve Bank of New York Quarterly Review*, Summer 1989).

Two conclusions may be drawn from the preceding discussion. First, the "Anglo-Saxon" model, in which bank loans are short-term, and long-term outside financing is obtained from capital markets, may not be the best way of providing long-term financing. Second, "universal banking" on the German model is not a necessary feature of a bank-based system of funding investment.

The differences between the various types of financial organizations discussed above are of great importance when considering policies to restructure the financial systems of developing and Eastern European countries. In many of these countries non-bank financial intermediaries and capital markets are non-existent, the dominant form of financial savings being bank deposits. As explained in chapter III below, in such conditions it may be better to increase the cost efficiency of the banking system, if necessary by means of sweeping reforms, rather than try to establish an Anglo-Saxon type of system.■

Chapter II

FINANCIAL FRAGILITY AND GLOBAL EXPANSION

A. Introduction

The organization of international financial markets has undergone major changes in the last three decades, with important consequences, direct or indirect, for developing countries. For instance, in the 1960s many United States banks established themselves offshore, where regulations were minimal, and were consequently able to take the lead in the "petrodollar recycling" of the 1970s. This process, together with the switch from officially-set to market-determined (i.e. floating) exchange rates, eroded the role of the official sector in international finance. The growth of commercial bank exposure to developing countries was made possible by the extensive use of rollover credits at variable interest rates. But this also made a crisis for both creditors and debtors inescapable when, at the end of the decade, dollar interest rates escalated and the world economy entered a deep recession.

The process of financial deregulation and innovation has continued apace, affecting many areas besides sovereign lending. This chapter explains how much the same factors that resulted in the weakening of bank balance sheets and fall in lending to developing countries are now once more eroding the financial strength of banks and depressing lending in a number of financial markets such as the United States and Japan. While this financial weakness will not by itself block global recovery, it could well serve to slow its pace, with adverse consequences for developing countries. In particular, a combination of weakening global growth and export markets, on the one hand, and financial stringency, on the other hand, would endanger the international debt strategy.

It is therefore even more necessary than ever to strengthen official sources of international financial intermediation for developing countries, and to take urgent steps to increase official financing, for instance on the basis of a new allocation of SDRs.

B. The United States

1. The structure of the United States financial system

The structure of the United States banking system is anomalous compared with that of other advanced countries. The United Kingdom and other West European economies have experienced a gradual process of consolidation in which a small number of large, multifunction commercial banks have come to dominate domestic markets, and are sufficiently large to compete against each other and their foreign competitors in the provision of financing and other services in international markets.

In the United States this process of concentration has been blocked by regulations which limit the growth potential of commercial banks in a number of ways. The United States system is characterized as a "dual" system of federal and state regulation of banks, and (as already noted in chapter I) a "unit" banking system, with controls which forbid inter-state, and strictly limit intra-state, branching.

This effectively limits a bank's operations to the geographical area in which it is located; and its growth is tied to the economy of that area. At the same time, there are limits on the proportion of bank capital which may be committed to a single borrower, which has often meant that even when a bank is located in a rapidly growing area with large, expanding corporations, it is unable to supply all the banking needs of its clients. Until recently banks were also regulated by legislation introduced in the aftermath of the 1929 stock market crash and the Bank Holiday of 1933, which gave the Federal Reserve powers to set limits on interest rates on deposits through regulation Q; these limits were generally set at zero for demand deposits and at low, fixed and relatively rigid rates on other deposit liabilities. This regulation eliminated price competition, both among banks and between banks and other financial institutions, for deposit liabilities. With the scope for expansion in domestic markets thus limited, banks could grow only by expanding their activities in international markets. However, regulations were introduced in the 1960s on international lending by banks located in the United States. In order to retain their international activities banks transferred their lending to branches outside the United States, to the Euro- and other offshore markets.[66]

At the same time, banks increased their efforts to reduce the impact of regulations on their domestic profitability via a series of domestic operating innovations, the best known of which was the introduction in the early 1960s of the negotiable Certificate of Deposit. Since these certificates fell outside regulation Q limits on interest rates payable on deposits, they provided a means of attracting funds, which came to be called "managed liabilities", via interest rate competition. With this and other devices for circumventing interest rate regulations, banks were able to attract funds away from other, more closely regulated, financial insti-

tutions, such as savings and loan banks. Savings banks, which were forbidden to provide their clients with transactions services, responded (in 1972) to this loss of funds by introducing the "negotiable order of withdrawal", which provided for the equivalent of checking service on a savings deposit account. Other financial institutions joined the competition for depositors' funds via "money market deposit accounts" (1973), and finally brokerage house "cash management accounts" (1980). As savings and loans banks and large stockbroker investment banks started to encroach on the provision of transactions deposits normally reserved to banks, large brokers and investment banks started to compete with banks for their large corporate borrowers by offering to underwrite for them the issue of short-term commercial paper. Commercial banks responded to this competition for their traditional services by seeking the elimination of New Deal legislation which reserved underwriting to non-bank financial institutions and prevented banks from offering similar services to their commercial clients.

These innovations in transactions accounts and other managed liabilities, all of which were used by the banks and other non-bank financial institutions to increase competition for depositors' funds via interest rates, were the basis for the subsequent calls for a "level playing field" for all financial institutions - commercial banks, saving and loans, securities houses and investment banks and insurance companies - nearly all of which were subject to different regulators and regulations with respect to their ability to compete for funds and to supply financial services.

The growth of the presence of United States banks in the Euromarkets and the introduction of financial innovations and the calls for deregulation in the domestic markets were thus all responses by United States banks to the decline in the position of the United States in providing international finance. To preserve their growth prospects in international lending, United States banks sought to escape domestic regulations by moving their operations abroad; and to increase growth potential in domestic markets they created new financial products exempt from regulatory control and sought the removal of prudential or historical regulations which limited the scope of their domestic activities.

---

66 From 1965 to 1970 the number of Federal Reserve System member banks operating foreign branches grew from 13 to 79, and had reached 125 by 1973; gross assets grew from $9.1 billion to $52.6 billion, and to $118 billion by 1973. The total number of foreign branches grew from 211 in 1965 to 532, and to 694 by 1973.

2. Implications of financial innovation and deregulation for the stability of financial flows

In 1979 the Federal Reserve shifted its policy from one of direct targeting of interest rates to one of controlling monetary aggregates, just when financial innovation and deregulation were freeing interest rates from controls and allowing financial institutions to use interest rates to compete for deposits and other borrowed (or managed) funds (see box 7). The result was to greatly increase variability in interest rates (and consequently also to increase variability in exchange rates). Since asset prices move with interest rates, the new environment was one in which asset price variability also increased.

The abrogation of state usury laws for most assets, which was included in the 1980 Monetary Control Act, also contributed to increased interest-rate variability, by eliminating ceilings on interest rates. More important, it made possible the introduction of adjustable interest rate financial instruments such as had already found widespread use in the Euromarkets. Variable interest rates eliminate the risk associated with traditional long-term lending at fixed rates against short-term liabilities by ensuring that rates on assets and liabilities move roughly in step, so that there is no risk of loss on past lending when rates rise. Financial institutions consequently thought that by issuing adjustable rate assets they could insulate the value of the assets on their balance sheets from changes in interest rates.

In addition, new financial markets grew up to trade the risks which had been created by the increased volatility of asset prices, just as foreign currency options and futures had grown as instruments to intermediate the risks associated with positions in foreign exchange when floating exchange rates were introduced. As financial markets were deregulated, derivative markets were developed for interest rate futures, and for futures and options for bonds and shares and market indexes of asset prices. These and other factors led to the widespread notion that it was possible to avoid the increased risk due to higher variability in asset prices, either by issuing adjustable rate assets or by buying "insurance" against the risk by assembling an appropriate package of products in derivative markets. But, adjustable rate assets simply transform the interest rate risk for the lender into a credit risk for the borrower. The viability of the borrower is more difficult to evaluate because it is less transparent and because it depends not only on his ability to pay interest but also on his ability to withstand increases in interest and falls in capital values. If the borrower's ability to withstand interest rate risk is less than the bank's, a shift to adjustable rates increases the overall level of risk. Besides, because the borrower's risk becomes less transparent it tends to be more easily underestimated or ignored.

The removal of restrictions on prices of assets, together with the apparent reduction in risks due to lenders' belief that the risks of variable rates could be traded, and the failure of borrowers to evaluate the real magnitude of the burdens they were undertaking, led to a rapid creation of financial assets via an overall increase in indebtedness of both households and businesses in the United States economy. The reason for this increase is also linked to changes in the way monetary policy affected the level of economic activity under the new operating procedures and the new "level playing field".

3. The transmission of monetary policy

A tightening of monetary policy in the United States had traditionally relied on open market sales of government securities by the Federal Reserve Board to push interest rates above the regulation Q-controlled time and savings deposit rates offered by commercial and savings banks. This led to a loss of reserves as funds were shifted into higher-yielding assets, requiring a reduction in lending, first to the construction sector and then to business generally as the economy moved into a (usually) brief recession. The financial institutions bore the cost of the change in interest rates through a fall in earnings, while the construction sector bore the brunt of the fall in the level of activity. But, the change in rates was accomplished with minimum variation in the value of the assets held on bank balance sheets, and thus minimal risk of bank insolvency.

With controls on deposit interest rates removed by the 1980 and 1982 legislation, banks could simply counteract any rise in interest rates on government securities caused by open market operations by raising their deposit rates. It thus became possible for rates on Government securities to push the costs of funds of financial institutions above the long-term rates being earned on assets such as mortgage lending. Instead of merely inflicting a fall in earnings on commercial banks, leading them to reduce their lending, an increase in interest rates could now cause technical insolvency for the savings and loan institutions,

Box 7

DEREGULATORY FINANCIAL LEGISLATION IN THE UNITED STATES

The initial response to the new conditions in United States financial markets resulting from the increased competition and financial innovation was the passage of the Depositary Institutions Deregulation and Monetary Control Act of 1980 which provided for the elimination of Federal Reserve regulation Q interest rate controls by 1986, introduced more uniform regulations to apply to all financial institutions acting as deposit takers, pre-empted state usury laws on certain types of lending such as mortgages (which removed a major obstacle to the introduction of adjustable interest rate lending) and increased federal deposit insurance maximum protection from $40,000 to $100,000 for all deposit-taking institutions.

This latter change was particularly important since at that time interest rate controls applied to deposits up to, but not including, $100,000, allowing CDs denominated in that amount to escape rate regulation so that during the phase-out period for regulation Q federal insurance guarantees applied to unregulated deposits. This is one of the major sources of the moral hazard problem of the deposit insurance system and of the high interest rates charged by troubled Savings and Loan banks, which could thus invest in high-risk, high-return assets and still offer a guarantee on investors' funds as long as each deposit was no greater than $100,000.

More importantly, these regulatory changes occurred in conditions of high inflation, which led the Federal Reserve in 1979 to shift its monetary policy objectives from interest rates to monetary aggregates and to initiate an anti-inflation policy based on monetary restriction. This change led to sharp increases in the level and variability of interest rates. The more "level playing field" introduced in the 1980 legislation, however, only applied to competition for deposit liabilities, not to already contracted long-term assets. Thus, the new freedom to compete for deposits at market-determined interest rates did little to resolve the difficulties faced by Savings and Loan banks, saddled with long-term housing loans at low, fixed interest rates. Even if Savings and Loans succeeded in warding off competition for their deposit liabilities from commercial banks, the difference between the competitive short-term rates they had to pay to keep deposits and the much lower fixed rates on their outstanding mortgages meant that most were technically insolvent after entering the more level playing field.

To meet the continuing difficulties of Savings and Loan banks the 1982 Depository Institutions Act eased the acquisition of failing units by purchase or merger with banks located in other states. The effect was a *de facto* abrogation of state laws controlling bank branching. In addition, the new legislation provided emergency government financing for failing Savings and Loan banks in the form of "net worth certificates" which in effect discounted bad loans. It also allowed savings banks to enter certain types of commercial lending and acquire securities which had previously been prohibited, in order to provide access to investment opportunities with higher interest rates to compensate the low rates on their outstanding mortgage lending. It was this provision which led to investments in property development, commercial real estate and in non-investment grade assets ("junk bonds") issued by such ventures which has been the cause of most of the fraud and continued losses of these banks. Thus, although most Savings and Loan banks were already insolvent as a result of the "level playing field" in the early 1980s, they were allowed to continue to operate, raising funds through the use of the interest control-exempt, but government-insured, $100,000 deposits to invest in assets with the highest, and thus riskiest, returns available in order to keep themselves from declaring insolvency. The result was the eventual bankruptcy of the federal insurance fund for Savings and Loan banks.

which would find themselves having to pay more for short-term funds than they earned on their long-term mortgage portfolio. The contraction in lending and the reduction in the level of economic activity sought henceforth had to come from the bankruptcy of the lending institution or of the borrower or both.

In these conditions, where the lending institution has substituted all its fixed interest assets by adjustable-rate loans, it simply passes a rise in deposit rates onto the borrower, whose interest payments consequently rise relative to his income. At the point when financing costs exceed income, default occurs and the loan becomes a charge against the lending institution's earnings. Thus, under the new transmission mechanism, lending is only seriously constrained when the borrowers and the lending institutions are threatened with insolvency.

Widespread use of variable interest rates thus means that bank profits are affected by changes in interest rates not only directly, but also indirectly through the financial position of their debtors. Moreover, since their profits now depend on turnover, banks are under a temptation to increase lending to higher-risk borrowers, or to under-evaluate risks. This produces a system in which increased use of price competition leads to an increase in overall lending, an underestimation of risk, and a considerable reduction in the influence of interest rates on the lending capacity of the banking system. In such conditions, and with operating procedures aiming at the control of quantitative monetary aggregates, the major channel through which monetary restraint can dampen economic expansion is a decline in asset prices large enough to drive financial and business institutions into financial difficulty. Moreover, the increased impact on bank equity resulting from the new channels of transmission of monetary policy has translated increased variability in interest rates and asset prices into increased variability in flows of funding at both the domestic and the international level.

4. The introduction of equity-based controls

As a result of the smaller impact of traditional monetary policy instruments on lending activity, and the resulting tendency to increase turnover and risk, alternative regulations have been proposed to safeguard the solvency of banks. Since its capital base is the ultimate determinant of the strength of a bank, these regulations have involved, in conformity with BIS guidelines,[67] setting minimum ratios of bank capital to the value of assets weighted by their risk. These regulations will be phased into effect for all banks operating internationally by the end of 1992. The first phase came into effect at the end of 1990.

If increases in interest rates on assets and liabilities no longer act to control expansion in banks' activity, under capital controls the expansion of a bank's assets is limited by its ability to increase equity capital. Any attempt to increase lending to more risky borrowers will now have to be met by borrowing in capital markets, at rates which presumably reflect fully the higher risks and therefore penalize excessively risky lending. While prudential capital

ratios can provide a substitute mechanism by which interest rates act as a brake on bank expansion, they can also establish a more direct connection between capital markets and money markets. Whereas the basis of the cost of funds to banks used to be the federal funds market, now it will be the cost of raising bank capital. The introduction of capital controls will also have an impact on supply and demand conditions in capital markets, for at precisely the time when there are increased demands on capital markets to fund long-term lending, the banks will also be competing for funds, first to increase their own capital, and second, as they attempt to reduce their asset portfolios through securitization, which increases the supply of assets in the capital market. Thus, controls on bank equity are increasing upward pressure on long-term rates by bringing banks to the capital markets as borrowers and by shifting some of their clients' traditional borrowing from banks to the capital markets.

5. Variability in capital flows

The transformation of the United States financial system has also increased the variability of the volume of lending to domestic borrowers, as well its interest costs (see box 8). By the 1980s, as domestic interest rates rose to double digits and expected dollar appreciation made the United States an attractive investment market, capital flowed back to the United States which became a net borrower in international capital markets. Because of the debt crisis United States banks steered clear of sovereign lending to developing countries and once again turned their attention to domestic financial markets. The decline in their short-term lending to corporations, together with the general decline in foreign trade finance and of the industrial sector, led banks and other financial institutions to shift their activity to the production and packaging of financial assets. Consequently, the indebtedness of households and firms expanded. The increase in the provision of funding for mergers and acquisitions via leveraged and management buyouts represented a shift in the determinants of bank profits from net interest margins to fees and commissions and also reflected the impulse to increase asset creation and turnover so as to replace 'normal' margin income from corporate lending. It also meant another sharp increase in the degree of risk and deterioration in the quality of the assets held on banks' balance sheets.

---

67 These guidelines are embodied in the Basle Agreement of July 1988 on International Convergence of Capital Measurement and Capital Standards (described in *TDR 1989*, annex 2).

Box 8

THE CAUSES OF HIGHER INTEREST RATES

Often ignored in discussions of the increase in interest rates in the 1980s is financial innovation and deregulation. They have had an important impact on both the short- and the long-term markets, as well as creating a tighter linkage between the two.

The average level of short-term rates has increased because of the elimination of controls over deposit rates and the increased use of interest rates by financial institutions to compete in order to increase size and market position. This increase in short-term rates need not have spilled over to an increase in long rates, but a number of factors have led to this result.

First, increasing government deficits may place a burden on asset markets to the extent that assets are issued merely to finance transfer payments which banks believe can find a place in portfolios only at lower prices, as is currently the case in the financing of German unification.

On the other hand, as noted above, the introduction of prudential capital ratios in conditions of increasing bank charge-offs of bad debts and depressed capital markets may lead to a shift in bank asset portfolios as low-weighted assets are substituted for those carrying higher weights. Thus, over the past year United States banks have increased the proportion of domestic treasury and agency securities, and in particular of mortgages and mortgage-backed securities, all of which have zero weighting, in their total assets. Since total assets have fallen, this need not have brought a net increase in such holdings. They have also sharply reduced their lending to commercial and industrial borrowers and engaged in large-scale securitization of consumer lending. Further, the creation and growth of the junk bond market reduced bank lending by small- and medium-size high-risk borrowers and generated additional demands on long-term bond markets. All these shifts meant that assets whose acquisition would previously have been financed in the short-term loan market by banks' money creation were being placed instead in capital markets. This shift in the stock of existing assets from the money market to the capital markets exerts a similar pressure on the schedule of asset preferences in capital markets.

To the extent that meeting capital adequacy ratios requires banks to change their asset composition, or shift their own borrowing to capital markets to support existing levels of lending, long-term rates will tend to be higher, even without any additional demand for finance for recovery or for reconstruction. Thus, while increased demand for investment funding need not increase long-term interest rates, a shift in funding from short-term bank financing to long-term capital market financing, which has been the basic result of the round of financial innovation and deregulation, i.e. a stock shift rather than an increase in flows, can lead to increased interest rates and lower asset prices. At the same time, the increase in variability of interest rates and asset prices increases the variability in capital flows and thus the overall efficiency of the financial system to satisfy the needs of developing country borrowers.

The greater variability of rates and the shifting of risk to the ultimate borrower has tended to cause an increase in long rates in addition to that caused by the shift of bank assets to capital market assets due to innovation and the application of prudential capital ratios shifting the supply of long-term assets without any concomitant current investment and is thus unmatched by any change in saving. Thus, the result has been a relative increase in long-term rates; other things being equal, this should feed through to an increase in real rates of interest stemming not from any shortage of real savings, but simply from the change in the institutional and regulatory environment.

As noted in the preceding chapter, the funding for new investment must compete with existing financial assets for investors' portfolios. Hence flows of new assets will tend to have a relatively small impact on prices, while shifts in investor preferences, in liquidity preferences and the efficiency of the financial system will tend to have more dominant effects. This is an area in which financial innovation has produced once-and-for-all shifts in the supply of assets to capital markets with a substantial impact on market conditions. With respect to international markets, the variability of exchange rates adds an additional element to interest rate variability which separates the assessment of risk by the borrower and the lender and increases the costs of intermediation and the long-term rate of interest.

The slowing of economic growth in the United States since 1989 has brought to the fore the hidden "credit risk" aspect of adjustable lending, and the tightening carried out by the Federal Reserve in the aftermath of the 1989 stock market crash has led to widespread private default and dramatic increases in impaired loans on the banks' books. These losses mean that many banks find it difficult to meet the new standards of capital adequacy. The conditions of their balance sheets and of the economy make it difficult for them to raise capital directly, so that the only way to meet the capital adequacy ratios is to cut lending. This has led to a further "credit crunch" as business now finds it much more difficult to borrow, either via commercial paper or via traditional bank lending. The impact of this reticence to lend on the part of the banks was reflected in sharp declines in the money supply (M2) during 1990.

The impairment of banks' lending ability due to changes in the value of their assets is mirrored in the difficulties faced by non-financial firms. As a result of the increase in borrowing to substitute for equity, net interest payments as a proportion of corporate gross profits have grown from 4.25 per cent in 1987 to over 5 per cent in 1989. This increase accounts for more than half of the fall in the gross profit share of corporations, from 9 per cent to 7.75 per cent, over the same period. By 1989 gross interest payments had reached an average of 50 per cent of corporate cash flow. Thus, the decline in earnings which is required to produce corporate default is now much lower than before, and both firms and banks are now more exposed to falls in income due to recession and to increases in interest rates due to tight monetary policy.

6. Debt deflation or credit crunch?

The increased variability of interest rates in conditions of widespread default on lending has created, for the first time since the 1930s, the potential for a credit contraction to turn into generalized debt deflation. When businesses and financial institutions are forced to sell assets in order to meet debt service, they can drive down asset prices very sharply and force otherwise viable institutions into distress sales and insolvency.

In a situation of debt deflation the assets of a financial institution do not generate sufficient cash to meet payments to creditors holding its liabilities; that is, in order to meet its financing commitments it has to sell those assets for which it has borrowed money to buy. The result is a further decline in asset values relative to the liabilities borrowed to finance them, driving a larger and larger wedge between asset values and liabilities which must be charged off against equity. This generates a circular process which leads rapidly to a generalized fall in asset prices. The inability to repay liabilities then produces a destruction of private sector wealth. Such conditions occurred in the "junk bond" market when the savings and loan rescue package passed by the United States Congress made it illegal for rescued banks to hold such assets. In disposing of them in the market they drove their prices down to such an extent that other institutions holding them found that their value was less than the value of liabilities plus equity and had to declare bankruptcy.

The current difficulties of the commercial banks, primarily related to commercial real estate assets whose prices have fallen precipitously over the last year, may be another early warning signal of a potential, generalized dramatic fall in asset prices and of financial collapse and insolvency. If that were to occur, the United States economy would not simply be in a cyclical downturn that normally follows a period of sustained expansion; it would have entered a period of turbulence, with a high risk that an initially mild recession turns into a sustained loss of jobs and wealth.

C. Japan

Because of the strength of the dollar and the deterioration of the United States trade account in the 1980s, the Japanese authorities were persuaded to introduce regulatory changes similar to those in the United States, in the expectation that this would strengthen the yen and provide new opportunities for United States banks to operate in Japan. Although the changes failed to influence the foreign exchange market in the manner expected, they did open considerably the financial system and, by virtually eliminating interest rate controls and allowing financial institutions to operate in new areas, increase competition amongst financial institutions which had previously been highly segmented. As a result, Japanese financial institutions rapidly embarked on international expansion: Japanese banks now deal in securities via their foreign subsidiaries, and securities houses have registered as banks outside the country.

A large proportion of bank assets in Japan consists of direct capital market investments in commercial and property companies. This explains why, in setting capital adequacy ratios, Japanese banks were permitted to count up to 45 per cent of their unrealized capital gains on such assets as capital. But it also means that prudential capital ratios now impose an important constraint. The rapid fall in the Tokyo stock market (by about 50 per cent) in the course of 1990, together with the difficulties and bankruptcies of a number of small property companies, had the result that at the end of 1990 Japanese banks had risk-adjusted capital ratios below the 8 per cent minimum. Like their counterparts in the United States, they responded by sharply reducing asset growth and new lending.

Financial markets have also been tightened by the practice of the trading corporations, most of which had no need for bank financing and enjoy extremely high credit ratings, to borrow heavily by issuing bonds convertible into shares at fixed prices or with warrants giving the right to purchase shares at fixed prices. Since demand for these convertible bonds and warrants was strong in the expectation that share prices would keep rising, the cost of funds to the companies was close to zero. They used the money to make extensive investments in property and securities markets; it is estimated that as much as 15 per cent of corporate profits in 1989 resulted from *zaitech* operations. However, the sharp fall in the stock market in 1990 rendered the warrant and conversion privileges worthless, and it is likely that the outstanding bonds will have to be refinanced at maturity instead of being converted at no cost into equity. This refinancing will require companies either to liquidate their property and security holdings or to borrow additional funds at interest rates which are now quite high. However, the companies are currently showing substantial losses. Thus, just as in the United States, there will be an increase in domestic demands on the capital market that is not linked to new investment. This could lead to a further fall in asset prices and to a further reduction in corporate earnings as borrowing costs rise.

Increased deregulation and financial openness has also put strains on monetary policy. Indeed, over the last few years the monetary authority has had to deal with a complex set of objectives including price stability, the exchange rate and financial market stability as well as the traditional objective of provision of cheap finance for industry. However, it has not always been easy to reconcile these objectives.

The boom on the Tokyo stock exchange (which reached its peak at the end of 1989) reflected the fact that monetary ease had led to asset price inflation rather than a lowering of bond rates, probably caused by the presence of a liquidity trap due to external factors. Given the massive Japanese trade surplus and the accompanying trade frictions, and the fact that interest rates were already lower than in the United States, there was little reason to expect Japanese rates to decline in the future. On the other hand, the Japanese stock market had been rising for sometime because of strong growth and trade performance. Liquidity expansion therefore led not to a fall in bond prices but to increases in equity prices. This helped Japanese companies further reduce their leverage. However, the bubble burst at the beginning of 1990. When interest rates rose in the United States (as fears of recession there subsided and inflation became the primary concern), and expectation became widespread that interest rates would rise in Germany (because of unification), there was a massive shift out of yen-denominated assets, forcing Japanese rates to be raised, i.e. considerably increasing the costs of both equity and debt finance. In the first four months of the year, the Nikkei index dropped by about 25 per cent (steeper, though slower, than the drop in Dow Jones in October 1987), the government bond index by more than 20 per cent and the yen by over 10 per cent.

Tighter monetary policy initially helped the authorities in their objective of bringing about an orderly reduction in stock market and land prices, which they considered had risen excessively. However, the fall in stock prices was so steep that in April 1990 they closed the primary market for equities to all issuers (including banks), with certain limited exceptions, forcing firms to resort to borrowing at higher interest rates. Nevertheless, the central bank resisted pressures to ease monetary policy for fear of aggravating inflation and encouraging a new spurt of speculative activity.

There was a further tightening of monetary policy and rise in the discount rate in August 1990. This reflected not so much a drive to continue with the policy of controlled debt deflation as concern with inflation following the invasion of Kuwait and the rise in oil prices. The Nikkei index fell by nearly 15 per cent in August, over 10 per cent in September, and continued to slide until December. As a result of the prolonged slump in the stock market and the downturn in property prices, Japanese banks have recently reported their second annual double-digit decline in earnings. Because of a fear of reviving speculative activity and because a lower yen would generate trade frictions and fuel inflation, the central bank none the less resisted all pressures to ease monetary policy and lower its discount rate until the "Nomura scandal" of June 1991 put further pressure on share prices. Besides, the brunt of the credit squeeze in manufacturing was borne by small, marginal firms.

In conformity with contemporary trends and in response to outside pressure, the Japanese financial system is undergoing a transition from a system that was administered, bank-based, and closed to one that will be market-based and open. The present crisis (slump in security and property prices and the difficulties of financial institutions) is partly the result of this transition; but it is also helping to speed up the transition by moulding new rules of behaviour. The much-noted deterioration of the relationship between securities houses and the Finance Ministry is only one instance of this trend. Another is the fact that moves in interest rates are not signalled in advance, as they used to be prior to the 1983-1985 deregulation. Yet a third example of change in behavioural norms is that Japanese institutional investors are now demanding high dividends to compensate for the decline in their asset growth and in their premiums. If the enforcement of anti-monopoly regulations begins to affect the traditional mutual financial support among members of *keiretsus*, the Japanese corporate sector will lose another distinct feature. These changes in rules and regulations may bring some benefits. But they will also mean that Japan, like the United States, will experience greater variability in interest rates and asset prices, as well as higher risk and interest rates, with adverse consequences on the level of international and domestic lending by banks.

D. Conclusions

The conclusions of the preceding analysis of the implications of the shocks to the financial sector and the real sector may be summarized as follows. Financial innovation and the process of deregulation of financial markets have made interest rates and asset prices more variable, rendering flows of funds more unstable, and has increased the potential instability of the financial system. These changes have so damaged balance sheets in the financial sector that refinancing will represent a major factor impeding the recovery from recession in the developed market economies. The shocks on the side of finance thus suggest that there will not be a rapid opening and expansion of developed economies' markets to the exports of developing countries, nor will there be substantial additional flows of finance to developing countries. Finally, the impact of deregulation has led to the removal of protection of banks in deposit markets, leading to increased competition, but also to increased short-term interest rates. This process of deregulation has also led o a major shift in the financing of existing assets from short-term to long-term finance. This increase in the supply of long-term financial assets in capital markets, in the absence of increased investment, has indeed placed pressure on the flow of savings and lead to an increase in long-term interest rates. Further, the introduction of capital adequacy requirements has also led to a closer linkage between money and capital market rates. This suggests that any current shortage of funds in capital markets is due neither to a shortage of savings nor to excessive increases in demands for funds, but to a stock shift on the supply side due to financial innovation.

The stimulus that might be expected from peace in the Persian Gulf does not seem to have been sufficient to offset the financial difficulties slowing recovery in the United States economy. Further, the expansion of the German and Japanese economies has slowed significantly, and both countries are applying monetary policies that are likely to slow growth further, and through exchange rate linkages, slow expansion in other EEC countries. Indeed, Japan has financial difficulties of its own and the real and financing difficulties associated with German unification suggest that these economies will be making a declining contribution to world activity in 1991. Thus, while current recessionary conditions are unlikely to be deep, they are likely to be persistent and cumulative. A process of balance sheet recovery for both financial institutions and families will be required before real, sustained expansion can take place. This is a process which will dominate 1991 and may persist well into 1992.

Thus, neither current economic conditions nor the developments in financial markets suggest that developing countries are likely to enjoy an improvement of their external trading and financial environment. More active measures will have to be taken to assure the basic conditions necessary for the successful functioning of the debt recovery programmes via increased institutional lending. Since the basic impediments are on the side of finance for development, rather than in terms of a lack of real savings, there is considerable merit in the proposal of Japan for a new SDR allocation of $20 billion to take place over 10 years through IMF. Developed countries would contribute their allocation to the Fund for lending to developing countries.■

FINANCIAL REFORM AND THE DEVELOPMENT PROCESS

A. Introduction

The external financial environment of developing countries has undergone a number of fundamental changes during the 1980s that are unlikely to be reversed in the foreseeable future. The average cost of international finance has become both much higher and much more variable. Similarly, the availability of external finance for these countries has generally not only decreased, but also become more unpredictable and apt to undergo extremely abrupt changes. For many developing countries increased financial stringency has been associated with a prolonged depression of export prices and the terms of trade. As a result, resources available for investment have contracted, disrupting stability and growth.

These developments have heightened the importance of raising the volume of domestic savings, and allocating and utilizing them to maximum effect in order both to combat debt and balance of payments problems and to sustain and accelerate growth and development. Even the few countries which continue to enjoy access to external finance are now seeking cheaper and more reliable resources for investment funds in their domestic markets. Close attention is thus being given to the character of the financial policies pursued by the developing countries themselves.[68]

In recent years many developing countries, supported by the World Bank and IMF, have reformed their financial policies in the context of adjustment programmes which emphasize the market mechanism. By and large, a liberal approach has been followed, including deregulation of interest rates, reduction or elimination of directed credit allocation, and the easing of restrictions on external finance. However, these policy efforts do not appear to have succeeded in lifting the level of domestic savings and investment. Savings and financial flows have failed to respond positively to incentives such as higher interest rates. A new look at the approach is therefore timely.

The financial policies appropriate for any particular country at any particular time are not easy to determine *a priori*. Finance concerns not only **assets** and their yield, but also **liabilities** and their cost. The impact of financial policies on debtors and creditors, and savers and investors, differs depending on their

---

[68] The ECLAC and UNCTAD secretariats have been studying this subject in a joint project, whereby ECLAC focuses on the experience of Latin American countries and UNCTAD on countries in other regions. The results of ECLAC's investigations are contained in the following documents published in 1990 by Grupo Editor Latinoamericano, Buenos Aires: C. Massad and N. Eyzaguirre, *Ahorro y formacion de capital - Experiencias latinoamericanas*; C. Massad and G. Held, *Sistema financiero y asignacion de recursos*; and G. Held and R. Szalachman, *Ahorro y asignacion de recursos financieros*. Those of UNCTAD are contained in the following UNCTAD documents: Y. Akyüz and D. Kotte, *Financial Policies in Developing Countries: Issues and Experience* (forthcoming); Y. Akyüz, "Financial System and Policies in Turkey in the 1980s", *Discussion Paper*, No. 25, Geneva, February 1989; A. Amsden, "Republic of Korea's Financial Reform: What are the Lessons?", *Discussion Paper*, No. 30, Geneva, April 1990; S. Chapple, "Financial Liberalization in New Zealand, 1984-1990", *Discussion Paper*, No. 35, Geneva, March 1991; J.Y. Lim, "The Philippine Financial Sector in the 1980s", *Discussion Paper*, No. 37, Geneva, March 1991; and M. Mrak *et al.*, "Financial System and Policies in Yugoslavia" (mimeo), Geneva, July 1990.

context. This makes it very hard to prescribe a single set of "correct" policies.

Discussions of interest rate policies generally emphasize their impact on savings and investment decisions - i.e. on flows, or additions to assets and liabilities. But interest rates also have important effects through the stock of debt already in place, all the more so when the rates on such debt are adjusted quickly in response to interest rate changes. This is particularly true in developing countries, where the equity base of firms is weak, their leverage high and the maturities on loans short. Consequently, the terms and availability of finance affect the level of both production and investment even if they have no effect on the propensity to save or on calculations of the rate of return on new investment.

Neglect of the effects of finance on investment and production decisions is a recent phenomenon. In the previous two or three decades, the main objective of financial policies was generally to help industrialization and development by providing low-cost finance to selected sectors and activities through controls over interest rates and patterns of lending. The public sector generally received preferential treatment, but those private sector investments that were viewed as necessary for rapid industrialization were also favoured. Typically, the Government set ceilings on deposit and lending rates, and refrained from altering them for macroeconomic management - something which caused real rates of return on a broad range of financial assets to turn negative when inflation rose. Lending rates were differentiated according to the sector's activity, and interest rate subsidies to industry were a major instrument of export promotion and import substitution. Credits were directed to key sectors by means of restrictions on bank portfolios, such as compulsory lending and high reserve requirements and liquidity ratios. The degree of financial openness was generally limited. Most countries erected barriers to the entry of foreign banks and restricted the access of non-residents to domestic capital markets. Similarly, the access of residents to foreign currency assets was restricted through controls over capital flows abroad, and residents were generally barred from holding foreign exchange deposits in domestic banks. Very few countries permitted domestic banks and/or non-financial corporations access to external credits without prior approval and guarantee.

These policies came under heavy criticism in the 1980s. This was partly because of the severity of the crisis in developing countries. But Governments in the major industrialized countries also embraced the doctrine of financial deregulation and liberalization, which came to be regarded as not only appropriate to contemporary conditions in those countries but also as being of general applicability. It is now widely believed that interventionist financial policies were one of the major causes of the crisis in developing countries, and that liberalization will make a major contribution to restoring growth and stability.

According to the theory of "financial repression" underlying current thinking, low or negative real rates of return on financial assets depress savings, render their allocation and use highly inefficient, encourage the holding of foreign exchange assets and capital flight, and induce savers to hold unproductive physical assets instead of lending funds to entrepreneurs for productive investment. Moreover, low interest rates and directed credit allocation lower the quality of investment and raise its capital intensity, thereby aggravating capital shortage and distorting the pattern of production and trade. Furthermore, lack of competition among banks creates inefficiencies in financial intermediation, while the unregulated, informal financial markets that typically mushroom under such conditions cause further distortions in resource allocation.

There can be little doubt that interventionist policies towards the level of savings and the allocation of resources have suffered from major shortcomings in many developing countries, and often continue to do so. But it is no less true that such policies contributed significantly to the rapid growth and industrialization registered in many countries in the 1960s and 1970s, including some that have been in crisis in the 1980s as well as others that have managed to continue growing. It is notable that interventionist financial policies played an important role in some "success stories": for instance, the Republic of Kórea did not leave interest rates entirely to market forces, allocated credit directly and differentiated the cost of finance among different sectors and activities as part of its active industrial and trade policy ("picking winners"). In Japan, too, the regulated financial system made an important contribution to industrial expansion. The experience in this respect is clear: while there have been many "failures" associated with interventionist financial policy, the only modern examples of industrialization based on purely market-oriented financial policies are a couple of "city states".

Why did much the same policy approach generate poor results in some countries and brilliant results in others? Two main lessons stand out:

- Macroeconomic stability is essential. Governments should not allow interventionist finance to degenerate into inflationary finance, and must resist excessive demand for credit and ensure fiscal discipline. Nor should they allow external shocks to trigger an inflationary process (something made extremely difficult in the 1980s by the sheer size of the shocks incurred by many countries and the rapid speed of adjustment required of them);
- Governments must ensure that the support and protection provided by them is well targeted and used for the purposes intended rather than as a handout. They must constantly monitor how far their policies are attaining their objectives, and undertake revisions as necessary.

In all but a very few cases, financial liberalization has ended in a crash. This was partly because although liberalization was typically adopted as a remedy for economic stagnation and instability, these had greatly weakened already fragile financial markets and institutions. But, in most cases there was also failure to strengthen prudential regulations and supervision to match the deregulation of interest rates and financial activity. This resulted in widespread speculation, excessive risk-taking, and fraud and irregularities, eventually giving rise to widespread insolvency among debtors and financial intermediaries, financial instability and significant damage to the real economy.

In the handful of cases where these problems were avoided, two factors were especially important:

- Financial liberalization was adopted after - not before - a considerable degree of industrialization had been achieved, and from a position of economic strength, not as a response to weakness. The presence of strong institutions and markets, and of competitive industries, proved to be essential preconditions for successful liberalization;
- Liberalization was undertaken gradually and without making it impossible to continue to pursue an active industrial policy. Governments continued to intervene directly in capital markets, financial intermediaries and corporate finance in order to preserve financial stability, and acted to strengthen existing market institutions and build new ones; they did not leave financial development to emerge spontaneously.

B. Financial policies and savings

1. Size and allocation of savings

There are significant differences in savings rates among developing countries; gross domestic savings during the 1980s were on average negative in a number of (mostly low-income and least developed) countries, whereas in some others they amounted to as much as 40 per cent of GDP. While countries with lower per capita incomes generally have lower average savings rates, there are some low-income countries where average savings rates are as high as, and even higher than, countries at much higher per capita income levels. Indeed, the dispersion of savings rates among developing countries is much greater than among the OECD countries, where the domestic savings rate as conventionally measured ranges from 18 per cent to 30 per cent. Moreover, over time the savings rate appears to be much less stable in developing than in developed countries, probably because of their greater vulnerability to shocks and disturbances. The relationship between savings rates and per capita income is more pronounced when comparison is between countries at different levels of income at a given point in time than for a given country at different points in time, implying a considerable degree of stickiness due to factors other than the level of income.

Similarly, there are wide differences in the distribution of domestic savings between the Government and the rest of the economy (i.e. the household and business sectors, including state economic enterprises). In many developing countries Governments either run deficits on current account, or their savings amount to no more than 1 or 2 per cent of GDP. These include not only low-income countries but also a number of middle and upper middle-income countries in Latin America and Asia. By contrast, in a number of other developing countries at various levels of development government savings constitute an important source of capital accumulation, ranging from 5 per cent to 10 per cent of GDP (e.g. Cameroon, Chile, Republic of Korea, Tunisia, Turkey, Venezuela and Yugoslavia). Available evidence also suggests that in most developing countries government savings are much less stable over time than aggregate domestic savings.

The household sector is often assumed to be the main source of private savings in developing countries. However, there is often very little information on the shares of the corporate and household sectors (including unincorporated business, where self-employment is very important in developing countries). Available evidence indicates that while in some countries corporate savings amount to less than 2 per cent of GDP (e.g. Chile, India, Philippines), in others they exceed 5 per cent, or even 10 per cent (Cameroon, Colombia, Malaysia, Mexico, Republic of Korea, Thailand), thereby accounting for an important and even the major part of private savings.

Empirical studies on inter-country differences in savings have failed to establish reliable and systematic linkages between the savings rate and the variables commonly thought to be its main determinants, including income and real interest rates. While income generally proves to be an important determinant of aggregate savings, differences in per capita income explain only part of the differences in savings rates. Evidence on the relationship between cross-country differences in savings rates and real interest rates is inconclusive. A few studies have found a positive but weak correlation, but others have either failed to do so or even found a significant negative correlation. These observations strongly suggest that structural and institutional factors play a much more important role than the real interest rate in determining differences in the savings rate.[69]

To analyze the response of the savings rate to changes in the real interest rate in developing countries, it is necessary to distinguish between what may be called "regime changes" and "changes within a given interest rate policy regime". Indeed, those favouring interest rate deregulation and financial liberalization stress that it is the regime changes that give rise to

strong savings responses. It has, for instance, been stated that "savers may ignore a possible transitory increase from, say, 4 to 6 per cent in rates of return, but they are less likely to maintain consumption-saving patterns when rates of return change, in a context of economic reform, from negative levels to positive 10 or 15 per cent and more".[70] It should be noted that such jumps in the real interest rate only occur under relatively rapid inflation.

The essential difference between these two types of change is not so much their size as their permanency. Many stabilization programmes have included sharp upward movements in nominal and real interest rates without any permanent change in the underlying philosophy in the determination of interest rates. It is expected that the effects of temporary adjustments made in interest rates, even when large on the behaviour of savers, will be much weaker than adjustments made in the context of structural reforms, even when small. Such reforms do not necessarily imply a need to deregulate interest rates completely: the Government may continue to set ceilings on interest rates without generating large and persistent imbalances in the credit market. However, the distinction between "regime changes" and "changes within a given interest rate policy regime" has usually not been made in studies on savings in developing countries, which makes it hard to interpret the time series data on savings and interest rates; in any case, these give mixed results and are no more conclusive than cross-country studies.

Numerous developing countries have changed their policy regime governing interest rates in the 1980s. The evidence from several such countries in Europe and Asia studied by the UNCTAD secretariat shows no simple relationship between financial liberalization and interest rates, on the one hand, and savings performance, on the other (see box 9). Similarly, a recent study by two World Bank economists of the financial liberalization experience of five Asian countries (Indonesia, Malaysia, Philippines, Sri Lanka and Republic of Korea) has concluded that "financial reform, whether comprehensive and sweeping or measured and gradual, does not seem to have made any significant difference to the saving and investment activities in the liberalized economies. It was

---

69 These factors determine not only the proportion of income saved, but also the degree to which the savings rate is responsive to interest rates. In other words, even if savings responded to interest rates within each country, aggregating countries that are heterogeneous structurally and institutionally would not be an appropriate procedure for analyzing the link between interest rates and savings because of differences in patterns of response. This may also be a reason why a number of studies pooling cross-country and time-series data (and, therefore, assuming implicitly the same savings response both within and across countries) have failed to find strong evidence of the effect of interest rates on savings.

70 E.S. Shaw, *Financial Deepening in Economic Development* (New York: Oxford University Press, 1973), p. 73.

Box 9

FINANCIAL LIBERALIZATION AND SAVINGS IN SELECTED DEVELOPING COUNTRIES IN ASIA AND EUROPE

- In the *Republic of Korea* both real interest rates and national savings rose in the 1980s. However, the two were not closely related to each other. Real interest rates rose as a result of the decline in inflation rather than liberalization, and the upward trend in savings started long before the rise in real interest rates. Econometric exercises also suggest that the two variables were weakly and insignificantly correlated with one another, whether savings are defined at the aggregate or household level. The main reason for the rise in household savings in the 1980s appears to have been the increased demand for housing combined with the paucity of mortgage financing.

- In *Turkey* ceilings on interest rates were lifted in mid-1980, and as the financial deregulation was accompanied by monetary restriction, real interest rates rose by 30-40 percentage points. Private savings as a proportion of GDP fell drastically in the early 1980s. This was initially associated with recession, but the decline continued until 1984, when growth picked up. The decline was primarily accounted for by corporate savings and the erosion of small savings. Corporate savings subsequently recovered as declines in real wages made up for much of the increase in the cost of finance. The private savings rate rose after 1984, but its level in the late 1980s was still below that of the late 1970s, even though income was one third higher and real interest rates higher still.

- In the *Philippines*, where financial liberalization started in 1981, savings were not significantly affected by interest rate movements. Between 1981 and 1985 the aggregate savings rate, and particularly the savings rates of households and small businesses, fell despite a sharp rise in nominal and real interest rates throughout the period. The fall was closely related to the movement of GNP: it was particularly pronounced during the years of deep recession (1984-1985), when real GNP fell and inflation accelerated. In 1988, real per capita income was still around 10 per cent below its level at the beginning of the decade. The aggregate savings rate recovered somewhat during 1986-1988, but it was still around 20 per cent lower than in 1980-1982, although real interest rates were higher. Initially, the rise in deposit rates attracted funds into banks, increasing the share of savings and time deposits in household portfolios. However, as macroeconomic and political instability intensified, there was a massive shift from domestic to foreign currency assets.

- In *Yugoslavia* the monetary authorities started to pursue a policy of positive real interest rates in 1986, and rates were completely liberalized in late 1989. Until 1986 savings rose even though real interest rates became increasingly negative. By contrast, savings fell sharply as a share of national income in 1990 after liberalization, as GDP fell sharply. The earlier rise in the savings ratio was entirely on account of household savings, which rose to unprecedented levels, whereas the share of enterprises in gross domestic savings declined sharply, reflecting a severe deterioration of corporate finances primarily due to increased interest payments abroad. Financial savings grew substantially as a percentage of national income throughout the 1980s. However, within this aggregate foreign currency deposits by households have grown much faster than domestic currency savings deposits. By 1989 their stock amounted to more than three times that of the latter. This increase, resulting from both foreign currency holdings by workers residing abroad and a substantial amount of currency substitution, was particularly strong after 1986 despite the rise of real domestic currency interest rates to positive levels. Accelerating inflation due to an intensified struggle over income distribution, together with increased macroeconomic instability, were the main reasons for currency substitution in the late 1980s. More recently, there has been a pronounced move out of bank deposits and into cash holdings, domestic and particularly foreign, as savers' confidence in the banking system has deteriorated and devaluation of the currency has appeared imminent. In response to these developments financial liberalization was partly reversed in the course of 1990, and interest ceilings were reintroduced.

believed until recently that removal of the repressive policies would boost saving. The survey in this paper of the consequences of reforms does not reveal any systematic trend or pattern in regard to saving ... It lends support to the by now well-acknowledged conclusion that decisions to save are determined by several factors and the relationship between savings and real interest rates is at best ambig-uous".[71] Recent academic studies of a number of sub-Saharan African countries (including Ghana, Kenya, Malawi, United Republic of Tanzania and Zambia) where financial liberalization and interest rate deregulation have also been an important ingredient of structural adjustment programmes come to much the same conclusion: interest rate changes have had very little effect on improving the size and allocation of savings.[72]

In Latin America, too, financial policies have increasingly relied on high real interest rates to raise private savings and have them deposited in domestic financial institutions. Real interest rates have been extremely volatile because of large and unpredictable changes in rates of inflation. The evidence suggests that in general real interest rates have not had a systematic and strong influence on real private savings (see box 10). They have at times been effective in checking capital flight, but the main influence on capital flight has been exchange rate expectations and general economic and political instability. Macroeconomic disorder and persistent payments disequilibrium have been the main factors discouraging the retention of financial assets at home, and encouraging speculation and capital flight.

One of the explanations advanced for the absence of a strong and stable relationship between household savings and interest rates is the presence of contractual and compulsory savings. Indeed, in a number of developing countries (e.g. Egypt, India, Malaysia, Philippines, Sri Lanka and Turkey) surpluses of compulsory provident and pension funds constitute an important part of household savings, sometimes reaching 25 per cent of the total. This is particularly true of countries where the social security system is relatively young, and where compulsory contributions to retirement funds consequently constitute the only source of savings for most of the working population. By contrast, contractual savings on a voluntary basis (such as life insurance) are very often small or negligible. Since in most developing countries surpluses of social security institutions are recorded as government revenues rather than as household savings, they should not introduce a significant bias in the estimates of the effects of interest rates on household savings.

There are no compelling reasons for household savings to rise in response to higher

interest rates. Even according to the conventional theory the impact depends on the relative strength of two contradictory effects. Higher interest rates imply a reduction of the present value of future goods, which should encourage the consumer to substitute future consumption for present consumption by raising current savings (the "substitution effect"). But they also raise expected future income from interest-earning financial wealth, which should raise current consumption, lowering current savings (the "income effect"). If the income effect dominates the substitution effect, savings will fall in response to a rise in the rate of interest.

The reaction of an individual to an increase in interest rates also depends on how his current income changes relative to his expected future non-interest income. If the increase in interest rates is accompanied by a decline in his current income relative to his expected future non-interest income, he may reduce his savings rate, and may even increase his level of consumption. In periods of falling per capita incomes and high inflation, it is known that small savers can react to interest rate increases by liquidating real assets (such as real estate) in order to invest in interest-yielding assets in an effort to prevent a fall in their accustomed level of consumption and to spend part of the nominal component of their interest income corresponding to inflation. This effect can be quite marked when financial liberalization is accompanied by stringent macroeconomic policies, particularly credit tightening with sharp declines in employment and wage income. Short-term bank deposits offering regular monthly incomes can then become instruments of dissaving rather than saving, and wealth can be further concentrated while small savings are eroded.

Moreover, individuals may in reality behave quite differently from the conventional assumptions. For instance, they may simply target a certain level of future income (rather than optimizing it by choosing carefully among all feasible intertemporal consumption paths as assumed in the conventional analysis), or save for the purpose of purchasing a durable physical asset (such as a house or a car). If so, a higher rate of interest can lower the rate of savings because the target level of future income or wealth can now be attained with a smaller amount of financial investment. For instance, in Japan and the Republic of Korea low interest rates combined with high real es-

71 Yoon-Je Cho and D. Khatkhate, "Lessons of financial liberalization in Asia. A comparative study", *World Bank Discussion Paper*, No. 50, Washington, D.C., 1989, p. 106.
72 See M. Nissanke, "Mobilizing domestic resources for African development and diversification. Structural impediments in the formal financial system", mimeo, Oxford, June 1990, p. 45.

FINANCIAL POLICIES AND SAVINGS IN LATIN AMERICA

- In *Mexico* the aggregate savings rate was considerably higher at the beginning of the 1980s than it had been during the 1970s although the real interest rate had become increasingly negative. Subsequently, financial policies caused a swing in real interest rates, in the order of 10 percentage points, to positive levels but savings remained depressed throughout the 1980s. Financial policies and higher interest rates in the 1980s were not capable of increasing private domestic savings to an extent that would compensate for the drop of public savings (more than 10 per cent of GDP between 1979-1980 and 1986) resulting from the rise of public sector interest payments on both domestic and foreign debt, and to allow for a rate of investment in line with the growth and development needs of the country.

- The aggregate savings rate in *Brazil* fell dramatically from the late 1970s until 1983, mainly on account of lower private savings in response to the economic crisis, which was expected by many households and enterprises to be short-lived. During the subsequent years the aggregate savings ratio recovered but still remained below its level of the late 1970s. With hyperinflation, private savings as conventionally measured almost doubled as a share of GDP between 1983 and the late 1980s, but much of this rise reflected the decline in the real value of net financial assets (i.e. government debt) held by the private sector. Indeed, while the public sector borrowing requirement soared, the decline in inflation-adjusted (operational) government savings was moderate since a very large proportion of government interest payments was due to meet the inflationary erosion of government debt.

- The financial reform undertaken in *Argentina* in the late 1970s led to a sharp rise in real interest rates from 1979 onwards, but the aggregate savings rate fell continuously, and halved by the mid-1980s. Substantially higher real interest rates caused severe problems for the indebted corporate sector and served to increase the number of insolvencies. As a consequence, the quality of banks' asset portfolios deteriorated, pushing interest rates further up in the absence of sufficient bank supervision, and causing the central bank to step in to protect small savers from the effects of bank insolvencies. Financial policies contributed to increased instability and to a sharp drop in private fixed capital formation. Capital flight has continued to be a major problem even though real returns on domestic financial assets have been rising.

- In *Chile* the financial liberalization in the 1970s led to sharp rises in real interest rates and a very fast expansion of the financial sector, which ended in a crash in the early 1980s. But the aggregate savings rate dropped markedly as high interest rates and restrictive policies reduced investment and GDP, with the investment/GDP ratio falling to 10 per cent in 1982-1984. The evolution of both investment and savings during the subsequent recovery suggests that it is not higher but lower interest rates which helped to restore the Chilean savings ratio, through their positive effect on investment and growth and by improving fiscal performance. Changes in the terms of trade and shifts in income distribution between wages and profits also seem to have had a major impact on savings.

tate prices have tended to raise household savings.

It is therefore very doubtful whether higher interest rates raise household savings. But there can be little doubt that they do affect debtors adversely, not only by discouraging new investment but also by damaging the balance sheets and even the financial viability of firms. The equity base of corporations in developing countries is generally very weak and their leverage (the debt-equity ratio) high. Moreover, maturities on loans are short, and the corporate debt is usually at variable rates. The corporate sector borrows heavily not only for investment but also for working capital. A sharp and sustained increase in real interest rates can therefore impose a very heavy burden. The impact is instantaneous, since it operates on the existing stock of debt; even without any new borrowing, the share of interest payments in the operating surplus can escalate suddenly.

The damage inflicted by liberalization of interest rates on corporate profits is very serious when liberalization is undertaken under conditions of rapid inflation and in the context of highly restrictive stabilization programmes. For one thing, interest rates increase very steeply and can push the interest bill of firms even above their wage bill. For another, sales will decline, pushing down revenues. Firms are thus doubly squeezed, like developing countries during the escalation of interest rates and global recession at the turn of the decade.

There is also a more permanent effect. In many countries the corporate sector saves more of its income than do households, and retained profits constitute an important source of business investment; in some countries retention ratios are 60-80 per cent. When income is permanently redistributed from the corporate sector to rentiers, the aggregate private savings rate will fall unless the interest rates have a particularly strong effect on the propensity to save of creditors, or unless the corporate sector can pass the increased debt burden onto wage earners.[73] Many attempts to offset the increase in debt servicing by declines in real wages have set off a wage-price spiral and disrupted social peace.

There is ample proof that high interest rates have had adverse effects on corporate profits and private savings. In the 1980s corporate profits in a number of highly-indebted developing countries (particularly the Southern Cone countries in Latin America, and in the Philippines and Yugoslavia) were hit first by sharp increases in interest rates on external debt, and then again when domestic interest rates were raised in an effort to achieve stabilization and structural adjustment. In a number of countries (Brazil, Chile, Philippines, Turkey, Yugoslavia) corporate profits and savings fell very drastically, depressing aggregate private savings, in some cases despite restoration of economic growth.

Much the same occurs with public savings. When interest-bearing public debt is large, higher interest rates can reduce public savings and increase budget deficits considerably. Since the increased interest payments by the Government will go partly into private consumption, unless government revenues are increased and/or other current expenditures are reduced, aggregate domestic savings can fall, and the indebtedness of the public sector can rise sharply. Public debt will also be pushed up by financial deregulation when that encompasses a shift in the financing of budget deficits from the central bank to private markets, even when the initial stock of interest-bearing debt is small.

The tax treatment of interest payments also influences the level and sectoral distribution of savings. In the 1980s there has been a general tendency to lighten taxation of financial incomes while continuing to allow interest payments by corporations to be deducted from taxable income. This has shifted part of the corporate interest burden onto the public sector and reduced its savings without generating a corresponding increase in private savings.

2. Interest rates and financial savings

Even if interest rate policies do not alter the propensity to save, they do have an important influence on the forms in which wealth is held. The range of assets available to savers depends on the level of economic and financial development, the extent and diversity of financial intermediaries and markets, the distribution of wealth, and the pattern of corporate ownership and finance. These assets will differ in liquidity, risk, return, storage and transaction costs, and the degree to which they provide a hedge against inflation.[74] A rise in interest rates as a result of financial liberalization may be expected to be followed by a switch towards bank deposits away from physical assets, international assets such as foreign currency and gold, and funds invested in unregulated, informal financial markets.

A rise in the size of the formal financial sector relative to GDP and investment (commonly referred to as "financial deepening") is generally thought to imply an improvement in the use of resources. However, this is not necessarily the case; whether it is so depends on how far it involves a genuine switch from unproductive to productive assets, and on the efficiency of financial intermediation, especially the banking system.

There can be little doubt that reducing unproductive commodity holdings and increasing the demand for financial assets instead can improve the use to which savings are put. However, for the most part, commodity stocks are held not because real interest rates on financial assets are negative but for other reasons. For one thing, they entail substantial

---

73 See Y. Akyüz, "Financial liberalization in developing countries: A neo-Keynesian approach", *Discussion Paper*, No. 36, UNCTAD, Geneva, March 1991.

74 In fact, one of the reasons why savings do not have a systematic relation with interest rates on financial assets (e.g. bank deposits, which are the single most important interest-bearing financial asset in developing countries) is the existence of physical and financial assets with different degrees of protection against inflation, since the return on such assets also influences the savings decisions. It can thus be expected that the greater the degree of influence of deposit rates on the allocation of savings among alternative assets, the smaller will be its influence on the volume of savings.

storage and transaction costs, making their own real rate of return typically negative. Interest rates on financial assets must become even more negative in terms of commodities for the latter to become a more attractive outlet for wealth. Secondly, under inflationary conditions prices of different commodities usually increase at different rates, an uncertainty which tends to reduce demand for commodities as a store of value.

Many studies of financial systems in sub-Saharan African countries have treated the large holdings of commodities by households as savings placed in unproductive physical assets, attributing them to low interest rate policies and estimated very high saving rates for rural areas (e.g. 50 per cent in rural Ghana, up to 60 per cent in parts of rural Kenya). However, these commodity stocks are a reflection not of portfolio decisions based on the interest rates prevailing, but of the nature of the production process and the fact that households and firms are not entirely separate entities. In the rural sector of low-income economies, not only savings but also incomes are largely in kind, and savings and investment decisions are closely connected. In agricultural activities, where income in kind is realized once or twice a year, the consumable produce must be stored to maintain the household and its livestock between¹ harvests. This stored produce is simply the necessary input of a production process. The amount of income saved each year should not be measured by the average stock of stored produce, but by the amount of remaining stock from the last harvest at the time the new harvest is in.

Decisions to save in physical assets are often explained by the non-monetization of agriculture in some areas of sub-Saharan Africa. Monetization indeed could transform savings in physical assets into financial savings, thus mobilizing them for national development. However, monetization of agriculture does not eliminate the need for society to hold stocks of produce necessary for the maintenance of the population; it may reduce the necessary volume of stocks and change the institution that does the storing. Monetization of agriculture in sub-Saharan Africa clearly cannot be brought about by interest rate policies, but by growth and the economic development of rural areas. There is ample evidence in this region that increases in deposit rates are often unable to induce liquidation of commodity stocks.

Land and real estate are other unproductive inflation hedges. However, reduced demand for land will lower its price (or the rate of its increase), not the quantity of it held; it will redistribute wealth but cannot release

savings. Much the same is also true for the existing stock of houses, except that an increase in interest rates, by lowering investment in new houses, can increase the bank deposits of households (in which case the financial deepening results not from a rise in household savings but from a fall in household investment). On the other hand, a shift from investment in housing to bank deposits (and even to business investment) will not necessarily represent an improvement in the way savings are used.

Gold and foreign currency are other hedges against inflation. It is very difficult to reduce demand for gold by raising interest rates where gold has traditionally been held as a safe store of value. Foreign currency holdings, by contrast, can be reduced by raising interest rates. However, many Governments have found it necessary also to legalize such holdings, typically in the form of foreign exchange accounts in domestic banks. Where this has been the case, the overall effect has often been to increase, rather than reduce, "dollarization" (see section F).

While it is true that low interest rates and the administrative allocation of credit encourage activity on informal markets, the main reasons for such markets lie elsewhere. In many poor countries, particularly in sub-Saharan Africa and Asia, informal markets render services which formal ones fail to do, dating back to colonial times, when banks concentrated on financing the export sector. They provide credit to small self-employed businesses and agricultural producers who are otherwise not catered to, and various services in physically remote areas without bank branches.

Informal lenders in low-income countries usually operate with their own capital, although in Africa collective revolving fund arrangements and mutual saving units are also widespread (see box 11). A second type of activity in informal markets involves financial intermediation - i.e. unlicensed brokers and bankers which collect deposits and lend (the "curb market"). These usually operate in urban areas and have access to bank credits. Their borrowers include corporate firms and their share in total credits can be very large. Raising bank lending rates often causes curb rates to rise sharply and generates instability in this market. However, financial liberalization does not always eliminate brokers because they are not subject to legal reserve and liquidity requirements, have lower overheads, and can easily evade taxes. In some countries, financial deregulation initially gave a major boost to such operators, encouraging unsound operations. For instance, in Turkey after the fi-

Box 11

INFORMAL FINANCIAL MARKETS IN DEVELOPING COUNTRIES

The informal financial sector consists of many institutions, including private bankers and brokers, who intermediate between ultimate borrowers and lenders, and moneylenders and pawnbrokers, who primarily lend on their own account. There are also a number of mutual fund institutions, such as rotating savings and credit associations (ROSCAs) and *susu* collectors.

ROSCAs are found in East, South-East, and South Asia, and in Africa, as are mutual savings groups, whose members make fixed contributions to a common savings pool with access to credit allocated according to a rule, such as the order of participation, drawing lots, auctions, etc. *Susu* collecting is a system whereby a certain person visits shops, homes, etc. to collect daily deposits, and at the end of a specified period (e.g. one to six months in Ghana) returns to each depositor his accumulated savings, less a payment to the collector for his services. No interest is paid on the deposits. A member may obtain an overdraft - with or without interest - and repay by means of daily deposits. The collector may use the fund to finance his own trade. In Ghana relatively large companies have also engaged in this business.

Moneylenders are the principal lending institutions in the informal sector. They usually are also engaged in other activities (land ownership, trade, etc.). Pawnshops are widespread in South-East Asia. They are licensed in Malaysia and Thailand, and government-owned in Indonesia. Unlicensed private bankers and brokers appear as a modern reaction to the deficiencies of the banking sector. They receive deposits, paying higher interest rates on them than banks, and they give loans, thereby performing intermediation. They are known to collude with banks to provide repayment guarantees to lenders (as in the Republic of Korea) and to market such instruments as certificates of deposits (as in Turkey). Their borrowers include corporate firms without access to bank credit.

Estimates of the size of informal financial markets are rough because of the unorganized, informal nature of the activities and the preference for discretion on the part of agents. One study on India estimated that as much as 20 per cent of total commercial credit outstanding in urban areas was accounted for by informal markets. Seventy-five per cent of rural credit in Malaysia in 1981-1982 was from the informal sector. A recent study of Malawi estimates that the credit extended by the informal financial sector to the private sector exceeds that extended by the formal financial sector. In Ghana, one study found that 45 per cent of financial savings in urban areas were placed in informal financial institutions. [1] In the Philippines they are estimated to account for a credit volume of between 30 per cent and 50 per cent of that of the banking system.

In some countries, lack of access to banks and high transaction costs involved in keeping savings in the formal sector explain why financial savings flow to the informal financial sector. According to one study, the average number of people per bank branch in Zambia was over 54,000. [2] In Ghana, it was around 30,000. The lack of an adequate network of bank branches creates high transaction costs for depositors in terms of time spent, and the lack of modern banking technology adds to the transaction costs. In Ghana, especially in large centres, as much as one to two hours may be required to withdraw cash, or make a deposit. Minimum limits for opening deposit accounts are also a factor in redirecting savings to the informal sector.

Moreover, there are problems of access and transaction costs in obtaining credit from formal financial institutions. Banks are reluctant to extend credit to small enterprises because they consider them too risky, and because allocating credit in small amounts increases operating costs. Minimum deposit requirements for credit, stiff collateral requirements and lengthy, arduous application procedures discourage many small and medium entrepreneurs from applying to formal institutions for credit, and consequently from depositing their savings there. In some sub-Saharan countries many farmers cannot use the customary land they till as collateral because it is not marketable. As a result, much of the potential credit demand is not directed to the formal financial sector, and this also diverts financial savings to the informal sector. The rural savings invested in formal institutions are mostly siphoned off to finance the corporate sector in urban areas.

In informal financial institutions transaction costs are low. The *susu* collector and the moneylender are readily accessible, local people who can assess credit risks; the collector himself visits the depositors. Transactions are simple and do not take time. Neither are there difficult

Box 11 (concluded)

procedures for obtaining loans, due to the web of personal relations and social sanctions surrounding the contact. These relations enable loans to be granted without the information costs and the collateral requirements that encumber bank operations. In addition, informal financial institutions are able to accommodate the borrowers' special needs concerning repayment conditions, etc. There are no restrictions on the use of the loans.

The most important attraction of informal institutions for savers is that placing deposits therein ensures the availability of credit. Many informal financial institutions can therefore compete with banks and thrive without paying interest on deposits. Interest may or may not have to be paid on loans from mutual fund institutions. When it is, however, the rate is usually somewhat higher than that of formal institutions.

The informal institutions are not capable of maturity transformation and therefore do not provide medium- or long-term financing. Although their borrowers are not always the same as those in the formal sector, excess demand for credit in the latter can easily spill over into the informal sector. Moreover, the two sectors can be linked in a variety of ways, leading to flows in both directions. The Ghanaian *susu* collector who places idle funds in deposits at banks is one link and serves as an intermediary for the mobilization of small savings. Evidence also shows that moneylenders and private bankers intermediate between formal and informal sectors, relending funds obtained from banks in the curb market. Studies of informal finance in India and the Republic of Korea indicate that interest rates and credit volume in the informal sector are affected by monetary policy. Informal markets can, however, create instability for the entire financial system if formal institutions collude with private bankers and brokers in Ponzi-type financing of high-risk business, as happened in Turkey in 1982-1983.

---

1 See C. Chipeta, "Mobilizing domestic savings for African development and industrialization: A case study of Malawi: part I", E. Aryeetey, Y. Asante, F. Gockel, A. Kyei, "Mobilizing domestic savings for African development and diversification: a Ghanaian case-study", papers presented at a Workshop on Mobilizing Domestic Savings for African Development and Diversification (International Development Centre, Queen Elizabeth House, University of Oxford, 16-20 July 1990).

2 See S. Musokotwane, "Domestic resources mobilization and development in Zambia, 1970-1986", *ibid.*

---

nancial liberalization of the early 1980s, brokers sold CDs issued by banks at large discounts and lent to high-risk business. Because of the increasing share of non-performing loans this process degenerated into Ponzi financing (i.e. obtaining the funds to pay interest by borrowing) and eventually broke down, making it necessary to liquidate a number of banks; the losses amounted to 2.5 per cent of GDP.

Since savings placed in the informal sector assures a small- or medium-size enterprise some access to credit, it is not always willing to shift to banks when deposit rates are raised; this has been observed frequently in sub-Saharan Africa. When funds are shifted on a large scale from informal to formal markets, the cost and availability of finance to small producers, farmers and traders can deteriorate considerably.

Being unable to extend long-term credit, "curb markets" are not the best solution to the problem of financing small-scale business. However, the criticism that they finance risky projects in return for high-risk premiums is no more than a description of the specific financial service these markets provide. Therefore, policies that shift funds from the informal to the formal sector should be accompanied by measures to improve considerably the access of small- and medium-size enterprises to formal financial institutions.

It is important to bear in mind that "financial deepening" does not always indicate an increase in savings or a desirable shift from other forms of holding wealth. Indeed, it can also be a symptom of a deterioration of the finances of the corporate and public sectors, and an accumulation of short-term debt by them for purposes other than the financing of new investment. This can happen when a rise in interest rates redistributes income in favour of rentiers, forcing the debtor sectors to borrow more, thereby raising the stock of financial assets and liabilities relative to output and investment. "Deepening" can also result from Ponzi financing. Financial deepening simultaneously with a fall in savings and investment has been experienced by a number of countries where financial liberalization redistributed income in favour of creditors and encouraged distress borrowing. There is no reason to view in a positive light an increase in the debtor-creditor relationships if it is not associated with rising levels of production and investment: it may indicate, rather, increased fragility in the financial system.

It is also dangerous to prescribe interest rate policies without reference to the specific macroeconomic and institutional environment. Fixed rules on real interest rates in developing countries are likely to prove no more useful or sensible than those on money supply growth have proved to be in industrialized countries.

Variations in inflation and interest rates tend to have a major influence on the behaviour of savers regardless of the level of the real interest rate. Indeed, an important impediment to resource mobilization in devel-

oping countries is macroeconomic instability and unpredictability. An environment of high and volatile inflation and sudden changes in key prices shortens the planning horizons of savers and investors, and encourages hedging and speculation rather than productive investment. Real interest rates can then turn very negative, but simply pushing up interest rates to match inflation can make matters worse: by reducing income and increasing price instability it can reduce savings and further distort resource allocation. When inflation is high, real interest rates need to be raised not so much by escalating nominal rates as by reducing inflation. On the other hand, when there is a reasonable degree of macroeconomic stability, and relatively little uncertainty and unpredictability, variations in the real rate of interest may not exercise a strong or systematic influence on the level and allocation of savings.

C. Efficiency, instability and regulation of finance

Non-bank financial intermediaries and capital markets are generally underdeveloped or non-existent in developing countries, where the main form of financial savings is bank deposits. The effect of interest rate policies on the use of resources thus largely depends on the efficiency of the banking system.

It is useful at this point to refer to the two concepts of efficiency discussed in chapter I, namely allocative and cost efficiency. Even if financial markets could be counted on to distribute finance to projects with the highest prospective profits, in developing countries this would not be enough to ensure allocative efficiency because private and social rates of return often diverge widely. Externalities, in particular the dynamic benefits of investment, are particularly important in the development process, but are not always reflected in the prices on which profit and loss calculations are made by private agents. Besides, the market structure in developing countries bears little resemblance to the competitive paradigm, with many imperfections and "missing" markets. Consequently, many Governments find it necessary, in the context of industrial policy, to intervene in the allocating and pricing of financial resources in developing countries (see section E).

The proportion of non-performing loans of the banking system and its profits are sometimes used as an indicator of allocative efficiency. This is appropriate when private and social rates of return are identical, but not when private returns differ significantly from social returns. For instance, external financial liberalization has often swollen bank profits by stimulating speculative inflows of capital (see section F). Or non-performing loans may be high because the Government has forced banks to lend on preferential terms to certain sectors and projects having high social but low private rates of return without providing commensurate subsidization.

As noted previously, the degree of cost efficiency in the banking system can be gauged by the spread between lending and deposit rates.[75] The size of the spread and the share of non-performing loans can be interrelated because banks can often pass the cost of bad loans onto borrowers, pushing otherwise viable borrowers into insolvency and increasing the number of non-performing loans. Almost all episodes of financial liberalization involving deregulation of interest rates and greater autonomy for banks in the allocation of credits have been followed by a rise in the proportion of non-performing loans in bank portfolios and widespread insolvency, and an increase in the

[75] The spread is also influenced by certain legal requirements regarding reserve and liquid asset holdings by banks, which are usually high in developing countries primarily because they are a source of financing for the Government. These ratios are typically lowered as part of financial liberalization.

spread (e.g. the Philippines, the Southern Cone countries, Turkey and Yugoslavia, though not in the Republic of Korea).

In some cases, this has been because liberalization was undertaken in adverse macroeconomic conditions: external shocks, declines in external resources, increased macroeconomic instability, reduced growth, and monetary restriction had together greatly weakened the balance sheets of the corporate sector and financial institutions. But experience shows that an equally important reason has been the presence of serious structural weaknesses in the financial sector. Because large non-financial corporations are typically able to exert strong influence over banks, the latter tend to concentrate their lending on a small number of firms, which increases their own vulnerability and diminishes financial discipline over the enterprise. Consequently, corporate distress borrowing and Ponzi financing are much more common in developing countries. They become especially visible and problematic during episodes of financial liberalization.

In many countries, interlocking ownership and practices of collusion survived or increased after liberalization, and the control of financial intermediaries by their main borrowers proved to be an important obstacle to efficiency in the financial sector, contributing significantly to the deterioration of bank portfolios. This institutional weakness has also raised the cost and reduced the availability of finance for other borrowers, and eroded confidence in domestic financial institutions and assets, thereby making foreign exchange assets more attractive.

Another structural weakness in developing countries is the weakness of prudential regulations and lack of effective supervision over banks. In many countries the Government imposes strict restrictions (e.g. on the acquisition of real estate, on lending to a single enterprise, or acquisition of shares in non-financial corporations) but fails to implement them. Legal provisions against bad assets are often either absent or ignored. Non-compliance with legal reserve requirements is widespread, not always because they are especially high, but because the monetary authorities are unable to impose sufficient penalties against non-compliance.

By contrast, many Governments have been all too ready to engage in financial rescue operations. The resulting moral hazard is often made worse by deposit insurance schemes designed to attract savings into banks. Banks often incur very little costs for the insurance coverage while having all the incentives to raise deposits at very high rates in order to invest in high-return, high-risk projects. Financial liberalization under such conditions thus often leads to excessive risk taking, speculation, and instability.

This discussion points to the dangers of undertaking reforms in an unstable macroeconomic environment and, more important, to the need for institutional reform. Experience has shown that increasing the role of the price mechanism in the allocation of resources will result in considerable waste in the absence of appropriate market institutions and supervisory mechanisms. All financial liberalization episodes in developing countries lacking them have ended in a financial crash.

In only very few countries were these problems avoided. The Republic of Korea followed a gradual and cautious approach, introducing financial liberalization after attaining stability and a considerable degree of economic and institutional development. Structural trade deficits and the foreign exchange shortage had been eliminated through a successful process of industrialization involving both import substitution and export growth; the savings ratio had been raised considerably, mainly through a sustained and rapid growth in incomes, especially corporate profits; monetary and fiscal discipline and price stability had been attained on a durable basis; and structural weaknesses in corporate finance and financial fragility had been reduced. Besides, even though interest rates were deregulated and directed credits phased out, a number of less visible levers of policy (e.g. "window guidance", "moral suasion", etc.) continued to be used both to avoid high interest rates and financial instability and to channel credit to targeted industries.

D. Capital markets

There is now much interest in developing countries, including low-income and least developed ones, in instituting and promoting domestic capital markets, and policies in this respect increasingly form part of the structural adjustment programmes supported by international financial agencies. In some countries one of the main reasons for privatizing public enterprises is precisely to promote capital markets. It is believed that the development of domestic capital markets can help overcome some of the structural deficiencies in the financial system. In particular, equity and bond issues can reduce the vulnerability of firms to sharp changes in the cost and availability of bank credit and provide them with more predictable, longer-term finance, while secondary markets in securities can accord savers liquidity. Moreover, capital markets provide competition for banks and other financial intermediaries, and thus reduce inefficiency.

These considerations are often invoked to argue in favour of maintaining tight credit policies in developing countries, on the grounds that cheap credit policies are the main reason for firms' excessive reliance on bank credits and aversion to equity issues. However, the nature of ownership of corporations is often a much more important impediment. Firms are often owned by families that do not wish to dilute their control. Besides, the owners are often unwilling to disclose the information and accept the supervision entailed by going public. Moreover, large firms tend to prefer bank to equity financing when they can obtain preferential treatment from banks under their control. In some countries, many large firms are transnational companies with little debt to the host country's financial markets and even less interest in broadening their equity base there.

Rather than high interest rates, a mix of restrictions and incentives may be needed to induce large firms to go public, including, for instance, limits on debt-equity ratios, tax exemptions and priority in government contracts for publicly-quoted joint stock companies. In the Republic of Korea, where restrictions and incentives of this kind have been applied, capital markets and equity finance have indeed emerged as serious alternatives to bank loans and have allowed firms to broaden their ownership. In Turkey, where the equity market has also developed rapidly in the 1980s, such direct incentives and restrictions have been generally absent. New issues by the corporate sector increased significantly only after the equity market experienced a speculative surge, greatly reducing the cost of equity finance (see box 12). In most other countries activity has been concentrated on secondary transactions, with few new issues and no tendency for corporate leverage to decline.

While capital markets may help stabilize corporate finance, they can also generate serious instability of other kinds. Since participants in secondary markets tend to be motivated by considerations of short-term capital gain, asset valuations tend to be extremely volatile, and do not gauge the rate of return on investment in productive capacity. These markets also tend to amplify disturbances in the rest of the economy. The problem of inefficiency and instability in capital markets can be serious, especially in developing countries, where the general macroeconomic environment tends to be more volatile. In some of the newly emerging capital markets prices have in fact been extremely erratic and subject to very large swings. One reason is that by removing credit constraints on many institutions and individuals financial liberalization has often triggered an increase in speculative activity. For instance, among fast-growing capital markets such as New Zealand's, which had developed well before the financial reform, increased speculative activity in the secondary market caused stock prices to rise during 1985-1987 even faster than in most of the world's major stock markets, and to fall, again far more than elsewhere, after October 1987. The speculative economy had become over-leveraged and a number of smaller financial institutions went bankrupt; one of the four major banks had to be rescued by the Government in an effort to prevent a financial collapse. Similarly, in Brazil between 1982 and 1985 share prices rose five-fold (in dollar terms); two years later they had dwindled to 28 per cent of their 1985 value. In Mexico in the first nine months of 1987 share prices rose six-fold, but following Black Monday in October 1987 they fell to a tenth of their pre-crash level. In Taiwan Province of China, which has the largest stock market in the third world, the index rose by 330 per cent between 1987 and February 1990, but fell to a quarter of its value by September 1990.

Another problem is that irregularities such as insider trading and fraud are often widespread and the administrative capacity to undertake effective supervision often weak. This makes it essential to strengthen the institutional and regulatory framework when incentives and restrictions aimed at developing capital markets are introduced.

The main question, however, is how much to expect from policies to develop capital markets. A close inspection of how modern industrialization has been financed raises questions on the relevance of the "Anglo-American" system of finance primarily based on direct security issues rather than bank debt (a subject already discussed in chapter I above). In Japan and the Republic of Korea, for instance, the corporate sectors have, for most of their history, relied on bank credits to meet their borrowing needs and operated with very high leverage; only recently have they started to reduce leverage through capital market funding. Corporate finance in Germany has

NEWLY EMERGING CAPITAL MARKETS - THE REPUBLIC OF KOREA AND TURKEY

The capital markets in the Republic of Korea and Turkey have gained importance in recent years among the "emerging capital markets". In terms of market capitalization the market of the former country is one of the largest of the group, while the Turkish market capitalization increased by more than 200 per cent in 1990, surpassing the levels reached in Greece and Portugal. The two markets have developed under policy regimes which differ considerably in the role they assign to government intervention.

The *Republic of Korea* embarked on a strategy to develop the domestic capital market in response to the increased stringency of external finance in the 1980s. The Ministry of Finance prevented companies from borrowing overseas and enforced debt/equity ceilings, thereby obliging the corporate sector to use the capital market for its finance needs, rescinded a regulation that required all share issues to be offered at par, gave permission for securities companies to increase their paid-in capital, and allowed other non-bank financial institutions such as insurance companies to hold securities in their portfolios. The authorities also took steps to spread the ownership of securities among small savers. They allowed 5 per cent of a company's new issues of debentures or stocks to be reserved for its shop-floor employees for sale at par value. On the other hand, the authorities limited the maximum number of market dealers to 30, which allows them to exercise influence over market behaviour.

As a result of these measures, the capital market gradually expanded, with the number of shares traded increasing more than four-fold from 1985 to 1989. The number of companies listed on the Stock Exchange was more than 660 by the end of 1990. By 1989 Employee Stock Ownership Associations covered some 700,000 workers in over 600 companies. The number of minor stockholders is now around seven million. The Composite Index of the Korean Stock Exchange rose by 571 per cent from 1985 to the middle of 1989, whereas consumer prices increased by 19 per cent. In November 1989 the index suffered a fall of 6.6 per cent, but apparently as a result of intervention through securities dealers, trust companies, insurance brokers, etc., it regained its original level within a week.

In *Turkey* a Capital Market Board (CMB) was established and protective legislation was put into effect after the financial liberalization and the brokers' crisis of the early 1980s. CMB was authorized to approve all public offerings of private sector companies, and to supervise joint stock companies. In 1987 bond rates were freed. Investment and development banks were allowed to issue short-term bills, and non-financial joint stock companies to issue commercial paper with maturities up to one year. Corporations were allowed to revalue their assets, to distribute stock dividends and to make rights issues. Dividends and capital gains were exempted from personal taxation. However, private firms were reluctant to submit to disclosure by going public, and the tax deductibility of interest payments by corporations made debt financing a more attractive option. As a result, the equity market remained rudimentary in terms of new issues and the volume of transactions.

This state of affairs began to change in 1989 with a surge of secondary transactions in the equity market, which drove the Istanbul Stock Exchange Index (ISEI) up by 770 per cent in the two years 1989 and 1990, while consumer prices increased around 160 per cent in the same period. The rise in the index coincided with negative real interest rates on deposits and an appreciation of the Turkish lira. The rise of the price/earnings ratio to 31.0 in September 1990 (compared to 19.1 in the Republic of Korea, 22.0 in Taiwan Province of China and 15.5 in Portugal) increased the flow of private sector new equity issues. The number of firms quoted and the number of licensed dealers and secondary market transactions have increased rapidly, and an informal secondary market has emerged for transactions of small volume. However, there is a high degree of concentration: ten large company shares account for three quarters of the market capitalization. The high price/earnings ratio has made equity financing cheaper. Consequently, firms quoted on the Exchange have been able to raise substantial equity capital and lower their leverage without any loss of ownership control. The increase in new equity issues appears to have anchored the ISEI at around 3500-4000 (January 1986 = 100).

also traditionally relied on bank credits not only for financing but also for funding investment, and the involvement of banks in industry has been important both in ensuring financial discipline and in reducing financing costs. Low-cost finance has given enterprises in these three countries an additional competitive advantage in world markets (see section E.2). In all of them, particularly the two late-comers to industrialization, financial policies have been an integral part of industrial policy. In those two countries the Government has exercised considerable control over the cost and allocation of finance to different industries; such controls are much easier to operate in a bank-based financial system than in a system based on capital markets.

Although capital markets provide long-term financing, they tend to value the enterprise on the basis of its short-term financial performance. By contrast (and as already noted in chapter I) bank-based financing of investment along German and Japanese lines has the great advantage of permitting the enterprise to take a long view on the basis of a reliable and predictable supply of finance. This is a particularly important consideration for developing countries, where most of the benefits of investment are realized over the long term via a learning process.

But at least two conditions must be met for a controlled bank-based system to work well. First, monetary stability is essential, since a bank-based system integrates finance with the monetary system. Second, finance must be effectively dovetailed with industrial policy so as to ensure that support is reciprocated by performance; otherwise close links between banks and industry will result in favourable treatment being given to inefficient, stagnant firms and not to efficient and dynamic ones. Most developing countries may be well advised to concentrate their energies in this direction, rather than pin their hope on developing capital markets. More industrialized developing countries may be able to combine the advantages of capital markets and bank finance by means of investment banks. These could be publicly owned or alternatively private (or mixed) enterprises. In either case, they could serve as an instrument simultaneously to assure long-term funds to priority sectors while imposing discipline on borrowers. The banks' lending levels could be supplemented by borrowing from the capital markets. Besides lending, the investment banks could help smaller corporations to gain access to domestic bond and equity markets, and improve their terms of access.

E. Internal financial liberalization, trade and industrialization

Internal financial liberalization means letting financial markets decide the allocation of financial resources and the level and pattern of interest rates on the basis of their own assessment of risks and rewards. In practice, this implies not only higher interest rates but also little or no direction of credit or preferential rates and subsidies for either public or private entities. It typically involves lessening or ending restrictions on bank portfolios, such as compulsory holding of government securities and minimum lending requirements to certain sectors and activities and differential loan rates. The impact of liberalization on resource allocation can have significant consequences for trade and industrialization, since finance is, after trade policy, perhaps the most important policy area for the performance of industry and trade.

1. Interest rates, trade and macroeconomic stability

In a developing country in a balance of payments disequilibrium internal financial liberalization is said to help raise production of export goods and import substitutes, making it possible to adjust external payments without significantly lowering domestic production. It is argued that higher interest rates reduce the demand for non-traded goods and their prices relative to traded goods (prices of the latter being determined by world prices, the exchange rate and the degree of protection). In short, their effects are like those of a devaluation. Provided that the resource shift in response to the change in relative prices and the real exchange rate takes place without friction, aggregate domestic output will not be changed. While some economists believe that liberalization is of direct help in stabilizing an economy and controlling inflation, most see a need to reduce budget deficits and inflation before deregulating internal financial markets.[76] This view is based on the failure of the "stabilization through liberalization" experiment of the Southern Cone countries in Latin America in the 1970s and early 1980s.

However, the immediate macroeconomic effects of financial liberalization may not be favourable to external adjustment for two reasons that are commonly overlooked. First, by raising costs, higher interest rates adversely affect the supply side, especially when the corporate sector is highly indebted. For this reason, orthodox policies have often proved to be unexpectedly stagflationary.

Second, and more important, imperfections in domestic goods markets can produce perverse results. Many firms in non-traded goods sectors enjoy monopoly power because of the small size of the domestic market, and are able to pass on the increased cost of finance by raising prices. The ability of firms producing for export to protect themselves in this way being much more limited, the increase in the nominal interest rate will reduce their profit margin instead and perhaps drive them out of business. The increase in interest rates may therefore act like a currency appreciation rather than a depreciation, and discourage investment in exports and import substitutes. It could in theory be offset by currency devaluation. However, strong doses of financial liberalization and devaluation taken together can be dangerous, particularly in debt-distressed countries which have already taken devaluation to the limit of tolerance in order to bring about a massive balance of payments adjustment and to compensate for trade liberalization. If the currency is depreciated, interest rates, prices of non-traded goods and wages will be pushed up. Strong wage resistance is very likely to be triggered, driving the economy into an inflationary spiral. The consequent distributional struggle

between wages, rentier incomes, and profits in traded and non-traded goods sectors can be extremely intense and disruptive. Perhaps it is for these reasons that many Governments have chosen to maintain preferential lending to export sectors when they have deregulated interest rates (see box 13).

2. Financial subsidies and industrialization

Almost all modern examples of industrialization have been accompanied by a considerable degree of government intervention in the determination of the cost and availability of finance in the pursuit of selective industrial policies. Such differentiation is still practised even in many successful industrialized countries as an instrument of sectoral and regional policy. Success in overcoming productivity handicaps in international markets has often stemmed not so much from lower wages as from selective incentives and subsidies; indeed, lower wages can lower productivity. Government intervention in the financial sector is needed to ensure that firms facing a prolonged learning process are not deterred by a lack of funds; in developing countries subsidized credit can mean the difference between establishing new industries or not, rather than the difference between financing more or less lucrative projects. Because of the problems of calculating the risks involved, financial intermediaries are naturally wary of financing new investment, especially by firms that are new and highly leveraged, and relatively small by world standards and thus unable to reap economies of scope and scale.

Indeed, such preferential credits made an important contribution to the successful industrialization of some Asian countries during the 1960s and 1970s. Contrary to widespread perception, interest rates were generally "suppressed" under tight ceilings, often resulting in negative real rates, and preferential rates were even lower. Two economists at the World Bank have found that in Thailand, which has generally pursued liberal economic policies, the *ex post* year-end figures for the real ceiling rates on various deposits and loans taken as a group

---

[76] If higher interest rates did, indeed, serve to foster trade adjustment, switching the financing of the deficit towards the financial markets would be more favourable than reducing its level. It is also inconsistent to argue in favour of liberalization only in the context of low inflation and to suggest that it will raise savings by substantially (and permanently) raising real interest rates; in practice big jumps in real interest rates only occur when inflation is rapid.

Box 13

FINANCIAL SUBSIDIES AND EXPORT PERFORMANCE - TURKEY AND THE REPUBLIC OF KOREA

- In *Turkey* interest rates on export credits were kept at around 20-25 per cent during the first half of the 1980s, when non-preferential lending rates had almost reached three-digit figures. The importance of credit subsidies for exports can be seen from the fact that export credits rose to over 40 per cent of the total value of exports. In the absence of such credits, it can be estimated that the Turkish lira would have had to depreciate by at least another 10 per cent in real terms. The evidence suggests that credit subsidies played an important role in export expansion during the first half of the 1980s. When in 1985 the Government eliminated preferential export credits partly as a result of a strong export performance and payments position, and partly due to external pressures for further liberalization, exports fell; preferential export credits were reintroduced at the end of 1986. It is particularly notable that the effect of abolishing credit subsidies for exports was much stronger than that of abolishing export tax rebates in 1990; in the latter instance exports did not fall even though there had been widespread over-invoicing.

- In the *Republic of Korea* preferential treatment of certain export industries was maintained after financial markets were liberalized in the 1980s, although liberalization was undertaken under much more favourable conditions with respect to the external payments position, growth and price stability than are typical of recent episodes of liberalization in developing countries; consequently, a significant increase in real interest rates was avoided. All preferential lending rates were ostensibly abolished in 1982 and the loan rates were unified, and there was a further move to liberalization in 1988 when interest rates were officially deregulated. However, in practice the Government "has tried to prevent a decline in export activity by arranging for certain exporters to receive preferential credit in a form other than subsidized export financing. This form of credit is the same form reserved for targeted industries. Targeted industries receive preferential credit in the form of access to bank loans which ... carry below-market interest rates, even if not the super 'preferential' ones they once carried." *1*

1 A. Amsden and Yoon-Dae Euh, "Republic of Korea's financial reform: What are the lessons?", *Discussion Paper*, No. 30, UNCTAD, Geneva, April 1990, p. 16.

---

were positive in only 24 out of 52 instances in the period 1970-1982.[77] Similarly, in the Republic of Korea "bank loan and deposit rates ... were consistently negative in real terms throughout the 1974-1980 period",[78] and targeted industries received loans at lower rates. Thus, "throughout most of the twenty-five years of Korean industrial expansion, long-term credit has been allocated by the Government to selected firms at negative real interest rates in order to stimulate specific industries".[79] Directed allocation of credits at preferential rates has also been applied to foreign capital tapped through official channels. Interest rate subsidies constituted the single most important incentive for sectors with export targets,

particularly to highly capital-intensive industries, which also had priority in credit rationing. Such subsidies amounted to 10 per cent of GDP in the 1970s. Early in 1991, the Government of the Republic introduced a plan to increase specialization among the country's large conglomerates (*chaebol*) by providing credit incentives to concentrate on a smaller number of activities, and to tighten existing credit controls on the others, on the grounds that more focused investment in technology was needed to increase competitiveness in international markets.

Evidence from developed countries also points to the importance of the cost of finance

---

[77] J.A. Hanson and C.R. Neal, "Interest rate policies in selected developing countries, 1970-1982", *World Bank Staff Working Paper*, No. 753, 1985, p. 137.

[78] Yoon-Je Cho and D. Khatkhate, "Lessons of financial liberalization in Asia. A comparative study", *World Bank Discussion Paper*, No. 50, 1989, p. 33.

[79] A. Amsden, *Asia's Next Giant. South Korea and Late Industrialization* (New York: Oxford University Press, 1989), p. 144.

for international competitiveness. As already noted in chapter I, international comparisons of cost of capital by the staff of the Federal Reserve Bank of New York indicate that corporations in the United States and United Kingdom suffer from a decided disadvantage in relation to those in Japan and Germany. In the latter two countries, where corporations are more leveraged, this advantage derives primarily from the lower cost of debt. The reasons include greater macroeconomic stability (i.e. stable growth and greater price stability) and the greater integration of industry with banking. In the United States, capital costs are now thought to have contributed to declining competitiveness both in industry and in international banking. It has been argued that lower capital costs have enabled Japanese firms to undertake longer-term projects whereas United States firms have been deterred from investing in research and development by the high cost of finance and the need for quick payoffs to investment.[80]

Clearly, there have been significant differences in success in directing credit and differentiating interest rates between the East and South-East Asian countries, on the one hand, and Latin American countries, on the other. The differences have been partly due to the selection of correct priorities, i.e. skill in "picking winners", and determining the nature and extent of subsidies needed. But even more important has been the extent to which South and South-East Asian Governments have made the provision of support and protection conditional upon good performance. Success came where the Government saw to it that its support and protection were really needed, and were actually used for the purposes intended, and not simply to sustain higher levels of profits and wages.

F. External financial liberalization, trade and competitiveness

1. Financial openness in developing countries

External financial liberalization consists of policy actions that serve to increase the degree of financial openness, i.e. the ease with which residents can acquire assets and liabilities denominated in foreign currencies and non-residents can operate in national financial markets (including the enjoyment of market access by foreign banks, discussed in part three, chapter IV, section C). This is not exactly the same thing as liberalization of capital-account transactions between residents and non-residents, since financial openness also includes financial transactions and debtor-creditor relationships among residents denominated in foreign currencies. The latter type of transaction, which is an important part of finance and banking, has international characteristics with effects on the national economy similar to conventional cross-border financial transactions.

In developing countries the real degree of financial openness does not always correspond to the restrictiveness of regulations ostensibly in force because the latter are not always fully implemented. Moreover, because financial institutions are underdeveloped, many financial transactions take place in informal, curb markets, which makes it relatively easy to circumvent regulations. Furthermore, a number of specific factors (such as high earnings from tourism and workers' remittances, the presence of transnational corporations, and physical proximity to hard-currency areas) can increase the ease of access to foreign currency and financial transfers abroad through informal channels. Nevertheless, the Government's policies and its resolve and capacity to implement rules and regulations play the most important role. It is therefore no coincidence that there has often been a close inverse correlation between capital flight and the degree of restrictiveness on external capital transactions.

Three broad areas of external financial liberalization may be distinguished. First, allowing residents, especially financial and non-

---

[80] See R.N. McCauley and S.A. Zimmer, "Explaining international differences in the cost of capital", *Federal Reserve Bank of New York Quarterly Review*, Summer 1989, and "Bank cost of capital and international competitiveness", *ibid.*, Winter 1991. See also J.M. Poterba, "Comparing the cost of capital in the United States and Japan: A survey of methods", in the latter source.

financial corporations, to borrow freely in international financial markets (and non-residents to lend freely in domestic markets) for reasons other than financing exports and imports. Second, allowing residents to transfer capital and to hold financial assets abroad (and non-residents to issue liabilities in domestic financial markets). Third, allowing debtor-creditor relations among residents in foreign currencies such as bank deposits and lending in foreign currencies (which often accompanies freedom to buy and sell foreign currency).

These three types of operation have not been liberalized in a strict sequence. The first wave of external liberalization in developing countries generally consisted of allowing the private sector to borrow abroad. The Southern Cone experience is the best-known, and was set in a broad programme of liberalization (see box 14). However, external borrowing by residents was liberalized also in a number of countries where domestic financial markets continued to be highly regulated (e.g. Turkey in the 1970s, Yugoslavia, and the Philippines). Resident banks were often involved as intermediaries between international capital markets and domestic borrowers. In countries with a sizeable flow of workers' remittances, a particularly important form of such borrowing took place, namely foreign currency deposits offering attractive terms and carrying government guarantees. In almost all these episodes there was a massive build-up of foreign exchange liabilities by private financial and non-financial corporations which contributed significantly to the subsequent debt crisis and payments difficulties.

Although a few developing countries have adopted capital account convertibility - some to an extent not found in most industrialized countries - most maintain many restrictions on transferring capital and holding financial assets abroad. However, there has been a tendency to permit and encourage residents to hold foreign exchange deposits with banks at home, both in countries where such deposits were originally permitted for migrant workers and in others with an acute foreign exchange shortage. The interest rates offered on such deposits have usually been above world levels; deposits are highly liquid; even sight deposits earn considerable interest; and they are much more easily accessible than their counterparts in most industrial countries, where they are subject to minimum limits and/or charges and commissions.

The purpose of introducing foreign currency deposits is generally to prevent capital flight and to draw holdings of foreign currency into the banking system. It is difficult to check capital flight by simply offering interest-bearing foreign exchange deposits at home so long as the underlying economic and political situation remains unstable and uncertain and the Government is unable or unwilling to restrict capital outflows. On the other hand, it is possible to draw foreign cash balances into the banking system, thereby providing sizeable foreign exchange resources. However, the effect is to increase the importance of foreign currency in the domestic monetary system, i.e. encourage currency substitution and dollarization of the economy. In many developing countries where such deposits were introduced, there was not just a once-and-for-all shift from holding foreign banknotes; rather, foreign exchange deposits have grown continuously and rapidly, and even come to exceed domestic currency deposits. Between 40 per cent and 60 per cent of total deposits in Bolivia, Costa Rica, Philippines, Turkey, Uruguay and Yugoslavia are in foreign exchange accounts. Even in London the share of total bank claims (including inter-bank claims) on residents in foreign currencies barely exceeds 20 per cent. Morover, some developing countries have started issuing dollar-denominated or dollar-indexed paper in domestic markets, and even quoting certain prices of certain public sector goods in dollars. It can therefore be concluded that the degree of financial openness of many developing countries is much greater than indicated by the degree of capital account convertibility.

2. External capital flows

Financial openness has significant effects on domestic asset prices, interest rates and exchange rates because it increases the substitutability of domestic and external funds for resident borrowers and, more important, between domestic and foreign currency assets for lenders. On the one hand, external capital flows make it very difficult to delink domestic interest rates from those prevailing in world markets and to decouple interest and exchange rates, giving rise to additional instability in both of these rates. On the other hand, increased competition between domestic and foreign currency assets tends to raise the cost of finance in developing countries relative to those in the financial centres. The consequences for trade and industrialization are significant.

The first effect is loss of "policy autonomy"; i.e. reduced ability of Governments to achieve national objectives by using the policy

THE SOUTHERN CONE LIBERALIZATION EXPERIMENT

In the face of balance of payments crises the three Southern Cone countries (Argentina, Chile, Uruguay) embarked on similar programmes to achieve stability through liberalization in the 1970s. In spite of some initial improvements, the programmes ultimately failed to achieve the objective of growth and stability, led to crises in the financial sectors and had to be abandoned.

The reforms were implemented in two phases. In the first (1974-1978 in Chile and Uruguay and 1976-1978 in Argentina) goods markets, the financial sector, labour markets and foreign trade were deregulated. In Chile, a step-by-step approach to capital account deregulation was taken while in Argentina and Uruguay most restictions on capital movements were lifted early on. In the second phase a preannounced exchange rate programme with diminishing devaluations (the *tablita*) was implemented in order to provide an anchor for inflationary expectations and to lower inflation.

Inflation did not slow down and the real exchange rate appreciated, increasing current account deficits. High domestic interest rates, overvalued real exchange rates, freedom to borrow abroad and plentiful international liquidity combined to induce capital inflows. Eventually the persistence of the real currency appreciation and growing foreign debts created expectations of a devaluation, which led to capital outflows. The experiments ended with the collapse of the domestic financial system which prompted large-scale bailout operations and heavy external indebtedness.

A number of interesting points emerge from the experience:

- In the first phase, while Chile and Uruguay were able to eliminate their fiscal deficits, Argentina only managed to reduce its own to a limited extent. The crisis engendered by financial liberalization increased deficits in Argentina because of the official guarantees on deposits. Deficits were financed first by borrowing abroad and then by monetization. Many writers draw the conclusion from Argentina's experience that stabilization cannot succeed without enforcing fiscal discipline and getting the fiscal deficit under control. However, Chile's budget surplus did not prevent serious financial crisis and acute macroeconomic turbulence.
- The retroactive wage indexation scheme in Chile harmed the stabilization efforts, especially during the *tablita* phase. It reinforced the "inertia" of inflation, prevented the inflation rate from converging to the rate of devaluation and caused widespread unemployment.
- The bail-out operations were at variance with the goal of relying on free-market mechanisms. Together with insurance deposits in Argentina, they created conditions for banks to engage in imprudent lending to high-risk borrowers. When distress borrowing began, the banks rolled over the bad loans and tried to finance them by attracting new deposits, which caused interest rates to rise. Easy access to foreign financial markets also facilitated imprudent lending.
- Experience shows clearly that financial deregulation should be accompanied by the introduction of prudential regulation and supervision by the authorities; that financial institutions should be insured but should themselves bear the cost of the insurance; and that measures are needed to prevent real interest rates from rising too high.
- In all three countries the *tablita* triggered an increase in capital inflow by increasing the spread between foreign and domestic interest rates. The lifting or absence of restrictions on short-term capital flows did not reduce the spreads in any of the three countries. The corporate sector was therefore led to borrow abroad. Many Argentine and Chilean firms moved into financial operations in order to profit from the difference in domestic and foreign interest rates. In all three countries the financial sector expanded, and enjoyed high profits from arbitrage. The capital inflow into Uruguay financed consumer credit and fuelled speculative bubbles in real estate and agricultural land. When the *tablita* policy could no longer be sustained and the currency had to be devalued by a significant margin, the bubbles burst, leading to widespread default. In Chile, a good deal of the inflow financed luxury consumption, instead of investment, a result of trade liberalization. In Argentina and in Uruguay the real currency appreciation harmed export activities; import-competing ones still enjoyed protection. The real appreciation and asset price booms led to increased spending generally and on imported durables in the three countries. The upshot was increased imports, loss of export competitiveness and wider current account deficits.

instruments at their disposal. Capital flows exert a considerable influence on exchange rates and hence trade, and are themselves influenced by volatile expectations regarding the returns on financial assets denominated in different currencies. This means not only that domestic policies have a new channel of influence on exchange rates and trade (namely, through their effects on capital flows), but also that exchange rates and trade will be influenced by financial policy abroad and by events at home and abroad that alter expectations.

Experience shows that leaving exchange rates to be governed by capital flows is a recipe for instability, and can undermine trade performance: exchange rate stability is essential for sustained export promotion and import substitution because of the need for firms to have long planning horizons. Exchange rate volatility has had adverse effects on investment in traded-goods industries even in industrial countries, where firms are better equipped to hedge against such effects.

There is a widespread belief, associated with the theory of sequencing of liberalization of markets, that external financial liberalization in developing countries gives rise to capital inflows provided that it comes after domestic capital markets have been liberalized (see box 15). The underlying assumption is that because of the relatively greater shortage of capital in developing countries, internal financial liberalization will raise interest rates above world levels, and a subsequent liberalization of the capital account will trigger capital inflow. However, the evidence strongly suggests that most capital movements are motivated primarily by prospects of short-term capital gains or losses, rather than by real investment opportunities and considerations of long-term risk and return. Consequently, they tend to generate gyrations in exchange rates and financial asset prices. The 1980s have shown how quickly capital movements can be reversed in developed countries for reasons unrelated to the underlying fundamentals. The systemic exposure to short-term, speculative capital flows is even greater for financially open developing countries because their instability provides opportunities for windfall profits. Moreover, the ability of developing countries to influence capital flows and exchange rates through monetary policy actions is much more limited.

In any event, interest rate differentials have proved to be an unreliable indicator of the direction of capital flows, especially for developing countries. Two countries with the same patterns of interest and exchange rates can have very different access to external financial markets and capital flows because of different perceptions by foreign creditors and domestic asset holders regarding the risk and uncertainty involved. The debt crisis has clearly shown that the foreign creditors' assessments of risk, return and creditworthiness can be changed suddenly by factors beyond the control of the debtors. Such changes can give rise to bandwagon movements which magnify their impact on the economy, which, in turn, alters the behaviour of domestic asset holders. Capital account liberalization in debt-distressed countries today cannot be expected to stimulate capital inflows as during the Southern Cone experiment, even though real interest rates are exceedingly high; rather, it will encourage capital flight and put pressures on domestic interest rates and the currency.

On the other hand, in a financially open economy with easy access to credit markets, the Southern Cone type of capital inflow problem can easily occur regardless in what order the markets have been liberalized, and even without any fiscal imbalance or policy-induced distortion in the exchange rate being present. Circumstances can arise that encourage short-term capital inflows, pushing up the exchange rate and hence encouraging further capital inflows. This often happens when domestic inflation and interest rates are much higher than abroad, and the country has a relatively high credit standing because of its export performance, terms of trade, etc. As short-term inflows lead to real currency appreciation, domestic financial institutions find they can borrow abroad at much lower interest rates than they can lend at home. If the process is not checked, the real exchange rate can continue to rise until the deterioration of the trade balance leads to a loss of confidence, triggering capital outflow.

Such a dynamic develops largely because, while internal financial liberalization strengthens the link between inflation and interest rates, external financial liberalization (unlike trade liberalization) weakens the link between inflation and the exchange rate, causing the latter to be dominated by capital flows instead of by the "fundamentals" of trade and the relative purchasing power of currencies. Any acceleration of inflation due to external shocks or domestic factors can raise nominal interest rates considerably and encourage short-term capital inflows. The central bank may not be able to block this process by altering monetary policy or by intervening in the currency market. When the capital inflow is large relative to the monetary base, the central bank cannot easily absorb it to prevent currency appreciation because of the monetary consequences. Nor may it be able to sterilize the monetary expansion through domestic open market operations without pushing up interest rates and acceler-

SEQUENCING THE LIBERALIZATION OF MARKETS

A particular policy measure may attain its intended objective, but at the same time prevent the attainment of other policy objectives. For instance, financial policies may undermine trade and fiscal objectives, or trade policies may impede the realization of fiscal objectives. This makes it necessary to consider a wide range of policy alternatives, and their *joint* effects over a whole range of policy objectives. Finding the optimal policy mix is not easy and no single answer fits all cases.

The literature on the sequencing of economic reforms argues that the liberalization of various markets (which is taken to be desirable) should be undertaken in a particular sequence. It has emerged in large part as an *ex post* theory of why the Southern Cone liberalization experiment failed (see box 6), rather than from general inquiry into the question of optimum policy in developing countries.

The need for a correct *sequence* of liberalization is drawn from the notion that deregulating one market may not eliminate the distortion there if distortions persist elsewhere. Therefore, the sequence of deregulation must follow the line of influence (or causality) from one market to another. *Timing* of the liberalization, on the other hand, addresses the question of whether a gradual or a once-and-for-all implementation of deregulation makes it easier for agents to adjust and encounters less political resistance.

- The main conclusion drawn is that liberalization is not a remedy for macroeconomic instability, but that stability is a precondition for successful liberalization. As inflation is generally seen as the result of monetization of fiscal deficits, this means that fiscal deficits must be brought under control before liberalizing the domestic financial sector. This is also needed to avoid public borrowing from abroad when the capital account is deregulated and private sector borrowing from abroad is putting upward pressure on the exchange rate. None the less, the opposite view - that it is difficult to control inflation without liberalizing the economy - is also defended by some economists on the argument that "anti-inflationary programmes structured to succeed only if the inflation rate declines are less likely to bring down the rate of inflation than are programmes designed to liberalize markets regardless of whether or not the anti-inflationary policies succeed". [1]
- A second conclusion is that the domestic financial market should be deregulated before capital account transactions are deregulated. Otherwise, the difference between international interest rates and regulated low domestic interest rates will induce a capital outflow.
- Views, however, differ on sequencing of trade liberalization and capital account liberalization. While all sides assume that capital account openness results in capital inflows, one view is that by making a higher level of imports possible this facilitates the adjustment of export and import-competing sectors to trade liberalization. The majority view is that trade liberalization should come first. Whereas trade liberalization involves adjustment to a new set of undistorted prices, temporary capital flows can alter the exchange rate and thereby convey misleading signals to the sectors trying to adjust.

[1] Anne Kruger, "Problems of liberalization", in A.C. Haberler (ed.), *World Economic Growth* (ICS Press, San Francisco, California, 1984), p. 413.

ating the capital inflow. The capital inflows can therefore cause a glut in the foreign exchange market and increase foreign exchange reserves and external indebtedness. It is only to the extent that import demand rises with the capital inflow (for instance, because tariffs are reduced) that appreciation of the currency can be slowed down; but then the trade balance will worsen due to increased imports.

This seems to have happened in Chile in the early 1980s when trade liberalization resulted in a substantial increase in imports of luxury goods, accompanied by large foreign capital inflows and increasing indebtedness. Almost a decade after its liberalization experiment, Chile seems to be suffering once again from a similar problem, except that this time the currency appreciation is market-generated rather than policy-induced. As noted by

ECLAC, the "substantial rise in interest rates ... and the stability of the (nominal) exchange rate encouraged a large increase in the inflow of short-term capital. This, together with the substantial inflow of direct foreign investment, made it more difficult to manage the monetary situation...".[81] Indeed, between mid-1989 and mid-1990 the average annual rate of interest on short-term loans was about 40 per cent, the consumer price inflation was around 25 per cent while the nominal exchange rate of the dollar against the peso rose by 10 per cent (which, incidentally, gave an arbitrage profit at the rate of about 17 per cent on dollars borrowed in the United States market at an interest rate of 10 per cent and lent in Chile in pesos). Export growth fell during the course of 1990 while imports and foreign exchange reserves rose considerably. There are also signs of such a process in Turkey following the lifting of restrictions on private borrowing. Domestic real interest rates have been barely positive, but the currency has been appreciating because of capital inflows, even though the massive increase in imports, particularly of consumption goods, also brought about by trade liberalization, has been absorbing most of the capital inflow; the rest has been reflected in a surge in the level of reserves, matched by an unprecedented trade deficit and debt accumulation.

When speculative capital inflows set off a vicious circle, the only way out may be to abandon either internal or external liberalization or both. Imposing ceilings on domestic lending rates can slow down the inflow by reducing arbitrage opportunities, but if taken too far will induce a switch to assets denominated in foreign currencies. A safer route might be to go back on external liberalization and restrict foreign capital inflows through direct controls (such as high reserve ratios for banks' foreign exchange liabilities). Experience shows that capital controls might have to be introduced anyway if the process develops into a payments crisis and capital flight. It may be easier to restrict capital inflows and prevent debt accumulation early on than to check capital flight in a crisis.

In some cases, the capital inflow may reflect a sharp increase in FDI, as in Chile recently. This is no cause for concern if the inflow is sustainable; then, the extent of currency appreciation will not represent a misalignment since it will be possible to finance a higher trade deficit by underlying, autonomous capital flows, and the investment will raise productivity growth and improve competitiveness. However, in practice direct investment, too, may be prone to bandwagon-type behaviour. A recently liberalized, well-performing economy can suddenly find favour with foreign capital of all sorts; but if things go wrong for some reason, the inflow can disappear just as rapidly.

When FDI has a substantial import content, it will absorb an important part of the foreign exchange inflow. However, if it consists not of new investment but of a transfer of ownership of existing private or public assets (privatization) to non-residents, or if it has very little import content, it can push up the exchange rate and hence depress exports. A corresponding increase in domestic investment (and capital goods imports) is the ideal response. But if private investment cannot be accelerated and the public sector lacks resources, slowing down FDI through licensing may be the least undesirable solution.

An important form of non-debt-creating financial flows that has been increasingly emphasized in recent years is equity investment by non-residents in the capital markets of developing countries. This is expected to alleviate foreign exchange shortage and to improve the efficiency of financial markets in developing countries. Many developing countries ("newly emerging capital markets") have opened up their capital markets to non-residents, and some have encouraged their participation in the privatization of public assets. Such a policy has advantages, but it is not risk-free. For one thing, it can make the corporate sector and the financial system even more vulnerable to business cycles abroad. For another, since opening up domestic capital markets requires some form of currency convertibility for non-resident equity investors, it increases the potential for the emergence of a foreign exchange crisis. Since the return on investment to the foreign investor depends partly on the movement of the exchange rate, expectations of a currency depreciation can trigger both a sharp decline in equity prices and an outflow of capital if the country suffers a serious shock (e.g. a terms of trade deterioration) that makes a devaluation appear inevitable; the capital outflow can multiply the problems of adjustment. Similarly, the mood in equity markets can exert a strong influence on the exchange rate - e.g. bullish expectations can cause capital inflows, leading to overvaluation.

A number of restrictions can be introduced in order to meet these problems. One common measure is to limit foreign ownership to approved country funds and allow trans-

---

81 ECLAC, *Economic Panorama of Latin America*, Santiago, Chile, September 1990, p. 39.

actions on such funds only among non-residents in order to control the flow of foreign funds in and out of the country via capital markets. This can be combined by the requirement that such funds be managed by local managers, who are more amenable to "moral suasion" by the authorities. It should be noted, however, that if such restrictions are effective, they tend to discourage capital inflow. It should also be noted that in several industrialized countries capital markets have been opened up to non-residents only very recently. In Japan, for instance, they were largely closed until the 1984 agreement with the United States, and even in Europe, where an integrated financial market is seen as an important step in the completion of a single EEC market, restrictions on entry into capital markets still remain in a number of countries (e.g. France and Italy). Again, the Republic of Korea only recently opened up its capital market to non-residents (apparently in order to help lift the prices after a massive drop), but restricted foreign acquisition to 10 per cent of total equity capital, and to 2 per cent in some strategic industries. As discussed in greater detail in *TDR 1990*, evidence in the 1980s suggests the presence of strong destabilizing influences among various capital markets as well as between financial and currency markets.

3. Cost of finance

By increasing the cost of finance, financial openness can place industry in developing countries at a disadvantage. This is due to risk and uncertainty, two factors typically neglected in discussions of interest rate determination and of financial liberalization but discussed in chapter I above. For asset holders risk and uncertainty vary with the identity of the borrower and the currency denomination of the asset. Lender's risk arises not only because of the possibility that the borrower's expectations regarding the return on his investment may not be realized (i.e. the borrower's risk), but because contracts may not be enforced (i.e. a moral risk) on account of dishonesty and/or the nature of the State and of the legal system. There is, further, capital-value uncertainty arising from the fact that the real value of assets can undergo substantial changes because of unforeseeable changes in interest rates, exchange rates and prices. These factors together

serve to raise the interest rate required by asset holders to become less liquid.

The fact that most developing countries are economically and politically more unstable than developed countries, together with the weaknesses in their financial and legal systems, makes investment in developing countries riskier. This explains why spreads over LIBOR in international lending are much higher for developing than for developed country borrowers, and why foreign exchange deposits in developing countries have to offer higher rates than those in world markets. Moreover, domestic-currency assets in developing countries often entail greater capital-value uncertainty than hard-currency assets. Consequently, when domestic and foreign-currency assets are left free to compete with each other, the former need to offer considerably higher real rates of return. Moreover, since savers tend to diversify their portfolios for reasons of safety regardless of the interest rate offered, the wealthy in developing countries will always put part of their savings abroad if they can. Offering still higher interest rates on domestic currency assets does not prevent this diversification. Indeed, if it is taken as evidence of underlying economic difficulties, it can accelerate currency substitution and capital flight. Moreover, foreign investors are often hypersensitive to signs of political and economic instability: sudden repatriation of funds can aggravate instability.

When enterprises in developing countries have to pay higher real interest rates than their counterparts in developed countries, even greater reliance has to be placed on lowering wages in order to compete in world markets. This may cause serious problems, particularly since there may not exist a level of wages that is compatible simultaneously with competitiveness, macroeconomic stability and social peace.

Given the drawbacks of external financial liberalization, tapping foreign capital through official channels may be the most effective way of alleviating the shortage of capital in developing countries. For instance, a principal feature of the external financial strategy of the Republic of Korea was for many years to control external borrowing through official approval and guarantees, and allocate foreign capital via the government-owned Development Bank. Even in the late 1980s the Government prohibited outright firms from borrowing abroad and tightly controlled short-run speculative capital inflows.

G. Conclusions

The main aim of financial policies in developing countries should be to ensure that resources are allocated at lowest possible cost for investment in areas with the highest social rate of return, without either causing instability or reducing the volume of resources mobilized for investment. Financial policies must therefore take account of the dual nature of interest rates: the *return* aspect, which primarily influences the distribution of asset holdings in different forms, and the *cost* aspect, which determines the capacity of the corporate sector to generate internal funds and to undertake investment.

Macroeconomic stability is of cardinal importance for the effective mobilization of domestic resources since instability leads to uncertainty, raises interest rates and shortens time horizons. Although there is now broader agreement that macroeconomic stability is an important precondition for successful structural reform, in a number of countries in the 1980s financial reforms have been undertaken in the midst of macroeconomic instability, with emphasis on the macroeconomic rather than the structural and developmental aspects of the reforms, and have been intended primarily as a remedy for stagnation and instability. As a result, they have not only failed to increase savings, but have also intensified instability in the corporate and financial sectors, and disrupted investment.

Also warranting greater attention is the organization of the financial system and of corporate finance, something which impinges directly on industrialization, development and stability. Many developing countries appear to be seeking to establish and/or develop all the financial institutions and markets that now exist in developed countries, rather than concentrate on those most suited to their own circumstances. Experience shows that no single type of financial system is suitable everywhere and at all times. For most developing countries, a system of bank-based finance combining investment banking with deposit taking appears to be more appropriate than one based on capital markets. Not only is it more susceptible to control - an important consideration since intervention in the allocation of credit is often needed to achieve development objectives - but also close relations between lenders and corporations can result in greater predictability in the

availability of funds and lower the cost of finance for firms, allowing them to take a long view in designing their business strategies.

However, a combination of intervention and bank-based finance can easily degenerate unless adequate precautions are taken:

- The authorities must ensure that all controls, regulations and subsidies serve the intended purposes, and monitor their policies constantly, revising them as necessary;
- Credit controls should not be used as a vehicle for facilitating financing of unproductive government expenditure;
- Macroeconomic stability must be ensured, since the dependence of the corporate sector on bank credits increases its vulnerability to large and unexpected changes in interest rates and credit volume;
- Closer relationships between banks and corporations can lead to waste and instability if corporations are allowed to control banks;
- Effective prudential regulations and strong bank supervision are essential to prevent excessive risk taking and speculation by the banking system, and all the more so when interest rates and lending are deregulated, and deposit insurance or enhanced lender-of-last-resort facilities are provided.

Despite the limitations of the Anglo-Saxon model of financing, capital markets can render useful functions, particularly at later stages of development, and can function alongside banks in providing funds for investment. But capital markets do not emerge spontaneously, and tax and other incentives to broaden the equity base of the corporate sector, as well as restrictions on corporate borrowing, may be needed. The promotion of capital markets should be accompanied by measures to prevent secondary market activity from becoming an additional source of financial instability, including regulations to prevent fraud and other irregularities as well as mechanisms to prevent excessive speculation. A tax on capital market transactions can help to deter short-term speculative moves into and out of equities.

It is also possible to combine the advantages of bank and capital market finance. One way is to introduce investment banks between capital markets and non-financial corporations, and allow them to raise funds in the capital markets. Another is to combine bank control over corporations, as in Germany, with equity holding by institutional investors such as provident and pension funds, as in Japan. Since large institutional investors are long-term holders, and more susceptible to official guidance, this can reduce capital market instability.

Particular care needs to be given to the design of external financial reforms, since mistakes in this area tend to be very costly and difficult to reverse. A complete isolation of the financial system in a developing country from the rest of world is neither feasible nor desirable if only because successful export performance requires close interaction of banks at home with international markets in order to provide trade-related credits and facilitate international payments. But, despite the difficulties involved, it is usually possible to separate trade-related financial transactions from capital transactions through restrictions on the size and maturity of banks' foreign exchange assets and liabilities.

Allowing domestic firms (whether private or public) uncontrolled access to international capital markets has proved damaging in many instances; short-term speculative capital flows have proved extremely troublesome even for industrial countries. Most developing countries need to exercise a considerable degree of control over external capital flows and the pace of accumulation of external debt. But that in itself will not stem capital flight if economic and political stability is absent. Foreign currency accounts can lead to dollarization, and are poor substitutes for sound policies.■

SELECTED ISSUES IN THE URUGUAY ROUND

Chapter I

REVIEW OF DEVELOPMENTS IN THE URUGUAY ROUND

After more than four years of negotiations, the Uruguay Round could not be concluded within the agreed time-frame at the Ministerial Meeting of the Trade Negotiations Committee (TNC), held at Brussels on 3-7 December 1990. The attainment of the ambitious and complex objectives of the negotiations was suspended, leaving the international trading system in a state of uncertainty as to the prospects for further liberalization and expansion of world trade and for the creation of improved multilateral trading rules and disciplines.

The negotiations had to be suspended because of a number of political deadlocks, first of all in the area of agriculture, where participants could not agree over "specific binding commitments" in the three related areas of domestic support, market access and export competition. There were also wide divergencies in the positions of participants in some other key areas, such as anti-dumping and trade-related investment measures, on which no draft texts were submitted to the Brussels Meeting. Moreover, practically all parts of the draft Final Act submitted to Ministers in Brussels contained fundamental political or technical points of disagreement, on which difficult compromises still had to be negotiated. The Brussels Ministerial Meeting concluded with a request to the Director-General of GATT to pursue intensive consultations in the early months of 1991 with the specific objective of achieving agreements in all the areas of the negotiating programme in which there were still differences outstanding, taking into account the considerable amount of work carried out by Ministers at the Brussels Meeting, although it did not commit any participant. These consultations led to a formal decision of the TNC in late February 1991 to restart the negotiations in all areas with the aim of concluding them as soon as possible. In April 1991 a new negotiating structure was agreed upon, reducing the number of negotiating groups from 15 to seven.[82] The new group structure was designed to encourage substantive negotiations and to help achieve political breakthroughs with the minimum delay. However, the new groups were able to start their work only in June 1991, and when the TNC met on 30 July the key political decisions still remained to be taken.

The practical resumption of the Uruguay Round was encouraged by the fact that the United States Congress in May 1991 extended the so-called "fast-track" authority of the President to negotiate multilateral trade agreements until 1 June 1993. The fast-track authority covers not only the possible agreements of the Uruguay Round, but also a tripartite United States-Canada-Mexico free trade agreement (NAFTA), which is already under negotiation.[83]

There are signs that a new political will is emerging to achieve "a wide-ranging, substantial, balanced and global agreement and a complementary institutional strengthening of the GATT system".[84] However, as recognized at the TNC meeting of 30 July 1991, in order to reach such a positive outcome by the end of 1991 participants will have to make genuine efforts to resolve the political and technical problems that are outstanding in virtually every negotiating area.

For the time being, the prospects of the Uruguay Round are often described as a matter of compromise between the divergent positions of the major trading nations, in particular, in the area of agriculture. In order to achieve

---

[82] The seven negotiating groups are: 1. Market Access (tariffs, non-tariff measures, natural resource-based products, tropical products); 2. Textiles and Clothing; 3. Agriculture; 4. Rule-Making and Trade-Related Investment Measures (TRIMs); 5. Trade-Related Aspects of Intellectual Property Rights (TRIPs); 6. Institutions; and 7. Services.

[83] See part one above, chap. III, sect. B.2.

[84] See for example, the Communiqué from the annual OECD Ministerial Session (4-5 June 1991), *Europe*, 1717/18, 12 June 1991.

their objectives more effectively, certain developing countries have aligned themselves with groups of developed countries where their interests coincide, as on agricultural reform and improved market access. In other areas, however, particularly that of the "new issues", where developed and developing countries find themselves in radically different situations, developing countries have effectively coordinated their positions and submitted joint proposals. Many developing countries, in anticipation of comprehensive and balanced results of the Round, have undertaken autonomous trade liberalization measures, covering tariff reductions and bindings, elimination of quantitative restrictions, and abolition of other non-tariff barriers. Countries in Central and Eastern Europe have also engaged in this process. However, there has yet been no agreement as to the approach for giving credit for such unilateral liberalization measures adopted since 1 June 1986, as agreed in the Mid-Term Review decisions in 1988.

It is still difficult to attempt to foresee the results of the Uruguay Round with any clarity. The negotiating groups will begin meetings again in September 1991 to enter the decisive phase of the negotiations on the assumption that the whole Uruguay Round will be concluded by the end of the year. However, it would seem appropriate to indicate some of the basic issues under consideration in each of the recently established negotiating groups, and to emphasize the concerns of developing country participants in relation to the attainment of the balanced outcome of the Round and the criteria for evaluating its results.[85]

In the *Market Access Group*,[86] in general no substantial progress has been registered since the Brussels Meeting. In particular, participants were unable to reach consensus on a common approach towards reduction, harmonization or elimination of tariffs and non-tariff measures. Moreover, different priorities are set for the results of negotiations. By the end of June 1991, over 50 participants had submitted proposals and offers aimed at the reduction of tariffs and non-tariff measures. These proposals and offers constituted the initial basis for bilateral and plurilateral negotiations, which were still in an early phase. In order to arrive at a mutually acceptable balance of reductions of tariffs and non-tariff barriers, participants will have to overcome a number of serious obstacles in each of the sub-areas of the negotiations. There is, first, the question

of the scope of the market access negotiations, as agricultural products, tropical products and natural resource-based products have so far been left largely outside the tariff offers of certain major participants. In addition, a number of industrial product areas have been excluded from the tariff offers (e.g. high tariffs on textiles and clothing, as well as on footwear, leather products and petrochemicals).

Market access negotiations and their results constitute a major component for developing countries in evaluating overall results in the Uruguay Round. Thus, it would seem essential to obtain a substantial package of concessions on the market access issues that would promote trade liberalization and effectively expand the opportunities for developing country exports to enter world markets. The negotiations would also need to address the issues of providing developing countries with compensation for the erosion of existing preferences and to give full recognition to the contribution made to the trade liberalization process by developing countries that have bound their entire tariff schedules in GATT.

In *Textiles and Clothing*, the Uruguay Round has concentrated on reaching agreement on modalities to bring this sector within the rules and principles of the multilateral trading system. The phasing out of the MFA and integration of trade in this sector into the General Agreement have been seen by many developing countries as a top priority in the Uruguay Round and as indispensable for the success of the negotiations. After the negotiations had been deadlocked for some time as a result of opposition to proposals for a "global quota" or "tariff quota" system put forward by certain developed importing countries, participants finally agreed to negotiate a mechanism that would phase out the MFA and "phase in" GATT disciplines so as to incorporate textiles trade into the General Agreement over a fixed period. While the draft agreement presented to Ministers at Brussels contains some positive elements for trade liberalization in this sector, certain outstanding issues remain to be resolved, such as: (a) the time span for the transition (probably 10 years); (b) the speed and coverage of the phase-out of quotas (suggestion of initial elimination followed by three more stages, but concern about how much would be left for the final stage); (c) growth rates of quotas during the phase-out (sufficiently high growth rates would partly obviate problems of excessive end-loading of quota eliminations);

85 Some of these issues have been analysed in detail in UNCTAD, *The Uruguay Round: Further Papers on Selected Issues* (United Nations publication, UNCTAD/ITP/42, New York, 1990).

86 This Group incorporates the pre-Brussels Groups on Tariffs, Non-Tariff Measures, Tropical Products and Natural Resource Products.

(d) circumstances in which safeguards, selective or not, can be applied to "snap back" quota eliminations or compensate for them during and immediately following the phase-out; and (e) whether, in the multilateral review of the progress made in winding up the MFA, conditional linkages may be made to policy behaviour and respect for commitments in other areas. During the final and critical phase of the negotiations, it is important to draw up an agreed programme for bringing trade in this sector within the purview of GATT rules and principles that will progressively reduce the flexibility of importing countries to restrict and discriminate against the exports of developing countries within a reasonable time-frame and prevent the extension of restrictions to new categories of products and to additional countries.

In the area of *Agriculture*, which is considered in more detail in chapter II below, in general the negotiations are awaiting a signal from EEC of an improvement in its existing offer linked to the anticipated progress in the reform of its Common Agricultural Policy. For developing countries it would seem important for a possible reform of GATT rules on agriculture to provide them with improved and secure market access for their agricultural exports, while containing specific provisions that would recognize the special developmental role of agriculture in their economies and societies, and offset any negative impact on net food-importing developing countries of a liberalization process.

The negotiations on *Rule-Making* are confronted with a variety of complex issues on which difficult compromises have yet to be made. This is particularly important for such sub-areas as anti-dumping, subsidies and countervailing duties, safeguards and a number of specific GATT articles, especially article XVIII, which permits developing countries to resort to quantitative restrictions to protect their balance of payments. The most difficult negotiations in this Group would seem to concern the review of the Anti-Dumping Code, where there is no common negotiating basis in the form of a draft agreement. Basic differences continue to persist among participants with respect to changes in the calculation of dumping margins, methods of establishing material injury, and anti-circumvention provisions. The negotiations in the Rule-Making area could make a substantial contribution to an overall balanced outcome in the Uruguay Round, *inter alia*, by: (a) tightening multilateral rules and disciplines regulating anti-dumping and countervailing measures so as to make a significant reduction in the scope for harassment of developing country exports; (b)

adopting an agreement on safeguards to impart stability and predictability to international trade, and to exclude any possibility of discriminatory action in violation of the most-favoured-nation (MFN) principle; (c) conserving in the GATT basic provisions permitting the flexible application of trade policy measures to developing countries on a provisional basis, especially in relation to balance of payments problems.

The negotiations on *Trade-Related Investment Measures* (TRIMs) have evolved into an area of major disagreement with little scope for convergence of views. The difficulties that were encountered in reaching agreement on a draft negotiating text on TRIMs before the Brussels Meeting reflected fundamental differences in interpreting the mandate of the negotiations on this issue. While some developed countries were seeking to establish a prohibition for investment measures *per se*, developing and certain developed countries considered that the Punta del Este mandate was solely to address the trade-restrictive and trade-distortive effects of investment measures. They were of the view that the right to determine whether and to what extent, and upon what terms, they would permit foreign investment was not only inherent in national sovereignty but was also necessary to ensure the maximum development impact of foreign investment and to counter or pre-empt anti-competitive practices of transnational corporations (TNCs). Developing countries, however, had indicated their willingness to accept disciplines to reduce or eliminate trade-restrictive and trade-distortive effects on trading partners when such effects could be demonstrated in specific cases. The prospect of arriving at a mutually acceptable agreement on TRIMs would seem to be clouded by fundamentally different perceptions as to how foreign direct investment can contribute to the development process and how to separate trade-related issues from those related to conditions for regulating investment regimes. Under the new negotiating structure, TRIMs have been merged with the other rule-making issues as one group. However, no text had emerged by the time of the TNC meeting on 30 July 1991, and the essential political differences have not yet been overcome.

The negotiations on *Trade-Related Aspects of Intellectual Property Rights (TRIPs)* are discussed in chapter III below. In general terms it can be emphasized that an agreement, which is emerging from negotiations on TRIPs, should promote rather than impede developing countries' access to technology and their development of indigenous technological capacities, and should not oblige countries to protect intellectual property rights in a manner that would constitute barriers to legitimate trade or would undermine public policy, and particularly social objectives. Developing countries remain concerned that the final result in this area should preclude any possibility of cross-sectoral retaliation between trade in goods and measures covered by the TRIPs agreement.

Negotiations on *Trade in Services* are proceeding on the basis of a draft text of a General Agreement for Trade in Services submitted at the Brussels Meeting. The draft contains three major elements: the text of the multilateral framework, annexes (on sectors and on labour mobility), and schedules of commitments. At present, work is progressing on the scheduling of initial commitments, which is essential for the process of exchange of offers and requests and the completion of the negotiations on specific commitments. By the end of July 1991, 35 preliminary offers had been submitted, and negotiations on initial commitments following a request/offer procedure are foreseen to begin in September 1991. As to the framework agreement, a number of outstanding issues remain, in particular those relating to the application of the MFN principle, from which a number of proposed derogations had been incorporated into the draft sectoral annexes dealing with transportation (air, maritime, land and inland waterways), "basic" telecommunication services, and audiovisual, broadcasting, sound recording and publishing services. Agreement on a labour mobility annex,[87] which is considered as a priority issue by developing countries, is particularly important for the progress of the negotiations on initial commitments.

The structure of the framework consists of an overall framework of general rules and principles, including that of unconditional MFN treatment, accompanied by lists of specific concessions with respect to market access and national treatment on a sectoral or sub-sectoral basis. These would all constitute integral parts of the General Agreement on Trade in Services. There would thus be a framework within which future negotiations aimed at the progressive liberalization of trade in services would be undertaken. In particular, developing countries would be able to obtain credit for any liberalization measures to which they were willing to commit themselves, in terms of reciprocal concessions, to provide effective access

for services of export interest to them in the markets of their developed trading partners.[88]

It is this question of "effective access" that presents particular problems for developing countries. Lacking large TNCs with global infrastructures, financial strength, mastery of advanced technologies and accumulated knowledge and established reputations, developing countries may find it virtually impossible to capitalize effectively on negotiated market access opportunities, particularly in those sectors where a relatively small number of corporations dominate world trade.

Developing countries have sought to correct what they have described as this "asymmetrical" situation by placing considerable emphasis on obtaining concessions with respect to the movement of labour, on arrangements for access to distribution channels and information networks, and on obtaining compliance with national policies to promote the transfer of technology by foreign firms benefiting from market access concessions. However, greater efforts seem to be required by the international community to assist developing countries to strengthen their service sectors so as to participate fully in and derive advantage from the process of progressive liberalization. It has been suggested that an action progamme to this effect could be drawn up at UNCTAD VIII.

The financial services sector has presented particular difficulties in the negotiations owing to divergent views on whether this sector should be governed by a self-contained agreement, presented in an annex to the multilateral framework, under which such services would be liberalized according to an agreed schedule and effectively isolated from the multilateral negotiating process. Developing countries have argued that such an approach would negate the principle of comparative advantage, undermine the coherence of the multilateral framework and nullify their possibilities of obtaining reciprocal concessions in sectors of export interest to them for liberalization commitments they might make in this sector, which is dominated by developed country enterprises.[89]

The work in the *Institutions* Group, which embraces negotiations on the Final Act, Dispute Settlement and Functioning of the GATT System, would seem to depend on the substantive progress in other areas of negotiations. The central issue here is the search for a new institutional framework to ensure the effective

---

87 Currently entitled "Annex on Movement of Natural Persons Providing Services Under the Agreement".

88 See discussion in such UNCTAD publications as *Trade in services: Sectoral issues* (UNCTAD/ITP/26), *Services in Asia and the Pacific* (UNCTAD/ITP/51) and *Mexico: Una economía de servicios* (UNCTAD/ITP/58).

89 The issues raised in the negotiations on financial services are discussed in chapter IV below.

implementation of the Uruguay Round results. Proposals have been advanced, and incorporated in the draft Final Act, to the effect, that as part of the outcome of the Round, GATT should be given a more permanent institutional character through the establishment of a new "Multilateral Trade Organization". At the same time, the initiative for the establishment of an international trade organization has been given a fresh impetus in the United Nations. In its resolution 45/201 of 21 December 1990 the General Assembly reaffirmed the request to the Secretary-General of the United Nations[90] to report to the Assembly at its forty-sixth session on institutional developments, taking into account all relevant proposals related to the strengthening of international organizations in the area of multilateral trade. These developments have refocused the attention of the international community on the incomplete and fragmented nature of institutional arrangements for governing international trade whose origin was the failure of Governments to implement the Havana Charter of 1948 for a comprehensive international trade organization. It would seem necessary that longer-term aims be kept firmly in view in current discussions of institutional arrangements, particularly in the Uruguay Round. The new institutional mechanism in the area of trade should be seen not in relation to a specific negotiating process but rather in the wider perspective of providing an economic basis for world peace and security.

The situation of the world economy would seem to call for an expeditious and successful conclusion of the Uruguay Round to regain momentum for trade liberalization and trade expansion in order to restore general economic growth. In this context a strict observance of the standstill commitment is particularly important, as well as a firm rejection of unilateralism in the conduct of national trade policies. There are a number of other aspects that would increase confidence in the success of the Uruguay Round, such as the avoidance of backsliding in areas where some positive results have already been achieved, as in the dispute settlement procedures, and the assurance of greater transparency in the negotiating process, which is of special importance for smaller and more vulnerable trading partners.

There are also a number of short-term factors that influence the pace of the Uruguay Round. One of the most important prerequisites would be a modification of the EEC position on agriculture to reflect the anticipated

reform of the Common Agricultural Policy. Developments at the regional level (reviewed in part one above, chapter III, section B) may also have some influence, such as negotiations on the completion of the single EEC market by 1992, on the European Economic Area (EEA), and on the formation of a free trade area in North America (NAFTA). It does not seem to be mere coincidence that the NAFTA negotiations have more or less the same structure as those of the Uruguay Round, in particular covering such issues as market access, trade rules, services, investment, intellectual property and dispute settlement.

It cannot be assumed that the new stage of the Uruguay Round is guaranteed to succeed, although there is a widespread awareness of the likely consequences of its failure. The maintenance of an open, multilateral trading system is of great importance to all countries. It is vital for many developing countries, as well as for Central and Eastern European countries that are undergoing a radical restructuring of their economies and economic systems and badly need a favourable environment in international trade. A retreat to protectionism and/or an exclusive focus on regional or bilateral arrangements would put the international trading system at great risk and could lead to a profound crisis of multilateralism. If the opportunities afforded by the Uruguay Round, despite all divergencies, are missed, a severe blow will be dealt to the principle of multilateralism.

Accordingly, if the Uruguay Round is to achieve a balanced and substantial package of results in all areas, it should address and satisfy the vital interests of all participants, in particular of the developing countries, which represent the majority of the participants. However, the current status of negotiations in different areas suggests that the real benefits that developing countries could derive from the Round are still somewhat limited. In particular, most of the provisions of the draft Final Act on differential and more favourable treatment are only proposals and remain in square brackets. In this context, it may be recalled that part I.G. of the Punta del Este Declaration called for the Group of Negotiations on Goods to conduct, before the formal completion of the negotiations, an evaluation of results in terms of the Objectives and General Principles Governing Negotiations as set out in the Declaration with a view to ensuring the effective application of differential and more favourable treatment for developing countries. This evaluation should afford the possibility of introducing corrective

---

[90] Economic and Social Council resolution 1990/57 of 26 July 1990.

measures to ensure that a balanced outcome is, in effect, reached. It would also seem important for such an evaluation to be conducted comprehensively within a sufficient time-frame to be able to influence the final outcome.

As indicated above, among the crucial and complex issues facing the negotiations in the present phase are those relating to Agriculture, Trade-Related Aspects of Intellectual Property Rights (TRIPs), and Financial Services, which are discussed in detail in the following chapters.■

Chapter II

EFFORTS AT AGRICULTURAL REFORM: ISSUES IN THE NEGOTIATIONS

A. Introduction

The Uruguay Round of multilateral trade negotiations has provided the framework since 1986 in which multilateral efforts are being made to achieve agricultural policy reform under the General Agreement on Tariffs and Trade (GATT). The Round was scheduled to conclude by the end of 1990. However, owing to the persistence of widely differing views among participating countries in some key areas of the negotiations - including, in particular, agricultural reform - it was not possible to end the Round as planned. It was suspended after the Uruguay Round Ministerial Meeting held at Brussels in December 1990, and subsequently restarted in February 1991. This chapter reviews developments in the agricultural negotiations since 1986, analyses the main issues and options under consideration for multilateral agricultural policy reform, and discusses the implications of these for the developing countries.

B. Agricultural production, trade and national policies

It will be useful as a background for understanding some of the contentious issues in the negotiations on agriculture, as well as the implications of various proposals under consideration, particularly from the perspective of developing countries, to review briefly world agricultural production and trade, the relative importance of agriculture in national economies and national policies affecting agricultural trade.

1. World agricultural production and trade: general pattern and relative importance to national economies

Although world trade in agricultural products, including temperate zone and tropical products, has been declining as a proportion of world merchandise trade since the Second World War, it remains substantial - amounting to more than $300 billion in 1990 - and is of vital importance to many countries, both exporters and importers.[91] Food products account for about three quarters of all agricultural trade, and raw materials for the remaining quarter. In terms of production and employment, although the share of agriculture in world production (GDP) and the proportion of the labour force it employs continue to decline over time, for a large number of countries, particularly developing countries, the agricultural sector is still of key importance in both absolute and relative terms.

For example, as table 27 illustrates, whereas in 1988 agriculture accounted for only around 2 per cent of the gross domestic product of developed market-economy countries, in the same year it accounted for about 15 per cent in developing countries as a whole (9 per cent in Latin America and the Caribbean, 22 per cent in East Asia, 33 per cent in South Asia and 34 per cent in sub-Saharan Africa). In fact, these aggregate figures understate the contribution of agriculture to monetary gross domestic product for a large majority of developing countries. In terms of employment, agriculture's share of the labour force is generally much greater than its share of GDP. Nearly 60 per cent of the labour force of developing countries (Africa, 66 per cent; Latin America and the Caribbean, 27 per cent; and Asia, 55 per cent) derived their income from the agriculture sector in 1989 compared with about 6 per cent in the developed market-economy countries.

The high relative structural dependence of developing countries on agricultural production translates into a high structural dependence on agricultural exports. For the majority of developing countries, the share of agricultural products in total merchandise exports ranges from 50 per cent to 100 per cent.[92] Among the developed market-economy countries only New Zealand has an agricultural share of exports in this range. Agricultural exports represent only 8 per cent of total OECD merchandise trade, ranging from around 60 per cent for New Zealand and 35 per cent for

Australia to more than 20 per cent for a number of EEC countries (Denmark, Greece and Ireland), about 13 per cent for the United States and less than 5 per cent for all non-EEC European countries and Japan.[93]

A distinction should be made between those agricultural products that are produced chiefly by the developing countries and for which there are no close substitutes in the developed countries (e.g. tropical products such as coffee, cocoa, tea, spices, bananas and natural rubber), and those that are also produced by or have close substitutes produced by the developed countries (e.g., cereals, meat, dairy products, fruit and vegetables, edible oils and sugar). The latter category, which comprises basic foodstuffs, often referred to as temperate zone products, accounts for the bulk of world agricultural trade in value. The developed countries are the major exporters of these, apart from sugar. While developing countries are highly dependent on exports of tropical agricultural products, they are also dependent as a group, with a few exceptions, on imports of temperate agricultural products, that is, basic foodstuffs such as cereals, dairy products, meat and edible oils.

The developed market-economy countries dominate world trade in agricultural products in terms of both exports and imports. On the export side, their share in world exports of food and agricultural raw materials increased from about 58 per cent to 67 per cent and from about 55 per cent to 66 per cent, respectively, between 1970 and 1989. In contrast, the share of developing countries in world agricultural exports has generally declined over the same period.[94] As indicated in table 28, there have been substantial losses in the world market shares of developing countries in products such as meat, cereals, sugar, tropical beverages, spices and vegetables.

On the import side, the share of the developed countries in world imports of agricultural products generally tended to decline in the 1970s and 1980s while that of developing countries tended to increase on the whole. In 1989, the gross food imports of developing countries rose to around $62 billion, with their net food imports attaining the unprecedented

---

91 If fishery and forestry products are included, the total figure for 1990 is about $419 billion. It should be noted that, since the Second World War, the value of world trade in agriculture has not declined in absolute terms, but its growth has been much slower than that of world trade in other products, owing to both the slower growth of the volume of trade and the declining trend in world prices of agricultural products relative to the prices of other merchandise, particularly manufactures.

92 For example, see UNCTAD, "Agricultural trade expansion and protectionism, with special reference to products of export interest to the developing countries" (TD/B/C.1/239).

93 See OECD, *Agricultural policies, markets and trade: Monitoring and outlook 1991* (Paris, 1991).

94 See "Trends in the international market for agricultural and tropical products and developments in the liberalization of international trade in agricultural and tropical products", report of the Secretary-General (E/1991/89).

Table 27

SHARE OF AGRICULTURE IN PRODUCTION AND LABOUR FORCE IN SELECTED REGIONS, 1965 AND 1988 OR 1989

(Percentage)

Region	Share in GDP		Share in total labour force	
	1965	1988	1965	1989
Developed market-economy countries	5.5	2.3	16.5	5.9
Developing countries	28.4	15.4	70.6	57.1
Africa	35.3	20.8	78.9	66.5
Sub-Saharan Africa	41.0	34.0		
Latin America	15.7	9.2	44.5	27.0
Asia	38.0	17.8	67.5	55.0
East Asia	41.0	22.0		
South Asia	44.0	33.0		

Source: GDP: UNCTAD, *Handbook of International Trade and Development Statistics, 1990*, New York, 1991; labour force: FAO, Agrostat files. Data for subregions of Africa and Asia are from World Bank, *World Development Report, 1990* (New York, Oxford University Press, 1990).

level of about $17 billion (see table 29). The net food imports of all net food-importing developing countries totalled nearly $36 billion, while those of low-income food-deficit countries totalled approximately $10 billion. According to FAO, the latter's capacity to enhance their food security through trade has been severely restricted in recent years owing to the decline in their export earnings, their high debt-service levels, other financial and economic constraints, and lower food aid availability.[95] In 1989, 28 developing countries were net food exporters, with net exports of about $19 billion.

Developed market-economy countries have traditionally been and still remain the major markets for the agricultural exports of the developing countries. However, these markets, increasingly protected in the 1970s and 1980s, have grown relatively slowly for such products. This is in large measure a reflection of the domestic agricultural and protectionist policies adopted by these countries, which have had the effect of reducing domestic dependence on imports through increased domestic production. The growth in exports of agricultural products from developing countries to developed market-economy countries has been much slower than in any other market. As a result, the developing country exports of such products received by developed market-economy countries declined in the 1970s and 1980s.

Given the developing countries' export dependence on the markets of the developed countries, so long as such countries, especially those dependent on agricultural exports, continue to have large and persistent balance-of-payments deficits with the developed countries (because of heavy debt-service obligations and essential capital goods imports), they will need to expand their agricultural exports to the developed countries.

2. National policies affecting agricultural production and trade

The international market for agricultural products is affected by a variety of policy measures applied by national governments. These measures include internal support policies (subsidies in various forms to domestic producers), the effect of which is to raise domestic production higher than it would otherwise be, thereby reducing domestic demand for imports or increasing export availability, border protection (tariffs, tariff escalation and non-tariff measures) to limit import access, and export subsidies (which distort competition among exporting countries). While policies falling into one or more of these categories are

[95] See FAO, "Assessment of the current world food security situation and outlook" (CFS: 91/2 and Supp. 1) and *Commodity Review and Outlook, 1990-91* (Rome, 1991).

Table 28

SHARE OF DEVELOPING COUNTRIES IN WORLD AGRICULTURAL EXPORTS, BY PRODUCT GROUP, 1970-1989

(Percentage)

Product group	1970	1980-1982	1989
Cereals	15.6	13.7	11.7
Meat	20.3	14.2	11.6
Edible oils	34.7	43.7	47.5
Dairy products	2.1	2.0	2.4
Sugar	68.2	60.7	52.2
Tropical beverages	91.2	84.7	78.4
Spices	85.6	81.6	72.4
Tobacco	25.4	27.9	24.7
Roots and tubers	32.9	42.7	41.9
Fruits	33.3	36.7	38.6
Vegetables	29.7	30.3	25.2
Total agriculture [a]	35.6	29.4	25.9

Source: FAO, *Trade Yearbook*, and UNCTAD secretariat calculations.
   a Excluding fishery and forestry products.

applied by many governments, those applied in the markets of the industrialized countries, because of their importance in international trade, have the greatest impact on the world market. (The policies of EEC and the United States in this respect are summarized in boxes 16 and 17 respectively.)

Whereas national support policies for agriculture, including subsidy programmes, were originally motivated by a desire to retain a minimum domestic agricultural capacity for national food security reasons and to provide assistance to rural areas in fulfilment of social policy objectives, policies of support and protection for the agricultural sector pursued in many developed market-economy countries have led to structural overcapacity in those sectors. Furthermore, in order to bolster domestic support policies, governments have instituted a variety of trade measures - ranging from conventional tariffs to a complex array of non-tariff measures (including variable levies, minimum prices, global and bilateral quotas, "voluntary" export restraints, import prohibitions, sanitary and phytosanitary regulations) - to restrict imports of agricultural products. Additionally, countries that are exporters of agricultural products have used export measures in support of domestic policy objectives, resorting in particular to export subsidies to reduce stocks of surplus products.

As a result of governmental policies in the agricultural sector, some developed coun-

tries that were previously major importers have become increasingly self-sufficient in agriculture or have gone beyond the stage of self-sufficiency to become large-scale exporters of a wide range of agricultural products. An important result has been not only to reduce, or shut off, the traditional markets for developing countries but also to displace developing countries on world markets, often through subsidized exports (see box 18). Subsidized exports from developed countries have affected developing country exports of cereals, meat, dairy products, oilseeds/vegetable oils and sugar, especially to third countries.

A major feature of the structure of tariffs and non-tariffs measures affecting agricultural exports of developing countries and in particular tropical products, is the tendency for tariffs to escalate with the stage of processing and for non-tariff measures to weigh more heavily on commodities in their processed forms. Many products of export interest to developing countries are particularly hard hit by this escalation of trade barriers, which has had a negative impact on the efforts of developing countries to enchance their participation in world agricultural trade in processed products.

The overall cost of the agricultural policies pursued by OECD countries, as measured by the sum of transfers from taxpayers (net of budget receipts from tariffs) and from consumers (through higher prices), rose to an estimated $299 billion in 1990, an increase of 12 per cent

Table 29

AGGREGATE FOOD [a] TRADE OF DEVELOPING COUNTRIES, 1989

(Millions of dollars)

	Imports	Exports	Net imports
Developing countries (132)	61 630	44 937	16 694
Net exporters (28)	12 550	31 407	-18 857
Net importers (104)	49 080	13 530	35 550
Low-income food-deficit countries (69) [b]	19 734	9 779	9 955
World	216 202		

Source: FAO, Agrostat files and UNCTAD secretariat calculations.

a "Food" is defined by FAO to include all products which are considered edible and contain nutrients in their raw or processed forms. For the present purpose the following commodities have been excluded from the definition: cocoa beans and products and other tropical beverages, fish and fishery products, feedingstuffs, alcoholic beverages, tropical fruits and spices and live animals.

b Defined by FAO as those food-deficit countries with per capita GNP less than $940 (in 1987 prices), which is the cut-off level for eligibility for IDA assistance.

over the 1989 figure.[96] This rise came after two successive years of decline from the peak level recorded in 1987. The decline in assistance to farmers in both 1988 and 1989 did not, however, reflect fundamental changes in government policy. The key influences were the recovery in some world market prices, particularly for major temperate zone commodities (due to drought-related reduction in supplies), and non-agricultural factors, such as changes in exchange rates. In 1990, the reversal of these short-term factors has seen the re-emergence of structural surpluses as domestic support prices remain high relative to world prices.

Estimates of producer subsidy equivalents (PSEs) for specific commodities are given in table 30, expressed as a proportion of the sales receipts for each commodity. As may be seen, this proportion is quite high, in particular for products such as sugar, cereals, and meat, which are of major trade interest to many countries. The table also shows that, although there were some declines in PSEs for specific products from the 1987 peak levels, these trends were largely reversed in 1990 in the major trading countries.

In contrast to the high degree of support provided to the agricultural sector in industrialized countries, the general policy stance towards the agricultural sector in developing countries has resulted in substantial discrimination against agriculture. In many cases, domestic pricing and taxation policies have kept producer prices well below border prices. An illustration of the bias against agriculture in developing countries is given in table 31 which provides an indication of how the differential protection given to industry has lowered the relative profitability of agriculture in several developing countries. With the exception of the Republic of Korea, all countries in the sample have discriminated against agriculture.

It is noteworthy that, in recognition of this situation, multilateral financial institutions have emphasized, in their stabilization and structural adjustment lending programmes of the 1980s, the need for changes in the policies of developing countries towards their agricultural sector, including changes in the structure of incentives (price and non-price) and trade liberalization designed to bring domestic prices in line with border prices. Also, in recognition of the underdeveloped state of agriculture in developing countries, the International Development Strategy for the Fourth United Nations Development Decade adopted by the General Assembly in December 1990,[97] has emphasized the importance of raising agricultural output in developing countries, both as a means of revitalizing their economic growth in the 1990s and of strengthening their food security and self-reliance. While not formally setting a target growth rate for agricultural or food production in developing countries, the Strategy maintains that "An annual rate of growth of the order of

96 See OECD, *op. cit.*
97 See General Assembly resolution 45/199.

Table 30

NET PRODUCER SUBSIDY EQUIVALENTS [a] FOR SELECTED COMMODITIES AND COUNTRIES, 1979-1990

Commodity	1979-86	1987	1989	1990	1979-86	1987	1989	1990	1979-86	1987	1989	1990
		Australia				*Austria*				*Canada*		
Wheat	10	14	11	17	32	73	38	62	26	54	26	43
Coarse grains	7	9	7	7	26	61	34	31	27	49	23	26
Rice	25	29	23	25	..	..	..	..	..	..	..	..
Oilseeds	8	12	16	12	..	..	..	..	20	30	23	21
Sugar	9	19	15	16	58	73	65	61	25	39	17	17
Milk	31	36	25	31	47	60	48	61	66	81	73	79
Beef	10	9	9	9	43	49	50	51	32	49	35	36
Pork	5	5	4	4	9	33	11	22	12	11	24	16
Poultry	5	4	4	4	14	2	52	49	28	45	37	40
		EEC [b]				*Finland*				*Japan*		
Wheat	32	60	27	46	62	82	77	81	96	103	95	99
Coarse grains	34	68	35	52	58	90	80	82	97	102	94	96
Rice	46	62	51	60	..	..	..	..	79	94	86	87
Oilseeds	45	70	60	69	64	90	80	96	82	79	67	69
Sugar	55	78	49	57	70	86	62	76	68	75	63	62
Milk	55	67	59	69	66	77	74	77	83	91	83	85
Beef	47	46	55	54	57	63	63	62	62	60	59	54
Pork	6	6	6	6	36	48	53	55	42	46	54	37
Poultry	20	22	26	28	46	56	52	56	17	13	13	13
		New Zealand				*Norway*				*Sweden*		
Wheat	9	25	14	10	63	78	76	79	35	65	41	73
Coarse grains	10	5	5	3	77	83	86	92	29	48	53	73
Rice	..	..	..	..	..	..	..	..	..	..	..	..
Oilseeds	..	..	..	..	..	..	..	..	36	42	61	68
Sugar	..	..	..	..	..	..	..	..	54	62	35	60
Milk	23	14	3	3	79	83	79	82	66	71	67	71
Beef	14	12	4	3	68	67	72	70	44	46	49	42
Pork	16	4	1	0	48	56	47	46	22	41	25	12
Poultry	29	47	49	57	56	64	65	59	26	36	38	29
		Switzerland				*United States*						
Wheat	72	85	76	81	28	64	25	44				
Coarse grains	74	91	84	89	21	46	30	24				
Rice	..	..	..	..	31	50	40	49				
Oilseeds	83	95	93	98	8	10	9	7				
Sugar	75	86	83	85	46	71	46	47				
Milk	73	85	76	84	63	70	55	62				
Beef	76	78	84	84	34	37	32	31				
Pork	45	62	38	44	7	7	7	6				
Poultry	80	83	82	81	8	35	10	10				

Source: OECD: *Agricultural policies, markets and trade: Monitoring and outlook 1991*, Paris, 1991. (Figures for 1989 are estimates; those for 1990 are provisional.)

a Total assistance for a given commodity as a percentage of the total value of receipts from sales of the commodity. PSE thus measures the value of transfers to farmers generated by agricultural policy.

b Excluding Portugal and Spain in 1979-1985.

Box 16

AGRICULTURAL POLICY IN THE EUROPEAN ECONOMIC COMMUNITY

The Common Agricultural Policy is one of the cornerstones of EEC. It was originally based on the principles of common pricing (Community-wide price support), a common market (free movement of farm goods covered by market organizations within EEC), and Community preference (protection for producers against non-EEC supplies). Domestic support prices and other policy guidelines are set annually by the Council of Agricultural Ministers of the member States, on the basis of proposals submitted by the Commission, which administers the CAP. Market price support represents about 80 per cent of total assistance provided to farmers in the Community, and is financed mainly by consumers (through the price impact of border measures). Price support exists for most commodities (grains, dairy, meat, fruits and vegetables, oilseeds, tobacco, wine, and sugar). Support is assured primarily through intervention purchases and border measures. Price support and import protection played a major role in the development of the Community from a net agricultural importer in the 1960s to self-sufficiency and subsequently to being a net exporter of a number of major commodities.

Import levies and export subsidies are calculated in relation to the difference between domestic support prices and world market prices. Levies (and minimum import prices or "compensatory amounts") serve to nullify price competition from imports, thus insulating domestic farmers from world market prices. Export subsidies are granted to dispose of internal surpluses on the world market, thus propping up prices on the EEC market but dampening world market prices to the detriment of competing exporters.

Border protection is somewhat attenuated for some developing countries by preferences. The Community provides tariff preferences under association agreements to Mediterranean countries, under the Lomé Convention to ACP countries, under the GSP to developing country beneficiaries, and to LDCs. However, these preferences are often limited by price or quantitative conditions.

Sanitary and phytosanitary regulations also sometimes serve to restrict imports; e.g. the ban on the use of hormones in meat production. United States concerns about stricter standards on a Community-wide basis after 1992 were behind the specific inclusion of sanitary and phytosanitary measures under agricultural trade reform.

Perhaps the greatest trade frictions between the Community and its partners have arisen over the last decade as a result of subsidized exports. Unresolved conflicts about the Community's increased share of the world market in sugar, wheat flour and dairy products, for example, and its practice of subsidizing the primary product component of processed products like pasta, contributed to the view that GATT disciplines on subsidies under article XVI and the Subsidies Code have been ineffective (see annex to this chapter). This is why the United States and Cairns Group are seeking significant specific reduction commitments on export subsidies from the Community.

4 per cent on average in food production would make a major contribution to food security and support agro-industrial development". The

Strategy calls for national and international action to raise agricultural production and productivity in developing countries.

C. Negotiating agricultural policy reform in the Uruguay Round

Since the inception of GATT, successive rounds of multilateral trade negotiations have, by and large, not covered agricultural products, and agricultural trade remains subject to some-

what looser disciplines than industrial products. This situation has been due primarily to the fact that at the outset a number of countries made it a precondition for their acceptance of

Box 17

AGRICULTURAL POLICY IN THE UNITED STATES

The Agricultural Adjustment Act of 1933 established the first major price support and acreage reduction programme of the United States. It set "parity" (the price which will give a unit of a farm commodity the same purchasing power as it had in a selected base period) as the goal for farm prices. Amendments to this Act made in 1935 gave the President the authority - and required him - to proclaim fees or quotas on imports (section 22), whenever he found that they interfered with agricultural support programmes. It also designated a percentage of customs receipts to promote agricultural exports and domestic consumption, and to help finance adjustment programmes. The Agricultural Adjustment Act of 1938 provided the first comprehensive price support legislation with nonrecourse loans and established marketing quotas for several crops. The Commodity Credit Corporation Act signed in 1948 established the legal entity through which USDA stabilizes prices and distributes agricultural commodities.

The United States was the chief architect of the exceptions in the GATT with respect to agricultural and commodity trade (see annex to this chapter). Notwithstanding the negotiators' attempt to accommodate United States farm legislation under the General Agreement, Congress adopted an amendment in 1951 which provided that no international agreement entered into shall be applied in a manner inconsistent with the provisions of section 22. As a result, the Administration sought and was granted, a waiver from obligations under GATT articles II and XI whenever necessary to comply with section 22. A goal of the agricultural trade negotiations under the Uruguay Round is to eliminate special exceptions and waivers under the GATT.

The United States operates a system of income support, price support, and acreage reduction programmes for wheat, feed grains, cotton and rice. There is also price support (loan rates) for oilseeds, peanuts, milk, sugar, wool and honey. Some provisions exist to limit costs of support; e.g. mandatory domestic marketing controls for sugarcane and sugarbeet if imports fall below 1.25 million short tons. Sugar and dairy products are also supported by tariffs and import quotas. Since the expiration in 1974 of the Sugar Act of 1948, a rather complex system of protection has been in place on imports of sugar and sugar-containing products, consisting of duties and quotas proclaimed by the President under the so-called headnote authority, and fees under section 22. Following legal complaints as to the conformity of this protection on sugar imports under the GATT, the United States established tariff rate quotas (the model it has proposed for tariffication in the Uruguay Round) in 1990.

The Meat Import Act of 1979 requires the President to impose quotas on imports of beef, veal, mutton, and goat meat when imports exceed a level adjusted by a counter-cyclical formula. Instead of mandated quotas on meat, the Administration has negotiated agreements on voluntary export restraints with its major suppliers from time to time over the last decade. VERs are considered grey-area measures which have largely escaped GATT control.

Sanitary and phytosanitary measures have affected imports of agricultural products, particularly as regards livestock and meat (e.g., restrictions for foot-and-mouth disease control), and fruits and vegetables (e.g., pesticide residue controls and the 1989 embargo on fruits from Chile). The United States also provides preferences to eligible Caribbean countries (e.g. on sugar) under the Caribbean Basin Economic Recovery Act.

The aims of the Export Enhancement Programme, which was established in 1985 and extended under the 1990 farm bill, are to counter "unfair trade practices" and to make United States commodities competitive. Sales have been directed in particular at markets where the United States believes its market share declined as a result of EEC subsidies. However, sales under the Programme have also affected other exporters, which is why the Cairns Group wishes to limit targeted export practices in any agricultural trade reform.

---

the General Agreement that special provisions be included to cover existing agricultural policies such as the maintenance of quantitative restrictions on imports and the use of production and export subsidies.[98] The disciplines were further weakened by the waiver granted to

---

[98] Unlike the case of industrial goods, countries are allowed to introduce, subject to certain conditions, quantitative restrictions on imports of agricultural products (article XI). In addition, the prohibition of export subsidies does not

SUGAR: NATIONAL POLICIES AND CHANGES IN THE PATTERN OF TRADE

Sugar is one product in which the pattern of trade has been changed drastically by agricultural policies in industrial countries. Cane sugar is produced in tropical climates while sugar beet is cultivated largely in Western Europe, the USSR and North America. Sugar also faces competition from other sweeteners, especially high fructose corn syrup produced from maize. Traditionally, the sugar trade has taken place between the low-cost tropical producing areas and the developed consuming areas of Western Europe, North America and Japan. However, this trade pattern has been changed by the policies of the traditional importing countries.

At the beginning of the 1970s the United States was the single largest sugar importer. However, sugar's share of the domestic sweetener market declined from 72 per cent in 1978 to 43 per cent in 1985. Sugar imports into the United States dropped by half between 1980 and 1985.

In 1967 the 12 countries now making up EEC were net importers of nearly 4 million tons of sugar. From 1967 to the early 1980s, however, domestic sugar production doubled under the protection of the Common Agricultural Policy (CAP), and by the mid-1980s EEC (including trade among its member countries) was the world's second largest exporter of sugar (with total exports of over 6 million tons and net exports of 4.5 million tons).

The losers in the sugar trade have been the developing countries that are low-cost cane producers (Brazil, India, the Philippines and Thailand, and a number of African, Caribbean and Pacific countries) and also Australia.

Prices in the United States sugar market have been maintained at a relatively high level by means of guaranteed loans for domestic producers and by limiting the supply of sugar through import quotas. The relatively high sugar price in the United States and the greater profitability of sugar than of other crops resulted in increased sugar production, but also in increased substitution of more competitively priced high fructose corn syrup (HFCS) for sugar in processed foods. Consequently, the United States import market has continued to shrink.

In the EEC sugar market, domestic prices and production have been supported through a system of mechanisms that include quotas on domestic production and preferential imports. There are guaranteed prices, expressed in terms of ECUs, intervention purchases of domestic sugar, variable import levies that effectively eliminate all imports except those from the ACP countries, and a system of export refunds to exporters whenever export prices for quota sugar are below the guaranteed domestic prices. The sugar regime has effectively insulated the EEC sugar market from the world sugar market and has converted the Community from a net importer of sugar in the 1970s to one of the world's four leading sugar exporters, and the single largest exporter to the free market.

Similarly, in Japan, the import stabilization fund, customs duties and consumption taxes have raised the import price of sugar substantially above the free market price. Sugar production increased by 16 per cent between 1982 and 1986 while consumption and net imports decreased by 6 per cent and 19 per cent, respectively.

As a consequence of the policy measures taken in many developed countries, in 1986 less than 27 per cent of world sugar production entered world trade and only 18 per cent was traded at free market prices.

the United States in 1955, the unbinding of certain tariff concessions of EEC member States and special provisions and protocols of accession (i.e. Switzerland). The result has been that agriculture was essentially "taken out of the GATT". The priority of domestic policy objectives in agriculture (national food security, social goals, and the need to counter market instability) has been asserted in order to avoid the application of GATT disciplines to this sector. (The GATT disciplines presently governing trade in agriculture are summarized in the annex to this chapter.) Uncertainty regarding agricultural trade has further been ag-

apply to agricultural products except to the extent that such subsidies lead to the subsidizing country obtaining "more than an equitable share of world export trade" in the products in question (article XVI, paragraph 3). The latter provision was also reiterated in the Code on Subsidies and Countervailing Duties that emerged from the Tokyo Round.

Table 31

PROTECTION OF AGRICULTURE COMPARED WITH MANUFACTURING IN SELECTED DEVELOPING COUNTRIES

Country and period	Year	Relative protection ratio [a]
In the 1960s		
Mexico	1960	0.79
Chile	1961	0.40
Malaysia	1965	0.98
Philippines	1965	0.66
Brazil	1966	0.46
Rep. of Korea	1968	1.18
Argentina	1969	0.46
Colombia	1969	0.40
In the 1970s and 1980s		
Philippines	1974	0.76
Colombia	1978	0.49
Brazil [b]	1980	0.65
Mexico	1980	0.88
Nigeria	1980	0.35
Egypt	1981	0.57
Peru [b]	1981	0.68
Turkey	1981	0.77
Rep. of Korea	1982	1.36
Ecuador	1983	0.65

Source: World Bank, *World Development Report, 1986* (New York, Oxford University Press, 1986), table 4.1.

a Calculated as:

$(1 + EPR_a)/(1 + EPR_m)$, where EPR_a and EPR_m are the effective rates of protection for agriculture and the manufacturing sector, respectively. A ratio of 1.00 indicates that effective protection is equal in both sectors; a ratio greater than 1.00 means that protection is in favour of agriculture.

b Refers to primary sector.

gravated by widely differing national norms and regulations related to animal, plant and human health and safety, which have the effect of protectionist barriers.

In recent years, because of the mounting budgetary costs to governments of agricultural support policies associated particularly with surplus production of certain products, and because of the ever-increasing frictions and disputes regarding trade in agricultural products among the major GATT members, due to intensified competition for export markets through the use of export subsidies, a consensus has developed that some remedial action must be taken.

The current round of multilateral trade negotiations is the first time that a serious attempt is being made to reduce the degree of protectionism in this sector and to bring agriculture under the rules and disciplines of the GATT. This section reviews developments in the Uruguay Round negotiations in relation to

agriculture, and analyses the main outstanding issues and options under consideration.

Evolution of the negotiations since 1986

When Ministers met at Punta del Este, Uruguay, in September 1986, to start the new Round, they agreed, *inter alia*, that the negotiations in the field of agriculture were to "aim to achieve greater liberalization of trade in agriculture, and bring all measures affecting import access and export competition under strengthened and more operationally effective GATT rules and disciplines". For the first time in the long history of trade negotiations in GATT, negotiations on agriculture were given a central role. Moreover, the focus of these negotiations was not to be limited to traditionally-defined trade policies, but would encompass all policies affecting agricultural trade, including domestic agricultural policies.

The initial phase of the negotiations, covering the first two years of the Round, was taken up mainly with the identification of the major problems affecting agricultural trade, general principles to govern future domestic and trade policies, technical matters and a number of initial proposals by participants for dealing with these issues.[99] A Mid-Term Review of the negotiations, begun in December 1988, was completed in April 1989. Agriculture was one of four subject areas of the Uruguay Round in which agreement could not be reached in the mid-term session of the Trade Negotiations Committee, held at the ministerial level in Montreal in December 1988. However, following intensive consultations, agreements on the four subject areas were adopted by the Committee in April 1989, which enabled the Uruguay Round negotiations to be resumed. Specifically in the area of agriculture, a "framework approach" was agreed, covering interrelated long- and short-term elements and arrangements on sanitary and phytosanitary regulations.

Regarding long-term reform, it was agreed that the objective is to establish a fair and market-oriented agricultural trading system and to provide for "substantial progressive reductions in agricultural support and protection" sustained over a period to be agreed upon, resulting in the correction and prevention of restrictions and distortions in world agricultural markets. Concerning the short term, during the remaining period of the Uruguay Round negotiations it was agreed that current domestic and export support and protection levels in the agricultural sector are not to be exceeded. In particular, tariff and non-tariff barriers are not to be intensified and not to be extended to additional products, while support prices to producers are not to be raised.

As regards sanitary and phytosanitary regulations, the agreement reached in April 1989 endorsed harmonization of national regulations as a long-term goal and a work programme embodying seven specific objectives. These included the development of harmonization of sanitary and phytosanitary regulations and measures, on the basis of appropriate standards established by relevant international organizations, including the Codex Alimentarius Commission, the International Office of Epizootics and the International Plant Protection Convention, and the strengthening of article XX of the GATT on General Exceptions so that measures taken to protect human, animal or plant life or health are consistent with sound scientific evidence and use suitable principles of equivalency.

The Mid-Term Agreement included important decisions concerning the interests of developing countries, which constituted a milestone in the negotiations on agriculture. These are highlighted in box 19.

Following the Mid-Term Review in April 1989, the Negotiating Group on Agriculture held a number of sessions in 1989 to discuss proposals submitted, principally in relation to the long-term reform process.[100] By the end of 1989, there were still wide differences in both basic perceptions and specific elements of this process. For instance, some participants considered that achievement of the agreed long-term objective should not imply the predetermination of specific goals regarding levels of government intervention or a specific time horizon for the attainment of such goals (e.g. elimination of export subsidies and trade-distorting support measures). Some others, however, advocated the inclusion of specific goals and time horizons among the eventual commitments. Fundamental differences also

---

[99] For a review of issues and proposals from the first two years of the Round, see, for example: Harmon Thomas, "Agriculture in the Uruguay Round: Interests and issues" in UNCTAD, *Uruguay Round: Papers on Selected Issues* (United Nations publication, UNCTAD/ITP/10, 1989).

[100] The Mid-Term Agreement also established the following work programme for the achievement of the long-term objective:

(a) By December 1989, participants would submit detailed proposals for the achievement of the long-term objective, including six specific areas: (i) the terms and use of an aggregate measurement of support (AMS); (ii) strengthened and more operationally effective GATT rules and disciplines; (iii) the modalities of special and differential treatment for developing countries; (iv) sanitary and phytosanitary regulation; (v) tariffication, decoupled income support, and other ways to adapt support and protection; and (vi) ways to take into account the possible negative effects of the reform process on net food-importing developing countries;

(b) By the end of 1990 participants should agree on the long-term reform programme and the period of time for its implementation;

(c) Implementation of the first tranche of agreed commitments on the long-term reform programme should take place in 1991.

Box 19

URUGUAY ROUND MID-TERM AGREEMENT ON AGRICULTURE AND THE INTERESTS OF DEVELOPING COUNTRIES

With regard to developing countries, the Uruguay Round Mid-term Agreement on agriculture, adopted in April 1989, specifies in relation to long-term elements, that:

(a) Special and differential treatment to developing countries remained an integral element of the negotiations, particularly on the strengthened and more operationally effective GATT rules and disciplines;

(b) Government measures on assistance, whether direct or indirect, to encourage agricultural and rural development were an integral part of the development programmes of developing countries;

(c) Ways should be developed to take into account the possible negative effects of the reform process on net food-importing developing countries.

Also, in relation to the short-term elements, it was agreed that "developing countries are not expected to subscribe to the short-term commitments."

---

remained regarding the importance to be attached to the objective of greater market orientation compared with non-trade factors, such as food security concerns, and the appropriateness of various policy instruments for the achievement of non-trade objectives. Moreover, a wide spectrum of views persisted concerning the six specific areas addressed in the long-term reform proposals.

The work of the Negotiating Group on Agriculture in the first part of 1990 focused mainly on the elaboration and clarification of elements of the detailed proposals submitted by participants pursuant to the Mid-Term Review decision.[101] Aspects of the proposals of the United States, EEC, the Cairns Group and Japan dealing with internal support, border protection and export competition, those of the net food-importing developing countries and those of the countries calling for due recognition of the importance of non-trade concerns (food security, environmental protection, etc.) were clarified with the aid of a number of questions. The process of formal and informal discussions associated with the clarification exercise gave a clearer idea of the possibilities of bringing positions closer together, for example on the disciplines to which certain internal support measures should be subjected, or on recourse to tariffication; they also showed large areas of divergence persisting, in particular in the field of export subsidies. The way in which

specific concerns expressed by some participant would be taken into account within a global agreement was also discussed.

In accordance with a decision in early 1990 of the Trade Negotiations Committee,[102] each negotiating group, including that on agriculture was to submit by mid-year a framework or profile of the text of the final agreement in each of these groups. However, at the conclusion of its July 1990 meeting, the Negotiating Group on Agriculture was unable to agree on such a framework. A draft text proposed by the Chairman of the Negotiating Group, and setting out a framework of modalities for the agricultural negotiations in the final phase of the Uruguay Round, was only accepted by participants as a "means for intensifying the negotiations". The Chairman's text called for participants to draw up and submit country lists indicating existing internal support, tariff and non-tariff measures and export subsidies by 1 October 1990. Offers by each country to reduce support and protection were also to be submitted in the course of that month. However, this process was not completed until late in November 1990. Although negotiations did start in the intervening weeks on the amount and duration of the substantial and progressive reductions in support and protection, little headway was made in them. In the end all the outstanding issues and offers tabled by participants were referred to the final Ministerial

---

[101] See boxes 21, 22 and 25.

[102] The Trade Negotiations Committee is responsible for co-ordinating the negotiations taking place in the different subject-matter groups (14 in all), including the Negotiating Group on Agriculture.

Meeting, held at Brussels on 3-7 December 1990.

At the Brussels Meeting, Ministers were unable to bridge the gap between the offers made by various participants on agriculture. There were widely differing views, particularly on: (a) the size and duration of the commitment to be entered into to reduce domestic agricultural support, border protection and export subsidies; (b) the modalities of reduction, including which subsidies and protective measures should be reduced; and (c) which products precisely should be covered. In the event, it was decided to suspend the formal negotiations to give participants more time to reconsider and reconcile their positions in some key areas of the negotiations, including agriculture. At the same time, the Director-General of GATT, in his capacity as Chairman of the Trade Negotiations Committee at the official level, was requested to pursue intensive consultations in the period from the close of the Ministerial meeting to early in the New Year with a view to achieving agreements in all the areas, including agriculture, services, intellectual property and textiles and clothing, in which differences between participating countries remained outstanding.

On 26 February 1991, the Committee reconvened in Geneva and decided to restart the Uruguay Round negotiations. With respect to agriculture, participants agreed to conduct negotiations to achieve specific binding commitments in each of the following areas: domestic support; market access; export competition; to reach an agreement on sanitary and phytosanitary issues; and to begin technical work immediately to facilitate these negotiations. No deadline was set for the conclusion of these negotiations.

Although formally restarted in February, the negotiations did not resume in earnest, owing to the wait-and-see attitude on the part of participants, until June 1991, after the United States Congress had approved a two-year extension of the President's "fast track" authority which would otherwise have expired on 31 May 1991.[103] In the last week of June 1991 the Chairman of the Negotiating Group on Agriculture circulated a paper to participants which listed unresolved problems in the main areas of the agricultural negotiations (i.e. domestic support, market access, and export competition) and set out options on which attention could concentrate as they prepared for substantive negotiations in the months ahead.

It is noteworthy that at their London Economic Summit (15-17 July 1991) the heads of State or Government of the Group of Seven major industrial countries confirmed their commitment to achieving "an ambitious, global and balanced package of results" from the Uruguay Round, called for the completion of the Round by the end of 1991 and with this aim pledged themselves to become personally involved in the negotiating process in order to resolve differences at the highest level. In this connection, the Chairman of the Summit stated that he was prepared to call a special Summit meeting if the negotiations became stalled and it seemed unlikely that they would be completed by the deadline.

D. Main issues in the negotiations

As mentioned earlier, from the outset of the negotiations there have been differing perceptions as to what they were supposed to achieve. Some participants have felt that the exercise should be limited to correcting the short-term imbalances on the world market for the major traded commodities. However, others have sought fundamental reform, not only in the degree but also in the form or manner in which governments support their farm sector. The central issue on which efforts to conclude the Round foundered last December was whether reduction commitments should be expressed as a general commitment to lower support, or whether there should be separate commitments on internal support, border protection and export competition. This is a substantive and not a procedural question, as it impinges on the extent to which new commitments and disciplines would restrain governments from supporting their agricultural sectors in ways that distort trade.

[103] Under fast-track procedures, the United States Congress must accept or reject a Uruguay Round trade agreement negotiated by the Administration as a whole, with no option to amend.

The consensus reached in February 1991 calls for negotiations on specific binding commitments on domestic support, market access and export competition. Other general questions under the negotiations concern the time period for implementation of reduction commitments, the depth or percentage of the cuts, and the product coverage. This section reviews the main outstanding issues and some of the options being considered for binding commitments in the areas of domestic support, market access, export competition, sanitary and phytosanitary measures, and differential and more favourable treatment for developing countries.

1. Domestic support

On the subject of domestic support, the main unresolved issues and proposals for commitments relate to which policies should be covered by, or exempted from, reduction commitments; how to express the reduction commitments; and the reinforcement of GATT rules and disciplines.

(a) Policy coverage

While it is generally accepted that in principle all governmental measures in the agricultural sector affect production and trade either directly or indirectly, a basic concern in the negotiations has been to reach agreement on reducing those policies that are most trade distorting. In addition, while it may be acknowledged that some policies may have a trade-distorting effect, they might be considered essential in the pursuit of developmental or non-trade objectives (e.g. regional development, employment, environmental conservation, food security). How are the policies that will be subject to reduction commitments and those that will be exempted to be defined? How are reduction commitments to be expressed and implemented? And how are strengthened and more operationally effective rules and disciplines to be developed?

A traffic-light approach has been used in the negotiations to differentiate between the policies to be exempted from reduction (green category), and those subject to reduction commitments (amber category). An attempt to prohibit certain policies considered to be the most trade distorting (red category) is no longer being pursued. It remains to be decided which or how policies should be assigned (e.g. by illustrative list or agreed criteria) to the green or amber category, and the relationship between the two (see box 20).

Some participants are concerned that without proper surveillance of, or conditions attached to, exempted or green policies, they could provide a loop-hole for circumventing reduction commitments on amber policies. How exempted policies will be monitored remains undefined. It has been proposed that they should be subject to an overall financial ceiling and/or regular monitoring. It has also been suggested that the following criteria should apply to exempted or green policies. They should be:

- funded by taxpayers, not consumers;
- not linked to production;
- not commodity-specific, but generally available;
- devoid of price support effects;
- limited, with respect to income safety-net programmes, to a specific level.

(b) Expression of reduction commitments

Whatever measures or policies negotiators agree should be reduced, there will also be a need for agreement on how to express or implement reduction commitments. Some delegations believe that reduction commitments should be made with reference to an aggregate measurement of support (AMS), which would serve as a common basis for expressing the value of assistance measures to producers and for implementing reductions. An AMS is generally calculated on the basis of direct budgetary expenditures and price gaps between domestic and world prices. In this connection, it will also need to be agreed how equivalent commitments should be determined for products where an AMS cannot be calculated. Other delegations have called for explicit commitments on specific policies in addition to, or instead of, the AMS.

In addition to the selection of the base year and agreement on the magnitude and implementation period of cuts, as mentioned above, it will also need to be decided whether an AMS would be expressed in total monetary value or per unit terms, and whether on a per commodity or per product sector basis. It will also need to be decided whether and how an AMS would be adjusted for inflation (e.g. through fixed external reference prices, commitments expressed in terms of hard currencies, use of inflation index, etc.) or for existing import ratios (e.g. in order to limit reductions for net importers).

Box 20

WHAT DOMESTIC SUPPORT MEASURES SHOULD BE REDUCED?

A key issue for decision in the area of domestic support concerns support measures that should be subject to reduction commitments (amber policies) and those that should be exempted (green policies). An illustrative listing, by no means uncontroversial, is given below.

Measures which might be considered for reduction commitments ("amber category"):

(a) Market price support , including any measure that acts to maintain producer prices at levels above those prevailing in international trade for the same or comparable products;

(b) Direct payments to producers;

(c) Input and marketing cost reduction measures, including credit and other financial inputs to the agricultural sector.

Measures which might be considered for exemption from reduction commitments ("green category"):

(a) General services (including research, advisory and training programmes, inspection, pest and disease control, marketing and promotion);

(b) Disaster relief, including crop insurance;

(c) Domestic food aid;

(d) Resource diversion and retirement programmes;

(e) Public stockholding for food security purposes;

(f) Developing countries' assistance to agriculture in pursuit of development objectives;

(g) Environmental and conservation programmes;

(h) Regional development programmes;

(i) Income safety-net programmes (e.g. decoupled deficiency payments);

(j) Investment aids;

(k) Payments linked to factors of production (land, livestock, farmers);

(l) Others: fuel tax rebates, tax incentives, incentives for farm improvements and productivity, structural/infrastructural aid.

(c) GATT rules and disciplines

Agreement on strengthened and more operationally effective rules and disciplines is an outstanding issue in domestic support as in other areas. The relationship between reduction commitments on domestic subsidies and existing rules on subsidies will need to be clarified. Specifically, would it be assumed that subsidies that are reduced in accordance with the reform package would be complying with the (revised) obligation under article XVI:1, second sentence, to limit subsidies that are causing or threatening to cause serious prejudice to other traders? Would "green light" policies be presumed to be non-injurious and not subject to countervailing action?

2. Market access

Major issues in the area of market access are related to the treatment of two broad types of policies: custom tariffs; and border measures other than normal customs duties. Key questions concern the conversion of non-tariff measures into tariffs (tariffication), modalities for the reduction of tariffs (and tariff equivalents), the amount and duration of the reduction commitment, maximum permissible protection levels or minimum access commitments (including rebalancing), and safeguard measures. A supplementary issue is whether current or new access opportunities should be extended only on a most-favoured-nation basis, and what arrangements, if any, should be made for preferential suppliers.

(a) Non-tariff barriers

An approach for dealing with non-tariff measures is to convert them into *ad valorem* or specific tariffs (i.e. tariffication). The conversion of non-tariff measures into an *ad valorem* or specific tariff rate is generally calculated on the basis of the difference between the domestic price and the world price for a product. There are unresolved questions concerning how to determine these prices, and whether and how to take into account variations in quality, degree of processing and currency fluctuations. Some participants seek to supplement tariff equivalents (fixed components) with a "corrective factor" - i.e. a variable charge to offset currency and other price fluctuations.

A major unresolved issue is the policy coverage of tariffication. For example, should all or some of the following measures be included: quantitative import restrictions, variable import levies, minimum import prices, non-automatic licensing, non-tariff measures maintained through State trading enterprises, voluntary export restraints and similar schemes, whether or not these measures are maintained under country-specific derogations from obligations provided for by rules and disciplines? The product coverage for tariffication also has to be agreed upon; for example, what "sensitive" products, if any, should be excluded, and for how long? If tariff quotas are introduced with tariffication, an important issue is how new access opportunities would be allocated. For example, would this be done in a non-discriminatory fashion for all potential suppliers?

(b) Tariffs and tariff bindings

An issue which has yet to be resolved is what approach should be adopted for the reduction of tariffs and tariff equivalents. Options include a linear approach, use of a harmonizing formula, or a request/offer procedure, including a target reduction in trade-weighted tariff averages. Some participants have advocated a harmonizing formula approach, in particular to deal with the problem of tariff escalation which affects many processed agricultural products. They have also suggested fixing a minimum reduction for each tariff line. The staging and implementation of reduction commitments has also to be decided; for example, should reductions be in equal annual steps or otherwise, and implemented over what period? A supplementary question is whether all tariffs should be ultimately bound or subject to a ceiling binding.

(c) Maximum rates of protection, minimum access levels, rebalancing

An issue related to tariffication is whether a ceiling should be placed (and at what level) on the height of agricultural tariffs after the conversion of non-tariff measures. A proposal has been made that at the end of the reform period tariffs should not exceed a fixed maximum level (e.g. 50 per cent). In addition, where no significant levels of imports exist as a result of non-tariff barriers, an issue is whether there should be a commitment to establish a minimum level of access - i.e. to earmark a percentage of domestic consumption (e.g. 1 per cent, 3 per cent or 5 per cent) for imports. Another unresolved question in this area concerns whether, in the tariffication exercises, countries should be allowed to "rebalance" their level of protection among products or to maintain tariff equivalents, after the conversion of non-tariff measures, at levels higher than existing bound tariffs.

(d) Safeguards

In order to facilitate the reform process, there is the issue of whether a special safeguard mechanism should be established to provide for emergency action, which would not require compensation, to deal with surges in imports or sudden declines in world prices for agricultural products subject to tariffication. In this connection, it will need to be decided whether the special safeguard would operate only during a transitional period or whether it would operate on a permanent basis. There is also the unresolved question of the form to be taken by safeguard action; that is whether only tariff action should be allowed or whether the possibility of imposing a quantitative restriction should also be included. Questions also remain concerning the level of prices or quantities of imports that would trigger special safeguards, as well as the level of tariff surcharge or quan-

Box 21

HIGHLIGHTS OF URUGUAY ROUND PROPOSALS FOR AGRICULTURAL TRADE REFORM BY THE UNITED STATES, EEC AND JAPAN

The following is a summary, in broad terms, of proposals tabled by the United States, EEC and Japan in 1990 for agricultural reform in the areas of domestic support, market access and export competition.

Domestic support

United States: Initially in the Uruguay Round the United State made a "zero-option" proposal; that is a call for the complete phasing-out of all agricultural subsidies and import barriers. This proposal was subsequently modified and by the end of 1990, in relation to domestic support, the United States called for reduction commitments of no less than 75 per cent over 10 years from 1991-1992 on a 1986 to 1988 average base period for commodity-specific support, and a 30 per cent reduction over the same period for non-commodity-specific support. There should be commitments on specific policies as well as on the AMS. For products for which the calculation of an AMS is not practicable, equivalent commitments should be based on producer price support and budgetary outlays.

EEC: For AMS products, a 30 per cent reduction implemented over 10 years from the base year 1986, for other products 10 per cent over the same period. Reduction commitments should be on the basis of the AMS, not specific policies. For products where an AMS cannot be calculated, the EEC offered, as equivalent commitments, reduction in production aid for certain products and border measures for others.

Japan: Reduction commitments of 30 per cent in real terms over 10 years from the base year 1986. Commitments should be based on the AMS. For some products for which AMS commitments, are not offered Japan proposed commitments on tariffs.

Market access

United States: All products affected by non-tariff measures should be subject to tariffication. Commitments should include the binding and reduction of all tariffs and tariff equivalents on a formula basis of no less than 75 per cent over 10 years commencing 1991-1992. A 50 per cent *ad valorem* equivalent ceiling should be established following the implementation period. There should be a special safeguard provision based on price fluctuations and import surges allowing temporary recourse to defined tariff surcharges without compensation.

EEC: Only AMS products plus wine, dried grapes, processed cherries and some fruit and vegetables should be subject to tariffication. Tariff equivalents (fixed components) should be adjusted by a "corrective factor" (a variable charge to offset currency and world price fluctuations). Rebalancing of border measures among products should be allowed with tariffication. Commitments would include the binding of and annual reduction in tariff equivalents (fixed components) by an absolute amount reflecting the incidence of the internal support reduction.

Japan: For those products for which an AMS commitment is not made and for which import restrictions are not applied, Japan proposes a target tariff reduction rate on a request/offer basis equivalent to the reduction rate for all agricultural products implemented by Japan in the Tokyo Round.

Export competition

United States: Commitments on export subsidies should include the reduction of both budgetary outlays and quantities exported by at least 90 per cent over 10 years from 1991-1992 on a 1986-1988 base. Export subsidies on processed products should be eliminated over 6 years. Producer-financed export subsidies should be subject to the reduction commitment.

Box 21 (concluded)

EEC: No specific reduction in export subsidies is proposed. It is indicated that the proposed reduction of support and protection will lead to a considerable reduction of export subsidies in global expenditure as well as in unit terms on the assumption that world prices remain stable. EEC is ready to quantify these and other elements in its offer. EEC proposes the following disciplines on the use of export subsidies:

- Limitation of export subsidies to the difference between the exporter's domestic price and the world market price;
- Limitation of export subsidies to the level of the import charge applied on the same product when imported into the exporting country;
- Enforcement of the notion of "equitable" market share in article XVI:3;
- Limitation of subsidies applied to exports of agricultural commodities incorporated in processed products to the difference between the exporter's domestic price and the world market price for the agricultural products concerned;
- Extension of the OECD "Consensus" on export credits to agricultural products and its incorporation into the GATT.
- No provision of export subsidies to commodities in respect of which export subsidies were not provided in the past.

Japan: No proposal.

titative restriction that could be imposed, and its duration.

(e) GATT rules and disciplines

Ways and means of strengthening GATT rules and disciplines on market access and making them more operationally effective will depend to a large extent on decisions concerning the nature and scope of special safeguard provisions for agriculture. An issue for decision would be whether a new agricultural safeguard mechanism should replace, or be additional to, article XI:2(c), which deals with agricultural import restrictions, whether or not modified.

3. Export competition

Given that export assistance measures, along with other forms of support and protection, are to be subject to reduction commitments, where should the line be drawn between commercial transactions and food aid? What commitments should apply to the gray area of concessional sales? Key issues in the discussion regarding commitments on export assistance relate to policy coverage (the forms of export assistance to be subject to reduction),

modalities for reduction (total outlays or per unit), food aid, subsidies on the primary product component of processed products, and reinforcement of GATT rules and disciplines.

(a) Policy coverage

A key issue in this area is whether to use a definitional criteria or a list approach to determine what kinds of export assistance measures are to be subject to reduction commitments. In any case, export assistance measures being considered for coverage in reduction commitments include:

- Direct financial assistance to exporters to compensate for the differences between the internal market prices in the exporting country and world market prices;
- Payments to producers of a product that result in the price or return to the producers of that product when exported being higher than world market prices or returns;
- Costs related to the sale for export of publicly owned or financed stocks;
- Assistance to reduce the cost of transporting or marketing exports;
- Export credits provided by Governments or their agencies on less than fully commercial terms;
- Provision of financial assistance in any form by Governments and their agencies to export income or price stabilization

---

THE CAIRNS GROUP

The Cairns Group is a coalition of developed and developing countries [1] originally formed to press for the inclusion of agriculture on the Uruguay Round agenda. Most members of the Group are net exporters of temperate zone agricultural products. The objective of the Group is to achieve fully liberalized trade in agriculture by eliminating distortive agricultural policies and by binding the necessary undertakings under strengthened GATT rules and disciplines.

On the various subjects of the reform programme (domestic support, market access and export competition) the views of the Group can be summarized broadly as follows: [2]

Domestic support: Reduction commitments should be not less than 75 per cent over 10 years from 1991-1992, with 1988 as the base year. Commitments should be on specific policies in addition to, or instead of, the AMS. Equivalent commitments for products for which the calculation of an AMS is not practicable should be based on producer price support and budgetary outlays.

Market access: All products affected by non-tariff measures should be subject to tariffication with the maintenance of existing, or the establishment of new minimum, access. Commitments should include the binding and trade-weighted 75 per cent reduction of tariff equivalents and existing tariffs over 10 years with a minimum 50 per cent reduction per tariff line and a ceiling binding of 50 per cent at the end of the transition period.

There should be a special safeguard provision based on price fluctuations and import surges allowing temporary recourse to defined tariff surcharges without compensation.

Export competition: Commitments on export subsidies should include reduction of budgetary outlays, per unit export assistance and quantities of subsidized exports by no less than 90 per cent over 10 years from 1991-1992 on an average 1987-1989 base. In addition, targeted export subsidies should be progressively eliminated and there should be no provision of export subsidies to products or markets in respect of which export subsidies were not provided in the 1987-1989 period.

---

1 The member countries are: Argentina, Australia, Brazil, Canada, Chile, Colombia, Fiji, Hungary, Indonesia, Malaysia, Philippines, New Zealand, Thailand, and Uruguay.
2 These views are not necessarily those of Canada, which has made separate proposals on the issues considered here.

---

schemes operated by producers, marketing boards or other entities that play *de facto* a dominant role in the marketing and export of an agricultural product;
- Export performance-related taxation concessions or incentives;
- Subsidies on agricultural commodities incorporated in processed product exports.

It has not yet been resolved which of the above-listed measures or practices should be covered by reduction commitments on export assistance. Another unresolved question is whether deficiency payments, which are not related to export performance but which can in practice operate to maintain or increase exports and to insulate producers from world price movements, should be treated as export subsidies for the purpose of reduction commitments.

A further issue is whether producer-financed export subsidies should also be subject to reduction commitments.

(b) Modalities for reduction

It will need to be decided whether reduction commitments on export assistance would be made in relation to budgetary outlays (and revenue forgone) on export assistance; per unit export assistance; the quantity of a product exported with assistance; or some combination of these approaches.

There is also the issue of whether a reduction in internal support in some countries would in itself lead to substantial reduction in export subsidies in terms of total expenditures and per unit assistance. Other outstanding questions relate to whether reduction commitments on export assistance should be made with respect to the entire agricultural sector or per commodity (or both), and whether - and - how to adjust commitments for inflation and world market price and currency fluctuations.

(c) Food aid

It is generally acknowledged in the negotiations that *bona fide* food aid would not be covered by reduction commitments under the agricultural reform programme. The question remains how to assure an adequate level of food aid, especially for food-deficit developing countries, to meet the food needs of their people, and at the same time prevent circumvention of the new disciplines on export subsidies. Various definitions of *bona fide* food aid (which would not be subject to reduction commitments) are being considered; for example:

* Food provided to meet internationally recognized emergencies;
* Food aid provided through non-governmental or private voluntary organizations or through international organizations; and
* Food aid provided in accordance with the system of usual marketing requirements (UMRs) under the FAO Principles on Surplus Disposal.

Another issue in this area is related to decisions on measures necessary to help net food-importing countries maintain their supplies of basic foodstuffs should world prices rise significantly during the reform process. Net food-importing developing countries have requested food aid and financial assistance as compensation for increased food costs arising from agricultural reform.

(d) Processed products

There has been a long-standing debate over whether subsidies on agricultural raw materials incorporated in processed products that were exported were prohibited or allowed under article XVI:4 (the ban on export subsidies of non-primary products) or under the Subsidies Code. It remains to be decided whether this practice should be eliminated or made subject to reduction commitments in itself or in conjunction with reduction commitments on internal support.

(e) GATT rules and disciplines

Whatever basis is chosen for the expression of reduction commitments on export assistance (total outlays, total quantities, and/or per unit), the question of how to incorporate them into the General Agreement will have to be faced. Some of the main issues concerning rules and disciplines over export subsidies include: targeted export subsidy practices; price undercutting of producer-financed export subsidies; subsidies on agricultural commodities incorporated in exported processed products; export credits; and food aid and concessional sales.

A fundamental issue that will need to be addressed is whether the equitable market share obligation in article XVI should remain the central principle governing export subsidies under the GATT or whether some other principle should be introduced (e.g. the total banning of all forms of export assistance, subject only to certain clearly-defined exceptions).

4. Sanitary and phytosanitary measures

There has been a general recognition from the outset of the negotiations that rules and disciplines would also be necessary to minimize the adverse effects that sanitary and phytosanitary measures can have on trade in agriculture, and to ensure that they are not used as unjustified barriers to trade. The negotiations on sanitary and phytosanitary measures have been an integral part of the agricultural negotiations.

Substantial progress has been made in negotiating a detailed text on sanitary and phytosanitary measures. It includes provisions on, for example, the requirement of a scientific basis for sanitary and phytosanitary measures; the objective of harmonization using internationally developed standards; the recognition of the equivalency of different measures; the use of risk assessment; recognition of pest- or disease-free areas; specific notification procedures; and use of GATT dispute settlement procedures.

The draft text does not attempt to establish sanitary and phytosanitary standards per se. Rather, it seeks to establish a multilateral framework of principles and procedures to

Box 23

NON-TRADE CONCERNS IN THE NEGOTIATIONS ON AGRICULTURE

Non-trade concerns in the area of agriculture, as described by several participants (Japan, Nordic countries, Republic of Korea, Switzerland and Austria), consist of such elements as food security, preservation of land and the environment, overall employment and maintenance of local communities. These concerns exist in varying degrees for all countries.

There are basically two options with respect to taking non-trade concerns into account: (1) to provide specific exceptions for domestic subsidies and import restrictions; or (2) to meet these concerns through measures that do not distort production and trade.

The participants that have attached particular priorities to non-trade concerns in the negotiations are all net agricultural importing countries. They would seem to favour the first option through a system of exceptions in the areas of (i) internal support (e.g. exclusion from the AMS of structural aid, production and surplus control expenditure, social welfare, research and development, and environment-oriented subsidies), (ii) import access (establishment of import quotas to assure that a certain level of domestic production is maintained, or that a certain level of the market is supplied domestically; or application of border adjustment measures to maintain domestic production levels in basic foodstuffs).

Japan, for example, defines agricultural products that are indispensable for the maintenance of the livelihood of a nation's citizens as follows: (i) those products, which have traditionally been the main source of nutrition for the citizens, and constituted an important part of their daily calorie intake; and (ii) those that will be produced and supplied on a stable basis in normal circumstances, and on a priority basis in times of food shortages.

On the other hand, the Cairns Group is of the view that food security and other non-trade concerns should be met through policies decoupled from production and trade, such as more secure and diversified import sources, stockpiling, and improved market orientation resulting from reform of trade in agriculture.

For the moment, a note submitted by the Chairman of the Negotiating Group on Agriculture in June 1991 defining options for negotiations simply states that "non-trade concerns will also have to be considered". However, the participants that place high priority on non-trade concerns insist that these concerns have to be an integral part of the operational rules of agricultural trade.

guide the adoption and enforcement of sanitary and phytosanitary measures. The draft decision would encourage the harmonization of standards - i.e., the establishment, recognition and application of common sanitary and phytosanitary measures - through the adoption of international standards. Such international standards are given status under the GATT through the provision that measures in accordance with international standards, guidelines or recommendations shall be presumed to be necessary to protect human, animal or plant life or health, and consistent with the decision and article XX(b). With respect to which international standards organizations would be deemed relevant for purposes of GATT-recognized international standards, there is agreement on the Codex Alimentarius Commission for food safety; the International Office of Epizootics for animal health, and the International Plant Protection Convention for plant health. For matters not covered by these bodies, appropriate standards promulgated by other relevant international organizations and their member regional organizations may also be deemed relevant.

The draft text essentially separates sanitary and phytosanitary measures into three categories. The first includes those measures that conform to international standards. If such measures are challenged under the GATT, the burden of proof would be on the importing country to provide scientific evidence that more stringent measures were necessary to protect human, animal or plant life or health. A second category includes sanitary and phytosanitary measures that are different from and more stringent than international standards. If such measures are challenged under the GATT, the burden of proof would be on the importing party to provide scientific evidence that more stringent measures were necessary to protect human, animal, or plant life or health.

A third category consists of measures that are less stringent than international standards. Contracting parties would accept as equivalent those measures applied by another contracting party that may differ from their own or from those of other contracting parties, but which provide the appropriate level of sanitary and phytosanitary protection (equivalence). Measures would be adapted to the sanitary and phytosanitary characteristics of the area of origin and that of destination.

The draft decision provides that contracting parties should use whenever appropriate the risk assessment techniques developed by the relevant international organizations. Guidelines are still being worked out to govern the biological and economic assessments for risk and appropriate protection. Governments should use, among the measures reasonably available that achieve the appropriate level of sanitary or phytosanitary protection, those measures that entail the least degree of trade restriction.

A rather extensive list of guidelines on control, inspection and approval procedures is included in the draft decision text. They aim to assure *inter alia* the smooth functioning of these systems, and no less favourable treatment for- imported products than for domestic products. Fees for applying for approval or registration in importing countries are to be at minimum cost to applicants, especially for products conforming to international standards. There is also an extensive list of guidelines on the publication of regulations, the establishment of enquiry points and improvement of notification procedures, with a view to enhancing transparency on sanitary and phytosanitary measures.

Under the draft text, GATT members would agree to facilitate technical assistance (including financial aid and technical expertise) to developing countries. Where the appropriate level of sanitary or phytosanitary protection allows scope for the phased introduction of new measures, developing countries should be given longer time-frames for compliance so as to maintain their export opportunities. Developing countries will also benefit from a longer period of time in which to bring their measures into conformity with this decision. Finally, recourse to technical expertise from relevant international organizations is to be encouraged for panels established under GATT dispute settlement.

There are several outstanding issues that need to be resolved in the draft text. One main issue relates to the scope of the agreement and its eventual legal form under the GATT (and its relationship to the Code on Technical Barriers to Trade). For example, while there appears to be a consensus that processing and production methods, testing, inspection, certification and approval procedures, quarantine treatments, packaging and labelling requirements directly related to food safety should be covered by the agreement, it still needs to be determined whether measures for the protection of animal welfare and of the environment as well as of consumer interests and concerns should be included in the decision. Other unresolved issues concern disciplines on national approval systems, the conditions under which the use of measures more stringent than international standards can be justified, and the extent to which countries will (or can) be required to ensure compliance with this decision by regional or local bodies within their territories; this concerns, for example, the relationship between EEC institutions and the member States, between the Canadian Federal Government and its provinces, and between the United States Federal Government and the states.

5. Special and differential treatment for developing countries

From the outset of the negotiations the special economic situation of developing countries and their need for differential treatment have been recognized. In the Ministerial Declaration launching the Uruguay Round negotiations it was agreed that the principal objective of negotiations was to "bring about further liberalization and expansion of world trade to the benefit of all countries, especially less developed contracting parties..." Concerning general principles to govern the negotiations, the Declaration further provides that the principle of differential and more favourable treatment would apply to the negotiations; that less developed contracting parties should not be required to make concessions that are inconsistent with their development, financial and trade needs; and that special attention should be given to the problems of the least developed countries and to the need to encourage positive measures to facilitate expansion of their trading opportunities. These general objectives and principles as they are to relate to the negotiations on agriculture were defined clearly in the Mid-Term Review decision. As mentioned earlier, in the Mid-Term Review decision on agriculture it was agreed that special and differential treatment is an integral element

THE DEVELOPMENT DIMENSION OF AGRICULTURE

Some developing countries (including, in particular, India) have stressed in the negotiations the close linkage between agriculture and the development process in most developing countries. They indicate that the special nature and role of agriculture in developing countries is evidenced by the high share of agriculture in GDP, high percentage of the population deriving their livelihood from agriculture, predominance of small and uneconomic (subsistence) holdings, and high proportion of foodstuffs in the allocation of household budgets. For developing countries with large segments of the population at subsistence level, price fluctuations of agricultural commodities can have extremely serious social and political repercussions. These special features of developing countries necessitate government intervention both to promote agricultural development and to maintain social welfare.

In their view, special and differential treatment for developing countries should be incorporated as an integral element in any agreement on agriculture, recognizing the right of developing countries to maintain incentive systems to protect and develop their agriculture sectors. In this context, it is stressed that governmental assistance by developing countries to their agricultural sector does not generate structural surpluses, as in the case of support policies of many developed countries, which generate trade-distorting structural surpluses. Accordingly, developing countries' assistance to agriculture should be exempted from reduction commitments in so far as it does not lead to structural surpluses.

As regards border protection, it is the view of these countries that commitments by developing countries should be commensurate with their trade, development and financial needs. In particular, developing countries should have the possibility of resorting to measures consistent with the present provisions of GATT article XVIII for balance of payments reasons.

The current status of the negotiations on agriculture indicates that the special concerns of developing countries regarding the development dimension of agriculture in their societies still remain to be addressed concretely in the light of the Mid-Term Review decision.

---

of the negotiations; that government assistance measures to encourage agricultural and rural development are an integral part of the development programme of developing countries, and that ways and means should be devised to take into account the possible negative effects of the reform process on net food-importing developing countries.

There are a large number of unresolved issues concerning the treatment of developing countries in a final agreement on agriculture (see box 24). One reason is that attention in the agricultural negotiations has so far been focused mainly on trying to put together the elements of a reform programme before defining the treatment of developing countries vis-à-vis this programme. However, in the individual areas of the agriculture negotiations (i.e. domestic support; market access; export competition; sanitary and phytosanitary measures), various options are being considered for the treatment of developing countries.

As regards domestic support, several options are being reviewed for the treatment of

developing countries. One is to allow developing countries lesser reduction commitments (e.g. smaller cuts) and/or a longer period to implement cuts in domestic support than developed countries. A further option is the total or partial exemption of developing country agricultural support measures from reduction commitments. This option is related to the Mid-Term Agreement that governmental measures to encourage agricultural and rural development are an integral part of the development programmes of developing countries. An unresolved issue is whether the policy exemptions that would be contained in the general "green box" would be sufficient to meet the needs of developing countries. In any event, some developed countries maintain that additional exemptions for developing countries should be based on effect-related, quantitative and qualitative criteria; while others maintain that only the least developed developing countries should be granted total exemption.

In the area of market access, the determination of special and differential treatment

Box 25

THE CASE OF NET FOOD-IMPORTING DEVELOPING COUNTRIES

Egypt, Jamaica, Mexico, Morocco and Peru have been principally responsible for arguing the case of net food-importing countries. They maintain that strong upward movements in the import prices of several major food items such as dairy products, vegetable oils, cereals and other foodstuffs since 1987 have already increased developing countries' expenditure on staple food imports. Increased food import bills are a major hindrance to development efforts, making economic adjustment with growth extremely difficult.

In addition, projected price changes arising from agricultural trade reforms suggest, for example, increases in net import costs of 29 per cent for Egypt, 30 per cent for Jamaica, 24 per cent for Mexico, 28 per cent for Morocco and 33 per cent for Peru, taking as a basis 1984-1986 average import expenditures. These increases will be difficult to absorb. Thus specific measures and commitments should be agreed upon at both bilateral and multilateral levels during the Round in order to offset the negative effects of the reform programmes on them. The objectives of these measures and commitments will be to alleviate the burden of increased prices on import bills and balances of payments, and to enhance the food production capacity of net food-importing developing countries.

These objectives can be achieved through the provision of increased financial resources and technical assistance, increased food aid, enhanced purchasing capacity through concessional sales, and an increase in the export earnings of these countries through improved and effective market access conditions. These measures and commitments could be implemented in cooperation with international financial and development organizations.

---

for developing countries is being considered in relation to two issues: the applicability of reduction commitments to developing countries, and commitments by developed countries to undertake greater and/or faster action on agricultural products (other than tropical products) of export interest to developing countries. On the applicability of reduction commitments to developing countries, two general options are being considered. One is to allow developing countries a longer time-frame for implementing reduction commitments than would be applicable to all countries; the other is to grant developing countries lesser reduction commitments (e.g. lower cuts or exemptions) and lesser market access expansion commitments (e.g. minimum access requirements).

There seems to be wide support for granting developing countries a longer time-frame for implementing reduction commitments (although some developed countries advocate linking the time-table to per capita income levels). There is, however, no consensus yet on the option of lesser commitments, including the scope for lower depth of cuts, and exemptions for particular products and/or policies. It has been suggested that the least developed countries be exempted from the tariffication process. The extent to which other developing countries would be allowed to use non-tariff measures

other than those provided under current or revised GATT rules has yet to be determined. It should be noted that a number of developing countries have already unilaterally liberalized their import regimes and have bound many of their tariffs.

While developed countries have already announced and implemented some reduction commitments of benefit to developing countries in the context of negotiations on tropical products, they have yet to indicate in their offers under the agricultural negotiations how they would undertake greater commitments (e.g. a faster rate of liberalization) with respect to other agricultural products of export interest to developing countries.

On the subject of export competition, the applicability to developing countries of options for reduction commitments on export assistance has yet to be considered. So far, exemptions for developing countries on the use of export assistance have not been envisaged.

The issue of food aid is often raised in the context of export competition. While it is important in terms of export subsidies in relation to the potential for the circumvention of commitments, it is more important in terms of continuing to provide assistance to developing countries, especially those that are net food-importers, in meeting the food needs of their people. Guidelines to assure a sufficient level of food aid to ensure that any increase in the prices of essential food imports does not affect access to food supplies have yet to be worked out. More generally, measures to deal with the possible negative effects of the reform programme on the least developed and net food-importing developing countries have not so far been given much attention. As indicated in box 25, net food-importing developing countries have called, *inter alia*, for increased financial assistance and food aid to offset possible increases in their food import expenditures due to the reform programme. LDCs have also put forward proposals to take account of their special problems (see box 26).

Special and differential treatment for developing countries is provided for in the draft text of an agreement on sanitary and phytosanitary measures. In particular, the text provides that contracting parties shall take ac-count of the special needs of developing contracting parties, and in particular of the least developed countries in the preparation and application of sanitary or phytosanitary measures. Where the appropriate level of sanitary or phytosanitary protection allows scope for the phased introduction of new measures of this kind, longer time-frames for compliance should be accorded on products of interest to developing contracting parties so as to maintain opportunities for their exports. In addition, with a view to ensuring that developing contracting parties are able to comply with the provisions of this decision, the Committee on Sanitary and Phytosanitary Measures (to be set up) would be empowered to grant such countries, upon request, specific, time-limited exceptions in whole or in part from obligations under this decision, in the light of their financial, trade and development needs. Contracting parties should also encourage and facilitate, through technical assistance, the participation of developing countries in the relevant international organizations.

E. Development considerations

Given the large number of outstanding issues to be resolved and the difficulties encountered so far in reconciling differences of views in the Uruguay Round negotiations on agriculture, it is perhaps too hazardous at this time to attempt a prediction of what the outcome of these negotiations will be in each of the areas of the reform programme - domestic support, market access, export competition, and sanitary and phytosanitary issues. The analysis made in this chapter, however, draws attention to some important considerations from the development perspective, which would need to be reflected in any eventual multilateral agricultural reform package.

For several decades now agriculture has escaped being subjected to the rules and disciplines of the General Agreement on Tariffs and Trade. Some developed countries have continued to provide considerable governmental support to exports and to domestic production. At the same time, the access of agricultural products to the markets of several developed countries has been inhibited by tariffs and various non-tariff measures. When the GATT rules would not permit certain policies and measures, recourse was taken to waivers under GATT and to special provisions in protocols of accession. The result has been the imposition of constraints on efficient producers and exporters, particularly among the developing countries, since they could not afford to engage in competitive subsidization. Their market opportunities have thus been seriously curtailed. As agriculture is an important source of foreign exchange earnings for many of them, this situation has had a serious adverse impact on their development process in general and debt servicing capacity in particular. It is in this context that the developing countries have drawn attention to the urgent need for liberalizing trade in agriculture.

The role of agriculture, in both absolute and relative terms, in the overall development context of a number of developing countries cannot be ignored. For many such countries, agriculture offers the only real possibilities for income growth and the generation of foreign exchange earnings. In addition, their prospects for eradicating hunger and malnutrition, and attaining a level of food supplies necessary for the promotion of economic development, also depend upon the development and expansion of their agricultural sectors. This is especially

Box 26

PROPOSALS BY LEAST DEVELOPED COUNTRIES

The least developed countries maintain that since development is synonymous with their agricultural and rural development, reforms and new disciplines that have been or may be agreed upon in the Uruguay Round should allow for their right to provide protection, support and assistance, including assistance to export development, in the agricultural sector.

Net food-importing LDCs may be adversely affected, at least in the short run, by the reform process in the agricultural sector. These countries should therefore be assisted to overcome any consequential erosion in their purchasing power of food through food aid, in the short run, and direct financial and technical assistance to their agricultural sector.

LDCs should be compensated appropriately for the continuing erosion of the margin of preference they enjoy under the GSP and other preferential regimes, due to the progressive elimination or reduction of tariffs on products of export interest to them.

Special consideration should be given to the LDCs within the framework of any agreement on sanitary and phytosanitary regulations, including their needs for technical assistance.

so as numerous developing countries, whose populations continue to grow rapidly, are finding it increasingly difficult to maintain a high level of food imports because of their balance of payments constraints. Furthermore, as agriculture in many developing countries is predominantly peasant agriculture, considerable public assistance is needed (in terms of infrastructural development, price and non-price incentives, research and extension services, a supply of inputs and credit) in order to improve productivity and realize their full agricultural potential. Accordingly, the reform programme on agriculture should be framed in such a way as to enable developing countries to undertake actions to expand and develop their agricultural sectors. This implies, for example, that in the areas of domestic support and border protection, developing countries should be accorded, as an instance of special and differential treatment, the necessary flexibility to continue with or to institute public programmes to develop their agricultural sectors. In addition, in order to give them an opportunity to expand their export earnings, their market access opportunities need to be significantly expanded. This implies greater and/or faster liberalization of access to the markets of

developed countries for products (including non-traditional tropical agricultural products, both raw and processed) of export interest to developing countries.

While the winding down of agricultural protection in the industrialized countries can be expected to provide developing countries with a long-term opportunity to expand their agricultural exports, the relative lag in agricultural production in many of these countries could cause difficulties for some of them in the short term. These difficulties are likely to arise on the import side as the large majority of developing countries are net importers of basic foodstuffs. Several studies[104] that have been undertaken on the possible consequences of reducing agricultural support and protection, principally in the industrialized countries, suggest in general that one overall effect would be an increase in the prices of temperate zone products (basic foodstuffs), leading to higher terms of trade for exporters and lower terms of trade for importers of these products. Clearly, net exporting developing countries of these competing-zone products would benefit from higher prices. However, for the developing countries that are net importers, the extent of

---

104 For example, see: K. Anderson and R. Tyers, "Liberalizing OECD agricultural policies in the Uruguay Round: Effects on trade and welfare", *Journal of Agricultural Economics*, 39 (2), May 1988; K.S. Parikh, G. Fischer, K. Frohberg and O. Gulbrandsen, *Towards Free Trade in Agriculture* (Amsterdam: Mortimers Nijhoff for IIASA, 1988); V.O. Ronningen and P. M. Dixit, *Economic implications of agricultural policy. Reform in industrial market economics*, ERS Staff Report (Washington D.C.: United States Department of Agriculture, August 1989); I. Goldin and O. Knudsen (eds.), *Agricultural Trade Liberalization: Implications for Developing Countries* (Paris: OECD, 1990); and UNCTAD/UNDP/WIDER, *Agricultural Trade Liberalization in the Uruguay Round: Implications for Developing Countries* (New York: United Nations publication, UNCTAD/ITP/48, 1990).

their net gains or losses would depend upon the consequences of trade liberalization in products of export interest to them. For many such countries, exports are concentrated on tropical products, sugar and certain natural resource-based products. Econometric studies of these products, with the exception of sugar, do not indicate that trade liberalization would result in significantly higher world prices. Moreover, given the low elasticity of demand for such products, trade liberalization is not likely to lead to a substantial increase of world consumption. This suggests that for those countries whose exports consist predominantly of such products, gains from trade liberalization, at least in the short to medium term, could be much smaller than the losses incurred through higher import costs on other agricultural products.

Although a rise in world food prices could eventually have the beneficial effect of stimu-lating food production, in the short run higher food prices would increase the pressure on the balance of payments of many food deficit countries with serious consequences for the well-being of the poor, whose food intake is already inadequate. This points to the need to adopt appropriate measures to offset the adverse effects of the reform programme on net food-importing developing and low-income countries. Accordingly, what needs to be envisaged for developing countries is a complete package of measures comprising understandings on trade liberalization (for products of export interest to them); on short-term balance of payments assistance (foreign exchange and/or food aid) to compensate for higher imported food prices; and on medium- to long-term assistance, in association with appropriate domestic actions, to accelerate the growth of domestic food production in food-deficit low-income countries.■

GATT RULES AND DISCIPLINES ON AGRICULTURE

From the beginning of the post-war multilateral efforts to liberalize trade, governments sought to draft or apply GATT rules and disciplines in such a way as to leave governmental restrictions or subsidies on farm products relatively unchecked. The vivid memory of food shortages in Europe and elsewhere during the Second World War led many governments to believe that agricultural production and trade merited special treatment. United States negotiators sought to accommodate domestic legislation for farm price support - with concomitant import quotas and subsidized surplus disposal - under a proposed charter for an International Trade Organization. Even so, concern that agricultural protection would be subject to international discipline of any kind eventually contributed to the failure of the United States to ratify the charter, thus spelling the collapse of ITO. Some but not all of the special provisions on agriculture worked out in the Havana Charter for an International Trade Organization found their way into the General Agreement, e.g. the exceptions for import quotas and export subsidies on certain agricultural products.

An objective of the Uruguay Round negotiations on agriculture is to strengthen GATT rules and disciplines with respect to agricultural trade, and make them more operationally effective. The following paragraphs provide details of relevant GATT provisions, particularly in regard to border protection, subsidies, sanitary and phytosanitary measures and special and differential treatment for developing countries as they relate to agricultural products.

1. Border protection

(a) Exceptions under the General Agreement (article XI:2)

Paragraph 1 of GATT article XI forbids "prohibitions or restrictions other than duties, taxes or other charges" on imports or exports of goods, but exceptions to this general ban are provided under paragraph 2 of the article. Of these exceptions, negotiators have focused in particular on 2(a) and 2(c)(i).

Article XI:2(a) permits export prohibitions or restrictions temporarily applied to prevent or relieve critical shortages of foodstuffs or other essential products. This constitutes the closest thing to a food security clause under the GATT, but applies only to an exporting country, which would have the right to decide for itself what products are "essential." The limiting factors are that the shortage should be a critical one and that the measures be temporarily applied. There is no provision under the General Agreement for an importing country to restrict imports of foodstuffs in order to assure domestic production for food security reasons *per se*. Some have argued in the negotiations that there should be a permanent exception for these purposes.

Article XI:2(c)(i) permits "import restrictions on any agricultural or fisheries product, imported in any form, necessary to the enforcement of governmental measures which operate to restrict the quantities of the like domestic product permitted to be marketed or produced, or, if there is no substantial domestic production of the like product, of a domestic product for which the imported product can be directly substituted". An interpretative note to the term "in any form" specifies that it "covers the same products when in an early stage of processing and still perishable, which compete directly with the fresh product and if freely imported would tend to make the restriction on the fresh product ineffective." It is further stipulated in article XI that the quantitative restrictions applied on imports under (c)(i), shall not "reduce the total of imports relative to the total of domestic production, as compared with the proportion which might reasonably be expected to rule between the two in the absence of restrictions", with due regard paid "to the proportion prevailing during a previous representative period and to any special factors...."

According to the drafting history of this provision, the exception under paragraph 2(c) was necessary because "agriculture and fisheries presented particular difficulties, since there were a multitude of small and unorganized producers who were often faced very suddenly with very large crops or catches, and the government accordingly had to step in and organize them."

Article XI:2(c) (i) is often referred to as the supply management exception. Originally designed to cover the United States sugar support programme at the time, the underlying premise of the provision is that a country is entitled to restrict imports quantitatively if it restricts domestic production or marketings quantitatively. A country invoking this exception must prove that it fulfils all of the requirements thereof. Governmental measures must include an effective limitation on the quantity that domestic producers are authorized to produce or sell. The provision does not, however, fix the ultimate level down to which production or sales are to be held, which could presumably exceed domestic consumption. The imported product must be a like product to - and therefore generally not at a further stage of processing than - the domestic product. The appropriate proportionality of imports to domestic production (or minimum access) must be maintained. This is difficult to determine where imports have been historically negligible.

Virtually every country that has invoked 2(c) (i) before GATT has been found wanting in fulfilling all the requirements of the exception. It might almost be concluded that there are no import quotas applied by any GATT member on agricultural or fisheries products that are fully justifiable under article XI:2(c).

Some have argued in the negotiations that the exception under article XI:2(c) (i)

should be eliminated. Others have proposed to modify it by making it either more restrictive or broader. Discussions have focused on finding a better definition of what constitutes effective governmental restrictions on domestic supplies, whether and which processed products should be subject to import restrictions, and what specific minimum levels of imports should be allowed access.

It should be noted that there is a safeguard clause under article XIX of the General Agreement for imposing quotas or increasing duties. This is generally available to all trade, agricultural and industrial when increased imports are shown to be causing or threatening injury to the domestic industry. The safeguard action should be temporary and may give rise to compensation. In practice few safeguard actions under this provision concern agricultural products. This may be because more permanent levels of protection are in place in this sector.

(b) Special exceptions (waiver, Protocol of Accession)

In some cases where the General Agreement failed to provide sufficient scope for subsequent or reinforced protective measures, additional special exceptions were sought and granted to individual countries. In 1955 GATT granted a waiver pursuant to article XXV:5 to the United States from its obligations under articles II and XI, "to the extent necessary to prevent a conflict with such provisions of the General Agreement in the case of action required to be taken by the Government of the United States under Section 22". Section 22 of the United States Agricultural Adjustment Act of 1933, as amended, requires that either fees or quotas be imposed on imported products by the President, whenever he finds that imports "render or tend to render ineffective, or materially interfere with" any USDA price support or similar agricultural programme, or "reduce substantially the amount of any products processed in the United States from any agricultural commodity or product thereof" which is covered by an agricultural programme. Import controls pursuant to section 22 are currently applied on certain dairy products, cotton, cotton waste and certain cotton products, peanuts, and sugar and sugar-containing products.

Switzerland has an exception specifically relating to agriculture incorporated into its 1966 Protocol of Accession. This country has reserved its position with regard to the application of the provisions of article XI of the General Agreement to the extent necessary to permit it to apply import restrictions pursuant to certain Swiss legislation concerning agricultural products.

It has been proposed in the negotiations that all specific exceptions allowed through waivers, Protocols of Accession, or "grandfather clauses" (i.e. mandatory legislation predating GATT) should be eliminated and/or made consistent with revised rules and disciplines.

(c) Measures not covered under the General Agreement

Certain kinds of restrictions on agricultural imports are not expresssly provided for in the General Agreement and have largely escaped GATT control. These include so-called gray-area measures like variable levies, voluntary restraint agreements, counter-trade and long-term purchasing agreements. Some countries, especially in Europe, rely on variable levies of one sort or another to ensure that imports do not undercut prices of domestic products. There has been no consensus on how the variable levy is covered under the General Agreement: whether it is a non-tariff or quantitative restriction, an unbound tariff whose level is variable, or in a class by itself (*sui generis*). It has been proposed in the negotiations that variable levies and minimum import prices should be eliminated. It has also been proposed that they should be maintained, but that the calculation of minimum import prices or of the differential between domestic and world prices should be more clearly defined.

2. Subsidies

Article XVI:1 contains the requirement to notify any subsidy, including any form of income or price support, which increases exports or reduces imports of any product directly or indirectly. It also obliges GATT members to consult on any subsidy granted that causes or threatens to cause serious prejudice to another member. An unresolved question regarding this GATT provision is how much is expected from a subsidizing GATT member by way of real commitment and action to limit the subsidy under these consultations. One view is that the member is required only to discuss the possibility of limiting the subsidization. In other words, if a subsidizing country is causing serious prejudice to its trading partners, all it is

obligated to do is talk. It need not reduce the subsidies.

Article XVI:3 declares that GATT members should "seek to avoid the use of subsidies on the export of primary products." These are not banned, however, but tolerated as long as they do not violate the equitable share obligation, i.e. they should not result in the subsidizing member "having more than an equitable share of world export trade in that product" over a previous representative period. Primary products are defined in Ad article XVI section B.2, as farm, forestry, fishery, or mineral products in natural form or as processed for bulk sales in international trade.

The Agreement on Interpretation and Application of Articles VI, XVI, and XXIII, also known as the Subsidies Code, attempted to give more precision to some of the terms used in article XVI:3. For example, under article 10:3 of the Code, signatories commit themselves not to undercut prices of other suppliers in a particular market.

The equitable share obligation governing export subsidies on primary products is based on *ex-post facto* evaluation of the trade effects of such subsidies, and has proved to be largely unenforceable. GATT case law on the subject is somewhat contradictory. Recent cases indicate that subsidies must not only be found to exist, but must be demonstrated to be the factor more important than any other factors taken together that could account for the subsidizing party's increased share of world export trade - and concomitant decreased share and displacement of other suppliers. Establishing such a causal relationship is an onerous task, given the plethora of special factors influencing world trade. It has been proposed in the negotiations that the equitable share obligation should be eliminated, and that export subsidies on primary agricultural products should be banned except for certain clearly-defined cases like food aid. It has also been proposed that the equitable share obligation should be retained and that a formula for defining market shares should be established.

Under the Subsidies Code, developed countries are prohibited from using export subsidies on non-primary products. However some of these countries do subsidize the primary product component of processed products. There are differing views as to whether this is allowed under GATT rules. It has been proposed that this practice should be eliminated or that it should be governed by whatever new rules are established for export subsidies on primary products.

3. Sanitary and phytosanitary measures

Article XX provides an exception from GATT obligations for the adoption or enforcement of measures necessary to protect human, animal, or plant life or health "subject to the requirement that such measures are not applied in a manner which would constitute a means of arbitrary or unjustifiable discrimination between countries where the same conditions prevail, or a disguised restriction on international trade...."

The Agreement on Technical Barriers to Trade sets down rules and guidelines to be followed by signatories in the preparation and application of technical regulations, standards and certification systems. However, this code has been considered ineffective as regards sanitary and phytosanitary measures, because essentially it does not cover production and processing methods on the basis of which many technical regulations and standards are established in the agricultural sector. An agreement governing the drafting and application of sanitary and phytosanitary measures is being worked out in the negotiations.

4. Provisions for developing countries

Article XVIII allows a developing country to modify or withdraw tariff concessions (section A), or to take other measures affecting imports (section C) in order to promote the establishment of a particular industry. These provisions have not often been invoked.

In order to safeguard their external financial position and to ensure an adequate level of reserves for their economic development, developing contracting parties are allowed (section B) to control the general level of their imports as necessary to forestall or stop a serious decline in monetary reserves, or to achieve a reasonable rate of increase in reserves. In applying such import restrictions, the developing contracting party may differentiate among products so as to give priority to the importation of products essential for its economic development. The justification for these measures must remain essentially to protect monetary reserves, and not to protect a particular domestic industry or agricultural sector.

Part IV of the General Agreement consists of best endeavour commitments on the part of industrialized countries to improve access for primary products from developing countries. It constituted the first formal statement of the principle that developing countries were not expected to offer reciprocity for benefits they derived under the GATT.

The decision on "Differential and More Favourable Treatment, Reciprocity and Fuller Participation of Developing Countries," also known as the Enabling Clause, allows GATT members to grant "differential and more favourable treatment" to developing countries without according such treatment to other contracting parties.[105] The Enabling Clause provided a permanent legal basis for the GSP, but such preferences are not obligatory. They can be granted on a discretionary basis by individual developed countries. In practice, benefits under the GSP for agricultural products have been limited. Most products that would compete with the preference-granting country's own domestic agricultural production are excluded or subject to quantitative or price limitations.

Other preferential schemes operated by industrialized countries include the Lomé Convention between the EEC and ACP countries (including a Sugar Protocol) and the Caribbean Basin Initiative of the United States. The latter is covered by a waiver granted under article XXV of the General Agreement, while the former was presented to the GATT under article XXIV (Customs Unions and Free-Trade Areas) and Part IV.■

---

[105] See chapter III below, footnote 109.

TRADE-RELATED ASPECTS OF INTELLECTUAL PROPERTY RIGHTS: IMPLICATIONS FOR DEVELOPING COUNTRIES

A. Introduction

In the late 1960s and the 1970s, developing countries campaigned to reform the international regime governing transfer of technology in general ánd intellectual property rights in particular, within the broad framework of proposals to establish a "New International Economic Order". A particular complaint of the developing countries was that the Paris Convention for the Protection of Industrial Property of 1883, and its successive revisions, established standards of international patent protection that were not geared to their domestic development needs. Consequently, the developing countries sought to obtain a better balance of public and private interests in the Convention through measures that, for example, strengthened a patentee's obligation to work a patent locally, limited the scope and duration of the patentee's exclusive rights in certain fields, and also regulated the conditions under which technology was transferred with a view to curbing restrictive and abusive trade practices. Many of these initiatives were implemented at the national level in various developing countries.

The developing countries' proposals were grounded on the conception that intellectual property law is to be viewed as an instrument for economic and technological progress that must strike a proper balance between the granting of exclusive rights to stimulate the creation of new technology and the dissemination of both new and old technological skills and knowledge. With this approach, the nature and scope of protection will necessarily vary from country to country and from one period to another, depending upon the degree of development reached and the policies chosen to implement differing national views of the public interest. These propositions hardly seem radical in that the developed countries, at earlier stages of their own industrial growth, often limited the scope of patent protection while denying protection altogether for certain technologies or product categories.[106] The international system of intellectual property rights

---

[106] The use of improvement patents and of a pre-grant opposition system were, for instance, key aspects of the Japanese strategy favouring diffusion of foreign technology over development, a strategy that lasted until Japan reached technological parity with the United States (see M. Borrus, "Macroeconomic perspectives on the use of intellectual property rights in Japan's economic performance", in F. Rushing and C. Ganz Brown (eds.), *Intellectual Property Rights in Science and Technology and Economic Performance* (Boulder, San Francisco and London: Westview Press, 1990), pp.261-275). Even the United States during its first 100 years seems to have behaved as many third world countries do today: "When the United States was still a relatively young and developing country ... it refused to respect international intellectual property rights on the grounds that it was freely entitled to foreign works to further its social and economic development" (Office of Technology Assessment, *Intellectual Property Rights in an Age of Electronics and Information*, Washington D.C., 1986, p.228). Many industrialized countries have only recently introduced patent protection of pharmaceutical products, while others still exclude them from protection.

(hereinafter IPRs) thus evolves gradually and consensually as the participating countries grow, establish innovation capabilities, and gain competitiveness in international markets.

After the failure of the Conference to Revise the Paris Convention during the 1980s, at which the developing countries' proposals were not accepted, the developed countries - led by the United States - mounted a strong counter-initiative aimed at strengthening the international intellectual property system by means of a radically new programme to be implemented both through bilateral and multilateral actions, particularly in the framework of the TRIPs (trade-related aspects of intellectual property rights) negotiations of the Uruguay Round. Succinctly stated, this programme is designed to ensure effective domestic enforcement of existing international obligations (including the possibility of retaliation against non-complying countries); to establish a universally applicable set of "minimum" standards that States would have to apply irrespective of their degrees of development; and to bring emerging new technologies (biotechnology, software, data banks, integrated circuits) within the international intellectual property framework on terms that would ensure maximum levels of protection.

This represents an altogether different scenario from that prevailing in the 1970s when the movement for reform was initiated by the developing countries, and its implications are profound. If the initiatives of the developed countries at the bilateral and multilateral level succeed, a basic feature of the present international intellectual property system - the freedom of each country to adopt, within certain limits, the regime of protection that it deems best suited to its own level of development[107] - will necessarily give way to a universal set of norms based on the current levels of protection

granted in the most technologically advanced countries. This would represent a drastic departure from the philosophy of the existing international intellectual property conventions based on the principles of "national treatment" and the gradual evolution of international mimimum standards, principles that were reaffirmed when The Hague Conference to Revise the Paris Convention in 1925 unanimously rejected a proposal by the United States to introduce the principle of "material reciprocity".[108] Such a principle, i.e., the notion that States must provide equivalent intellectual property protection to all other States, regardless of their respective national interests, was never accepted in the Berne or Paris Conventions. Moreover, the principle of material reciprocity clashes with explicit undertakings contained in Part IV of GATT and reiterated in the Enabling Clause of 1979, in which the industrialized countries solemnly pledged not to seek reciprocity in their trade relations with developing countries and renounced the imposition of "concessions that are inconsistent with the latter's development, financial and trade needs".[109]

It should be remembered that the subject of intellectual property protection was first introduced into the GATT negotiations during the Tokyo Round, on the basis of a draft proposal put forward by the United States and EEC with specific regard to anti-counterfeiting measures. Because no agreement was reached at that time, the United States circulated a new draft in 1982, and a GATT Group of Experts held several meetings on the matter in 1985. WIPO also prepared model provisions for national laws in 1988.

Counterfeiting mainly pertains to the use of false brand names on consumer goods and to the outright copying of copyrighted works, such as audio cassettes. Although an economic

---

107 The Paris Convention - with only one exception (article 5 *quater*) - leaves member States a large measure of discretion in determining the scope of protection to be granted to various forms of industrial property. Although the Berne Convention does establish more minimum standards, it recognizes the principle of national treatment and the gradual formation of consensual norms.

108 See S. Ladas, *Patents, Trademarks and Related Rights: National and International Protection* (Cambridge, Mass.: Harvard University Press, 1975), p.2700. According to Ladas, the methodology of the Paris Convention, by relying on national treatment, is inherently "opposed to the principle of reciprocity", which is instead sufficiently assured by the obligations flowing from adherence to the Convention (*ibid.*, p.269).

109 Differential and more favourable treatment, reciprocity and fuller participation of developing countries (decision of 28 November 1979). See GATT, *Basic Instruments and Selected Documents, Twenty-sixth Supplement* (Geneva, 1980), pp.203-205, hereafter referred to as the Enabling Clause. Para. 5 of the Enabling Clause states:

"The developed countries do not expect reciprocity for commitments made by them in trade negotiations to reduce or remove tariffs and other barriers to the trade of developing countries, i.e., the developed countries do not expect the developing countries, in the course of trade negotiations, to make contributions which are inconsistent with their individual development, financial and trade needs. *Developed contracting parties shall therefore not seek, neither shall less-developed contracting parties be required to make, concessions that are inconsistent with the latter's development, financial and trade needs*" (emphasis supplied).

evaluation of the drive to repress counterfeiting gives inconclusive results, the developing countries on the whole have acquiesced in the need to establish international rules covering this matter within the TRIPs context. This position recognizes the damage that counterfeiting may cause to legitimate vendors in terms of direct sales losses and lost reputation, and it also acknowledges the producers' need for incentives to maintain high quality standards. By the same token, negotiations on counterfeiting issues do not require developing countries to establish new substantive standards. Most legislation in developing countries already provides sanctions for the use of false trademarks and for the slavish copying of some copyrighted works. In these cases, developing country legislators have sought not only to defend title-holders' interests but to protect the public against deceptive trade practices as well.

The developing countries find it easier to address this issue because counterfeiting does not normally co-involve technological undertakings, unlike questions about the role of reverse engineering. Nor does the practice of counterfeiting confer advantages in terms of national policy aimed at building up industrial and technological capabilities. However, owing to the insistence of the developed countries, the discussions in the TRIPs negotiations of the Uruguay Round turn more on the establishment of substantive and uniform standards involving a higher level of protection for intellectual property rights.

B. The drive towards uniform standards on intellectual property

The reasons behind the new wave of reforms advocated by the developed countries have been analysed elsewhere.[110] The main arguments for an enhanced system of protection stress the magnitude of the losses incurred by innovative firms due to trade distortions and piracy as well as the benefits that would accrue to all countries from greater encouragement of innovation. A deeper analysis reveals a number of other explanatory factors for the proposed changes in intellectual property regimes, mainly:

- The increase in research and development expenditures which, in developed countries, have grown more rapidly than GDP;
- The ease with which extremely valuable intellectual goods can now be imitated, particularly those in certain fields, such as software, pharmaceuticals and audiovisual works;
- The intensification of technology-based competition and, very importantly, the relative decline of the technological leadership of the United States in certain fields (e.g. microelectronics);
- The threat posed by those developing countries that have acquired a capacity to imitate, adapt and compete in international markets;[111]
- The globalization of the world economy and the advantages that large corporations may derive from a harmonized legal framework and, particularly, from a system free of stringent working obligations;[112]
- The lobbying strength of organized industry groups, such as those representing the

110 See A. Mody, "New international environment for intellectual property rights", in Rushing and Ganz Brown (eds.), *op.cit.*; C. Correa, "Propriedad intelectual, innovación tecnológica y comercio internacional", *Comercio exterior*, vol.39, No.2, Mexico, December 1990; C.A. Primo Braga, "The economics of intellectual property rights and the GATT: a view from the South", *Vanderbilt Journal of Transnational Law*, vol.22, 1989, pp.243 *et seq.*; P. Almeida, "The "new" intellectual property regime and its economic impact on developing countries" in Giorgio Sacerdoti (ed.), *Liberalization of Services and Intellectual Property in the Uruguay Round of GATT* (Fribourg: University Press, 1990).

111 As mentioned by R. Evenson, "Intellectual property rights, R and D, inventions, technology purchase, and piracy in economic development: an international comparative study" in R. Evenson, and G. Ranis (eds.), *Science and Technology: Lessons for Development Policy* (Boulder: Westview Press, 1990), p.235, it is hardly coincidental that the "U.S. Department of Commerce's list of pirating nations is almost exactly the list of countries that most economists would regard as having made significant progress in economic development over the past thirty or forty years".

112 The softening of working obligations has been one of the main features of the process of revising the patent system throughout this century. The latest proposals take a new step in this direction.

pharmaceutical, software and semiconductor chip sectors.

The main complaints of developed countries as regards the level of intellectual property protection available in developing countries pertain to: (a) the lack of subject-matter protection in certain fields (primarily pharmaceutical products) and the uncertainty about the extent of protection concerning applications of the new technologies (software, integrated circuits, data banks, biotechnology); (b) limitations on title-holders' rights (e.g., as regards imports, forfeiture and compulsory licensing); (c) inadequate enforcement of conferred rights (lack of rapid administrative and judicial procedures, questions about the applicable burden of proof, etc.); (d) inadequate duration of protection (particularly in the patent field), which is said to discourage innovators from introducing new products or processes and to limit their ability to recover the expenditures incurred in research and development.

The tools employed by developed countries to bring the laws of developing countries into conformity with the former's desired standards have combined bilateral and multilateral negotiations with various forms of political pressure and trade retaliation.

1. Bilateral actions

The United States Tariff and Trade Act of 1984 ties the application of the GSP to developing countries to the willingness of those countries to adopt higher standards of intellectual property protection. In addition, section 301 of the Act allows the President to limit the import trade from these countries in the case of unjustifiable or unreasonable trade practices. The United States Omnibus Trade and Competitiveness Act of 1988 extends this action further by authorizing the United States Trade Representative, through a new "Super 301", to draw up a list of countries that have been given deadlines for an improvement of their intellectual property protection and threatened with sanctions should such improvements not occur.

The United States has repeatedly employed these unilateral instruments with a view to inducing particular developing countries to change their intellectual property laws. As re-

gards Latin America, two inquiries were opened with regard to Brazil, one of which ended with the application of trade sanctions (consisting of the imposition of 100 per cent duties on Brazilian exports worth $US 39 million).[113] Although Brazil resisted this pressure and complained to GATT (where a dispute panel was convened), the Government recently prepared a bill that largely satisfied United States demands. In response to similar pressure, Chile also adopted a law in 1991 that meets these same demands. Argentina and Venezuela are likely to revise their patent laws in the short term and to recognize, in particular, pharmaceutical patents.

Several Asian countries were subject to proceedings brought under section 301. After Thailand suffered a loss of privileges under the GSP, the Thai Government's attempts to comply with United States demands in the software area provoked a political crisis in 1988 that led to a call for new elections. The Republic of Korea rapidly responded to United States complaints by amending its patent law in 1987 and by subsequently enacting a software protection law, but complaints about enforcement are still pending. The United States also initiated bilateral negotiations on these issues with Taiwan Province of China, Indonesia and other countries in the region. India and China are now high on the list of targeted countries.

The European Economic Community has also pursued intellectual property objectives in its dealings with the developing countries, notwithstanding its reservations about United States unilateral actions designed to obtain adequate and effective protection.[114] EEC activities in this field were facilitated by the adoption of a new trade policy in 1984. One pending case concerned the Republic of Korea which, under United States pressure, had extended United States nationals' intellectual property rights on terms that differed from those granted to nationals of other countries. In 1987, the Community suspended generalized tariff preferences for products originating from the Republic of Korea. A more recent case concerned videogram products from Indonesia.

To date, unilateral action seems to have produced mixed results. In many cases it did lead to legislative changes in targeted countries that were implemented faster than could have been expected if matters had been left to multilateral negotiations. However, these changes did not always quash the underlying

---

113 The United States decision was based on the lack of product and process protection for pharmaceuticals. The other proceeding related to the informatics sector, and it ended without sanctions in 1989.

114 EEC supported the formation of a GATT panel to review the United States decision to retaliate against Brazil, as mentioned in the text.

controversies, and problems of interpretation or implementation still subsist. Another short-coming is that the discretionary character of the measures actually adopted does not always contribute to the establishment of common standards, the goal of those who pressed for change. Thus, the Brazilian law on software grants a 25-year term of protection, while the term adopted in the Republic of Korea was 50 years, and in both cases the duration is shorter than that generally accepted under interna-tional copyright law.

Notwithstanding these limitations, United States trade strategy continues to em-phasize the use of bilateralism in intellectual property matters. In Latin America, the United States recently entered into agreements to establish a framework of principles and pro-cedures for consultations on trade and invest-ment relations with eight countries. These agreements recognize the importance of pro-viding "adequate and effective protection and enforcement of intellectual property rights," and they institute a system of bilateral consul-tations to deal with this subject.[115]

From the developing countries' perspec-tive, the reform of domestic intellectual prop-erty laws in response to the developed countries' demands hardly constitutes a ra-tional approach to their own economic needs. In the short term, it may enable them to avoid trade sanctions, the economic implications of which depend upon a number of factors, par-ticularly the volume of exports to the country demanding the reform (always bearing in mind that these exports do not necessarily fall in areas related to the intellectual property dis-putes).[116] In the long term, however, reforms that do not stem from developing countries' perceptions of their own interests and needs, and that are not articulated in keeping with broader economic and technological policies,

are unlikely to result in stable and predictable rules or to be properly enforced. True, a reform of intellectual property legislation has some-times been considered an element of a broad domestic programme to modernize the scien-tific and technological infrastructure, as oc-curred in Mexico,[117] but this is the exception rather than the rule. In most cases, legislative changes are introduced to avoid trade sanctions without a proper evaluation of their economic consequences.

2. Multilateral initiatives: the TRIPs negotiations

The most comprehensive and far-reaching multilateral efforts to establish international standards of intellectual property protection have been channelled through the TRIPs ne-gotiations in the Uruguay Round.[118] The Punta del Este Ministerial Declaration established a mandate to negotiate on the trade-related as-pects of intellectual property rights, including trade in counterfeit goods.[119] The attitudes of developed and developing countries varied considerably in regard to this mandate.

The developing countries were initially prepared to discuss only the clarification of ex-isting GATT rules and provisions dealing with intellectual property, such as articles IX and XX (d), as well as measures to restrict trade in counterfeit goods that could be understood as clarifying article 9 of the Paris Convention.[120] These countries regarded any discussion of substantive intellectual property norms as be-yond the competence of GATT and within the exclusive jurisdiction of the World Intellectual Property Organization (WIPO). This follows from GATT article XX (d), which appears to reserve substantive intellectual property law to

---

115 The countries that signed these agreements include Mexico, Colombia, Ecuador, Bolivia, Costa Rica, Honduras, Chile and Venezuela.

116 In the case of Chile, for example, the basic United States claim concerned pharmaceutical products, but the main threat of eventual retaliation pertained to fruit exports, a crucial item in Chilean foreign trade.

117 See Secretaria de Programación y Presupuesto, *Programa Nacional de Ciencia y Modernización Tecnológica 1990-1994* (Mexico City, 1990).

118 Another important development is taking place under WIPO auspices, with the goal of harmonizing certain substan-tive and procedural aspects of patent law. See, "History of the preparations of the patent law treaty", Memorandum prepared by the International Bureau (PLT/DC/5) in *Industrial Property*, March 1991.

119 The mandate reads as follows: "In order to reduce the distortions and impediments to international trade, and taking into account the need to promote effective and adequate protection of intellectual property rights, and to ensure that measures and procedures to enforce intellectual property rights do not themselves become barriers to legitimate trade, the negotiations shall aim to clarify GATT provisions and elaborate as appropriate new rules and disciplines. Ne-gotiations shall aim to develop a multilateral framework of principles, rules and disciplines dealing with international trade in counterfeit goods, taking into account work already undertaken in the GATT. These negotiations shall be without prejudice to other complementary initiatives that may be taken in the World Intellectual Property Organiza-tion and elsewhere to deal with these matters."

120 Article 9 of the Paris Convention deals with "Seizure, on Importation, etc., of Goods Unlawfully Bearing a Mark or Trade Name".

the Berne and Paris Conventions, while conditioning ancillary measures to enforce intellectual property rights on a showing of "necessity" and on the avoidance of any "disguised restriction on international trade" or any "arbitrary or unjustifiable discrimination between countries where the same conditions prevail".[121] On this interpretation, the drive for material reciprocity initially clashes with the language in article XX(d) that implicitly *allows* "discrimination between countries where the same conditions *do not* prevail".

In contrast, the developed countries interpreted the Punta del Este Declaration as allowing the relevant Negotiating Group to elaborate new substantive rules of international intellectual property law. In due course, the developed countries - notably, the United States, EEC, Japan and Switzerland - made detailed submissions concerning the international minimum standards to be adopted, and it became increasingly difficult for developing countries to remain outside the negotiations.[122]

The developed countries subsequently began to indicate a preference for an integral package deal that would require all GATT Contracting Parties to accept the results of the Uruguay Round as a whole and that would deny single States the right to choose among the various agreements to which they wished to adhere. It should, however, be recalled that the Punta del Este mandate recognized only negotiations on trade in goods as constituting an organic and legal undertaking under the GATT framework. The broader dimensions of the Uruguay Round were recognized only in a political or policy sense. Nevertheless, should the view of the developed countries prevail, it could have the effect of making the benefits of market access negotiations conditional upon acceptance of the entire package of results, including those pertaining to intellectual property, despite the inconsistency between this position and the MFN principle enshrined in GATT article I. Moreover, a "single undertaking" could render developing countries liable to cross-sectoral retaliation for noncompliance with prescriptive norms governing intellectual property rights.

Faced with this challenge, and with the Mid-term Review decision of 8 April 1989,[123] a

---

121 See GATT article XX (d); J. Reichman, "Intellectual property in international trade: Opportunities and risks of a GATT connection", *Vanderbilt Journal of Transnational Law*, vol.22, 1989, pp.834-836.

122 The position papers of the developed countries reflected different opinions concerning the proper coverage and extent of the prospective regulations. See, generally, A.A. Yusuf, "Developing countries and trade-related aspects of intellectual property rights", in UNCTAD, *Uruguay Round: Papers on Selected Issues* (United Nations publication, UNCTAD/ITP/10, 1989).

123 The Trade Negotiations Committee's Mid-Term Review decision clarified the issues to be negotiated and gave a clear mandate to the Negotiating Group by stating that:

"Negotiations on this subject shall continue in the Uruguay Round and shall encompass the following issues:

(a) the applicability of the basic principles of the GATT and of relevant international intellectual property agreements or conventions;

(b) the provision of adequate standards and principles concerning the availability, scope and use of trade-related intellectual property rights;

(c) the provision of effective and appropriate means for the enforcement of trade-related intellectual property rights, taking into account differences in national legal systems;

(d) the provision of effective and expeditious procedures for the multilateral prevention and settlement of disputes between governments, including the applicability of GATT procedures;

(e) transitional arrangements aiming at the fullest participation in the results of the negotiations.

Ministers agree that in the negotiations consideration will be given to concerns raised by participants related to the underlying public policy objectives of their national systems for the protection of intellectual property, including developmental and technological objectives.

In respect of (d) above, Ministers emphasize the importance of reducing tensions in this area by reaching strengthened commitments to resolve disputes on trade-related intellectual property issues through multilateral procedures.

The negotiations shall also comprise the development of a multilateral framework of principles, rules and disciplines dealing with international trade in counterfeit goods.

The negotiations should be conducive to a mutually supportive relationship between GATT and WIPO as well as other relevant international organizations."

number of developing countries (notably Chile, India, Peru and Brazil) first prepared individual submissions of a general nature that were followed by a mid-1990 paper containing concrete counterproposals officially advanced by a group of 14 developing countries.[124]

This was a turning point for the negotiations, viewed in its North-South dimension, in part because it permitted the Chairman of the Negotiating Group to consolidate the texts and to prepare a comprehensive proposal for purposes of discussion at the Brussels Ministerial Meeting in December 1990.

A number of factors persuaded the developing countries to change their original position as regards entering into concrete negotiations. First, several of these countries, including certain newly industrialized countries held responsible for significant trade losses due to inadequate intellectual property protection, have brought their laws closer to that of the developed countries' own standards since the beginning of the Uruguay Round. Second, separate negotiations on particular issues, such as integrated circuit designs and plant varieties, contributed to clarifying the respective positions and to reaching a measure of agreement,

at least on basic principles. Third, discussions among developed countries themselves led in some cases to the formulation of more flexible positions put forward by those countries as a group, particularly in regard to new technologies. Fourth, the developing countries have agreed, at least in principle, to assume obligations to combat counterfeiting and to make the legal and procedural changes this entails. In other words, developing countries have shown a willingness to combat the slavish copying of a wide range of products that accounts for a substantial part of the losses attributable to inadequate intellectual property protection. Finally, developing countries have softened their initial position concerning WIPO's exclusive jurisdiction over intellectual property matters, without prejudice to the eventual role that this Organization could play in the implementation of the agreements to be reached in the future.

Although conflict of interests concerning agriculture at the Brussels Ministerial Meeting of December 1990 prevented further progress on other negotiating areas, including TRIPs, the work accomplished so far makes it possible to identify the areas of current agreement and those where divergencies still prevail.

C. Main areas of tension

While all the factors mentioned above have contributed to lessening the degree of conflict in a North-South perspective, many issues remain controversial and unresolved. The following are of primary importance.

1. Patentable subject matter

Efforts by the developed countries to make virtually all fields of technology eligible for domestic patent protection as a matter of international law still encounter resistance from countries seeking to preserve a certain degree of freedom to legislate in accordance with their

own assessment of the relative costs and benefits of protecting specific subject matters. Pharmaceuticals, not surprisingly, are of major concern, as are various branches of bio- technology. Although many developing countries now seem prepared to accept product patents in pharmaceuticals, they are likely to seek measures that limit the exclusive rights to be conferred (e.g. right of importation) and that provide a lengthy transitional period before the duty to issue such patents enters into force. In biotechnology, the developing countries can be expected to resist accepting the patentability of plant varieties, animal varieties and substances that already exist in nature, in keeping with their position on the use and conservation of biological diversity, an issue still open for appropriate international action.

[124] These were: Argentina, Brazil, Chile, China, Colombia, Cuba, Egypt, India, Nigeria, Pakistan, Peru, United Republic of Tanzania, Uruguay and Zimbabwe.

2. Scope and duration of patent protection

If many developing countries have been persuaded or have decided to broaden the list of patentable subject matter, their position on the scope and limits of the patentee's rights are still likely to elicit controversy. Developed countries appear willing to reduce local exploitation requirements drastically and to soften the conditions governing the availability of compulsory licences, in conformity with the aim of their enterprises to conduct trade in invention-based products on a global world market unhampered by nationally imposed working obligations. This reflects the current emphasis in developed countries on stimulating innovation by means of private incentives and rewards.

In contrast, the developing countries as net importers of patented technology logically emphasize the need to balance rewards to distant innovators against the strong public interest in promoting industrialization and the effective transfer of up-to-date technologies. They view the working requirements and compulsory licences recognized in article 5A of the Paris Convention as an integral component of the domestic public interest, as they perceive it, even if this means striking a different balance between private incentives and public benefits from that applicable in highly developed countries. In this connection, statistics tending to demonstrate the inefficacy of the compulsory licensing system remain unpersuasive, because the very existence of these licences serves to induce patent owners to grant voluntary licences where they would not otherwise have considered doing so. It can be argued, indeed, that the introduction of compulsory licences in favour of developing countries u nder the Berne Convention has played a comparable role in holding foreign proprietors of translation and reproduction rights more closely to local market conditions. In any event, it hardly seems logical, from the developing countries' viewpoint, to seek to weaken or remove long-established compulsory licensing procedures based on the Paris Convention when comparable procedures were added to the copyright conventions in 1971 for the specific purpose of alleviating abuses reported by the developing countries.

Of particular importance for many developing countries is the possibility of establishing compulsory licences applicable to areas of special public interest, such as health, food and the environment. In fact, several developed countries have used (and still use) this type of system, particularly to protect consumers against abusive prices or inadequate supply. For the poorer developing countries, the need to ensure adequate supplies of basic necessities at affordable prices goes well beyond "consumer protection" and involves the ability of governments to ensure that basic living conditions meet minimum acceptable levels. As one commentator observed, it is not "really so difficult to understand that countries suffering from starvation and epidemic diseases ... have a different approach to the patentability of foodstuffs and pharmaceuticals than most industrialized countries ... half a century after their industrialization".[125]

The duration of patent rights is another area of divergence. The developed countries argue that the importance of the resources devoted to R and D requires long periods of recovery if the continuity and expansion of the innovative process is to be ensured. Hence, they want a uniform 20-year period. But the developing countries view this arrangement as contrary to their need to master new technologies and to expand their own industrial capacity, needs that become all the more acute when the foreign technology is neither worked locally nor effectively transferred by other means. In other words, the ability of the developing country enterprises ever to aspire to a degree of competitiveness in international trade depends on faster access to superior technology than occurs in the advanced countries, an advantage that is more than offset by a slower technological learning curve. These needs are further aggravated by the trend towards short product cycles, particularly in high technology fields.

For these and other reasons, they believe that a uniform 20-year period of protection for all patentable subject matters could only retard their access to foreign technologies and create further constraints to technology transfer. Thus, they have suggested, as a compromise solution, to seek to ensure a minimum period of effective protection beyond which the specific development needs of single developing countries could be taken into account. This would entail the extension of the period of protection only for those patented technologies that are effectively worked in a developing country. It would thus imply differential and more favourable treatment geared to the needs

---

125 Ullrich, "GATT: Industrial property protection, fair trade and development" in F.K. Beier and G. Schricker (eds.), *GATT or WIPO: New Ways in the International Protection of Intellectual Property* (Max Planck Institute for Foreign and International Patents, Copyright and Competition Law, IIC Studies, 1989), p.142, N. 41.

of the developing countries, at least until the latter graduate to a higher competitive status, and create an incentive to use proprietary technologies in the country granting protection.

3. Computer software

Copyright protection of software has become more controversial than ever, notwithstanding attempts to paper over the underlying differences with a formal appearance of consensus. In reality, despite the fact that many developing (and developed) countries have followed the initial United States position of recognizing copyright law as the primary vehicle for software protection, the trend in the United States now favours concurrent patent protection for those computer programmes that satisfy the requirements of patentability.[126] This poses the question as to whether the developing countries ought to be locked into copyright law at all, with the attendant risks of overprotection, when the major world producer in this field has still not clearly resolved the issue of whether copyrights or patents are the appropriate legal framework for software protection. For the time being, it appears that the consensus on copyright protection hinges mainly on fears that the developing countries will not otherwise agree to provide adequate and effective levels of protection for computer programmes.

A workable compromise at the international level that combines effective protection against wholesale copying for the one side with access to technological concepts for the other could enable innovators, producers and users to agree on a modified copyright approach that might benefit the market for computer technology everywhere. While providing reasonable guarantees to software producers, this would ensure that innovators retain access to technological ideas and, when necessary, to the technical information required to attain interoperability and compatibility between systems. If such a compromise were then broadened to cover slavish imitation of new technologies generally, it could be brought within article 10 bis of the Paris Convention

without requiring the premature elaboration of international standards on which no real consensus exists.

A second problem arises from the proposed qualification of software as a "literary" work. The fear of the developing countries is that this could considerably limit the right of any country to subject software to domestic rules that specifically take account of its functional nature (as France, Japan, Brazil and other countries have done in the past). A third and crucial issue pertains to the scope of protection to be given to software, with a view to ensuring that underlying ideas and concepts remain available to those engaged in further innovation and competition. Recent United States case law has broadly protected the "look and feel" of copyrightable computer programmes, including standardized elements of user interfaces, and these precedents narrow second comers' "reverse engineering" rights, as do certain provisions in the European Economic Community's new directive on software.

Analytical use of computer programmes - a method that is clearly accepted in the field of integrated circuit designs - is important to the creation of competing products, to the task of ensuring the interoperability or portability of systems and data, and to the maintenance of high performance standards. Indeed, the authors of both leading copyright treatises in the United States believe that exclusive reproduction rights cannot be used to deny access to underlying ideas,[127] and one affirms that reverse engineering in the sense of analytical use is guaranteed by statutory fair use provisions.[128] Some language in EEC's directive also tends in this direction, although the courts will ultimately determine the degree of analytical use that is consistent with the various domestic laws. Strict rules prohibiting all forms of reverse engineering would adversely affect the developing countries' capacity to create or expand domestic software industries. Indeed, many fear that undue constraints on reverse engineering will undermine competitiveness in developed countries, too, which partly explains why those lacking the capabilities to establish industry standards have actively opposed the protectability of interface information, as illustrated by the recent debate on the EEC's software directive.

---

[126] See P. Samuelson, "Benson revisited: The case against patent protection for algorithms and other computer program-related innovations", *Emory Law Journal*, vol.39, 1990, p.1025.

[127] See, for example, M. and D. Nimmer, *Nimmer on Copyright* (New York: Matthew Bender, 1990 rev.ed.); P. Goldstein, *Copyright: Principles, Law and Practice* (Boston: Little, Brown & Co., 1989 plus 1990 supplement), p.198.

[128] See P. Goldstein, *op.cit.* (1990 supplement), pp.60-66.

4. Rights related to or neighbouring on copyright law

Developing countries have also expressed concern that proposals advanced by some developed countries would extend neighbouring rights protection, at the international level, to noncopyrightable compilations of data, and to the protection of performers, and the producers of sound recordings and broadcasts. Some of these subject matters are covered by existing conventions to which some developing countries may or may not be a party, and other subject matters - notably, compilations of data - are not yet covered by international agreements. Even when the subject matter is covered by one or more neighbouring rights conventions, the treatment proposed within the TRIPs framework usually exceeds existing minimum standards. If these proposals are approved and are then applied to developing countries by one means or another, some of these countries could find themselves subject to heavy external charges that have not hitherto entered into their balance of payments schedules.

5. Geographical indications of origin

The drive to enhance the protection of these indications has aroused significant controversy in the developed countries themselves. The willingness of the United States, for example, to adapt its law either to existing or proposed international standards remains unclear. Heightened protection of this subject matter would obviously affect the economies of the developing countries in which existing production might have to be cut back. Some of them could only accept the protection of geographical indications if various specific conditions were met,[129] while the dislocation costs ensuing from cutbacks of existing production should be compensated by one means or another.

6. Undisclosed information

Know-how and trade secrets constitute assets of great value to modern enterprises. Although a large share of the most valuable technologies currently falls under the heading of non-patented or otherwise unprotected know-how, and this share is destined to grow even larger over time, world intellectual property law does not confer any internationally recognized proprietary rights in know-how that are equivalent to patents or other proprietary titles granting exclusive rights against third parties. Know-how is not even perceived as the subject of a property right under many continental laws. The protection of know-how, whether in traditional or modern forms, is thus entrusted to trade secret or confidentiality laws that prohibit misappropriation by unethical means, such as commercial bribery or theft. However, these laws protect know-how only so long as the innovator takes reasonable precautions to maintain secrecy, and they allow third parties not under contractual restraints freely to reverse engineer all unpatented discoveries.

Although the Paris Convention makes no mention of trade secret protection as such, the developed countries have proposed the inclusion of a specific chapter in the TRIPs negotiations on "undisclosed information", a broad expression including know-how and the protection of trade secrets generally. The developing countries have responded by showing some willingness to restate the canons of unfair competition law applicable to the misappropriation of trade secrets, particularly by unethical conduct. This would help to clarify and perhaps expand article 10*bis* of the Paris Convention.

However, the developing countries are wary of engaging in a standard-setting exercise on the margins of intellectual property law, where no international minimum standards exist and where even the leading industrial power - the United States - lacks a single federal law to protect trade secrets. Some developing countries do not feel the need to enact trade secret laws at all. Others want such laws to be strictly geared to their domestic development needs. They perceive little need to establish specific schemes of protection for data relating to pharmaceutical and agrochemical products, for example. On the contrary, many experts

---

[129] For example, the Latin American countries hold that such indications should not be protected when they are considered generic in the territory of one participating country, when they have been used for a long time, or when they have become part of the common language. See SELA, "Evaluacion sobre la Rueda Uruguay", communication from the Permanent Representative of Uruguay on behalf of SELA, Geneva (29.11.90), 1991.

contend that acceptance of a multilateral system of protection for undisclosed information would significantly undermine the patent system, which makes adequate disclosure a condition of protection.

Finally, the regulation of trade secrets under any future international regime cannot logically be separated from the developing countries' own drive for an international regime to govern transfer of technology and the regulation of restrictive practices, including the transfer and licensing of unpatented, noncopyrightable know-how. The developing countries feel that, in the absence of such a regime, higher standards of protection would only serve to buttress the monopolistic imbalance that is already inherent in the existing means of keeping undisclosed data beyond the reach of fair competitors.

7. Transfer of technology and restrictive practices

Precisely because the developed countries control the bulk of all patented technology and the incentive to innovation in the developing countries afforded by the grant of patents is often marginal, these countries need to redress this imbalance by ensuring a more effective transfer of both patented and unpatented technologies to their industrial establishment. At present, this goal is undermined by certain restrictive licensing practices, among others, that cause the developing countries to devote scarce resources to the acquisition of technological know-how that has not been effectively transferred or absorbed. Such practices include grant-back provisions; unreasonable requirements of exclusive dealings; restrictions on independent research and the use of personnel; price-fixing conditions; limitations in product adaptation; tying arrangements and burdensome exclusive distribution clauses; export restrictions and limitations on advertising; obligations to pay after the expiration of industrial property rights; and other burdensome clauses including unreasonable cross-licensing constraints and post-contractual limitations.

As a result of concerns expressed during the 1970s, a major effort to establish international voluntary standards in this field was undertaken within the framework of negotiations for a code of conduct on the Transfer of

Technology, under UNCTAD's auspices. The substantive negotiations pertaining to this draft Code have covered both the transfer of technology through essentially private transactions, with emphasis on the identification of undesirable practices and conduct, and the regulatory action to be taken by Governments to meet their obligations under the Code. While the benefits of such a code of conduct for the developing countries' own economies are evident, these countries believe that it would also increase the opportunities available to small and medium-sized firms in the industrialized countries to participate in the international market for technology. The draft Code of Conduct is thus aimed at removing existing barriers to entry for all participants and at augmenting fair trade in technology generally, in keeping with goals that are widely attributed to the TRIPs initiative as a whole.

In reality, the developed countries seem disinclined to discuss these issues, even though several of them initially called attention to the need to combat abuses of intellectual property rights while assuring adequate protection for such rights. One major obstacle to progress on the Code in the past was the difficulty of adopting an agreed concept for the "restrictive practices" in question, and this remains controversial despite a certain evolution in the developing countries' position. The matter is of particular importance in view of the lack or weaknesses of antitrust and competition laws in most developing countries.

Concerns about restrictive licensing practices are just one aspect of the developing countries' deeper preoccupation with access to technology in the emerging international framework. The strengthening and expansion of intellectual property protection is viewed as one component of a larger global strategy by developed countries to protect the technological assets of their enterprises and to increase the financial returns therefrom. Besides this growing recourse to technological protectionism, a trend towards the privatization of scientific knowledge has also been discerned. As one recent report observes, "there is a growing trend toward imposing very strict restrictions on the disclosure, distribution and transfer of scientific and technological achievements. This trend is seen in the research on applied sciences and development work, but there are fears it will also affect basic research, in part because the differences between basic research and research on applied science have become less and less distinct".[130] For example, more than 40 per cent of pre-competitive re-

---

130 See Council for Science and Technology of Japan, *Ad hoc* Committee on International Affairs, *Toward the Globalization of Science and Technology* (1990), p.4.

search falling under the ESPRIT programme turned out, in 1986, to have been susceptible of direct industrial application.[131]

Although present trends thus indicate that the prospects for developing countries' access to foreign technologies are likely to present more difficulties than in the last two decades, the TRIPs negotiations fail to address the main issues and problems associated with access to and transfer of technologies. Developing countries may, nevertheless, still use the negotiations in the Uruguay Round as a forum in which to formulate long-desired rules on technology transfer, and propose the consideration not only of the static aspects of intellectual property rights, as has been the case up to now, but also of their dynamic aspects, including the impact on international transfer of technology and licensing arrangements.

8. Enforcement and dispute settlement

While the main areas of North-South disagreement are likely to centre on the elaboration of substantive standards, procedural matters pending on the TRIPs agenda are also controversial. The stricter enforcement of agreed procedural standards sought by developed countries would certainly increase the costs of administering intellectual property systems, costs that many developing countries already find extremely burdensome. Enforcement provisions, including border control measures, would also imply changing various aspects of national legislation (including rules of jurisdiction) that might be difficult to implement in view of the differences in administrative and judicial systems.

Of particular concern to developing countries is the insistence on reversing the burden of proof in relevant infringement cases. Such a reversal is viewed as a derogation from general *onus probandi* principles that unjustifiably increases the power of the title-holder at the expense of small and medium-sized enterprises.

Finally, the proposed linkage between compliance with intellectual property standards and eventual trade retaliation is a matter of deep concern to all developing countries. The hope of achieving such a linkage has been a primary reason why the developed countries introduced intellectual property into the Uruguay Round negotiations in the first place. Developing countries have continued to emphasize the role and jurisdiction of WIPO, and they note that existing conventions already provide dispute settlement mechanisms. Meanwhile, WIPO has begun to consider an instrument for the settlement of disputes in connection with its efforts to retain jurisdiction over international intellectual property issues.

D. Implications for developing countries

1. General considerations

Economists continue to debate about the value and functions of intellectual property systems in market economies generally, and the drive for enhanced international regulation of intellectual property has only intensified this ongoing controversy.[132] Despite a formidable body of theoretical and empirical work on this subject, there are no conclusive answers to those who question the relative costs and benefits of the system as a whole, particularly when an asymmetric technological relationship is introduced into the analysis.

The economic rationale for intellectual property protection, simply stated, is to reward the often large expenditures for research and

---

131 L. Mytelka, "Les alliances stratégiques au sein du programme européen ESPRIT", *Economie Prospective Internationale 5*, 1989, p.17.

132 See generally R. Benko, *Protecting intellectual property rights: Issues and controversies* (Washington, D.C.: American Enterprise Institute, 1987); W. Siebeck (ed.) with R. Evenson, W. Lesser and C.A. Primo Braga, "Strengthening protection of intellectual property in developing countries. A survey of the literature", *World Bank Discussion Paper No. 112* (Washington, D.C., 1990).

development that become necessary to develop new processes or products that promote the general welfare of society. This assumes that, on the one hand, investment in innovation would be sub-optimal in the the absence of protection; and, on the other, that the social benefits from productivity gains and economic growth, on balance, offset the added costs created by legal monopolies.

In countries that have already attained a certain degree of industrial and technological development, intellectual property protection may well be an important tool in fostering innovation to the extent that it ensures the exploitation of R and D results through the vehicle of exclusive rights. It is not surprising therefore that developed countries, which control an overwhelming share of the world's scientific and technological resources, advocate the benefits of such protection and the need to strengthen it at the international level.

Developing countries, however, do not view the relationship between protection and innovation through the same lens. These countries account for barely 3 per cent of world R and D expenditure, and their levels of domestic patenting are extremely low compared with those of the developed countries. Only a few developing countries that have recently attained high rates of industrial growth show significant improvement in their innovative capacities. These are the very ones - Republic of Korea, Taiwan Province of China, Singapore, Brazil - that were criticized for maintaining particularly weak levels of intellectual property protection. Depending upon the point of departure in terms of technological and industrial development, strong systems of protection may limit the possibility of following an imitative path of technological development, based on reverse engineering, adaptation and the improvement of existing innovation. A premature strengthening of the international intellectual property system can then be viewed as a one-way scheme that favours monopolistically controlled innovation over broad-based diffusion through free-market competition, a scheme that does not conform to the practices of many of today's most developed countries at earlier stages of their growth.

While legal protection by itself is clearly insufficient to stimulate innovation in countries with low industrial capabilities that lack qualified human resources and other enabling factors, it has also become evident that, in the present international situation, developing countries are bound to provide a certain degree of intellectual property protection in their own interests. Perhaps the proper focus of discussion should be the type and extent of such protection, and the measures needed to mitigate its undesirable monopolistic effects, rather than the issue of whether intellectual property as such should be recognized at all.

The weakness of research capabilities in most developing countries has led some observers to hope that foreign firms will increase the level of direct R and D investments in those developing countries that strengthened their legal framework. These hopes are unlikely to materialize, however, because intellectual property protection by itself will not offset the lack of trained personnel, equipment and general infrastructure and the benefit of proximity to major university research centres that are key factors in determining the location of R and D facilities in developed countries.

The exact relation between a strong system of intellectual property protection and increased transfers of technology remains uncertain. On the one hand, potential suppliers are reluctant to transfer their knowledge to countries where technology can be easily copied. The willingness of a firm to license its technology (often its most valuable asset) thus appears strongly linked to the guarantees it can obtain to ensure respect for its property rights. On the other hand, even if the attitude of potential technology suppliers seems likely to improve in a protectionist environment, more legal protection will not automatically lead to an enhanced process of technology transfer.

This conclusion follows from a number of premises that are worth articulating. First, technology transfers will not occur, regardless of the legal protection available, if other conditions pertaining, for example, to market size and expected growth, or to the competitive ability of potential licensees, are not met. Licensing decisions are generally based on a multiplicity of factors, among which intellectual property is not necessarily decisive. It may be argued, for instance, that the decision to license depends much more on the solidity of a particular licensing agreement than on the degree of legal protection itself.

Secondly, the availability of broader legal protection will naturally strengthen the bargaining position of proprietary rights holders, particularly if local working obligations are eroded, if the duration of protection is lengthened, and if other limits on the scope of protection are not recognized (such as non-voluntary licences implementing public interest concerns). A strengthened bargaining position will then probably be reflected in demands for higher royalty rates and in the imposition of restrictive clauses of various kinds. If legal protection arguably increases the willingness of innovators to license their technology, it thus also augments the possibility of inhibiting access to this same technology in terms of price and other considerations. The level of royalty rates charged in some fields may altogether deter developing countries' firms from gaining access to the most competitive technologies. Furthermore, given the globalization of the world economy and the spread of technological protectionism, technology holders will be strongly tempted to exploit innovation - whenever possible - through trade rather than through the decentralization of production activities and the transfer of technology.

The impact of intellectual property protection on foreign direct investments is thus quite uncertain. There is no empirical evidence showing a positive correlation between a strong system of protection and managerial decisions to undertake such investments. The availability of legal protection is one factor taken into account when considering such a decision; but market size and growth prospects, freedom for profit remittances and other economic conditions play a far more significant role. Moreover, as suggested by Dunning's eclectic theory of FDI, it is the very lack of protection, rather than its availability, that in many cases can stimulate a firm to establish a branch or subsidiary abroad.[133] A study of the abolition of pharmaceutical patents in Turkey indicates, for example, that foreign investment continued to flow into Turkey's pharmaceutical industry, despite the elimination of patent protection, because foreign-owned firms desired to increase their capital for a variety of reasons.[134]

Thirdly, while the impact of legal protection varies significantly with the economic and technological conditions of the country where it applies, it may also differ in strength from one industrial sector to another. Certain sectors, such as pharmaceuticals and, more recently, computer software, are particularly sensitive to the level of intellectual property protection because the nature and rate of innovation depends on the relative ease of copying (or of inventing around) any new product. This is not the case in other sectors (e.g. mechanical engineering) where protection is more clear-cut, infringement is more easily identifi-

able, and products do not necessarily embody the producer's most valuable know-how.

Furthermore, intellectual property protection may produce different effects even within a single industry when different products are involved. For instance, contractual agreements are more important in protecting custom-made computer programmes than copyright law because these programmes are not distributed on the open market. As regards pharmaceuticals, monopoly rights could more significantly affect new biotechnology-based drugs (such as human proteins), which replicate unique molecules existing in nature, than conventional drugs based on chemical synthesis. In still other sectors, protection against imitation may be built into the product itself or may be susceptible of simple measures to preserve trade secrecy.

Lastly, the full impact of intellectual property protection on consumers also depends on market structure, on the characteristics of the products in question and the extent of the proprietary rights conferred. As a rule, the stronger and broader the exclusive rights granted, the higher the risk of exorbitant prices and of other abusive practices that may harm consumer interests. The high prices charged for patented pharmaceuticals have often triggered corrective measures by governments, including the establishment of special compulsory licensing mechanisms.[135] Higher prices may also retard the rate of diffusion of technology, as is occurring in the case of software and informatics. It can be argued, of course, that without certain price levels the innovative firms would not obtain sufficient resources to justify continued R and D activities. But this argument is not compelling when applied to developing countries because it fails to consider that R and D expenditures are largely recovered in the markets of developed countries. In this calculus, the developing countries' markets are in most cases marginal - or ignored - and would not normally constitute a primary factor in determining the rate of investment in R and D.

2. Specific policy considerations

Several basic principles that could affect the entire TRIPs negotiations need to be put in

---

133 See J. Dunning, "The eclectic paradigm of international production: a restatement and some possible extensions", *Journal of International Business Studies*, No.19, Spring 1988, p.13.

134 See A. Kirim, "Reconsidering patents and economic development: a case study of the Turkish pharmaceutical industry", *World Development*, February 1985.

135 One interesting example is provided by the patent legislation of Canada.

evidence. The most fundamental is that, if the developing countries cannot ignore the developed countries' need to repress counterfeiting in their own markets (as well as those of third countries), the developed countries cannot ignore the need of the developing countries to tie the provision of intellectual property protection in their markets to domestic development needs. Such an approach is consistent with that taken at the Paris Diplomatic Conference in 1971, which saved the international copyright conventions, and it is consistent with the principle of non-reciprocity embodied in the General Agreement via paragraph 5 of the Enabling Clause adopted in 1979.

To the extent that a standard-setting exercise ignores the legitimate needs of the developing countries for differential and more favourable treatment, and overrides the element of consensus that has hitherto characterized the formation of international intellectual property norms, it may well cause disruption to a system that has survived over a century owing to its flexibility and capacity of adaptation to the needs of countries at different levels of development. By the same token, efforts to reach a good faith compromise in which "adequate and effective protection" is correlated with economic status and capabilities could end by reinforcing the commitment of the developing countries to the principles underlying the Paris Convention, just as occurred after differential and more favourable treatment was introduced into the Berne Convention and the Universal Copyright Convention (UCC) in 1971.

It may be assumed that all countries need public interest exceptions to the basic norms governing patents and other modalities of intellectual property protection, just as all countries impose immunities and exceptions on copyrightable works in addition to broad fair use exceptions. In this regard, rather than constituting an endless list of specific exceptions, it might facilitate matters if a basic principle were formulated that tied general norms ensuring "adequate and effective" (but not maximum) levels of protection to language that explicitly recognized the developing countries' offsetting conditions. For example, article 14, paragraph 5, of the Subsidies Code requires a developing country to "endeavour to enter into a commitment to reduce or eliminate export subsidies when the use of such export subsidies is inconsistent with its competitive and development needs".

In the present context, given the proper incentives, the developing countries might consider a more strongly worded commitment, based on the "adequate and effective principle," that also took account of their need for special public interest exceptions. From the developed countries' point of view, such a commitment to "adequate and effective protection" would be much stronger in principle than that made under article I of the Universal Copyright Convention because the TRIPs negotiation envisions a solid dispute-resolving apparatus that would put teeth into the agreement as a whole. On the one hand, the parties would agree that, just as the Universal Copyright Convention bridged the gap between countries at different levels in regard to copyright law, so a proper TRIPs agreement must bridge the gap between developed and developing countries in regard to industrial intellectual property protection. On the other hand, a failure to provide adequate and effective protection within fair-minded parameters agreed by the TRIPs exercise would become an actionable issue, even though the relevant dispute-resolving panel would be empowered to evaluate the developing countries' defences cast in terms of local development conditions.

E. Main conclusions

Developing countries face the need to devise intellectual property systems in response to international requirements, on the one hand, and to their own development goals, on the other. The task is difficult, because most of these countries have not yet reached levels of technological development that would permit them to extract the full benefits obtainable from these systems in the immediate future. However, greater benefits may be expected as their economies grow and the scientific and technological infrastructure develops.

The reinforcement and expansion of intellectual property protection in developing countries is not likely to create, of itself, more favourable conditions for technological development. Nor will it necessarily foster FDI and the transfer of technology. Legal protection is to be viewed as just one component of a larger framework conducive to innovation; the general macroeconomic environment, the investment rate, the availability of qualified personnel are far more decisive factors. In this connection, a major shortcoming of the present negotiations is their narrow focus on the static aspects of intellectual property rights. The dynamic aspects, and particularly those related to technology transfer and diffusion, are virtually absent from the current debate.

The outcome of the Uruguay Round is still uncertain. If further progress is made and extended to TRIPs, a stronger and more harmonized intellectual property system seems likely to emerge. Although significant disagreement persists, expecially in a North-South context, and this endangers a positive result, considerable progress towards a workable agreement has already been made. The increasingly flexible attitude of the developing countries suggests that a final consensus lies within reach, provided that their special needs and requirements are taken into account by the proponents of stronger IPR protection.

This new framework, if finally adopted, will make it harder to follow the "catching up" practices used in the past, and will entail better devised strategies for technological development. The challenge for developing countries is great, as is the responsibility of the international community to ensure that the new rules do not deepen the present economic and technological asymmetries. The search for new mechanisms of international cooperation to ensure that all countries have access to the fruits of technological progress should thus rank high on the agenda of the international community for years to come.■

THE MULTILATERAL NEGOTIATIONS ON BANKING SERVICES: CONTEXT AND SELECTED OUTSTANDING ISSUES

A. Introduction

The principal focus of this chapter is a set of issues relevant to North-South aspects of the current multilateral negotiations on international trade in financial services. However, many of these issues are also important to Eastern European countries, since their development of more market-oriented banking sectors and of concomitant regulatory regimes is still at a fairly early stage. The current negotiations are global in scope, and must thus also take into account matters involving primarily competition between enterprises from OECD countries in each others' markets.[136] Some preliminary remarks may serve to highlight certain forces associated with ongoing internationalization of banking within the OECD area.

As far as the mutual relations of OECD countries are concerned, an agreement liberalizing trade in banking services needs to be seen in the context of broader movement towards more open markets and regulatory convergence.[137] While the internationalization of banking in the OECD area would not have begun in the absence of government measures making it possible, internationalization in turn has generated pressures on policies in the regulatory field. Differences in national regulations can be a source of competitive

advantages and disadvantages to banks in international markets. Thus such differences themselves constitute a force for increased regulatory convergence. At the national level the resulting trend has been generally in the direction of a reduction of controls over banks. But there is also recognition that deregulation needs to be accompanied by steps ensuring that banks are subject to stronger and more uniform regimes of prudential supervision. Measures in pursuit of this objective at an international level have entailed an extension of cooperation among countries' regulators. Notable manifestations of the process are various initiatives under the auspices of the Basle Committee on Banking Regulations and Supervisory Practices concerning such subjects as the distribution of supervisory responsibilities for international banks between authorities in parent and host countries, and the international convergence of measurement and minimum levels for banks' capital.

This combined movement towards greater liberalization and regulatory convergence presupposes a certain degree of homogeneity among the economies of the countries in question. An analogous process is thus not to be expected in the case of banking re-

---

[136] The negotiations on financial services include insurance as well as banking, but the discussion here covers only the latter.

[137] Several aspects of this broader movement are described in R. de C. Grey, "'1992', financial services and the Uruguay Round", *UNCTAD Discussion Paper No. 34*, Geneva, March 1991.

lations between OECD countries, on the one hand, and developing ones or the countries of Eastern Europe, on the other. Here account must be taken of the much more disparate levels of both financial and overall economic development.

B. Protectionism and market opportunities in developing countries

Part of the impetus behind attempts to achieve an agreed framework for international trade in banking services has come from banks in the OECD area, which believe that such an agreement would facilitate the exploitation of market opportunities in the developing world. The evidence suggests that the markets of most interest to banks from the OECD area in this context are located mainly in certain middle- and high-income developing economies. There are indications that in many low-income economies, which are likely to provide less attractive markets, the prevalence of protectionist restrictions directed at foreign banks is lower.

No global survey of restrictions on the entry and operations of foreign banks has been undertaken since that of the United States Treasury in 1979 (henceforth referred to as *National Treatment Study 1979*).[138] The follow-up has taken the form of three studies (published in 1984, 1986 and 1990) surveying subsequent developments in a limited number of countries. The studies published in 1984 and 1986 (henceforth referred to, respectively, as *1984 Update* and *1986 Update*)[139] covered Argentina, Brazil, India, Mexico, Philippines, Republic of Korea, Singapore, Taiwan Province of China, Thailand and Venezuela. With the exception of Argentina, all the above economies were found to follow protectionist policies towards the entry and operations of foreign banks in 1979.[140] Thus three of them

prohibited by law, policy or administrative practice the entry of foreign banks except in the form of representative offices, and five of them entry in the form of branches. One of the latter group prohibited any purchase by foreign banks of an equity interest in indigenous ones, and the remaining four limited such purchases to less than a controlling interest. The updating exercises identified a measure of liberalization of restrictions on both the entry and the operation of foreign banks in some of the economies.[141]

The most recent study in the series (henceforth referred to as *National Treatment Study 1990*)[142] covers 12 developing economies, the group already mentioned plus Indonesia and Turkey. Unlike its predecessors this study provides information concerning the access of foreign firms to the securities business in developing countries, relatively detailed surveys of the subject being included for Argentina, Brazil, India, Mexico, Republic of Korea, Singapore, Taiwan Province of China and Venezuela.

Table 32 summarizes the major findings of the study concerning the position regarding market access for foreign banks in the 12 economies. In only two of them is the entry of foreign banks considered to be free of discriminatory legal or administrative impediments. But even in the absence of such impediments the granting of market access

---

138 The full title is Department of the Treasury, *Report to Congress on Foreign Government Treatment of U.S. Commercial Banking Operations* (Washington, D.C., September 1979). There is more detailed discussion of some of its findings in *TDR 1990*, part two, chap. II, sect. G.

139 The full titles are Department of the Treasury, *Report to Congress on Foreign Government Treatment of U.S. Commercial Banking Organizations. 1984 Update* (Washington, D.C., July 1984), and *National Treatment Study: Report to Congress on Foreign Government Treatment of U.S. Commercial Banking and Securities Organizations. 1986 Update* (Washington, D.C., Dec. 1986).

140 Although the authors of *National Treatment Study 1979* felt that they had insufficient information to permit the application of their system of classifying restrictions on the entry of foreign banks to Taiwan Province of China in 1979, the remarks in table II-1 of that study (p. 176) and in *1984 Update* (pp. 53-57) indicate that such restrictions were substantial.

141 *TDR 1990*, pp. 152-153.

142 The full title is United States Department of the Treasury, *National Treatment Study. Report to Congress on Foreign Government Treatment of U.S. Commercial Banking and Securities Organizations 1990* (Washington, D.C., 1990).

remains subject to the dictates of national policy towards the banking sector. Thus, for example, in Argentina, one of the two economies classified in the table as maintaining no discriminatory prohibitions on the entry of foreign banks, applications for the establishment of new banks, domestic and foreign, have none the less been denied by the authorities since 1984. Likewise the granting of the other forms of market access specified in the table is generally subject to administrative discretion, and can thus be expected to reflect various policy considerations.

The incidence of controls over market access for foreign banks varies considerably among the countries covered by *National Treatment Study 1990*. In only a limited number of cases do restrictions appear to reflect generalized opposition to foreign investment in the financial sector. Much more frequently the controls seem to be geared to the achievement of objectives with respect to particular banking submarkets or to the avoidance of problems which a more liberal regime of market access for foreign banks might cause for the pursuit of broader macroeconomic and development policies. Some of the controls described in the study are clearly designed to make possible the tapping of foreign expertise in the context of otherwise restrictive regimes. For example, in Indonesia since 1988 new entry for foreign banks must take the form of joint ventures with indigenous participation.[143] Reciprocity is a criterion taken into account by some of the developing countries covered.[144] For example, India applies a reciprocity test in the case of access to banking business generally, and the Republic of Korea applies such a test in the case of access to securities business.[145]

The study also reveals considerable variation in the extent to which foreign banks are subject to discriminatory restrictions on their operations in the sub-markets to which they have been granted entry.[146] The instances of discrimination covered by the study include not only that under a country's internal taxes, laws and regulations (discrimination analogous to the denial of national treatment in the case of trade in goods) but also that due to the less well defined concept of unequal competitive opportunity.

The two countries classified in table 1 as imposing no discriminatory restrictions on the entry of foreign banks (Argentina and Turkey) were also found to provide non-discriminatory treatment for such banks' operations.[147] In all the other economies surveyed foreign banks' operations were found to be subject to a measure of discrimination under current regulations or administrative practices (or both). In certain cases the discrimination is favourable to foreign banks. In India, for example, such banks are required to channel a lower proportion of their lending than domestic ones to priority sectors defined by the Government.[148] In the Republic of Korea foreign banks are fully or partially exempt from various restrictions imposed on domestic banks' management of their assets as part of policies regarding credit allocation and liquidity control.[149] Among the types of discrimination unfavourable to foreign banks the most widespread relate to funding, particularly important under this heading being restrictions on such banks' branching networks and their rights to instal automatic teller machines (ATMs).

Unequal competitive opportunity was found to exist in a number of instances where equal treatment under a country's legal and fiscal regime co-existed with some form of competitive disadvantage for foreign banks in relation to domestic ones. Such situations were generally attributed to controls of various kinds. For example, controls on foreign exchange operations are capable of having a differentially unfavourable impact on foreign banks if they are more dependent than domestic ones on international business, and controls on domestic operations may impede such banks

---

[143] *Ibid.*, pp. 356 and 360.

[144] Reciprocity in this context denotes the linking by a country of its policies towards foreign banks to the treatment accorded by their countries of origin to its own banks.

[145] *National Treatment Study 1990*, pp. 191, 194, and 268.

[146] It should be noted that the concept of non-discriminatory treatment is subdivided for purposes of the present Report in a way different from that followed by the authors of *National Treatment Study 1990* itself, who do not distinguish between discrimination with regard to market access, on the one hand, and with regard to operations in banking sub-markets to which access has been granted, on the other. The justification for the approach adopted here lies in the importance of control over market access as a policy instrument for developing countries. For further discussion of this distinction see subsections E.1 and E.2 below.

[147] One exception to the otherwise non-discriminatory treatment in Turkey with respect to operations relates to capital requirements. Foreign banks are not permitted to revalue their fixed assets in line with inflation in the same way as domestic banks. However, the authors of *National Treatment Study 1990* apparently do not rate this as a major deviation from non-discriminatory treatment (p. 397).

[148] *National Treatment Study 1990*, pp. 191-192 and 195-197.

[149] *Ibid.*, p. 251.

Table 32

MARKET ACCESS OF FOREIGN BANKS IN SELECTED DEVELOPING COUNTRIES, [a] 1990

Extent of access	*Number of countries*
No discriminatory restrictions	2
Prohibition [b] of entry of foreign banks in form of branches, subsidiaries and affiliates	2
Prohibition [b] of entry of foreign banks in form of branches	4
Of which:	
Accompanied by prohibition of purchase of controlling interest in indigenous banks [c]	4
Entry in form of branches permitted [b]	4
Of which:	
(i) Accompanied by prohibition of purchase of interest in indigenous banks [d]	2
(ii) Accompanied by prohibition of purchase of controlling interest in indigenous banks	1
(iii) accompanied by other limitations [e] on purchases of interest in indigenous indigenous banks	1

Source: United States Department of the Treasury, *National Treatment Study 1990. Report to Congress on Foreign Government Treatment of U.S. Commercial Banking and Securities Organizations 1990* (Washington, D.C., 1990), supplemented as necessary by the earlier national treatment studies and updates referred to in the text.

a Argentina, Brazil, India, Indonesia, Mexico, Philippines, Singapore, Republic of Korea, Taiwan Province of China, Thailand, Turkey, Venezuela.
b By law, policy or administrative practice;
c For one of the economies in this group the prohibition does not apply to merchant banks in the form of joint ventures.
d For one of the economies in this group the prohibition does not apply to a non-controlling interest in an integrated securities company.
e Prohibition of purchase of interest in existing indigenous banks but permission for establishment of new banks in form of joint ventures.

from taking advantage of superior innovativeness in designing new financial products and services.

It is reasonable to assume that the developing countries singled out for inclusion in *1984 Update, 1986 Update and National Treatment Study 1990* are of particular interest to banks in the United States, and the same presumption is likely to apply to banks in most other OECD countries. Only India of the countries in the group had a level of GDP per capita in 1985 below $500, and a number of

them have also achieved high rates of economic growth in recent years.

The widespread use of protectionist policies towards foreign banks in countries covered by the studies just described furnishes an interesting comparison with information concerning the presence of such banks in sub-Saharan Africa. Many of the countries in this region are among the world's poorest, and their financial sectors are in general underdeveloped. The findings of *National Treatment Study 1979* indicate relatively low levels of restrictiveness in policies towards the

Table 33

PRESENCE OF FOREIGN BANKS IN SELECTED AFRICAN COUNTRIES ᵃ IN THE LATE 1980s

Number of foreign banks *b* present per country	0	1	2	3	4	5	6
Number of countries	3	12	5	1	4	3	2

Number of foreign banks *b* present per country	7	8	9	10-19	20 or more
Number of countries	2	3	1	2	1

Source: *Bankers' Almanac and Year Book 1988* (East Grinstead, West Sussex, England: Thomas Skinner Directories, 1988); *Who Owns What in World Banking 1986* (London: Financial Times Business Information, 1986); *New African Yearbook 1991-92* (London: IC Publications, 1990).
a 39 countries of sub-Saharan Africa.
b Branches, but also subsidiaries or affiliates in some cases. Information is not always complete.

entry of foreign banks among African countries.[150] The data concerning the presence of foreign banks in the late 1980s provided in table 33 no doubt reflect to a significant extent the financial legacy of the colonial period, and should thus not be taken as an indicator of the current degree of restrictiveness of the regulations and administrative practices faced by foreign banks in the region. Nevertheless, the data are broadly consistent with expectations based on the findings of the above-cited study. Only in a small number of the economies covered by the table is there virtually complete exclusion of foreign banks. In several other countries the presence of such banks would appear to be important (especially in view of the small size of many of the economies in question).

C. Salient features of positions expressed at the negotiations

Liberalization of international trade in banking services generally entails both costs and benefits. The divergent positions of different groups of countries participating in the negotiations have concerned the respective weights to be given to these costs and benefits, and the nature of the measures required if liberalization is to lead to a favourable balance between them. The potential costs and benefits of liberalization have been discussed in the

150 *TDR 1990*, p.152. In 15 (or almost 40 per cent) of the 38 countries of sub-Saharan Africa covered by the study no restrictions on the entry of foreign banks were found. By contrast only six (or little more than 15 per cent) of these countries prohibited the entry of foreign banks by law, policy or administrative practice either completely or in any form other than representative offices.

literature as well as in *TDR 1990*,[151] so that only the briefest of recapitulations will be undertaken here. In arguments supporting liberalization the emphasis is on the way in which barriers to trade in banking services restrict the choices of economic agents, thereby raising their costs and otherwise reducing their opportunities to increase their incomes. Thus, for example, it is pointed out that restrictions on the establishment of foreign banks lead, via lower levels of competition, to reduced innovativeness and microeconomic efficiency in a country's financial sector. Similarly, operating restrictions can lead, via the increased costs imposed on the banks affected, to higher interest rates and other charges to borrowers and to lower levels of lending. The dangers of liberalization, on the other hand, stem from potential loss of autonomy and flexibility in macroeconomic and development policies, and from harmful forms of competition. Key areas of economic policy which may be affected by liberalization include exchange control, monetary policy and the allocation of credit. Moreover, liberalization is capable of sharply reducing or eliminating the scope for providing infant industry support to national financial institutions and thus harming the development of indigenous banking systems.

By and large OECD countries participating in the negotiations have stressed the advantages resulting from liberalization, while developing countries have drawn greater attention to its difficulties and risks. Positions expressed by the latter have reflected the wide variety of particular situations and levels of development which characterize them. While developing countries have not denied the potential benefits from at least a measure of liberalization, they have emphasized the need to maintain control over the process, so that its costs are minimized and policy autonomy is not threatened. A well articulated statement of such views was contained in the communication to the Working Group on Financial Services including Insurance by SEACEN countries.[152] The communication draws attention to the relatively high degree of liberalization already achieved in a number of SEACEN members (in certain cases greater than in some OECD countries), and to the commitment of most of them to liberalization, but as a gradual process consistent with national objectives and aspirations. Thus liberalization must not be of such a kind as to have

harmful effects on national institutions or the general functioning of the economy, and must allow flexibility in the design and implementation of banking and credit policies. It should also take cognizance of the levels of development of the financial sectors of SEACEN countries vis-à-vis those of more developed countries.

Opposition among developing countries to, in their view, excessively tightly drawn or onerous obligations under an agreement has been expressed in various ways. One example was widespread resistance to draft annexes to the overall multilateral framework for trade in services put forward by certain OECD countries that elaborated in substantially greater detail various aspects of obligations applying to the sector. Another example was the pressure from many developing countries regarding not merely the financial sector but also other services for the adoption of a "positive list" approach to commitments under a multilateral framework for trade in services. Under this approach commitments regarding the granting of market access, the modes of delivery to which it would apply (a matter discussed below in section D), and national treatment would apply only as specified in countries' schedules of bindings. Under the alternative "negative list" approach, liberalization in accordance with the multilateral framework would apply to all sectors and subsectors not specifically excluded from countries' commitments. It was felt that this latter approach might result in substantial reductions in countries' flexibility regarding both economic policy and regulatory measures affecting their banking sectors, unless they were prepared to specify broad lists of exceptions during the negotiation of commitments. Such an approach was also widely viewed as likely to be biased against countries (such as the great majority of developing ones and those of Eastern Europe) whose legal regimes for banking are still relatively underdeveloped and are thus likely to require substantial adaptation and extension in future. In the event, the conditional offers so far submitted by countries as part of the negotiation of commitments have broadly followed the "positive list" approach.

Other aspects of different groups of countries' positions come up naturally in the discussion which follows of particular principles and other matters that have been singled out during the negotiations as major likely constituents of an agreement.

---

151 See for example, *National Treatment Study 1979*, chap. 4, and *TDR 1990*, pp. XIII and part two, Introduction and chap. II, sects. C-F.

152 Indonesia, Malaysia, Myanmar, Nepal, Philippines, Republic of Korea, Singapore, Sri Lanka and Thailand.

D. Cross-border trade

So-called international trade in banking services takes place by means of both cross-border transactions and the provision of such services through a commercial presence in the importing country. In practice the latter form of trade cannot be separated from foreign direct investment (though in some cases the presence in question may require only the renting of office space). Issues under the heading of trade involving a commercial presence are taken up in subsequent sections.

Cross-border transactions are defined in the most recently circulated draft of a general agreement on trade in services as involving supply of a service (a) from the territory of one country into that of another, (b) in the territory of one country to the consumer of another, or (c) by persons from one country in another. In banking it is not possible to draw tight distinctions between those three forms of supply. For example, important instances of (a) would be the supply of payments and financing facilities or investment instruments by banks in one country to residents of another. An example of (b) might be the provision of deposit facilities by a bank in one country to residents of another. In many cases supply under (a) or (b) might be difficult in the absence of the movement of persons (salesmen or other agents) from the supplying to the importing country. It should also be noted that cross-border movement of persons from the supplying country is generally an integral part of the establishment of a commercial presence.

In the case of cross-border transactions of types (a) or (b) a crucial question is the extent of the relaxation of control over external payments which the liberalization of trade in banking services would require. Many of these payments (for example, those for the purchase of financial assets of various kinds) would be classified as capital transactions for the purpose of foreign exchange control.[153] Moreover, many countries may be unwilling to relax limitations on residents' rights to open bank accounts abroad on the grounds that such action would facilitate capital flight and other kinds of evasion of exchange control. Thus the obligations under an agreed framework for international trade in banking services, unless appropriately qualified, are capable of having important implications for countries' regimes for the control of external capital movements.

In this connection it should be recalled that only a minority of the member countries of IMF have accepted even the obligations of article VIII, which refer only to the convertibility of currencies for payments and transfers for current international transactions and not to those for capital transactions. The remaining member countries of the Fund have article XIV status that permits transitional arrangements under which a country "may maintain and adapt to changing circumstances the restrictions on payments and transfers for current international transactions that were in effect on the date on which it became a member".

Various proposals submitted at the negotiations by OECD countries would have entailed obligations as to the freedom of external payments and transfers that went beyond those of IMF article VIII.[154] However, during the most recent phase of the negotiations there appears to have been a softening of the stance of major countries in this group concerning the issue. For example, in the proposed text of an annex for financial services put forward by Canada, Japan, Sweden and Switzerland, the freedom to be given to residents of a party to the agreement as regards the purchase of financial services from another party was qualified in that it was to apply only so far as the associated capital movements were liberalized. Moreover, the rights and obligations of member countries of IMF under its Articles of Agreement concerning such matters as the use

---

153 In IMF article XXX (d) payments for capital transactions are distinguished from payments for current ones on the basis of a definition of the latter which includes the following: (1) all payments due in connection with foreign trade, other current business, including services, and normal short-term banking and credit facilities; (2) payments due as interest and as net income from other investments; (3) payments of moderate amount for amortization of loans or for depreciation of direct investments; and (4) moderate remittances for family expenses.

154 One example was a draft proposal for a general agreement on trade in services and its accompanying annex on financial services submitted by EEC in the summer of 1990.

of exchange controls and exchange restrictions in conformity with these articles were accepted as taking precedence over an agreement on financial services.[155]

E. Trade involving a commercial presence in the importing country

As mentioned in the previous section, the question of trade involving the provision of banking services by means of a commercial presence in the importing country is related to that of foreign direct investment. The reservations of many developing countries concerning inclusion of such trade in a multilateral framework for international trade in services stem partly from the belief that GATT provides an inappropriate framework for an agreement concerning FDI. Some more general considerations (which may partly explain developing countries' reservations in this regard) are taken up in the discussion in section F of connections between the negotiations on trade in services and other multilateral initiatives regarding guidelines for FDI and TNCs. In this section attention will be limited to certain specific issues related to the liberalization of regulations concerning the entry and operations of foreign banks.

1. Market access

The banking sector consists of several different activities and submarkets. Thus control over the access of foreign banks can be exercised at a disaggregated level, permission to enter being granted only in respect of certain activities and submarkets. Such control is generally a key instrument for the pursuit of policy objectives regarding banking, in particular objectives involving the subjects discussed in section C which are a source of concern to developing countries in the context of the liberalization of banking services. During the negotiations OECD countries have tended to favour an approach which would involve commitments of a broad character to granting market access in all except certain fairly restricted circumstances. At least some of these countries, however, would appear to want one major exception to such commitments, namely the right to include reciprocity with regard to the banking sector among the criteria which would be taken into account under this heading.[156] However, in other respects the position of OECD countries regarding market access is in accord with the "negative list" approach to commitments which many of these countries favour. By contrast, developing countries (as might be expected from their support for a "positive list" approach) have been concerned to retain the flexibility to grant market access of a limited and more narrowly specified kind.

It should be noted that if countries limit the entry of foreign banks for reasons of economic policy rather than according to standard licensing rules concerning subjects such as fitness to conduct banking business, the result will generally be a form of quota for such banks. This has implications for the application of the MFN principle in a multi-

---

[155] IMF proposed to the Group of Negotiations on Services in November 1990 that an acknowledgement along those lines of member countries' rights and obligations regarding exchange controls under the Articles of the Fund be inserted in article XI of the draft general agreement on trade in services available at that time.

[156] For example, under the Second Banking Directive of EEC the granting of market access to foreign banks currently lacking a subsidiary in an EEC country is subject to reciprocity. Another example is furnished by the conditional offer submitted in December 1990 at the negotiations by an OECD country not a member of the Community. Among the limitations and conditions on market access in this offer there is a reference to the regard paid to reciprocity in the process for approving the establishment of branches or subsidiaries by non-resident financial institutions.

In their conditional offer the Community and its Member States express readiness to abandon reciprocity measures so long as there are mechanisms in the agreement on trade in services "to ensure an adequate balance of commitments in certain sectors and the assumption by others of a satisfactory level of commitment".

lateral framework for international trade in financial services, a subject taken up below.

2. National treatment

Both the meaning of national treatment and its relation to market access have been the subject of important differences among the groups of countries at the negotiations. Major OECD countries have pressed the view that market access as well as national treatment should be comprehended in the overall concept of non-discriminatory treatment of foreign suppliers. Such an approach is embodied in several Treaties of Friendship, Commerce and Navigation (FCN).[157] Developing countries, on the other hand, have tended to emphasize the need to make a clear distinction between market access and national treatment, a position which in fact accords with that in the OECD's own Declaration on International Investment and Multinational Enterprises of June 1976.[158] The SEACEN countries, for example, in the communication to the Working Group on Financial Services including Insurance mentioned in section C above, stated that market access through commercial presence should not be granted automatically but only subject to several policy criteria, and that national treatment should be considered as a separate issue.

The position of developing countries in this regard is in accord with the handling of this principle for goods trade in GATT article III, which states that national treatment under internal taxation and regulations is to be accorded to imported goods after they have crossed a country's border (in other words, after they have received market access). In the versions of the draft multilateral framework for trade in services recently circulated at the negotiations this position now appears to have been accepted in so far as commitments regarding market access and national treatment are the subjects of separate articles.

Once a distinction has been made between national treatment and market access, it must still be decided what obligations as to non-discriminatory treatment of foreign suppliers should be included in the former. Here many OECD countries have appeared to favour obligations going beyond the scope of GATT article III, which is almost entirely concerned with the treatment of imported goods under internal taxation and regulation.[159] In this context these countries have put forward the broader concept of equality of competitive opportunity.discussed above in the account in section B of the findings of *National Treatment Study 1990*. The examples of unequal competitive opportunity in developing countries cited by that study were mainly cases of the coexistence of *de jure* equal treatment regarding certain controls over banks' operations with discriminatory effects in practice on those of foreign banks. Inclusion in the multilateral framework for trade in services of provisions designed to handle discrimination in the form of unequal competitive opportunity is potentially capable of leading to far-reaching intrusions into countries' domestic policies. In cases like those just described such intrusion might be directed

---

[157] An example of the way in which the right to market access is often linked to the principle of national treatment in FCN Treaties is furnished by article VII, paragraph 1, of the 1954 treaty between the United States and the Federal Republic of Germany (as quoted in C.D. Wallace, *Legal Control of the Multinational Enterprise. National Regulatory Techniques and the Prospects for International Controls* (The Hague, etc.: Martinus Nijhoff, 1982), p.52):

> Nationals and companies of either Party shall be accorded, within the territories of the other Party, national treatment, with respect to engaging in all types of commercial, industrial, financial and other activity for gain, whether in a dependent or an independent capacity, and whether directly or by agent or through the medium of any form of lawful juridical entity. Accordingly, such nationals and companies shall be permitted within such territories: (a) to establish and maintain branches, agencies, offices, factories and other establishments appropriate to the conduct of their business; (b) to organize companies under the general company laws of such other Party, and to acquire majority interests in companies of such other Party; and (c) to control and manage enterprises which they have established or acquired. Moreover, enterprises which they control, whether in the form of individual proprietorships, companies or otherwise, shall in all that relates to the conduct of the activities thereof, be accorded treatment no less favorable than that accorded like enterprises controlled by nationals or companies of such other Party.

[158] In its remarks on national treatment the Declaration states that "this Declaration does not deal with the right of Member countries to regulate the entry of foreign investment or the conditions of establishment of foreign enterprises".

[159] An exception to this limitation to treatment under internal taxation and regulation is contained in paragraph 9, where it is acknowledged that measures controlling prices, even if they accord with the principle of non-discriminatory treatment of imports, may have effects that are prejudicial to the interests of their suppliers, so that "contracting parties applying such measures shall take account of the interests of exporting contracting parties with a view to avoiding to the fullest practicable extent such prejudicial effects".

against countries' regimes of exchange control. Another important subject which might become an issue under the heading of equality of competitive opportunity is legislation conferring on Governments powers to control monopoly and mergers which were not enacted with the objective of deterring or excluding foreign direct investment but may none the less be used for protectionist purposes. Here the intrusions under the multilateral framework might be directed at matters covered by countries' antitrust policies.

Statements at the negotiations by developing countries concerning national treatment have tended to favour a looser set of obligations than those envisaged by OECD countries. The communication of the SEACEN countries, for example, emphasized that these obligations should not be such as to preclude the application of conditions to the operations of foreign banks designed to take account of such matters as a large existing presence of such banks and the competitiveness of such banks in relation to domestic ones. In this context it is worth recalling that the concept of national treatment in GATT article III is compatible with infant industry tariffs levied at the border. When banking services are provided through a commercial presence in the importing country, this option for furnishing protection to domestic suppliers is not available. Thus it can be argued that, in the case of developing countries, obligations as to national treatment should provide for the possibility of infant industry protection in the form of differentially high taxation for foreign banks, limits on access to retail deposits or refinancing facilities at the central bank, etc. (restrictions which are sometimes described as "tax-like" owing to their effect of raising banks' costs in a manner analogous to a tax).

3.   The most-favoured-nation (MFN) principle

Two major issues under this heading do not appear to have been resolved during the negotiations so far. One is the compatibility with MFN treatment of procedures that have the effect of putting a limit on the total number of foreign banks to which market access is granted (a matter already raised in subsection E.1 above). The other concerns countries' eligibility to receive the benefits of concessions under an agreed multilateral framework for trade in services (through the application of the MFN principle).

Cross-border trade in banking services would not appear to present any conceptual problems as to the application of MFN treatment very different from those arising in the case of trade in goods. But when banking services are supplied through a commercial presence in the importing country, the question arises of how to reconcile ceilings on the number of foreign banks admitted under the country's licensing procedures with non-discriminatory treatment of parties to an agreement in accordance with MFN. In the case of goods GATT article XIII prescribes that in the application of quantitative restrictions "contracting parties shall aim at a distribution of trade ... approaching as closely as possible the shares which the various contracting parties might be expected to obtain in the absence of such restrictions". However, the procedure is not practicable when it comes to the allocation of a permitted level of commercial presence for foreign banks, since measurement of the hypothetical distribution of business in the absence of restrictions on market access will generally be impossible. One solution to this problem which might be accepted as fair would be to allocate the limited number of slots to foreign banks on a first-come first-served basis equally open to all.[160] Acceptance of such a procedure as a substitute for traditional MFN treatment might be enhanced by a high degree of transparency concerning the modalities of its application. However, obligations with respect to transparency in administrative guidelines and decisions remain a point of contention for several developing countries. For example, in the communication of the SEACEN countries mentioned earlier obligations of this kind are rejected as onerous and impracticable. Another possible solution to the problem of reconciling a ceiling on market access with fairness would be an auction in which the limited number of places would be allocated to the foreign banks submitting the highest bids.

Eligibility to receive the benefits of concessions under an agreement in accordance with the MFN principle may be a source of serious difficulties if many countries, particularly developing ones, include extensive limitations and conditions with regard to market access and national treatment in their offers submitted during the negotiation of commitments. Such

---

160 In the opinion of a former General Counsel to the United States Office of the Trade Representative, under such a procedure "MFN seems realized". J.H. Jackson, *The World Trading System. Law and Policy of International Economic Relations* (Cambridge, Mass.: The MIT Press, 1989), p.140.

inclusion is capable of greatly complicating the attainment of a widely acceptable agreement. Indeed, it is noteworthy that a number of countries which have already submitted offers have prefaced them with reservations concerning their right to modify the contents in the light of the number of offers by other parties to the negotiations and of the degree to which they are "equivalent and mutually acceptable" (as well as of the final text of the multilateral framework for trade in services and its annexes).

A possible approach to this problem would be agreement concerning ground rules as to the character of conditions and limitations that could be accepted in countries' offers (with particular reference to those likely to be forthcoming from developing countries). Such ground rules would form part of the negotiating guidelines and procedures whose establishment is prescribed in the article concerning negotiation of commitments in the most recent draft multilateral framework for trade in services.[161] In the absence of such ground rules the negotiation of commitments is susceptible to breakdown or fragmentation owing to the difficulty of achieving a generally accepted reconciliation of conditional offers submitted subject to reservations such as those described in the preceding paragraph. The eventual result of a fragmentation of the negotiations might be a tiered agreement under which a group of countries decided to restrict to each other eligibility for the concessions contained in their schedules of bindings.

There remains the question of the character of these ground rules. One point which, as is noted in subsection E.4 below, is implied by the relevant parts of the current draft framework for trade in services but might none the less be worthy of explicit emphasis among the ground rules is that solution of the problem of eligibility for concessions would be facilitated by a negotiating process that balances limitations and concessions in countries' offers for services as a whole. In this way countries

only prepared to make very limited concessions in one sector (which might be banking) can receive offsetting credit for greater commitments regarding others. Ground rules referring to the overall negotiating process might be supplemented by others covering particular sectors. In the present state of knowledge about trade in financial services, and thus the likely effects of negotiated liberalization, there are limits to the amount of precision which could be furnished by such supplementary sectoral ground rules. The article in the draft multilateral framework concerning the negotiation of commitments already refers to the need to take account of countries' levels of development, and to provide for a degree of flexibility which would enable developing countries to engage in a more gradual process of liberalization adapted to achieving the goal of greater participation by them in the supply of services. One way of going beyond such a general statement of intentions would be to provide in an annex on financial services annotations concerning such subjects as market access, national treatment, domestic regulation and transparency that would list categories of limitations and conditions regarding banking that would be acceptable in developing countries' offers during the negotiations.[162]

4. Cross-sectoral suspension of benefits

During the current multilateral trade negotiations an important source of concern to the less powerful participant countries, in particular developing ones, is the possibility that eventual agreement might furnish the major trading powers with extended justification for the imposition of retaliatory trade restrictions.[163] One result of this concern has been resistance to incorporating a services agreement into the General Agreement, since

[161] Article XVIII of the draft of November 1990.

[162] The history of GATT provides a precedent for the acceptance of more limited commitments on the part of developing countries. In their admittance of new developing-country members contracting parties have generally accepted relatively short schedules of concessions by the applicants in question, being influenced in this respect by paragraph 8 of GATT article XXXVI, which states that "the developed contracting parties do not expect reciprocity for commitments made by them in trade negotiations to reduce or remove tariffs and other barriers to the trade of less-developed contracting parties".

[163] According to a former veteran trade negotiator several countries did reach the conclusion that such an extension of the justification for retaliatory action was part of the "hidden agenda" of the negotiations. R. de C. Grey, *Concepts of Trade Diplomacy and Trade in Services*, manuscript of *Thames Essay No. 56*, submitted for publication on behalf of the Trade Policy Research Centre (1989), pp. 144-145. Support for cross-retaliation between trade in goods and that in services within the United States Administration and Congress is exemplified by remarks in *Uruguay Round Negotiations on Financial Services*, Hearing before the Subcommittee on Financial Institutions Supervision, Regulation and Insurance Task Force on International Competitiveness of U.S. Financial Institutions of the Committee on Banking, Finance and Urban Affairs, House of Representatives, One Hundred First Congress, Second Session, 17 July 1990 (Washington, D.C.: U.S.Government Printing Office, 1991), pp. 2 and 16.

such incorporation might enable a country to withdraw from another contracting party concessions regarding trade in goods in retaliation for alleged restrictions on cross-border trade in services or on the entry and operations of service firms.

As far as the various service sectors are concerned, the position regarding cross-sectoral actions to suspend benefits appears to be still the subject of differences. The most recently available draft framework for trade in services specifies negotiations of commitments that are clearly designed to include several different service sectors in a single process. As already mentioned in subsection E.3 above, such a procedure has advantages for developing countries, which should thus have greater flexibility regarding sectoral differences in their willingness to liberalize, credit being accorded for sectors where they are prepared to make greater commitments as to liberalization balancing limitations on their concessions elsewhere. The natural corollary of this approach is that there should be no restriction as to the service sector regarding which a country suspends its obligations to other parties whose failure to fulfil their obligations has been identified as the cause of a nullification and impairment of benefits under the agreement. In the article on Dispute Settlement and Enforcement in the draft framework[164] there is indeed no limitation of the suspension of benefits to the service sector in which the nullification and impairment is identified. However, in a draft annex for financial services put forward by four OECD countries in December 1990 (and mentioned above in section D) it is proposed that measures authorized in settlement of a dispute should be limited to the sector which is the subject of that dispute. The same limitation is included in a draft annex also submitted in December 1990 by the SEACEN countries.

5. *Restrictive business practices and anti-dumping policy*

The term, "restrictive business practices", covers a broad spectrum of anti-competitive practices by enterprises. In the Set of Multilaterally Agreed Equitable Principles and Rules for the Control of Restrictive Business Practices approved by the United Nations Conference on Restrictive Business Practices in April 1980 and subsequently adopted by the General Assembly, in its resolution 35/63 of 5 December 1980, such practices are defined as "acts or behaviour of enterprises which, through an abuse or acquisition and abuse of a dominant position of market power, limit access to markets or otherwise unduly restrain competition, having or being likely to have adverse effects on international trade, particularly that of developing countries, and on the economic development of these countries, or which through formal, informal, written or unwritten agreements or arrangements among enterprises, have the same impact".[165] The enterprises in question may be private or government-owned. The definitions of the Set contain a long list of activities capable of having the anti-competitive effects at which the Set is directed, including various types of collusive and collective arrangements and behaviour, discriminatory and predatory pricing, certain restrictions on trade for the purpose of price fixing, and various types of exclusive dealing. The predatory pricing for the purpose of weakening or eliminating competitors specified in the Set comprises practices which in the case of international trade are classified as dumping.

Restrictive business practices are the subject of two articles in recently circulated drafts of a multilateral framework for trade in services, those dealing with Monopolies and Exclusive Service Providers, and with Behaviour of Private Operators.[166] The first of these articles is designed to ensure that suppliers of services from one party are not adversely affected by RBPs on the part of another party's government-owned monopolies or private entities granted monopoly or other special rights and privileges by its Government. The second concerns RBPs on the part of private enterprises but limits obligations to the exchange of information and other unspecified forms of cooperation. No article in the drafts of the multilateral framework is explicitly directed at dumping. However, the article on Emergency Safeguard Measures[167] permits the suspension of obligations by a party if as a result of unforeseen developments and of the effect of a specific commitment assumed under the agreement a service is being imported into its territory in such increased quantities and under such conditions as to cause or threaten serious injury to domestic suppliers. This article is clearly modelled on GATT article XIX, which does not concern dumping as such, the subject

---

[164] Article XXIII of the draft of November 1990.
[165] Sect. B, para. 1 of the Set (TD/RBP/CONF.10/Rev.1), United Nations publication, Sales No. E.81.II.D.5.
[166] Articles VIII and IX of the draft of November 1990.
[167] Article X of the draft of November 1990.

of separate treatment in article VI. Nevertheless, one can envisage circumstances in which the article on Emergency Safeguard Measures might be used as a justification for protectionist measures against dumping.

The prevalence of RBPs in the banking sectors of OECD countries has probably been declining in recent years. This decline is the result of a general movement in the direction of greater competition and openness and away from previously widespread cartel agreements concerning such matters as interest rates, fees and commissions. Moreover, the absence of copyright or patent laws for banking services and products removes a source of RBPs which is frequently important in other sectors.[168] Nevertheless, some RBPs continue to characterize banking in OECD countries. One potential vehicle for such practices is so-called "club arrangements", which include some of a primarily social nature, professional associations and groupings with specific objectives involving such matters as payments systems, quotation, dealing, clearing and settlement systems for the markets for securities and other financial instruments, and data banks.[169] The danger that such arrangements can be used to discriminate against foreign suppliers of banking services is acknowledged in the proposed annex for financial services put forward by four OECD countries (and mentioned earlier) through inclusion of a provision that where membership of bodies of the kind described here as "club arrangements" is a prerequisite for the provision of banking services by foreign suppliers on an equal basis with domestic ones, the obligation of national treatment applies to these arrangements as well as the measures of Governments.

The other major subject which should be taken up under the heading of RBPs is price discrimination for predatory purposes which, as noted above, in international trade is denominated as dumping. Banking is one of a number of service sectors that offer both possibilities and incentives for the use of price discrimination.[170] There are considerable impediments for purchasers of banking services to arbitrage between lower-price and higher-price markets, impediments that will tend to be greater in the case of markets in different countries. Moreover, during any relatively short period the share of banks' fixed costs in their total costs is high,[171] thus increasing their incentives to obtain extra business by reducing prices to levels which still cover the additional costs incurred but might be classified as "below normal" in the context of allegations of dumping. In international banking these incentives may be particularly important for entities whose market power in their countries of origin assures them of profits from which their activities in foreign markets can be subsidized. Allegations have recently been made in at least one OECD country that banking services have been dumped in its market as a means of increasing market share. It is thus scarcely surprising that concern should be felt in several developing countries over the vulnerability of their financial enterprises to predatory price discrimination by international banks.

Although opportunities and incentives for dumping are present in international banking, considerable difficulties (in many ways analogous to, but none the less probably greater than, in international trade in goods) can be expected to confront efforts to establish that the prices charged in particular cases actually constitute dumping.[172] The difficulties include

168 Concerning patent licence agreements as an instrument for RBPs as to selling prices, markets and marketing, qualities and volumes of output, etc. see, for example, F. Machlup, *The Political Economy of Monopoly. Business, Labour and Government Policies* (Baltimore: The Johns Hopkins Press, 1952), pp. 92-93, 207-210 and 282-285.

169 "Club arrangements" with restrictive membership policies also exist in a number of developing countries. See, for example, *National Treatment Study 1990*, pp. 256, 296, 385 and 393.

170 The existence of price discrimination in certain services sectors, its effects, and appropriate measures for regulating it have a long history as subjects of economic analysis. For the purpose of better understanding questions in this area involving banking services, a fruitful source of such analysis is the economics of railroad regulation owing to similarities in the two sectors' cost structures and their problems of cost allocation among different outputs. For a particularly succinct account of such analogous aspects of costing, prices and competition in railroad transportation see J.M.Clark, *Standards of Reasonableness in Local Freight Discriminations* (New York: Columbia University Press, 1910), chaps. 1 and 2.

171 The high burden of costs fixed in the short run reflects the importance of staff and premises. A clear breakdown of short-run costs in banking between variable and fixed is not possible owing to imprecision as to the degree of fixity of different expenses on staff. Nevertheless, the following typical cost structure for retail banking (taken from N. Coulbeck, *The Multinational Banking Industry* (London and Sydney: Croom Helm, 1984), p.134) may be of some interest in this context: staff costs (salaries, pensions, concessionary loans): 70 per cent; occupancy of leasehold premises and notional rental of freehold premises: 8 per cent; equipment and depreciation: 8 per cent; communications: 5 per cent; miscellaneous items and bad and doubtful debts: 9 per cent.

172 There were several references to dumping of financial services at the hearings of a subcommittee of the United States House of Representatives mentioned in subsection E.4 above (*op.cit.*, pp.21-22, 32, 34, 36, 38-40 and 68). Concrete supporting evidence, however, was not submitted and Bryce L. Harlow, an Assistant Secretary of the Treasury, in a letter included in the report of the hearings (*ibid.*, pp. 39-40), drew attention to the difficulty of demonstrating such

widespread use of cross-subsidization by banks in their domestic markets (prices which are a possible benchmark in dumping investigations) and the somewhat arbitrary nature of banks' assignment of many of their expenses to their different activities as part of their cost accounting. The article of the draft framework on Emergency Safeguard Measures which, as noted above, might be invoked by countries in instances of alleged dumping, contains no guidelines as to the procedures to be followed in such cases. GATT article VI and the Agreement on the Implementation of Article VI of the General Agreement on Tariffs and Trade (concluded at the 1979 Tokyo Round of multilateral trade negotiations) do describe procedures to be followed in the case of trade in goods but are felt in many quarters to have served in recent years as vehicles for rationalizing unjustified sectoral protection.[173] Notwithstanding these misgivings concerning

the uses to which procedures for handling dumping in a multilateral framework for trade in services may be put, omission of the subject risks being in contradiction with some basic and widely held views about fairness in international trading relations. There would thus appear to be an argument either for making dumping the subject of a separate article in the multilateral framework or for appropriate extension of the article concerning Behaviour of Private Operators to cover dumping. Absence of explicit procedures for handling dumping in an eventual international agreement on trade in services may well simply increase the likelihood of action at a national level. Such action might take the form of tighter control over the market access of foreign banks, discriminatory measures against such banks already in a country, or even the withdrawal of their permission to operate.

F. The relevance of work in other forums on guidelines for foreign direct investment

As stated at the beginning of section E, the reservations of many developing countries concerning the inclusion of services in the current multilateral trade negotiations has been due at least in part to the conviction that the General Agreement is not an appropriate model for a multilateral agreement on FDI. One noteworthy difference between a framework for trade in services based on GATT, on the one hand, and various multilateral guidelines for FDI either agreed or still being negotiated, on the other, lies in the balance prescribed between the rights and responsibilities of investors.

A framework for trade in services modelled on GATT can be expected to emphasize the rights of foreign direct investors subject to

specified limitations. By contrast, a series of OECD declarations, decisions and recommendations concerning international investment and multinational enterprises, whose starting-point is a highly positive view of the contribution that both can make to economic and social progress, sets out guidelines concerning not only the obligations of member countries towards multinational enterprises but also the responsibilities of such enterprises regarding disclosure of information, competition, financing, taxation, employment and industrial relations, science and technology, etc.[174] Likewise, the negotiations on the United Nations Code of Conduct on Transnational Corporations have considered not only such corporations' responsibilities in the areas cov-

---

dumping in particular instances. For earlier discussion of dumping of financial services in the context of banking relations between Japan and United States see D.D. Hale, "Global finance and the retreat to managed trade", *Harvard Business Review*, Jan.-Feb. 1990, pp. 152 and 161.

173 See, for example, R. de C. Grey, *Concepts of Trade Diplomacy and Trade in Services*, pp. 64-66.

174 Declaration on International Investment and Multinational Enterprises (21 June 1976); Annex to the Declaration of 21 June 1976 by Governments of OECD Member Countries on International Investment and Multinational Enterprises; Decision of the Council on Intergovernmental Consultation Procedures on the Guidelines for Multinational Enterprises (21 June 1976); Decision of the Council on National Treatment (21 June 1976); Decision of the Council on International Investment Incentives and Disincentives (21 June 1976); Recommendation of the Council on the Determination of Transfer Prices between Associated Enterprises (16 May 1979); and Recommendation of the Council concerning Action against Restrictive Business Practices Affecting International Trade including those involving Multinational Enterprises (20 July 1978).

ered by the OECD guidelines (as well as various others) but also standards for the treatment which such corporations should receive in host countries.[175]

Failure to address the responsibilities as well as the rights of foreign direct investors in the context of a multilateral framework for international trade in services can be expected to affect the conditional offers put forward by countries during the negotiation of commitments, and thus the character of any agreements reached concerning both banking and other services. The responsibilities outlined in the OECD declarations, decisions and recommendations and in the draft provisions of the United Nations Code cover matters widely considered to be legitimate subjects for policy measures towards foreign direct investment. If such responsibilities are omitted from, or inadequately treated in, the multilateral framework, then many countries may wish to retain greater latitude for action at a national level in the policy areas in question. Since this action will in many cases impinge on both market access and national treatment for foreign enterprises, it is reasonable to anticipate as a consequence of this attitude an increase in the number of limitations, conditions and qualifications included in conditional offers.■

---

[175] In a discussion of the relevance of the negotiations on the United Nations Code of Conduct on Transnational Corporations to a multilateral framework for services trade, a former United States representative to the United Nations Commission on Transnational Corporations has drawn attention not only to the coverage of subjects in the negotiations but also to the character of developing countries' participation in them. As he puts it, "[The] Code has been negotiated, over the course of all too many years, with the full participation of the developing countries. Those countries have always felt that the original General Agreement on Tariffs and Trade (GATT) was negotiated without their participation". S.J. Rubin, "Corporations, conduct and codes: investment and trade in the Uruguay Round", *The CTC Reporter*, No. 29 (Spring 1990), p. 21.